Chaos

Tom O'Neill is an award-winning investigative journalist whose work has appeared in *Premiere*, *New York*, *The Village Voice* and *Details*.

Dan Piepenbring is an advisory editor for *The Paris Review* and a contributor to *The New Yorker*'s website.

- Praise for *Chaos*

'[Full of] scandalous findings ... As it develops, O'Neill's tale embroils an increasingly stellar cast of accomplices or enablers ... No unified field theory of malfeasance would be complete without a link to the JFK assassination and the ensuing cover-up. O'Neill supplies one, and to me it seems only too plausible. Inevitably there are contemporary resonances ... O'Neill's intricately sinister "secret history" often sounds incredible; that doesn't mean that it's not all true.'

Observer

'[A] true crime masterpiece. O'Neill persuasively revises the accepted narrative that Manson was a freak of 1960s California, arguing that he was ingrained in state surveillance ... The riveting story of the story unfolds, as O'Neill details the physical and mental toll of his reporting. Several painful, thankless decades in the making, *Chaos* stands as a heroic testament to the perspicacity of journalism.'

Times Literary Supplement, Books of the Year

Chaos

The Truth Behind the Manson Murders

Tom O'Neill
with Dan Piepenbring

Windmill Books

5 7 9 10 8 6

Windmill Books
20 Vauxhall Bridge Road
London SW1V 2SA

Windmill Books is part of the Penguin Random House group of companies
whose addresses can be found at global.penguinrandomhouse.com.

Penguin
Random House
UK

First published in Great Britain by William Heinemann in 2019
First published in the United States by Little, Brown and Company in 2019
First published in paperback by Windmill Books in 2020

www.penguin.co.uk

A CIP catalogue record for this book is available from the British Library.

ISBN 9781786090621

Printed and bound in Great Britain by Clays Ltd, Elcograf S.p.A.

For my parents

CONTENTS

CHAOS

Vincent Bugliosi was on another tirade.

"Nothing could be worse than accusing a prosecutor of doing what you're implying that I did in this case," he barked at me. "It's extremely, extremely defamatory."

It was a sunny day in February 2006, and we were in the kitchen of his Pasadena home. The place was cozy, with floral patterns, overstuffed furniture, and—literally—a white picket fence out front, all belying the hostility erupting within its walls. Bugliosi wanted to sue me. It would be, he soon warned, "a hundred-million-dollar libel lawsuit," and "one of the biggest lawsuits ever in the true-crime genre." If I refused to soft-pedal my reporting on him, I'd be powerless to stop it.

"I think we should view ourselves as adversaries," he'd tell me later.

Vince—I was on a first-name basis with him, as I guess adversaries must be—was a master orator, and this was one of his trademark perorations. Our interview that day dragged on for more than six hours, and he did most of the talking, holding forth as expertly as he had when he prosecuted the Charles Manson trial more than thirty-five years before. Seventy-one and in shirtsleeves, Vince still cut an imposing figure, hectoring me over a Formica table strewn with legal pads, notes, tape recorders, pens, and a stack of books—all written by him. Wiry and spry, his eyes a steely blue, he would sit down only to leap up again and point his finger in my face.

Riffling through the pages of one of his yellow legal pads, he read from some remarks he'd prepared. "I'm a decent guy, Tom, and I'm going to educate you a little about just how decent Vince Bugliosi is."

And so he did—reciting a prewritten "opening statement" that lasted for forty-five minutes. He insisted on beginning this way. He'd dragooned his wife, Gail, into serving as a witness for the proceedings, just in case I'd try to misrepresent him. Essentially, he'd turned his kitchen into a courtroom. And in a courtroom, he was in his element.

Bugliosi had made his name with the Manson trial, captivating the nation with stories of murderous hippies, brainwashing, race wars, and acid trips gone awry. Vince was sure to remind me, early and often, that he'd written three bestselling books, including *Helter Skelter,* his account of the Manson murders and their aftermath, which became the most popular true-crime book ever. If he seemed a little keyed up that day, well, so was I. My task was to press him on some of his conduct in the Manson trial. There are big holes in *Helter Skelter:* contradictions, omissions, discrepancies with police reports. The book amounts to an official narrative that few have ever thought to question. But I'd found troves of documents—many of them unexamined for decades, and never before reported on—that entangled Vince and a host of other major players, like Manson's parole officer, his friends in Hollywood, the cops and lawyers and researchers and medical professionals surrounding him. Among many other things, I had evidence in Vince's own handwriting that one of his lead witnesses had lied under oath.

I sometimes wonder if Vince could see what a bundle of nerves I was that day. I'm not a churchgoing person, but I'd gone to church that morning and said a little prayer. My mom always told me I should pray when I need help, and that day I needed all the help I could get. I hoped that my interview with Vince would mark a turning point in my seven years of intensive reporting on the Manson murders. I'd interviewed more than a thousand people by then. My work had left me, at various points, broke, depressed, and terrified that I was becoming one of "those people": an obsessive, a conspiracy theorist, a lunatic. I'd let friendships fall away. My family had worried about my sanity. Manson himself had harangued me from prison. I'd faced multiple threats on my life. I don't consider myself credulous, but I'd discovered things I thought impossible about the Manson murders and California in the sixties—things that reek of duplicity and cover-up, implicating police departments up and down the state. Plus, the courts. Plus—though I have to take a deep breath before I let myself say it—the CIA.

If I could get Bugliosi to admit any wrongdoing, or even to let a stray detail slip, I could finally start to unravel dozens of the other strands of my reporting. Maybe soon I could get my life back, whatever that might look like. At the very least, I could know that I'd done all I could to get to the bottom of this seemingly endless hole.

Sitting in his kitchen, though, and watching the hours wear on as Vince defended and fortified every point he made, my heart sank. He was stonewalling me. I could hardly get a word in edgewise.

"It's a tribute to your research," he told me. "You found something that I did not find." In the closest thing I got to a concession, he said, "Some things may have gotten past me." But, he added, "I would never in a trillion years do what you're suggesting. Okay? Never. My whole history would be opposed to that. And number two, Tom, even if I had the thought that you're suggesting"—of suborning perjury—"it goes nowhere. It's preposterous. It's, it's *silly . . . Who cares?* It means nothing!"

Who cares? I've asked myself that a lot over the years. Was it worth investing so much of my time and energy in these, some of the most well-known, worn-out crimes in American history? How did I end up falling into this, anyway? I remember glancing over at Gail, Vince's wife, during his long, stentorian "opening statement." She was leaning against the counter looking exhausted, her eyelids drooping. Eventually, she excused herself to go upstairs and lie down. She must've heard it all a thousand times before, his scripted lines, his self-aggrandizement. When I'm down on myself, I imagine everyone feels like Gail did that day. Oh, no, not the Manson murders, *again*. We've been through this. We've processed this. We know everything there is to know. Don't drag us back into this story.

I was almost heartened, then, to see that Vince was so anxious. That's what kept me going, knowing that I'd gotten under his skin. Why would he be so committed to stopping this? And if what I'd discovered was really "nothing," why had so many of his former colleagues told me otherwise?

Another one of my sources had tipped off Vince about my reporting, giving him the ludicrous idea that I believed he'd framed Manson. That was dead wrong. I've never been a Manson apologist. I think he was every bit as evil as the media made him out to be. But it *is* true that Stephen Kay—Vince's coprosecutor on the case, and no friend of his—had been shocked by the notes I'd found in Vince's handwriting, telling me they could be enough to overturn all the verdicts against Manson and the Family. That was never my goal, though. I just wanted to find out what really happened. "I don't know what to believe now," Kay told me. "If he [Vince] changed this, what else did he change?"

I wanted to know the same thing, but Vince always found a way to change the subject. "Where does it go?" he kept asking. "What's the point?" The point, as I saw it, was that an act of perjury called the whole motive for the murders into question. Vince was too busy patronizing me about *my* motives to take that into consideration. How could I dare insinuate that he'd done something wrong? How could I live with myself if I tarnished his sterling reputation? He liked to bring up "the Man in the Mirror," as if he, and not Michael Jackson, had popularized the phrase. "You cannot get away," Vince said, "you cannot get away from him!" I tried to steer the conversation back to Manson, but Vince was having none of it. He wanted to recite some "testimonials" about his good character, to "read them into the record."

Both of us had showed up that day with two tape recorders—I was as scrupulous as he was, and neither of us wanted to risk having an incomplete account of the conversation. Over and over, whenever the intensity mounted and Vince had something sensitive to say, he would demand that we go off the record, meaning each of us had to shut off two machines, sometimes just for a few seconds, only to turn them all back on again. Often he'd forget one of his, and I'd have to say, "Vince, you didn't turn it off."

Off the record, he'd lash into me again, his eyes piercing under that silver crescent of hair. "If you do the book and it's legally defamatory, you have to realize one thing," he said. "You have to realize I have no choice. I *have* to sue you."

By the time I left his house, I had a headache from all his shouting, and the sun had set behind the Hollywood Hills. Gail had never bothered to come downstairs again. Outside, before I got to my car, Vince grabbed my arm and reminded me that a blurb from him could boost the sales of my book—and he'd be happy to offer one, provided the manuscript passed muster with him. "That's not a quid-pro-quo offer," he added. But it seemed like one to me.

Driving away, I felt despondent. I'd just gone toe-to-toe with one of the most famous prosecutors and true-crime authors in the world. Of course I hadn't broken him. I knew I wasn't alone, either. Other reporters had warned me that Vince could be ferocious. One of them, Mary Neiswender of the *Long Beach Press Telegram and*

Independent, told me that Vince had threatened her back in the eighties, when she was preparing an exposé on him. He knew where her kids went to school, "and it would be very easy to plant narcotics in their lockers." Actually, I didn't even need other sources—Vince himself had told me mere minutes before that he had no compunction about hurting people to "exact justice or get revenge."

As it turned out, my reprieve was short-lived. I arrived at my home in Venice Beach to find that he'd already left me a message, wanting to talk about "a couple of follow-up things." I called him back and we talked for another few hours. The next day, we had another phone call—then another, then another. When he saw that I wouldn't back down, Vince only grew more exasperated.

"If you vaguely imply to your readers that I somehow concealed evidence from the Manson jury," he told me on the phone, "whether you believe it or not, the only thing you're going to be accomplishing is jeopardizing your financial future and that of your publisher." Demanding an apology, he assured me that I was treading "in dangerous waters": "It's possible the next time we see each other I'll be cross-examining you on the witness stand."

Fortunately, that never happened. The next time I saw Vince, it was June 2011, and he was striding past me in an auditorium at the Santa Monica Library, where he was giving a talk. He'd noticed me—his adversary—in the crowd and paused as he made his way forward.

"Are you Tom O'Neill?"

"Yes. Hi, Vince."

"Why are you so happy?"

I must've been smiling out of nervousness. "I'm happy to see you," I said.

Studying me a bit, he asked, "Did you do something to your hair?"

"No."

"It looks different." He kept walking. And that was it. We never spoke again. Vince died in 2015. Sometimes I wish he were alive to read what follows, even if he'd try to sue me over it. I feel foolish for having expected to get firm answers from him. I replay the scenario in my head, figuring out where I could've caught him in a lie, where I should've pressed him harder, how I might've parried his counterattacks. I really thought that, with enough tenacity, I could get to the truth under all this. Now, most of the people who had the full story, including Manson himself, have died, and the questions I had then have continued to consume me for almost twenty years. But I'm certain of one thing: much of what we accept as fact is fiction.

1

The Crime of the Century

Two Decades Overdue

My life took a sharp left-hand turn on March 21, 1999, the day after my fortieth birthday—the day all this started. I was in bed with a hangover, as I'd been after countless birthdays before, and I felt an acute burst of self-loathing. I was a freelance journalist who hadn't worked in four months. I'd fallen into journalism almost by accident. For years I'd driven a horse and carriage on the night shift at Central Park, and over time, my unsolicited submissions to magazines like *New York* had led to bigger and better assignments. While I was happy, now, to be living in Venice Beach and making a living as a writer, I missed New York, and mine was still a precarious existence. My friends had obligations: they'd started families, they worked long hours in busy offices, they led full lives. Even though my youth was behind me, I was so untethered that I could sleep into the afternoon—actually, I couldn't afford to do much else at that point. I felt like a mess. When the phone rang, I had to make a real effort just to pick it up.

It was Leslie Van Buskirk, my former editor from *Us* magazine, now at *Premiere,* with an assignment. The thirtieth anniversary of the Manson murders was coming up, and she wanted a reported piece about the aftershocks in Hollywood. So many years later, Manson's name still served as a kind of shorthand for a very American form of brutal violence, the kind that erupts seemingly from nowhere and confirms the nation's darkest fears about itself. The crimes still held great sway over the public imagination, my editor said. What was it that made Manson so special? Why had he and the Family lingered in the cultural conversation when other, even more macabre murders had faded from memory? *Premiere* was a film magazine, so my editor wanted me to talk to Hollywood's old guard, the generation that had found itself in disturbing proximity to Manson, and to find out how they felt with three decades of perspective. It was a loose concept; Leslie trusted me to find a good direction for it, and to shape it into something unexpected.

I almost said no. I'd never been particularly interested in the Manson murders. I was ten years old when they happened, growing up in Philadelphia, and though my brother swears up and down that he remembers me keeping a scrapbook about the crimes, I can't recall how they affected me in the slightest. If anything, I thought I was one of the few people on the planet who'd never read *Helter Skelter.* Like an overplayed song or an iconic movie, Manson held little interest to me precisely *because* he was ubiquitous. The murders he'd ordered were often discussed as "the crime of the century," and crimes of the century tend to be pretty well picked over.

But I needed the job, and I trusted Leslie's judgment. We'd worked together on a number of stories at *Us* — it was a monthly magazine then, not a weekly tabloid — and a piece like this, pitch-black, would be a welcome departure from my routine as an entertainment writer, which called for a lot of sit-down meetings with movie stars in their cushy Hollywood Hills homes, where they'd trot out lines about brave career choices and the need for privacy.

That's not to say the work was without its twists and turns. I'd gotten in a shouting match with Tom Cruise about Scientology; Gary Shandling had somehow found a way to abandon me during an interview in his own home; and I'd pissed off Alec Baldwin, but who hasn't?

I had some chops, in other words, but not much in the way of investigative bona fides. For a recent story about an unsolved murder, I'd chased down some great leads, but because my case was mostly circumstantial, the magazine sensibly decided to play it safe, and the piece came out toothless.

This time, I thought, I could do better. In fact, through the fog of my hangover, I remember thinking: this will be easy. I agreed to file five thousand words in three months. Afterward, I thought, maybe I could move back to New York.

Twenty years later, the piece isn't finished, the magazine no longer exists, and I'm still in L.A.

"A Picture Puzzle"

Before I interviewed anyone, I read *Helter Skelter*. I saw what all the fuss was about: it was a forceful, absorbing book, with disquieting details I'd never heard before. In their infamy, the murders had always seemed to exist in a vacuum. And yet, reading Bugliosi's account, what had seemed flat and played out was full of intrigue.

I made notes and lists of potential interviews, trying to find an angle that hadn't been worked over. Toward the beginning of the book, Bugliosi chides anyone who believes that solving murders is easy:

In literature a murder scene is often likened to a picture puzzle. If one is patient and keeps trying, eventually all the pieces will fit into place. Veteran policemen know otherwise... Even after a solution emerges—if one does—there will be leftover pieces, evidence that just doesn't fit. And some pieces will always be missing.

He was right, and yet I wondered about the "leftover pieces" in this case. In Bugliosi's telling, there didn't seem to be too many. His picture puzzle was eerily complete.

That sense of certitude contributed to my feeling that the media had exhausted the murders. The thought of them could exhaust me, too. Bugliosi describes Manson as "a metaphor for evil," a stand-in for "the dark and malignant side of humanity." When I summoned Manson in my mind, I saw that evil: the maniacal gleam in his eye, the swastika carved into his forehead. I saw the story we tell ourselves about the end of the sixties. The souring of the hippie dream; the death throes of the counterculture; the lurid, Dionysian undercurrents of Los Angeles, with its confluence of money, sex, and celebrity.

Because we all know that story, it's hard to discuss the Manson murders in a way that captures their grim power. The bare facts, learned and digested almost by rote, feel evacuated of meaning; the voltage that shot through America has been reduced to a mild jolt, a series of concise Wikipedia entries and popular photographs. In the way that historical events do, it all feels somehow remote, settled.

But it's critical to let yourself feel that shock, which begins to return as the details accumulate. This isn't just history. It's what Bugliosi called, in his opening statement at the trial, "a passion for violent death." Despite the common conception, the murders are still shrouded in mystery, down to some of their most basic details. There are at least four versions of what happened, each with its own account of who stabbed whom with which knives, who said what, who was standing where. Statements have been exaggerated, recanted, or modified. Autopsy reports don't always square with trial testimony; the killers have not always agreed on who did the killing. Obsessives continue to litigate the smallest discrepancies in the crime scenes: the handles of weapons, the locations of blood splatters, the coroner's official times of death. Even if you could settle those scores, you're still left with the big question—Why did any of this happen at all?

Something to Shock the World

August 8, 1969. The front page of that morning's *Los Angeles Times* described an ordinary day in the city. Central Receiving Hospital had failed to save the life of a wounded policeman. The legislature had passed a new budget for schools, and scientists were optimistic that Mars's south polar cap could be hospitable to alien life. In London, the Beatles had been photographed crossing the street outside their studio, a shot that would become the cover of *Abbey Road*. Walter Cronkite led the *CBS Evening News* with a story about the devaluation of the franc.

The space race was in full swing, and Americans were dreaming, sometimes with a touch of trepidation, about the science-fictional future. Less than three weeks earlier, NASA had put the first man on the moon, an awe-inspiring testament to technological ingenuity. Conversely, the number one song in the country was Zager and Evans's "In the Year 2525," which imagined a dystopian future where you "ain't gonna need to tell the truth, tell no lies / Everything you think, do, and say / Is in the pill you took today." It would prove to be a more trenchant observation about the present moment than anyone would've thought.

Late that night at the Spahn Movie Ranch, a man and three women got in a beat-up yellow 1959 Ford and headed toward Beverly Hills. A ranch hand heard one of the women say, "We're going to get some fucking pigs!"

The woman was Susan "Sadie" Atkins, twenty-one, who'd grown up mostly in San Jose. The daughter of two alcoholics, she'd been in her church choir and the glee club, and later at a parole hearing claimed that her brother and his friends would often molest her. She had dropped out of high school and moved to San Francisco, where she'd worked as a topless dancer and gotten into LSD. "My family kept telling me, 'You're going downhill, you're going downhill, you're going downhill,'" she would say later. "So I just went downhill. I went all the way down to the bottom."

Huddled beside her in the back of the car—they'd torn out the seats to accommodate more food from the Dumpster dives they often went on—was Patricia "Katie" Krenwinkel. Twenty-one, from Inglewood, Krenwinkel had developed a hormone problem as a kid, leading her to overeat and fear that she was ugly and unwanted. As a teen, she got into drugs and started to drink heavily. One day in 1967, she'd left her car in a parking lot, failed to collect the two paychecks from her job at an insurance company, and disappeared.

In the passenger seat was Linda Kasabian, twenty, from New Hampshire. She'd played basketball in high school, but she dropped out to get married; the union lasted less than six months. Not long after, in Boston, she was arrested in a narcotics bust. By the spring of 1968, she'd remarried, had a kid, and moved to Los Angeles. She sometimes introduced herself as "Yana the witch."

And at the wheel was Charles "Tex" Watson, twenty-three and six foot three, from east Texas. Watson had been a Boy Scout and the captain of his high school football team; he sometimes helped his dad, who ran a gas station and grocery store. At North Texas State University, he'd joined a fraternity and started getting stoned. Soon he dropped out, moved to California, and got a job as a wig salesman. One day he'd picked up a hitchhiker who turned out to be Dennis Wilson of the Beach Boys—a chance occurrence that changed both of their lives forever.

That night in the Ford, all four were dressed in black from head to toe. None of them had a history of violence. They were part of a hippie commune that called itself the Family. Living in isolation at the Spahn Ranch—whose mountainous five hundred acres and film sets had once provided dramatic backdrops for Western-themed movies and TV shows—the Family had assembled a New Age bricolage of environmentalism, anti-establishment politics, free love, and apocalyptic Christianity, rounded out with a vehement rejection of conventional morality. More than anything, they lived according to the whims of their leader, the thirty-four-year-old Charles Milles Manson, who had commanded them to take their trip that night.

The four arrived at 10050 Cielo Drive, where the actress Sharon Tate lived with her husband, the filmmaker Roman Polanski. He was away in London at the time, scouting locations for *The Day of the Dolphin,* a movie in which a dolphin is trained to assassinate the president of the United States.

The drive to Cielo would've taken about forty minutes. It was just after midnight when they arrived. Benedict Canyon was quiet, seemingly worlds away from the hustle and sprawl of Los Angeles. The house, built in 1942, had belonged to a French actress, who'd modeled it on the Norman country estates of her youth. A long, low rambler at the end of a cul-de-sac, invisible from the street, it sat on three acres of bucolic, isolated land. Nestled against a hillside on a bluff, it afforded views of Los Angeles glittering to the east and Bel Air's fulsome estates unfurling to the west. On a clear day, you could see straight to the Pacific, ten miles out.

Watson scaled a pole to sever the phone lines to the house. He'd been here before, and he knew where to find them right away. There was an electric gate leading to the driveway, but instead of activating it, the four elected to jump over an embankment and drop onto the main property. All of them were carrying buck knives; Watson also had a .22 Buntline revolver. Kasabian remained on the outskirts, keeping watch. The other three crept up the hill toward the secluded estate.

At the top of the driveway they found Steven Parent, an eighteen-year-old who'd been visiting the caretaker in the guesthouse to sell him a clock radio. He was sitting in his dad's white Rambler, having already rolled his window down to activate the gate control. Watson approached the driver's side and pointed the revolver at his face. "Please don't hurt me, I won't say anything!" Parent screamed, raising his arm to protect himself. Watson slashed his left hand with the knife, slicing through the strap of his wristwatch. Then he shot Parent four times, in his arm, his left cheek, and twice in the chest. Parent died instantly, his blood beginning to pool in the car.

Those four shots rang out through Benedict Canyon, but no one in the house at 10050 Cielo seemed to hear them. It was a rustic home of stone and wood, its clapboard siding often described, in the many newspaper stories soon to follow, as tomato red. Beside the long front porch, a winding flagstone path led past a wishing well with stone doves and squirrels perched on its lip. There was a pool in the back and a modest guesthouse. The yard had low hedges, immense pines, and welcoming beds of daisies and marigolds. A white Dutch door opened into the living room, where a stone fireplace, beamed ceilings, and a loft with a redwood ladder provided a warm ambience.

Finding no open windows or doors, Watson cut a long horizontal slit in a window screen outside the dining room and gained entry to the house; he went to the front door to let Atkins and Krenwinkel in. In the living room, the three killers came across Wojiciech "Voytek" Frykowski, a thirty-two-year-old Polish émigré and an aspiring filmmaker, asleep on the couch with an American flag draped over it. Frykowski was coming off a ten-day mescaline trip at the time. Having survived the brutal Second World War in Poland, he'd gone on to lead an aimless life in America, and friends thought there was something "brooding and disturbed" about him; he was part of a generation of Poles who'd been put on "a crooked orbit."

Now, rubbing his eyes to make out the figures clad in black and standing over him, Frykowski stretched his arms and, apparently mistaking them for friends, asked, "What time is it?"

Watson trained his gun on Frykowski and said, "Be quiet. Don't move or you're dead."

Frykowski stiffened, the gravity of the situation beginning to seize him. "Who are you," he asked, "and what are you doing here?"

"I'm the devil and I'm here to do the devil's business," Watson replied, kicking Frykowski in the head.

In a linen closet, Atkins found a towel and used it to bind Frykowski's hands as best she could. Then, on Watson's instructions, she cased the house, looking for others. She came to a bedroom, the door ajar, where she saw a woman reclining on a bed, reading: Abigail Folger, twenty-five, the heiress to a coffee fortune. She'd been staying at the house with Frykowski, her boyfriend, since April. Now she glanced up from her book, smiled, and waved at Atkins, who responded in kind and continued down the hall.

She peered into a second bedroom, where a man sat on the edge of a bed, talking to a pregnant woman who lay there in lingerie. The man, Jay Sebring, thirty-five, was a hairstylist. His shop in Beverly Hills attracted a wealthy, famous clientele; he'd been the first one to cut hair in a private room, as opposed to a barbershop. He'd served in the navy during the Korean War. An intensely secretive man, he was rumored to allow only five people to keep his phone number.

On the bed with him was his ex-girlfriend, Sharon Tate, then twenty-six and eight months pregnant with her first child. She'd recently filmed her biggest role to date, in *The Thirteen Chairs,* and her manager had promised she'd be a star someday. Born in Dallas, Tate was the daughter of an army officer, and she grew up in cities scattered across the globe. Her beauty was such that she'd apparently stopped traffic, literally, on her first visit to New York. She'd been a homecoming queen and a prom queen; even at six months old, she'd won a Miss Tiny Tot contest in Texas. A film career, she hoped, would get her noticed for something beyond her good looks. There on Cielo Drive, at the home she called the "Love House," Tate was optimistic about the future. She believed her child would strengthen her marriage to Polanski.

Having reported back to Watson, Susan Atkins retied Frykowski's hands with a piece of nylon rope. She went to bring the others into the living room, returning with Folger at knifepoint, and then with Sebring and Tate. "Come with me," she'd told them. "Don't say a word or you're dead."

In their shock and confusion, they offered the intruders money and whatever they wanted, begging them not to hurt anyone. Watson ordered the three who'd come from the bedrooms to lie face-down on their stomachs in front of the fireplace. Tate began to cry; Watson told her to shut up. Taking a long rope, he tied Sebring's hands behind his back and ran a length around his neck. He looped the rope around Tate's neck next, and then Folger's, throwing the final length over a beam in the ceiling.

Sebring struggled to his feet and protested—couldn't this man see that Tate was pregnant? He tried to move toward Tate, and Watson shot him, puncturing a lung. Sebring crumpled onto the zebra-skin rug by the fireplace. Since they were all tied together, his collapse forced the screaming Tate and Folger to stand on their toes to keep from being strangled. Watson dropped to his knees and began to stab the hairstylist incessantly; standing up again, he kicked Sebring in the head. Then he told Krenwinkel to turn off all the lights.

Tate asked, "What are you going to do with us?"

"You're all going to die," Watson said.

Frykowski had managed to free his hands. He lurched toward

Atkins, attempting to disarm her, but she forced her knife into his legs, stabbing him constantly as they rolled across the living room floor, a tangle of limbs glinting with steel. He pulled her long hair. His blood was spraying everywhere, and he'd been stabbed more than half a dozen times, but Frykowski staggered to his feet. Atkins had lost her knife, so he made a run for the front door and, with Atkins still pummeling him, got as far as the lawn. Watson halted him with two bullets and then tackled him to the ground, pounding the butt of his gun against the back of his head again and again, with such force that the right grip shattered, and Frykowski's skull cracked.

Inside, Tate was sobbing. Then Folger, who'd lifted the noose from her neck, ran down the hall and out of the house through a side door. She was halfway across the front lawn, her nightgown flowing behind her like an apparition, when Krenwinkel caught up to her and brought her knife down, stabbing her twenty-eight times. Watson joined in and Folger went limp, saying, "I give up. I'm already dead. Take me."

Drenched in blood and their own sweat, the two killers rose to see Frykowski, yet again, on his feet stumbling toward them. Soon they were stabbing him with the same mechanical precision, forcing steel through flesh, bone, and cartilage. The coroner tallied fifty-one stab wounds on the Pole, plus thirteen blows to the head and two bullet wounds.

Atkins had remained in the house with Tate, who was whimpering, sitting on the floor—still in only lingerie, and still bound by the neck to the dead body of her former lover, Sebring. She was the only one still alive. She was due to give birth to the child, a boy, in two weeks. Watson came back inside and ordered Atkins to kill her. Tate begged her to spare her life, to spare her unborn child. "I want to have my baby," she said.

"Woman, I have no mercy for you," Atkins responded, locking her arm around Tate's neck from behind. "You're going to die, and

I don't feel anything about it." She stabbed her in the stomach. Watson joined in. The pair stabbed her sixteen times until she cried out for her mother and died.

Atkins dipped her fingers into one of Tate's wounds and tasted her blood. It was "warm, sticky, and nice," she'd recall later. "To taste death and yet give life," she said, "wow, what a trick." She soaked a towel in Tate's blood and brought it to the front door, where, following Watson's instruction to "write something that would shock the world," she scrawled the word "Pig." Their work was done.

When Watson, Atkins, Krenwinkel, and Kasabian returned to the Spahn Ranch early that morning, they went to their beds and slept soundly. "I was gone," Atkins later recalled. "It was like I was dead. I could not think about anything. It was almost as if I passed out, blacked out...My head was blank. There was nothing in me. It was like I had given it all."

At 10050 Cielo Drive was a scene of such callous, barbarous devastation that it shook something loose in the national psyche. August 8, 1969, and August 9, 1969, suddenly seemed to describe different realities. Media accounts were quick to infer something more sordid than ordinary homicide, something occult. One paper called the murders a "blood orgy"; others reported "ritualistic slayings" and "overtones of a weird religious rite." The facts were unavailable or misreported. Maybe drugs were involved, maybe they weren't; maybe Sebring had been wearing the black hood of a Satanist, maybe he hadn't. The big picture was one of supernatural ruin. An officer at the scene said the bodies looked like mannequins dipped in red paint. Another said, "It's like a battlefield up there." Pools of blood had soaked into the carpets. According to *Time* magazine, stray bullets were lodged in the ceiling.

In Roman Polanski, whose films were arrantly, even proudly occultist, the public found someone onto whom it could project its fatalism. A popular press account said that, mere minutes before he learned of the murders, Polanski, at a party in London, had been discussing a friend's death. "Eeny meeny miney mo," he said, "who will be the next to go?" With that, the phone rang, and he was summoned to hear that his wife and friends had been brutally murdered.

It wasn't over. The next night at the Spahn Ranch, the same group convened, with three additions. There was the eighteen-year-old Steven "Clem" Grogan, a musician and high school dropout, and the nineteen-year-old Leslie "Lu-Lu" Van Houten, a former homecoming princess from the suburbs of Los Angeles who'd played the sousaphone in junior high.

And there was Charles Manson. Their leader.

The seven of them piled into the beat-up Ford on a search for more victims. After nearly three hours of restive driving through Los Angeles and its environs, Manson finally settled on a home in Los Feliz, at 3301 Waverly Drive, next door to a house he'd once stayed in. With no idea of who lived there, he broke into the house by himself, armed with a pistol and a knife. Others maintain that he brought Tex Watson with him. In any case, he spotted Leno LaBianca, forty-four, a grocery store owner, asleep on the couch, a newspaper over his face. Leno's wife, Rosemary, thirty-eight, was in the bedroom. Rosemary was paranoid that people had been breaking in and moving their furniture around lately—and, like the whole city, she was spooked by the Tate murders the previous night. Even so, Manson was apparently able to walk right in through an unlocked side door, and he tied up the couple by himself. Then he rejoined his acolytes at the bottom of the long driveway, where they were waiting in the car.

Manson chose Watson and Krenwinkel, again, as his executioners. This time he added Van Houten to the mix. She'd never so much as struck another person before that night. He told the three of them to go inside and kill everyone. They had only buck knives.

They burst into the house, separated the couple, and stabbed Leno twenty-six times; they cut the word "War" into his stomach and impaled a carving fork beside it, its handle jutting out of his belly. They left a steak knife protruding from his throat. Rosemary suffered forty-one stab wounds, many inflicted after she'd died. Before they left, the killers scrawled "Healter [sic] Skelter" in blood on the refrigerator—misspelling the Beatles song "Helter Skelter." On the walls, they smeared "Rise" and "Death to Pigs" in Leno's blood.

"Almost Dead Inside"

The bloodshed, in its primitive defiance—a pregnant star slaughtered, a man perforated with kitchen utensils—confirmed a sense of rupture in America. The decade's subversive spirit had come on with too much fervor. Some reckoning was bound to come, or so it seemed in retrospect; the latent violence couldn't contain itself forever.

The nation was immured in these events: in the motive, the manhunt, and then, in 1970, the sensational nine-and-a-half-month-long trial. But Manson and his cohort weren't brought to justice for nearly four months. With the suspects unknown and at large, rumors proliferated and the tension reached a fever pitch. For a while, the police maintained that the two sets of murders were unrelated; the LaBiancas were victims of a copycat attack. Even Truman Capote, whose *In Cold Blood* was only a few years old, fell into the speculative fervor, appearing on *The Tonight Show* to provide a "fantasy" explanation of the murders. He blamed them on one person, with the motive a fit of rage and a heaping portion of paranoia.

As days turned into weeks and weeks to months, two separate teams of LAPD detectives—one assigned to Tate, the other to LaBianca—failed to share information, believing the crimes unconnected. As they lost valuable time pursuing false leads, doubt and ridicule followed them in the press. For almost four months, the police would say that they had no real idea who had committed some of the most appalling murders in the history of the country.

Talk about the murders long enough, and inevitably someone will bring up Joan Didion's famous remark from *The White Album*: "The sixties ended abruptly on August 9, 1969...The tension broke that day. The paranoia was fulfilled." There's the germ of truth in that. But the process wasn't so abrupt. It began that day, but it wasn't over, really, until December 1, 1969, when the police announced the crimes had been solved and the nation got its first glimpse of the killers. Here was the final fulfillment of paranoia, the last gasp of sixties idealism.

At LAPD headquarters, the chief of police, Edward M. Davis, stepped up to an array of fifteen microphones and announced to a stunned crowd of two hundred reporters that the case was solved. Warrants were out for Charles Watson, Patricia Krenwinkel, and Linda Kasabian. More people would be named pending grand jury indictments. Davis added, to everyone's astonishment, that the Tate and LaBianca murders were connected. The suspects may have been responsible for a series of other unsolved homicides, too.

He didn't name Manson or Susan Atkins that day because they were already in custody. In mid-October, Manson, with a welter of his followers, had been apprehended on auto-theft charges at the Barker Ranch, a hideaway in forbidding Death Valley; its seclusion surpassed even that of the Spahn Ranch. Atkins had been charged with another, unrelated murder—that of Gary Hinman, an old friend of Manson—and was being held at the Sybil Brand Institute, a jail for women in Los Angeles County, where she bragged to cellmates about her complicity in the Tate murders. Those off-hand remarks broke the case open for the LAPD, who began to connect the dots they'd been staring at for nearly four months.

Journalists dug into the story. Images and mug shots of Manson and the Family were emblazoned on front pages and TV screens around the world. The cognitive dissonance was intense. These weren't the faces of hardened criminals or escaped lunatics. They were hippies, stereotypical flower children, in the bloom of wide-eyed youth: the men unshaven and long-haired, wearing beads and buckskin jackets; the women in blue jeans and tie-dyed tops, no bras, their hair tangled and unwashed.

They talked like hippies, too, spouting an ethos of free love, eschewing monogamy and marriage in favor of sexual experimentation. They lived in roving communes, caravanning along the Golden Coast in Technicolor-bright buses and clunkers cobbled together from spare parts. They believed that hallucinogens strengthened the spirit and expanded the mind. They gave birth naturally and raised their children together in rustic simplicity.

In other ways, though, their philosophy was gnostic, verging on theological. Time did not exist, they proclaimed. There was no good, no bad, and no death. All human beings were God and the devil at the same time, and part of one another. In fact, everything in the universe was unified, one with itself. The Family's moral code, insofar as it existed at all, was riven with contradictions. While it was wrong to kill animals—even the snakes and spiders in their bunkhouses had to be carefully spared—it was fine to kill people, because a human life was inherently valueless. To kill someone was tantamount to "breaking off a minute piece of some cosmic cookie," as Tex Watson later put it. If anything, death was something to be embraced, because it exposed your soul to the oneness of the universe.

Where had these beliefs come from? The murderers had been raised and educated in solid, conventional American communities, but no one wanted to claim them. The Family, with its starry-eyed communalism, sexual frankness, and veneration of LSD, offered a screen onto which anyone could project his insecurities about the era's politics and pressures. The promise of the hippie movement had been in its willingness to forgo cherished institutions in favor of the new and untested. After the Tate murders, it seemed that hippies and freaks were more than a risible sideshow: they could really undermine the status quo. Their promiscuity had always earned a lot of finger wagging from concerned moralists, while others had looked on with thinly veiled envy. Parents were worried that their kids would drop out, become hippies, and never get decent jobs. Everywhere, kids were hitchhiking. The consensus from the straight world was that hippies were mostly harmless—but you didn't want to be one. While there had been isolated incidents of violence attributed to hippies, none of it was as horrific, premeditated, and systematic as the murders committed by Manson's Family. And so much about the crimes was mired in uncertainty, from the motive to the body count. By some estimates, over that four-month period in 1969, as many as thirty-three people may have been killed simply because one man ordered it. This was something altogether different.

On December 12, with the nation still reeling from the indictments, a piece in *Time* magazine drew specious parallels between hippies and violence. In the movement's "invitation to freedom," the magazine warned, "criminals and psychotics" blossomed as easily as innocents and pacifists did. But how, *Time* asked, could "children who had dropped out for the sake of kindness and caring, love and beauty, be enjoined to kill"? Dr. Lewis Yablonsky, a sociologist who'd written a book called *The Hippie Trip,* argued that many hippies were "lonely, alienated people":

> Even when they act as if they love, they can be totally devoid of true compassion. That is the reason why they can kill so matter-of-factly...Many hippies are socially almost dead inside. Some require massive emotions to feel anything at all. They need bizarre, intensive acts to feel alive—sexual acts, acts of violence, nudity, every kind of Dionysian thrill.

"The Mechanical Boy"

And this Charles Milles Manson, whose face was suddenly everywhere—was he not the epitome of the Dionysian thrill seeker? A thirty-five-year-old ex-con, roughly half his life whiled away in federal institutions, had ensnared the lives and minds of his followers, mainly young women. Numbering variously between two to three dozen, the majority of the Family members had been under Manson's influence for less than two years, some not even close to that. Yet all of them would do anything Manson asked, without question, including slaughtering complete strangers. He had cultivated extreme compliance.

Manson was an unlikely candidate for a charismatic leader. Born in Cincinnati, Ohio, to a sixteen-year-old mother and a father he never met, he'd known little but privation and suffering. Few would be naturally inclined to look up to him, and in the most literal sense, not many could: he was only five foot six.

Manson spent his earliest years in neglect. When he was still an infant, his mother would leave him to go on benders with her brother, during one of which the pair decided to rob a guy who looked wealthy. Within hours, they'd been arrested, and Manson's mother was imprisoned for several years. He was eight when she was released, and they spent the next months with a succession of unreliable men in seamy locales, his mom racking up another arrest for grand larceny. Eventually, she pursued a traveling salesman in Indianapolis, marrying him in 1943 and trying to cut back on her drinking. Manson, not yet nine, was already a truant, known to steal from local shops. His mother looked for a foster home for him. Instead, he was made a ward of the state and sent to the Gibault School for Boys, a Catholic-run school for delinquents in Terre Haute, Indiana. He ran away. His mother took him back. The separation must have weighed on him, at least to go by his acolyte Watson, who later wrote that Manson had "a special hatred for women as mothers... This probably had something to do with his feelings about his own mother, though he never talked about her... The closest he came to breaking his silence was in some of his song lyrics: 'I am a mechanical boy, I am my mother's boy.'"

The "mechanical boy" made short work of the Gibault School. Ten months in, he ran away again, turning to burglary to keep himself afloat. His crimes soon landed him in a correctional facility in Omaha, Nebraska. He ran away from there, too, and started breaking into grocery stores. At age thirteen, Manson was sent to the Indiana Boys School, a tougher institution, where he claimed the other boys raped him. He learned to feign lunacy to keep them at bay. And he kept running away: eighteen times in three years.

In February 1951, when he was sixteen, Manson broke out again, this time with a pair of other boys. They drove a stolen car across state lines—a federal offense. When a roadblock in Utah brought their escapade to an end, Manson was sent to the National Training School for Boys, in Washington, D.C. Thus began a long stint in the federal reformatory system. From there, Manson went to the Natural Bridge Honor Camp, where he was caught raping a boy at knifepoint; to a federal reformatory in Virginia, where he racked up similar offenses; and to a reformatory in Ohio, where a run of good behavior earned him an early release in 1954, though caseworkers had taken frequent note of his antisocial behavior and psychic trauma.

In less than a year's time he had a wife, and a baby on the way. He took on various service jobs, but he couldn't give up stealing cars, several of which he drove, again, across state lines. Those crimes, plus his failure to attend a hearing related to one of them, netted him a three-year sentence to Terminal Island, a federal prison in San Pedro, California. By the time he got out, in 1958, his wife had filed for divorce, and he turned to pimping to make a living. The following May, he was arrested yet again, this time for forging a government check for $37.50. This got him another ten-year sentence, but the judge, moved by the plea of a woman who said she was in love with him and wanted to marry him, suspended the sentence right away, letting him go free.

Manson kept pimping, stealing cars, and scheming people out of their money. The FBI was surveilling him, hoping to bust him for violating the Mann Act, which forbade the transportation of prostitutes across state lines. They were never able to bring the charge, but when Manson disappeared to Mexico with another prostitute, he was found in violation of his probation, and the ten-year sentence he'd received earlier was brought into effect. The same judge who'd granted him probation now decreed: "If there ever was a man who demonstrated himself completely unfit for probation, he is it."

Stuck in prison for the long haul, Manson took up the guitar and dabbled in Scientology. The staff noted his gift for charismatic storytelling and his enduring "personality problems." He made no secret of his musical aspirations. From behind bars, he observed, with great interest and envy, the meteoric rise of the Beatles.

When he was released at age thirty-two, he'd spent more than half his life in the care of the state. He preferred life in prison, he said, so much so that he asked if he could simply remain inside. "He has no plans for release," one report said, "as he says he has nowhere to go."

"Bloodthirsty Robots"

Reading early press accounts of Manson and the Family, I found it hard to separate hyperbole from veracity. Manson was often made out as an artful seeker—"an evil Pied Piper," as one paper put it, with reserves of obscure power. About a week after the Family's arrests, a photograph of a wild-eyed Charles Manson, looking for all the world like a modern-day Rasputin, appeared on the cover of *Life* magazine. Inside the issue, the "Manson women," many of them barely teenagers, posed with babies slung over their slender shoulders. They spoke of their love and undying support for "Charlie," whom they deemed the second coming of Christ and Satan in one.

The media had already started to label the Family "a nomadic band of hippies" and a "pseudo-religious cult"; the *New York Times*, striking a dramatic note, claimed that they "lived a life of indolence, free sex, midnight motorcycle races and blind obedience to a mysterious guru inflamed with his power to control their minds and bodies."

The underground press, though, had a swell of sympathy for Manson. People thought he was innocent, that his status as a left-leaning communard had been overblown. *Tuesday's Child,* an L.A. counterculture paper geared toward occultists, named Manson their "man of the year." Some didn't even care if he *was* behind the murders. Bernardine Dohrn, of the Weather Underground, put it most outrageously: "Offing those rich pigs with their own forks and knives, and then eating a meal in the same room, far out! The Weathermen dig Charles Manson."

I watched the first television footage of Manson. Cameras followed as bailiffs led him to a pretrial hearing, shackled, stooped, and glaring. I saw few traces of his fabled charisma, but I understood how his unsocialized air of pseudomysticism and jailhouse aggression seemed authentic. Manson brought a rollicking exhibition of controlled insanity whenever he appeared before the bench. He quarreled with the judge, arguing that he should be allowed to represent himself. The "girls," for their part, mimicked their leader's behavior, publicly battling the judge and their court-appointed defense attorneys at every opportunity and refusing to obey even the most fundamental rules of courtroom decorum.

That Manson had been apprehended in Death Valley—as abyssal a place as any in the United States—made him all the more transfixing. Reporters played up the Rasputin comparison, emphasizing his desert-wanderer sorcery. He was a "bearded, demonic

Mahdi," wrote one journalist, who led "a mystical, semi-religious hippie drug-and-murder cult." Another described him as a "bushy-haired, wild-bearded little man with piercing brown eyes," with the Family "a hippie-type roving band." Manson's malevolence was seemingly inexplicable. Even in the doodles that he left behind on a courtroom legal pad, psychiatrists saw "a psyche torn asunder by powerful thrusts of aggression, guilt, and hostility."

Beneath this spectacle, I could glimpse the public's truer, more profound interest in the case, the same puzzle that would consume me: How and why had these people devolved into criminals? And, more pointedly, could it happen to any average American child—could anyone go "too far"?

The trial started in July 1970. The jury was sequestered at the Ambassador Hotel, where, two years earlier, Bobby Kennedy had been assassinated. The Superior Courthouse in downtown Los Angeles became the center of a media circus unlike any the nation had ever seen. The six defendants—Charles Manson, Patricia Krenwinkel, Susan Atkins, Leslie Van Houten, Steve Grogan, and Linda Kasabian—received the kind of scrutiny known only to the most famous celebrities in the world. (Tex Watson was tried separately from the other Family members; he'd fled to Texas and had to be extradited to California.)

Vincent Bugliosi became the public face of the state, and Manson's de facto foil. Though you'd never know it to look at them, the two were the same age—Manson was actually Bugliosi's senior by three months. Both were thirty-five when the trial began. But Bugliosi, with his three-piece suits and his receding hairline, was the very picture of the straight world, with its authority and moral gravity; sometimes he looked old enough to be Manson's dad.

In *Helter Skelter,* Bugliosi claims an aversion to "the stereotyped image of the prosecutor" as "a right-wing, law-and-order type intent on winning convictions at any cost." But that's exactly how he came across. In file photographs he's often haloed in microphones, his solemn pronouncements helping the world make sense of the senseless. Journalists lauded his "even-toned arguments."

With his opening statement, Bugliosi, no less colorful a character than Manson, made what was already a sensational case even more so. The motive he presented for the murders was spellbindingly bizarre. In Bugliosi's telling, it crossed racism with apocalyptic, biblical rhetoric, all of it set to a melody by the Beatles—"the English musical recording group," as he primly referred to them:

> Manson was an avid follower of the Beatles and believed that they were speaking to him through the lyrics of their songs…"Helter Skelter," the title of one of the Beatles' songs, meant the black man rising up against the white establishment and murdering the entire white race, that is, with the exception of Manson and his chosen followers, who intended to "escape" from Helter Skelter by going to the desert and living in the Bottomless Pit, a place Manson derived from Revelation 9.

Nothing like this had ever been heard in a courtroom. People kill one another for all kinds of reasons, but they're usually personal, not metaphysical. Seldom had threads like these—racism, rock music, the end times—been woven together in a single, lethal philosophy. When Paul Watkins, a former Family member, took the stand to elaborate on Helter Skelter, the details were even more jarring. Watkins spoke of "a big underground city," secreted away in a hole wide enough that "you could drive a speedboat across it." From the book of Revelation, the Family knew the city would have no sun and no moon, and "a tree that bears twelve different kinds of fruit." Subsisting on that fruit in their subterranean Elysium, the Family would multiply into 144,000 people.

As insane and illogical as it sounded, Bugliosi explained, Manson's followers subscribed to his prophecy of Armageddon as if it'd been delivered from the Holy Mount. They were willing to kill for him to make it a reality.

But none of this explained why Manson had chosen the Tate and LaBianca homes as his targets. Manson had known the former tenant at the Tate house, Terry Melcher, a record producer and the son of Doris Day. Melcher had flirted with the idea of recording Manson, who had dreams of rock stardom, but he decided against it. Sometime in the spring before the murders, Manson had gone looking for Melcher at the house, hoping to change his mind, but a friend of the new tenants told him that Melcher had moved out. Manson didn't like the guy's brusque attitude. Consequently, the house on Cielo Drive came to represent the "establishment" that had rejected him. When he ordered the killings, he wanted to "instill fear in Terry Melcher," Susan Atkins had said, sending a clear signal to the stars and executives who'd snubbed him. As for the LaBianca house: Manson had once stayed in the place next door. That house was no longer occupied, but it was no matter. The neighbors, Manson decided, would suffice as targets, because they, too, no matter who they were, symbolized the establishment he sought to overthrow with Helter Skelter.

The trial was the longest and most expensive in U.S. history at the time. It wasn't as straightforward as it might seem, because Manson himself hadn't actually murdered anyone. He hadn't set foot in the Tate home at all, and though he'd entered the LaBianca home, he left before his followers killed the couple. That meant Manson could be convicted of first-degree murder only through a charge of conspiracy. According to the legal principle of vicarious liability, any conspirator was also guilty of the crimes committed by his coconspirators. In other words, if the prosecution could prove that Manson had ordered the killings, he would be guilty of murder, even having not laid a finger on any of the victims. Bugliosi had to show that Manson had a unique ability to control his followers' thoughts and actions—that they would do whatever he asked, even kill complete strangers.

It would have been a complicated case even had things proceeded smoothly. But the Family did all they could to throw sand in the gears. On the very first day of the trial, Manson showed up at the courthouse with an X carved into his forehead, the wound so fresh it was still bleeding. The next day, Atkins, Krenwinkel, and Van Houten arrived with their own bloody Xs. The women skipped down the courtroom hallways, three abreast, holding hands, singing nursery rhymes that Manson had written. They laughed at the photographers who jostled to get their pictures. During the trial, if Manson took umbrage at something, they took umbrage, too, mimicking his profanity, his expressions, his outbursts.

The judge, Charles Older, would often threaten to remove Manson. On one occasion, Manson returned the reproach: "I will have *you* removed if you don't stop. I have a little system of my own...Do you think I'm kidding?" Grabbing a sharp pencil, he sprang over the defense table, flinging himself toward Older. A bailiff intervened and tackled him, and the girls jumped to their feet, too, chanting unintelligible verses in Latin. As he was dragged from the courtroom, Manson remained defiant, shouting, "In the name of Christian justice, someone should cut your head off!" It was a glimpse of the raw pugilism that ran beneath Manson's philosopher-guru facade. The judge began to carry a .38 revolver under his robes.

Things were no more orderly outside the courtroom, where, at the corner of Temple and Grand, members of the Family gathered each morning to hold sidewalk vigils. Barefoot and belligerent, they sat in wide circles, singing songs in praise of their leader. The women suckled newborns. The men laughed and ran their fingers through their long, unwashed hair. All had followed Manson's lead and cut Xs into their foreheads, distributing typewritten statements explaining that the self-mutilation symbolized their "X-ing" themselves "out of society."

Bugliosi called the defendants "bloodthirsty robots"—a grandiloquent phrase, but an apt one. It captured the unsettling duality of the killers: at once animal and artificial, divorced from emotion and yet capable of executing the most intimate, visceral form of murder imaginable. Tex Watson would later hymn the detached, automated ecstasy of stabbing: "Over and over, again and again, my arm like a machine, at one with the blade." Susan Atkins told a cellmate that plunging the knife into Tate's pregnant belly was "like a sexual release. Especially when you see the blood spurting out. It's better than a climax." And behind them was Manson, who lived for sex even as he described himself as "the mechanical boy."

"A Stage of Nothing"

After seven grueling months, the first phase of the trial drew to a close, and the jury, after ten days of deliberation, arrived at unanimous guilty verdicts. Now, in the second phase, the prosecution had to present an argument for putting the defendants to death. Their case, and the defense's counterarguments, led to some of the most unnerving testimony yet, including a kind of symposium on LSD—not as a recreational drug, but as an agent of mind control. This death-penalty phase of the trial entertained some of the same questions that engrossed and vexed me for the next two decades. Had Manson really "brainwashed" people? If so, how? And if one person was truly under the psychological control of another, then who was responsible for that person's actions?

For the first time, the three convicted women—Atkins, Krenwinkel, and Van Houten—took the witness stand. One by one, they explained their roles in the murders, absolving Manson of any complicity and proclaiming their utter lack of remorse. The families of the victims looked on in stunned silence as the women described their loved ones' final moments in clinical detail. To kill someone, the women explained, was an act of love—it freed that person from the confines of their physical being.

Almost unblinkingly, Susan Atkins recalled how Tex Watson had told her to murder Tate: "He looked at her and he said, 'Kill her.' And I killed her...I just stabbed her and she fell, and I stabbed her again. I don't know how many times I stabbed her." Did she feel animosity toward Tate or the others? She shrugged. "I didn't know any of them. How could I have felt any emotion without knowing them?" She knew that what she was doing "was right," she added, "because it felt good."

Patricia Krenwinkel said she'd felt nothing when she stabbed Abigail Folger twenty-eight times. "What is there to describe? It was just there, and it's like it was right." Why would she kill a woman she didn't even know? "Well, it's hard to explain. It was just a thought and the thought came to be."

" 'Sorry' is only a five-letter word," Leslie Van Houten told the courtroom. "It can't bring back anything." She'd helped stab Rosemary LaBianca forty-one times. "What can I feel?" Van Houten said. "It has happened. She is gone."

As unrepentant as the women were, Bugliosi had his work cut out for him when it came to securing the death penalty. His reasoning relied on a seeming contradiction. He'd argued during the first phase of the trial that the women were "brainwashed zombies," totally in Manson's thrall. Now he had to prove the opposite: that they were as complicit as Manson was. Although they were "automatons," Bugliosi said, "slavishly obedient to Manson's every command," the women still had, "deep down inside themselves," such "bloodlust" that they deserved the death penalty.

The defense argued that the women were merely pawns. Manson had used an almost technologically precise combination of drugs, hypnotism, and coercion to transform these formerly non-violent people into frenzied, psychopathic killers. At that point, scientists in the United States had been studying LSD for only a little more than a decade—it was far from a known quantity. Manson, the defense said, had used the drug to ply his impressionable followers, accessing the innermost chambers of their minds and molding them to his designs.

Former members of the Family have often recounted Manson's systematic "brainwashing" methods, beginning with the seduction of new recruits by "bombarding" them with love, sex, and drugs. On the witness stand, Paul Watkins outlined the near weekly orgies that Manson orchestrated at the Spahn Ranch. The leader would hand out drugs, personally deciding everyone's dosages. And then, as Bugliosi writes in *Helter Skelter*,

> Charlie might dance around, everyone else following, like a train. As he'd take off his clothes, all the rest would take off their clothes... Charlie would direct the orgy, arranging bodies, combinations, positions. "He'd set it all up in a beautiful way like he was creating a masterpiece in sculpture," Watkins said, "but instead of clay he was using warm bodies."

If any of those bodies had "hang-ups" or inhibitions, Manson would eliminate them. He'd force someone to do whatever he or she most resisted doing. "One thirteen-year-old girl's initiation into the Family consisted of her being sodomized by Manson while the others watched," Bugliosi wrote. "Manson also 'went down on' a young boy to show the others he had rid himself of all inhibitions."

Tex Watson, in his 1978 memoir *Will You Die for Me?*, tells a similar story. "There was a room in the back of the ranch house totally lined with mattresses," he wrote, essentially set aside for sex. "As we had any inhibitions we still weren't dead, we were still playing back what our parents had programmed into us."

Having made them feel freed and wanted, Manson would isolate his followers from the world beyond the ranch, giving them daily tasks to support the commune and forbidding them from communicating with their families or friends. His was a world without newspapers, clocks, or calendars. Manson chose new names for his initiates. "In order for me to be completely free in my mind I had to be able to completely forget the past," Susan Atkins testified. "The easiest way to do this is to have to change identity."

Their induction was complete after they participated in lengthy LSD sessions—often stretching over consecutive days, with no breaks—during which Manson only pretended to take the drug, or took a much smaller dose. Clearheaded, he manipulated their minds with elaborate word games and sensory techniques he'd developed in the two years since his release from prison. With only negligible downtime between acid trips, detachment was all the easier. Every experience led the Family to drift further from reality until, eventually, even basic contradictions seemed tenable: death was the same as life, good was no different from bad, and God was inseparable from Satan.

Paul Watkins believed that Manson wanted to use LSD "to instill his philosophies, exploit weaknesses and fears, and extract promises and agreements from his followers." And it worked. Watkins recalled an instance in which Manson told Susan Atkins, "I'd like half a coconut, even if you have to go to Rio de Janeiro to get it." Atkins "got right up and was on her way out the door when Charlie said, 'Never mind.'" Manson excelled, Watkins said, at "locating deep-seated hang-ups." He "took up residence in people's heads," leaving them with "no point of reference, nothing to relate back to, no right, no wrong—no roots." They lived in a "new reality" summoned by LSD, which left them "melt-twisted and free of pretension in timeless spirals of movement."

Ironically, as his followers became more and more robotic, Manson taught them that people in the straight world "were like computers," the Family's Brooks Poston wrote. Their worldviews were simply a matter of society's programming, and any program could be expunged. On the stand, Susan Atkins described Sharon Tate as an "IBM machine—words came out of her mouth but they didn't make any sense to me."

For a Family novitiate, the goal was to burn yourself out, to take so much LSD and listen to so much of Charlie's music that you returned "to a purity and nothingness" resembling a new birth, Tex Watson wrote. This was called going "dead in the head," and it let you incorporate into the collective, sharing "one common brain."

Bugliosi had to use a little prosecutorial hocus-pocus to tell stories like these. He argued that the Manson women had been psychologically compromised, but he didn't assert that Manson had actually *created* his killers. Despite Manson's talk about "reprogramming," there was no template for one person's ever having done such a thing to another. Instead, Bugliosi purported that Manson's followers must have had some preexisting homicidal impulse buried in their subconsciouses. Manson had learned to recognize and exploit that impulse, but even so, each woman was responsible for her actions. Then as now, this position fascinated and perplexed me: it posited a form of brainwashing in which the brainwashed were still, to some degree, "themselves."

When it came time to decide on the death penalty, though, the defense called a series of psychiatric experts who disagreed. Manson *had* brainwashed his followers, they said, and those followers couldn't be culpable for the murders. LSD had given him a portal to the most labile parts of the subconscious. The scientists explained how acid could break down and reconstruct someone's personality—how a sober "guide," intended to lead someone peacefully through the many hours of an acid trip, could abuse the role, inserting violent ideals and beliefs into their minds. With repetition and reinforcement, these beliefs took root and flourished even when the followers were sober. Throw in other coercive techniques like sensory deprivation and hypnosis—both of which Manson embraced—and it was possible to rewrite someone's moral code such that she acknowledged no such thing as right or wrong.

Dr. Joel Fort, a research psychiatrist who'd opened the nation's first LSD treatment center, was one of the defense witnesses. He believed that Manson had used LSD to produce "a new pattern of behavior for the girls," resulting in "a totally neutral system which saw death or killing in a completely different way than a normal person sees it," free of "social concern, compassion, [and] moral values."

In one of the most remarkable exchanges in the trial, Manson's attorney, Irving Kanarek, asked Dr. Fort if "a school for crime" could exist, peopled with social rejects and fueled by LSD: "Let us say with your knowledge of LSD, you have a school for crime, and then you take them here and you program them to go out and commit a murder here, there, everywhere...Are you telling us that this can be done, that you can capture the human mind by such a school for crime?"

"I am indeed telling you that," Fort said. And he'd never seen anything like it. He compared it to a government's ability, through the nebulous powers of patriotism, to condition soldiers to kill on its behalf.

What no one brought up was how someone like Manson, with little formal education and so much prison time under his belt, had mastered the ability to control people this way. Whether you thought it was full-on brainwashing or merely intense coercion, the fact remained: He'd done it. No one else had. This remains the most enduring mystery of the case. It's the one that still keeps me up at night. And while all this back-and-forth about LSD is provocative, it feels like an insufficient explanation.

In *Helter Skelter,* Bugliosi grapples with this unfathomable riddle: How did Charles Manson, a barely literate ex-con who'd spent more than half his life in federal institutions, turn a group of previously peaceful hippies—among them a small-town librarian, a high school football star, and a homecoming princess—into savage, unrepentant killers, in less than a year? Bugliosi conceded that he still didn't have the answer. "All these factors contributed to Manson's control over others," he writes,

> but when you add them all up, do they equal murder without remorse? Maybe, but I tend to think there is something more, some missing link that enabled him to so rape and bastardize the minds of his killers that they would go against the most ingrained of all commandments, Thou shalt not kill, and willingly, even eagerly, murder at his command.
>
> It may be something in his charismatic, enigmatic personality, some intangible quality that no one else has yet been able to isolate and identify. It may be something that he learned from others. Whatever it is, I believe Manson has full knowledge of the formula he used. And it worries me that we do not.

In the end, Manson and his followers got the death penalty anyway. Bugliosi said that they had, "coursing through their veins," the willingness to kill others. For the jury, as for the public, that was a much more comfortable truth: these people were an aberration. Brainwashing, complete loss of agency—these were difficult to contemplate, let alone to accept.

"When you take LSD enough times you reach a stage of nothing," Manson had said in court. "You reach a stage of no thought." No one wanted to dwell on that. Ingrained evil, teased out of young women by a mastermind—that was *something*. And something was better than "a stage of nothing."

When the jury delivered death sentences to the four defendants—Manson, Krenwinkel, Atkins, and Van Houten; Kasabian had become a witness for the prosecution and was granted immunity—the three women sprang to their feet. Their heads were freshly shaved, as Manson's was. They'd enlarged the Xs on their foreheads, as Manson had. And they were livid.

"You have judged yourselves," Patricia Krenwinkel screamed at the jury.

"Better lock your doors and watch your own kids," Susan Atkins warned.

"Your whole system is a game," Leslie Van Houten shouted. "You blind, stupid people. Your children will turn against you."

Out on the street, Sandy Good, one of Manson's fiercest loyalists, looked into a TV camera and said, "Death? That's what you're *all* going to get."

With that, the Family was swept off the national stage, and the public could relegate these grisly crimes to the past. Seven people had been brutally murdered. But the nation was confident that we knew how and why, and that the evil people were behind bars.

2

An Aura of Danger

"Live Freaky, Die Freaky"

When I started interviews for my *Premiere* piece, in April 1999, much of what you've just read was unknown to me. I'd gotten through *Helter Skelter*, and I knew the murders had left a mark on Hollywood, but that was about all. In a few years I'd develop a deep obsession with the case; I'd have the trial transcript at my fingertips and binders full of press clippings at my disposal. But in the beginning, I was flummoxed.

Helter Skelter had captured the story definitively. Its author had ensured that Manson was locked away. How could a magazine feature top that? Leslie, my editor, had given me leeway in finding an angle. But her first suggestion—how did the crimes change Hollywood?—wasn't enough for me, and I suspected it wouldn't be enough for her, either.

My earliest weeks of interviews pulled me in wildly different directions. At first, I was compelled by the way the murders had sundered friendships in Hollywood, revealing strong opinions about the era's morality, or lack thereof. As I cycled through Hollywood cliques, I found that I was reigniting thirty-year-old rumors and rivalries. Everyone, over time, assigned the blame for the crimes a little differently. I was dealing in memories that had survived decades of erosion. Even my most reliable sources were shaky on the details. As for the *un*reliable sources, I kept reminding myself that many of them were washed-up Hollywood personalities, often in their dotage. Their memories had warped to accommodate their bruised egos, their ulterior motives, and, above all, their sense that they were at the center of any story worth telling.

A lot of the contradictions I heard centered on the house at Cielo Drive, and the decadent scene there in the months before the murders. That house still signified a lot in Hollywood. For some, the death of Sharon Tate and her friends aroused as much fear as it did grief.

After the murders, the media had blamed Hollywood's "unreality and hedonism," as the *New York Times*'s Stephen Roberts put it, for having fostered an atmosphere where mass homicide was all but guaranteed. Roberts, then Los Angeles bureau chief of the *Times*, talked to a lot of Hollywood people in those first weeks. Bugliosi quoted him in *Helter Skelter:* "All the stories had a common thread: That somehow the victims had brought the murders on themselves...The attitude was summed up in the epigram: 'Live freaky, die freaky.'"

The problem was, thirty years later, no one could agree on who had brought the "freakiness" into the home, and why. I had to wonder if there was a conspiracy of silence in Hollywood. It had taken months for the LAPD to crack the case. In that time, Manson and the Family had almost certainly killed others. If Hollywood hadn't circled the wagons, it seemed there was a good chance the investigation could have ended sooner. So many of the people I spoke to had strong ideas about why these murders had happened—and yet none of them had spoken to the police, and many remained unwilling to go on the record with me.

The one thing everyone seemed to agree on—everyone outside of the DA's office, that is—is that Bugliosi's Helter Skelter motive didn't add up. It had worn thin with police and Hollywood insiders, and it was wearing thin with me, too. I tried to unpack this idea that Manson chose the Cielo house to "instill fear" in Terry Melcher, the record producer whose rejection had apparently so enraged Manson that he activated a race war.

One problem was that Melcher, by all accounts, had no idea that this was why the Family attacked his former home. They never told *him* that they wanted him to be afraid—they didn't follow the murders with any kind of communication to him. According to Bugliosi, Melcher never realized the crimes had anything to do with him until months later, when the police got in touch with him. How was this motive supposed to work if Melcher was never apprised of it?

The grander scheme underlying Helter Skelter—to start a massive race war by making it look as if Black Panthers were behind the murders—didn't land, either. Although Manson was clearly a racist, and while he had a wild, eschatological philosophy, no one believed even for a second that black militants were behind these killings, as he'd hoped it would seem.

So was the Family just too dumb, or too drugged, to pull it off? Or was there another reason for the murders that had nothing to do with race wars and scaring Melcher? It seemed to me that the Manson murders had garnered much of their infamy—and Bugliosi much of his fame—from the Helter Skelter motive. A hippie race war spawned by an acid-drenched, brainwashing ex-con: it was such a fantastical conceit that the murders lived on in pop culture. With a more commonplace explanation—a drug burn, say, or Hollywood infighting—they would've faded into history after a few years, and Bugliosi would never have written the most popular true-crime book of all time.

With an eye on other possible motives, I focused on three questions in my first weeks of reporting. First: Did the victims at the Tate house have something to do with the killers?

Second: Had Terry Melcher known who the killers were immediately after the crimes, and failed to report them to the authorities?

Third, and most sensationally: Were the police aware of Manson's role in the crimes much earlier than it seemed—had they delayed arresting the Family to protect the victims, or Melcher and his circle, from scrutiny?

Here, as neatly as I can tell it, is what I learned in the early, frantic weeks of my reporting. Just as important is what I *didn't* learn—which goes a long way toward explaining how a simple three-month magazine assignment turned into a twenty-year obsession.

"The Dancing Was Different"

Julian Wasser, a photographer for *Life* magazine, was my first interview. Almost right away, I felt the kind of cognitive dissonance that followed me through my reporting. I'd meet my sources at a fancy restaurant of their choice—in this case, Le Petit Four, a sunny sidewalk café in West Hollywood—and, within minutes, as the conversation turned toward violence, the plush setting would feel totally incongruous. Such was the case with Wasser, who told me over a tuna niçoise salad about one of the saddest days of his life.

Days after the murders, as part of an editorial for *Life,* Wasser had accompanied Roman Polanski on his first return visit to the house on Cielo Drive. One of Wasser's pictures from that day is a study in grief. Polanski, in a white T-shirt, sits slumped and devastated on the front porch of his home, his eyes carefully averted from the faded word "Pig" written in his wife's blood on the front door.

"It was too soon," Wasser told me. He'd shadowed Polanski as he moved through the bloodstained rooms. It wasn't a home anymore; it was evidence. "There was fingerprint-dusting powder all over the bedroom and the phones, and there was blood in the carpet. It was thick like Jell-O." And there was so much of it that it hadn't even dried yet, Wasser said. "You could still smell it … Salty, carnal." The odor reminded him of a slaughterhouse.

Right away, Wasser regretted the assignment. But Polanski wanted him there, even at his most vulnerable moment. It wasn't an exercise in vanity, at least not entirely. Hoping to help solve the murders, Polanski had invited along a psychic, Peter Hurkos, whose alleged clairvoyance had made him a minor celebrity. Wasser was enlisted to provide duplicates of his photos to Hurkos, who could glean "psychic vibrations" from them.

Polanski led them to the nursery, which Tate had carefully furnished and decorated in anticipation of the baby. "Roman went over to the bassinet and just started crying. I said, 'This is such a private moment, I shouldn't be here,' and he said, 'Please, don't take any more pictures right now.' It was just the saddest thing I've ever seen in my whole career. I've never seen anything, in my mind, so intrusive, even though he had invited me … The enormity of it," Wasser added, "going into this pregnant woman's bedroom and seeing her intimate area covered with fingerprint powder and realizing what happened there."

Hurkos, it turned out, didn't share Wasser's sense of solemnity. A week before the *Life* story ran, pirated reproductions of Wasser's photos appeared on the front page of the tabloid the *Hollywood Citizen News*. The psychic had sold his copies, vibrations and all.

Wasser described the "great fear" that descended on Los Angeles after the murders. "I lived in Beverly Hills. If you went to someone's house they wouldn't let you in. The normal selfishness and paranoia was magnified a hundredfold. It was another reason for not answering your door."

I heard a lot of that in my first interviews. Sales of burglar alarms and security systems had apparently soared after the murders, and people were quick to ditch their drug stashes. There's a famous, anonymous line from *Life*, from the very article featuring Wasser's pictures, actually: "Toilets are flushing all over Beverly Hills; the entire Los Angeles sewer system is stoned."

Others took more drastic precautions. At the funeral of his friend Sebring, Steve McQueen carried a pistol in his belt, his publicist Warren Cowan told me. The actor was in the throes of an anxiety that pervaded Hollywood, where everyone suspected that the killer might be among them. Dominick Dunne, the *Vanity Fair* journalist known for his reporting on the entertainment industry, told me, "Hollywood did change...The dancing was different. The drugs were different. The fucking was different." He and his wife were so frightened that they sent their kids to stay with their grandmother in northern California.

Tina Sinatra, Frank's daughter, said that her father had hired a security guard. "He was there from sundown to sunrise for months," she explained. "Mom fed him to death, I think. He was uniformed with a gun and he sat in the kitchen *all* night. I can remember the whole tone of this city afterward...it defined fear."

In 1999, apparently, that fear was still alive and well, at least among Hollywood's A-list, many of whom declined to speak to me, even though thirty years had passed. I was rebuffed by the intimates of Tate, Polanski, and Sebring—sometimes with vehemence, sometimes with tersely worded emails or phone calls. "No interest." "Doesn't want to be involved." Or just the one word: "No." Warren Beatty and Jane Fonda said no. Jack Nicholson and Dennis Hopper, both reputedly close to Tate and Polanski: no, no. Candice Bergen, Terry Melcher's girlfriend at the time of the murders, said no, too—as did David Geffen, Mia Farrow, and Anjelica Huston, among others.

As the rejections piled up, I had my own bout of paranoia. Had some memo gone out? My request had asked simply if they'd like to discuss the aftereffects of the murders on their community; it didn't feel like I was prying. And *Premiere,* since it was dedicated entirely to the movie business, usually garnered some enthusiasm from this crowd. Bruce Dern: no. Kirk Douglas: no. Paul Newman: no. Elliott Gould, Ann-Margret, Hugh Hefner: no, no, no. All told, more than three dozen people turned me down. Some were household names, but plenty of the decidedly nonfamous found reasons to decline, too. It was looking like I'd have a story about Hollywood with no one from Hollywood in it.

Hoping for something more revelatory, I went to less well-known names. Peter Bart, the longtime editor in chief of *Variety,* had been close to Polanski, and what he told me gave me some semblance of a lead.

"I must confess that that crowd was a little scary," Bart said, referring to Polanski and Tate's circle. "There was an aura of danger around them...there was an instinctive feeling that everyone was pushing it and things were getting out of control. My wife and I *still* talk about it," he said. "Anybody who underestimates the impact of the event is full of shit."

This was my first taste of the "live freaky, die freaky" view: the idea that Polanski's circle, with its bacchanalian parties and flexible morals, had brought about their own murders. I thought there might be something here. After all, the murders had been solved and the victims had done seemingly nothing to instigate them—but Bart, and others I'd soon speak to, still claimed that their lifestyles were to blame.

I had to get closer to those who'd known Sharon and Roman, anyone who'd attended these supposedly lurid parties. But the rejections kept coming. I'd been in touch with Diane Ladd's manager, having heard that Ladd, who'd been married to Bruce Dern at the time of the murders, ran in some of the same circles as Tate and Polanski. Her manager promised to set up an interview. The next day she called back, saying that Ladd had had an "emotional, visceral reaction." The manager said, "I don't know what happened with Diane back in the sixties, but she adamantly refused to have anything to do with the piece. She even told me that if her name was in it, she was going to contact her attorney."

Peter Fonda gave me yet another no. Not long afterward, I came across him at a gas station in the middle of the Mojave Desert, of all places, some five hours outside L.A. True to form, he was in leathers and on a Harley. I approached him with my business card and tried to explain the story as succinctly as possible. He seemed receptive. But later, when I followed up again, the answer was still: no.

I mentioned the rash of rejections to Peter Bart. His observation stayed with me, especially as the months wore on and I began to see that Manson might have been more plugged into Hollywood than anyone cared to admit. "Just the fact that they're all saying no," he said, "is fascinating."

Bugliosi's First Slip

There was one major player who agreed to talk to me: Vincent Bugliosi. Not only did he sign on for an interview, he invited me to his new home in Pasadena, the same one where, years later, he would threaten to "hurt [me] like [I'd] never been hurt before" if I published my findings.

There was no sign of that animosity during our first meeting. On a sunny spring day, Bugliosi gave me six hours of his time, driving me around to show me various landmarks related to the crime and enjoying a long lunch with me in one of his favorite restaurants. I was flattered to have captured his attention—here was the man who'd put away one of the monsters of the twentieth century. Later I would question the motive behind all his generosity.

A prosecutor makes a lot of enemies over the course of his career, and Bugliosi, I'd learn, made more than most, both in and out of the DA's office. But considering that he'd once fielded death threats from Manson himself, he lived in a surprisingly unprotected home, quintessentially suburban. He and Gail, his wife of forty-three years, were still moving in when I visited that April of 1999; Bugliosi, white haired, lean, and blue eyed, greeted me with a firm handshake and a litany of apologies for the unpacked boxes. In the living room, flowers of all kinds, dried, artificial, and real, burst from pots and vases.

Their kitchen, adorned with Gail's chicken and rooster tchotchkes, could've been right out of a fifties sitcom. Bugliosi picked up a hairless cat that brushed against his leg—a rare Siamese breed, he told me. The cat's name was Sherlock, "because he snoops everywhere." Gail put out a plate of cookies and a pair of iced teas for us.

Bugliosi was a fast talker. He sent a tsunami of words in my direction, sometimes jumping out of his chair for no apparent reason. Gail, an island of repose by comparison, busied herself at the kitchen counter. I caught her rolling her eyes as her husband told me that the movie version of *Helter Skelter,* from 1976, "was number one that year" and "had the biggest ratings in TV history, prior to *Roots.*" He'd essentially been on a thirty-year victory lap, and he had his talking points down cold. It was hard to get him off script. As he drove me around that day, he was still reliving his encounters with Manson in the courtroom. Sometimes it seemed he was quoting almost verbatim from *Helter Skelter.* On the surface, he seemed chatty and forthcoming, but everything he said—for hours—was canned.

Still hoping for a good angle, I tried to probe, however gently, at the holes I'd noticed in *Helter Skelter.* For one, how had the cops missed so many clues in the case—why hadn't they solved it much sooner? As he did in his book, Bugliosi blamed sloppy police work. They never would've cracked the case without him, he told me.

I wanted his take on the Cielo house's caretaker, William Garretson, who'd been the only one on the property to survive that night. Garretson lived in the modest guesthouse separated from the main home. His story was so unlikely that, at first, he'd been the LAPD's number one suspect. He swore that his stereo had been playing loud enough to drown out the murders. He'd heard no part of the brutal slaughter, even though the screaming and the gun-shots had occurred only sixty feet from his bedroom window. And Bugliosi concurred, albeit reluctantly. The police, he reminded me, had conducted sound tests that supported Garretson.

I moved on to Terry Melcher. If Manson had wanted to teach him a lesson, why did he order the killings of people who had no real connection to him, other than that they'd lived at the same address at different times? Melcher didn't know any of the victims at the Tate house. I couldn't even find evidence that he'd *met* any of them. Plus, by Bugliosi's own account, Manson sent his followers to the Cielo house knowing full well that Melcher *didn't* live there anymore.

Bugliosi dodged those questions, instead reiterating the terror that Melcher felt during the trial and for years afterward—fearing that Manson or someone from the Family still wanted him dead. Could he put me in touch with Melcher? The mere fact that I'd asked seemed to unnerve him a bit. He said I'd have a hard time getting him to talk. Later, when I did manage to track down Melcher, I'd find out why.

As the sun was setting after many hours of talk, I asked Bugliosi if he could share anything with me about the case that had never been reported before—the journalist's Hail Mary. I could see by the furrow of his brow that he was really thinking about it. I pulled a book from my bag: Barney Hoskyns's *Waiting for the Sun,* a his-tory of L.A.'s music industry. I'd been reading it for research—what with all the rejections I'd gotten, I had a little more free time on my hands than I'd expected—and I wanted Bugliosi to look at a passage I'd highlighted. Hoskyns alleged that a few S&M movies had been filmed at the Tate house, and that a drug dealer had once been tied up and flogged against his will at a party there. Other sources, including Ed Sanders's 1971 book *The Family,* had made the same claims, but Bugliosi had conspicuously omitted the anecdote from *Helter Skelter.*

Bugliosi seemed to be in the midst of some kind of internal debate. After what felt like a long silence, he told me to turn off my recorder. "This can never be attributed to me," he began. "Just say it's from a very reliable source." (I'll explain later in the book why I'm treating this as an on-the-record response.)

Bugliosi claimed that, when he'd joined the case, the detectives told him they'd recovered some videotape in the loft at the house on Cielo Drive. According to the detectives, the footage depicted Sharon Tate being forced to have sex with two unidentified men. Bugliosi never saw the tape, so could not verify what the detectives claimed. How could they be sure it was non-consensual sex? But Bugliosi claimed he told them, "Put it back where you found it. Roman has suffered enough. There's nothing to gain. All it's going to do is hurt her memory and hurt him. They're both victims."

It was a tawdry aside, I thought, and anyway, Bugliosi had reported most of this episode before. In *Helter Skelter,* he wrote that the cops had recovered a tape of Roman and Sharon "making love," and that it had been discreetly returned to their home. Polanski had found it not long after, on the same visit with Julian Wasser and the psychic. He "climbed the ladder to the loft," Bugliosi writes, "found the videotape LAPD had returned, and slipped it into his pocket, according to one of the officers who was present."

The more I thought about it, the more startled I was that the footage was so sordid. It gave yet more weight to the "live freaky, die freaky" motto. Was it rape? Bugliosi wasn't in a position to say, but if he was telling the truth about his conversation with the detectives—and that was a big *if,* I soon acknowledged—the tape seemed like something that the police should've at least retained.

I hoped that I could verify Bugliosi's story. It was the first piece of new information I'd found so far. In my haste to keep reporting, I failed to see that the revelation came with a slipup on his part, one that would take me more than six years to recognize. He couldn't have told the detectives to put the tape back in the loft. As a DA, he wasn't assigned the Tate murder case until November 18, 1969, months after Polanski's August 17 return visit to the house.

In the early phases of a case, police need to talk to DAs like Bugliosi to authorize search warrants. If he'd learned about the tape from the detectives back in August—if he'd been the one, as he claimed, who ordered its return to the house—then something in the police investigation had necessitated his involvement much earlier than he'd ever acknowledged. Maybe it was something trifling; maybe it was something he felt he'd had to cover up to protect some celebrities' reputations. The point was, we'd never know, because it was something he'd hidden from his readers. Though I hadn't caught this mistake, there were more variations to come. When I finally found them, it would change the whole tenor of our relationship.

Ugliness and Purity

Helter Skelter opens with a famous sentence: "It was so quiet, one of the killers would later say, you could almost hear the sound of ice rattling in cocktail shakers in the homes down the canyon." The first half of the book, concerning the police investigation, traffics in the dread of that sentence. Given Bugliosi's revelation to me, it was the first place I started looking for a break. If he had changed one detail about the case, could he have changed others? That question would recur throughout my entire investigation.

The LAPD had assigned two separate teams of detectives to the cases, one for the Tate murders and one for the LaBiancas. Despite the similarities in the crimes, the LAPD had concluded, as mentioned earlier, that the LaBiancas were the victims of a copycat crime. After all, there was seemingly little common ground between the luxe Beverly Hills set at Cielo and the suburban couple in Los Feliz.

The police fanned out in what would become the largest murder investigation in Los Angeles history. The LaBianca team operated in relative anonymity; the press couldn't muster much interest in their case, at least not when Sharon Tate's killer was on the lam. On the other side of town, by contrast, the Cielo crime scene was like a carnival. The LAPD had assigned twenty-one men to the case. Helicopters hovered over the hilltop property. Guards stood watch around the clock at the entry gate.

Detectives moved to lock down their initial suspect right away. William Garretson, the lone survivor of the night's massacre, was dragged out of the guesthouse sleepy-eyed, shirtless, and barefoot, shoved into a patrol car, and driven straight to headquarters, where he was read his rights and charged with five murders. Garretson, only nineteen, couldn't explain why he hadn't heard anything that night, except to say it might have been because he had the stereo on. For three days, he was on front pages around the world as he languished behind bars. Finally, police concluded he was just a slow kid in the wrong place at the wrong time.

In those same first twenty-four hours, the Tate detectives got a tip. A friend of the victims had been telling people that he knew who the murderers were; convinced that his knowledge would get him killed, the friend had gone into hiding. He was Witold Kaczanowski, an artist and Polish émigré who'd known the Tate crowd through his countryman Voytek Frykowski. Police tracked him down through Roman Polanski's manager. Lured by the promise of twenty-four-hour police protection, Kaczanowksi finally consented to be interviewed.

He believed that Frykowski had been involved in the drug trade with a host of career criminals and other unsavory characters. One of these was a man named Harris "Pic" Dawson, who had, at a recent party, threatened to kill Frykowski. Remember how Susan Atkins wrote the word "Pig" on the front door of Cielo Drive, in Sharon Tate's blood? Kaczanowski thought that word was "Pic," as in Pic Dawson.

The police found him credible, especially because they'd learned about another altercation at the Cielo house that past spring, when Tate and Polanski had thrown a going-away party. (Although the couple had moved in only on February 15, by the end of March they had to leave for separate film jobs in Europe, where they'd remain for most of the summer.) At their farewell party, attended by more than a hundred guests, three gate-crashers had behaved so aggressively that Polanski had them kicked out. They were Billy Doyle, Tom Harrigan, and Pic Dawson.

Hoping to ask Polanski about these three, police anxiously awaited his return from London, scheduled for the evening of August 10, the day after the bodies had been discovered. Polanski flew back to L.A. under heavy sedation, with his longtime producer Gene Gutowski and two friends, Warren Beatty and Victor Lownes. At the airport, he was spirited through a side exit to a waiting car while Gutowski read a statement to the throngs of press.

The chairman of Paramount Pictures had arranged a suite for Polanski on the studio lot—a place where he could avoid the prying eyes of the press, and the killers, too, if they were out to get him. But before he arrived at Paramount, Polanski had his car stop at a Denny's parking lot for a hushed conversation with Kaczanowski. Bugliosi never reported this in *Helter Skelter*. The media never knew about it. To me, it was something to explore.

After they chatted at Denny's, Kaczanowski got in the car and headed to Paramount with the director; they talked all the way to the lot. When the LAPD arrived at the studio that evening, they were barred from entering Polanski's suite until he'd finished the debriefing. Bugliosi didn't find that worth mentioning; he only wrote that "Polanski was taken to an apartment inside the Paramount lot, where he remained in seclusion under a doctor's care. The police talked to him briefly that night, but he was, at that time, unable to suggest anyone with a motive for the murders."

Polanski's friends Lownes and Gutowski confirmed the secret Denny's meeting in interviews with me. Both defended it as a simple exchange of information between Polanski and Kaczanowski. And yet Polanski, in a polygraph exam with the LAPD, had denied knowing Kaczanowski.

Sensing there was more to the story, I sought out Kaczanowski, who, like so many others connected to the victims, had never spoken to reporters about the murders. Over the phone, somewhat to my surprise, he promptly agreed to discuss the case with me. Yes, he said, the Denny's meeting had happened, but, despite its seeming urgency, there was nothing so furtive about it. He'd only answered some of Polanski's questions about Frykowski's possible drug dealing. Kaczanowski emphasized that his suspicion—that Pic Dawson had targeted Frykowski—sent the police on a months-long chase that amounted to nothing.

And yet it was easy to see how Frykowski may have gotten in over his head in those months before the murders. It was a turbulent time at the Cielo house, I learned—much more fraught than Bugliosi had reported. When Tate and Polanski left, they gave Frykowski and Abigail Folger the run of the place, and things got weird. The couple threw parties all the time. The door was open to anyone and everyone. The crowds grew rowdier, the drugs harder—not just pot and hash, but an abundance of cocaine, mescaline, LSD, and MDA, which was then a new and fairly unheard-of synthetic. Frykowski was especially enamored of it.

Dawson, Doyle, and Harrigan, the same trio who'd been booted from the party in mid-March, were now regular guests at the house, sometimes staying for days at a time. They also supplied most of the drugs. By July, the three men, all international smugglers, had cornered the market on MDA, which was manufactured in Doyle and Harrigan's hometown, Toronto. Frykowski wanted in. Although he didn't have much cash—Folger, his heiress girlfriend, kept him on a tight leash financially—he negotiated a deal with his new friends, making himself a middleman between them and Hollywood.

Soon after we spoke on the phone, Kaczanowski visited Los Angeles. I met him in the backyard of his friend's home in West Hollywood. A handsome man with a craggy face, thick black hair, and robust blue eyes, he spoke with a heavy accent and a reserved, contemplative air. Though it was maybe three in the afternoon, he opened a bottle of red wine and poured us each a generous glass.

He'd been the last of Frykowski's friends to see him alive. The two had gotten together at his gallery just hours before the murders; he'd intended to visit the Tate house that night, but he was too tired. Frykowski had called him around midnight, likely just minutes before the killers arrived, to try to talk him into coming over.

Now he showed me a large manila envelope full of old ephemera, including Frykowski's airline ticket to the United States, dated May 16, 1967, and a reference letter Polanski had written for him on Paramount stationery. These artifacts seemed to transport Kaczanowski. The sixties, he said, were often on his mind.

"I can close my eyes and I feel that it's still 1969. I hear people's voices, I see their faces," Kaczanowski said. He was amazed at how the usual indicators of class and status had disappeared in Hollywood at the time, where "the most extreme ugliness with total purity was mixed up." This blurriness was the inevitable outcome of the open-door policy they'd all subscribed to at the end of the decade. "Totally primitive, uneducated people" could dress and act like visionary artists. "And you couldn't know absolutely who was who. You could have a Manson and you could have a great poet and it was impossible to make a distinction."

Accordingly, Kaczanowski remembered "so many strange people" coming and going from the house on Cielo Drive, where he would sometimes stay with Frykowski for days at a stretch. "I didn't trust them," he said of the guests. "They walked so freely through the place." He would ask Frykowski who these people were, and the answer always came with degrees of removal—they were friends of this guy, or friends of friends of so-and-so. That was why, after the murders, he felt he'd gotten a bead on who the killers were: the same set of drug dealers that Bugliosi mentions passingly in *Helter Skelter*.

"I remember Voytek telling me that they threw Pic Dawson out of a party," he said, taking a sip of wine. "They told Pic Dawson to take his backpack and fuck off." Kaczanowski remembered another party, a few weeks before the murders, where he'd had to kick out two very drunk guys. At the gate, "they were standing on the other side, looking at Voytek and me, and they said, 'You sons of bitches, we will be back, and we will kill you.'"

All the months of partying with Frykowski had a cumulative effect. He met so many threatening characters that, when his friend turned up dead, he was convinced one or more of them was to blame. He'd wondered if Frykowski, or even Polanski or Sebring, had ever encountered Manson or his followers. His concern and uncertainty still felt raw. Here was someone who'd been so close to the victims that he'd held on to their possessions for all these years—and he still couldn't rule out the possibility of a revenge motive. As I sat across from him, the elaborate puffery of the Helter Skelter motive, and all the panicked headlines that came with it, seemed to recede into the afternoon smog.

If Frykowski were alive, I ventured, and Kaczanowski could ask him one question, what would it be? Looking down into his wine, he said quietly, "Did you ever meet anybody from the group of people who came to kill you?"

"He Who Dies with the Most Toys Wins"

Having finished what would be her final film, *The Thirteen Chairs* (also known as *12 + 1*), Sharon Tate came back to the Cielo house in July 1969, more than seven months pregnant. She wanted to have her baby in the house she loved. But Polanski, who was supposed to have returned by then, deferred his homecoming. He needed to continue scouting locations for his next film. Assuring her that he'd be back in time for the baby's arrival, he asked his old friend Frykowski to stick around with Folger and keep Tate company.

That, at least, is the version Bugliosi provides. Once I'd heard from him about the tape from Polanski's house and the seedier side of Cielo, I started pushing harder in my interviews, and diverging stories developed. Polanski's intimates said that Tate was grateful for the company. She didn't want to be alone in the secluded estate, especially at the end of her pregnancy. As for Polanski himself, his friends described him as careful, conservative, even square, and deeply in love with his wife. If he said he had to stay on in London for work, then that's what he was doing.

Others remembered it differently. Tate had been horrified at the scene that greeted her upon her return to Los Angeles. She was leery of Folger and especially of Frykowski, whom she suspected of drug dealing—she wanted the couple, and the crowd attached to them, out of her house. As I won the confidence of some of her closest friends, they came out with intensely disturbing stories. Her marriage was in shambles, they said, and many of them didn't want her to fix it—they wanted her to leave it.

According to those I spoke to, the Sharon Tate they knew, warm and vivacious, was diminished in Polanski's presence. "The difference in Sharon was incredible," said Elke Sommer, the German actress who appeared with her in *The Wrecking Crew.* She "just wasn't herself when she was with him. She was in awe, or frightened; he had an awesome charisma."

Dominick Dunne, who'd been close to Tate, Polanski, and Jay Sebring, was confident that Polanski hosted orgies at the house. "I never went to their orgies, but I know they existed, and I think Jay was in on it, too," he said to me. The director James Toback—who would himself be disgraced, nearly twenty years later, by more than two hundred allegations of sexual harassment (which he strongly denies)—was even more certain. One night, Warren Beatty had invited him to a party at the Tate house. Toback brought Jim Brown, a football all-star who'd become an action-film hero. At the party, people began to whisper about an orgy. "I was going to be included because I was with Jim," Toback told me, "and I was certainly up for it, but Jim declined."

And yet: "James Toback is full of shit," Paul Sylbert, a production designer and a friend of Polanski, told me. "Nothing crazy went on up there. There were no orgies, not that I ever have been to, and I was up there frequently." He conceded that Polanski was "peculiar," but "whatever his kinkiness was, it was on a small scale and quite private. He might've been hinting at orgies, but there were never any."

Orgies or no, at a certain point Tate felt that she'd suffered enough. As the humiliations accumulated, she approached Elke Sommer for her advice. Sommer remembered telling her, "I'd take the next heavy object, whether it's an iron or a frying pan or a spade out in the yard, and I'd just brain him."

Tate wasn't about to do that, but she did, on a few occasions, warm to the idea of leaving Polanski. Sommer thought she was always too much in her husband's thrall to follow through. "There was a tremendous sickness when I worked with Sharon," Sommer said, "a horrendous sickness surrounding her relationship. She was quite lost."

A number of Tate's friends were quick to mention the undesirable company she kept—with Frykowski and Folger at the top of the list.

Tate "couldn't stand them," said Joanna Pettet, another actress who'd become close to her. The two had had lunch together at the house on the day of the murders. Pettet was surprised to see Frykowski and Folger, whom she'd never met before, walking around like they owned the place. "I asked, who are these people? Why are they here? She said, 'Roman didn't want me to be alone.'" Tate tolerated the pair only because her husband insisted on it. A friend described her on the phone with Polanski, so depressed that she fell into tears, complaining that the two had brought too many drugs into the house, too much chaos. But Polanski apparently refused to turn them out. She asked constantly when he would come home, but he kept postponing his return trip. Moreover, she told Pettet she'd tried to stay with him in London, and he wouldn't let her—he didn't appear to want her there.

I'd gone to great lengths to track down Pettet, who had quit the movie business in the nineties. She lived in the high desert beyond Palm Springs, where she was something of a recluse, with no phone. It had dawned on me that I might be able to reach her through the Screen Actors Guild—they would have her address on file, since they were responsible for mailing her residual checks. Through them, I sent her a long letter, and she agreed to meet me for lunch at a strip mall near her house. She was slightly apprehensive when she first arrived. Then fifty-seven, she cut a striking figure, dressed head to toe in denim, with dark glasses that obscured her piercing eyes, until she felt comfortable enough to remove them.

"I lost it when Sharon was killed," she said. "I had to be hospitalized and missed the funeral." She made no attempt to conceal her contempt for Polanski. "I hated him," she said flatly. As others had, Pettet described a marriage in which he exuded an almost casual cruelty toward his wife. For four months in the summer of '67, Pettet had stayed with the couple at a rented beach house, and she began to notice how often Polanski bossed Tate around. She said he had a malicious streak; sometimes it reached Pettet herself. "He would throw a brick in the pool and watch my dog dive for it and try to retrieve it. He stood there laughing. The dog wouldn't give up."

After Sharon's funeral, Polanski called Pettet. "On the phone he was strange with me, cold as ice. There was no despair. And I was sobbing." He wanted to know what she'd told the police. It made her wonder what was behind her friend's murder. "At the time I suspected it was maybe friends of his who did it. All I know is, he never came [when she asked him to come back], and she was here."

Figuring that Polanski's confidants would want to tell a different story, I coaxed Bill Tennant, his manager, into talking to me. Tennant had never given an interview about the murders, in part because the events of 1969 had sent his life into a tailspin. He'd had the somber task of identifying the bodies at the Tate house. A 1993 piece in *Variety* (by Peter Bart, as coincidence would have it) described Tennant's fall from grace. Through the sixties and seventies, he'd found great success in Hollywood, discovering the script for *Butch Cassidy and the Sundance Kid* and agenting Peter Fonda's deal for *Easy Rider*. But Bart had found him, "a gaunt, battered figure," "sleeping in a doorway on Ventura Boulevard." A cocaine addiction had done away with his marriage and his money, leading him to trade "even the gold inlays in his teeth for a fix." In Bart's assessment, "the shock of the Manson murders began unraveling him."

I tracked down Tennant in London, where he was sober, remarried, and managing Michael Flatley, the Lord of the Dance. He'd become a born-again Christian, but he displayed little compassion or forgiveness for Polanski, his onetime client and friend. "Roman is a shit," he said. Echoing what I'd heard from other friends of the couple, Tennant said there were two versions of their story. "Which one do you want to tell?"

On one hand, Polanski had fallen into dissolution in London, where he was working on a movie and sleeping around while, back in California, his pregnant wife was putting together a home. Tate "wound up getting murdered because he was fucking around in London," he suggested. But that was just one side of it.

"The other story is sitting in the Bel Air Hotel with Roman after the funerals and having to address his financial situation, which was not very good," Tennant said, "and Roman looking across the table at me and saying, I wish I had spent more. I wish I had bought more dresses. I wish I had given more gifts. So what story do you want to tell? The one about this little prick who left his wife alone . . . with Jay Sebring and Gibby [Folger] and Voytek, these wankers, these four tragic losers, or do you want to talk about a poor kid, Roman Polanski?"

Tennant resisted the idea that the murders represented a loss of innocence for Hollywood. "There was nothing innocent about it," he said. "It was retribution." The big value in Los Angeles when he was there, Tennant said, was this: "He who dies with the most toys wins. I think it's pretty self-serving to call that period, and what was going on, innocent . . . What's innocent about drugs? What's innocent about promiscuous sex? . . . You tell me where the innocence was." Within a week of the murders, Polanski was "partying it up" with Warren Beatty, he claimed. In his opinion, the brutal reality was that "nobody cared or gave a shit about Sharon Tate. Not because they weren't nice but because she was expendable. As expendable as an actor whose option comes up and gets dropped."

After his wife's murder, Polanski stayed on the Paramount studios lot as much as he could. It was the only place he felt safe. And not just from the killers or the media—from the LAPD. "You found the police surveillance units and you found that the police in Los Angeles knew everything about everybody," Tennant said: "that there was a kind of FBI-slash-CIA aspect of the Los Angeles Police Department, and that they knew everything there was to know."

Although he had no way of knowing it in 1969, Tennant wasn't being paranoid when he wondered how the LAPD knew so much about his friends. Many law enforcement agencies, including the LAPD, the Los Angeles County Sheriff's Office, and the FBI, had maintained units to surveil and even infiltrate groups that they considered subversive or threatening. At this stage, I wasn't inclined to view law enforcement with anything approaching suspicion. Even so, I was beginning to see the official version of the case with a jaundiced eye.

"In California, Everybody Has a Tan"

I found it difficult to sort through the stories coming out of the house on Cielo Drive. Picture a spiderweb so dense with connections and tendrils that it looks like a solid sheet of fabric. That's what I felt I was working with. The Hollywood cliques that had seemed, at the start, so discrete and isolated were all mixed up with one another, much more than Bugliosi had made it appear. Plus, then and now, people weren't always willing to be up-front about who they hung out with.

Tate was right to be wary of Frykowski, assuming she had been. He'd fallen in with a dangerous crowd. Many of the "primitive" people that Kaczanowski met had extensive rap sheets, and their names kept coming up when people mentioned the gravest excesses of Cielo Drive. Pic Dawson, who'd threatened Frykowski's life and been thrown out of Polanski's party, had been the subject of Interpol surveillance for drug smuggling as early as 1965. The young son of a diplomat, he'd gained entrée in the Polanski crowd through his friendship with Cass Elliot, one of the singers in the popular sixties group the Mamas and the Papas. Like most of the men in the troubled singer's life, he'd used her for her money and connections. Elliot's biographers would later write that her infamous 1966 London arrest—she'd been caught stealing hotel towels and keys—was actually a ruse to force her to share information about Dawson's drug-smuggling operations. Dawson's colleagues in the drug business, Billy Doyle and Tom Harrigan, also wormed their way into Polanski's circle through Mama Cass.

According to police reports, Dawson, Doyle, and Harrigan—all twenty-seven, and all romantically involved with Elliot—were joined by a fourth partner, "Uncle" Charles Tacot, a New Yorker who was more than a decade older. A former marine, the six-foot-six strongman was renowned for his prowess with knives; he was rumored to have maintained ties to military intelligence, and he'd been selling drugs in Los Angeles since his arrival in the mid-1950s. Curiously, despite their many years of drug peddling and several drug arrests among them, only Doyle had ever been convicted of any crime—and his conviction was later overturned and changed to an acquittal on his record. Like Charles Manson, the four men seemed to have little fear of law enforcement.

Helter Skelter paid only passing attention to these guys. They were among the few figures in the book who were given pseudonyms. Although Bugliosi noted Pic Dawson's death threat against Frykowski, he omitted an even more disturbing incident, one that makes a revenge motive much more plausible—and that reveals the extent to which the victims were mixed up in the seamier side of the counterculture.

As the story goes, at some point in the months before the murders, the residents of Cielo threw one of their endless parties, with Frykowski and Sebring leading the charge. Billy Doyle showed up and, in the spirit of the times, drank, smoked, and snorted himself to unconsciousness. Frykowski and Sebring wanted to get even with Doyle for something. Some say he'd sold them bad drugs. So, before a crowd of onlookers, they lowered Doyle's pants, flogged him, and anally raped him.

This has become the kind of apocrypha that Manson conspiracy theorists can't get enough of. It's the same incident referenced in Barney Hoskyns's *Waiting for the Sun*, the book I showed Bugliosi that day after our lunch. The story feels almost mythological, in its ugliness and in the extent to which its most basic details—who, what, when, where, why—are in flux. Candice Bergen, in an interview with the LAPD a few weeks after the murders, said that it was a rape, most likely at Sebring's place or at his friend John Phillips's (also of the Mamas and the Papas); Dennis Hopper told the *Los Angeles Free Press* that it was at the Cielo house. He described it as "a mass whipping of a dealer from Sunset Strip who'd given them bad dope." Ed Sanders, in *The Family,* reports that Doyle was "whipped and video-buggered," and the location varies depending on which edition of the book you're looking at.

So what really happened? I hesitated to report on this in 1999; it felt like another lurid departure from Manson, and it's not as if my deadline afforded me time to explore every strange byway. But it bothered me that Bugliosi had left this out, and that so many people close to the victims regarded it as a flashpoint in the case. It was another instance of the resilience of the "live freaky, die freaky" mind-set. Plus, even if Pic Dawson, Billy Doyle, and the other dealers hadn't murdered anyone, they could still be behind the crimes, or adjacent to them. If I could connect them to Manson, for instance—couldn't they have contracted him for the murders? And if they were selling a lot of drugs to anyone who'd died at the Tate household, might there have been some kind of cover-up at work?

So, down I went.

Thanks to Kaczanowski and a few others who spoke with the LAPD, detectives were quickly suspicious of Doyle and his companions after the murders. And Doyle himself was getting around quite a bit at the time. He was back and forth between Los Angeles, Jamaica, and his native Toronto. It was in this last city that police caught up to him in late August. I wouldn't get a transcript of the LAPD's interview until many years into my investigation, but it's worth including here because it gives his side of the story. And Doyle is quotable — there's something almost farcically hard-boiled about him.

In short, he told the LAPD's Lieutenant Earl Deemer that he didn't remember being raped, but he couldn't be sure; it might've happened anyway. He recalled going over to see Frykowski at the Cielo house on the night in question, sometime in early July. Frykowski, thinking it would be a funny prank, slipped some mescaline in his champagne. Folger was there, too. "It was out at the swimming pool," Doyle told Deemer, "and there was two cases of champagne by the pool... And apparently [Frykowski] put some in my drink, and I said, Jesus...I am high...I am really out of my bird."

He wanted something to bring him down, and Frykowski was happy to oblige, producing some pills that he said belonged to Sharon Tate. Doyle swallowed "about eight of them," and soon enough, as Frykowski started to laugh at him, he realized that the pills were something else entirely, and that he was dealing with some wild people:

> They were crazier than hell. I didn't realize they were so
> crazy. I am using the word 'crazy,' I mean drug-induced

crazy...in California, everybody has a tan. Now, if people don't have a tan, they look a little different. You can see things in their face[s] that a tan covers up...They were all tan and looked healthy. They looked very straight to me when I first got there. And, uh...I don't remember much more than that.

His observation about California, where "everybody has a tan," reminded me of Kaczanowski's remark: it was impossible, back then, to separate geniuses from charlatans. Everyone blended in.

Of course, by most reckonings, Doyle himself would count as one of the charlatans. He admitted that he was a naturally paranoid person. In recent months he'd developed a coke habit, which only exacerbated the paranoia. Convinced that someone, somewhere, was out to get him, he started carrying a gun. It didn't help that he often bragged about how much cocaine he had, especially when there were women around. "They all wanted to get laid," he said to Deemer, "and the price of admission was a nose full of coke, and I learned that." He would show up at parties with a silver coke spoon and tell everyone he had "pounds of it." His good friend Charles Tacot said, "'For Chrissakes, Billy, what do you tell people that kind of stuff for?' And I said, 'I want to get laid, Charles.'"

That day, higher and higher on drugs that he couldn't even name, Doyle became convinced that Frykowski meant to harm him. So he pulled out his gun and pointed it at the Pole, threatening to kill him. Frykowski, the bigger man—and the more sober, too, if only by a hair—wrested the gun from him.

Here Doyle's memory got hazy; he apparently lapsed into unconsciousness, and Voytek called up Charlie Tacot, asking him to come collect his deranged friend. It was possible, Doyle conceded, that he had been raped after that. He admitted that he might've told his friend Mama Cass something to that effect. "I was unconscious," he told Deemer. "I wasn't sore the next day ... not there. But I was sore everywhere else."

In another LAPD officer's account of that interview, Doyle puts it even more frankly: "I was so freaked out on drugs I wouldn't know if they'd fucked me or not!"

It took a lot of asking around, but eventually I tracked down both Billy Doyle and Charles Tacot. (As for the other two: I'd learned Dawson had died of a drug overdose in 1986, and Harrigan was nowhere to be found.) Neither had given an interview before, and though they could be cagey, they were also eager to relive their underworld glories. Both were old men now, but they were still operators who acted as if they were at the height of their criminal powers. Impressively foulmouthed, both of them threatened to have me killed at various points in our interviews, although I didn't take either seriously.

In our first phone call, Tacot filled in some of the blanks from Doyle's story. He remembered driving over to pick up Doyle, who was passed out somewhere on the Cielo Drive property. His belt had been split, apparently with a knife. A friend who'd come along for the errand said, "I think Voytek fucked him."

They took Doyle, still unconscious, to Mama Cass's place in the Hollywood Hills. Tacot remembered thinking, "If we don't take care of him, he's going to go back there and have a beef. I carried him out, laid him by a tree, went back to my car and got about twenty feet of welded link chain, which I had in there for somebody else, originally. I put it around his ankle and a tree with a good padlock and snapped it all together—so I know he's not going anywhere. Cass was in the hospital at the time. She said, 'Get the Polaroid! Get the Polaroid!'"

Doyle came to a few hours later, still very high, and simmering with rage. "'I'm going to shoot that motherfucker,'" Tacot remembered him saying. "And I said, 'No, no, we're leaving town. We're going to Jamaica...but first you're going to get sober and you're going to be on this fucking tree until you are.'"

I asked Tacot: "Do you think Voytek did fuck Billy?"

"Yeah, that's why Billy was so pissed at him," Tacot said. "Voytek would have been killed if I hadn't intervened."

"Would Billy have hired killers?" I asked, thinking of Manson.

"No. He would've taken all the pleasure himself."

In his interview with the police, Doyle had allowed that he was furious at Frykowski and his set. "When I was chained to the tree," he said, "they were the object of my rage. Which was an unreasonable and unnatural rage." To calm him down, Doyle said, Tacot had "chained a sign to the tree that said 'You are loved.'" Doyle was stuck there for more than a day.

After that, Tacot told me, the pair headed off to Jamaica, where apparently they were making a movie about marijuana. (No footage from this film has ever surfaced. Others have said the two were involved in a large narcotics deal.) On August 9, while they were away, "Manson goes up and kills those people and everyone's looking for [Doyle]," Tacot said. He and Doyle were suspects within days. "I picked up the phone one day and the *Toronto Star* informed me that me and Billy were in the headlines: two wanted for murder." A couple of days later, back in the United States, "I took a lie-detector test," Tacot told me. "They knew I had nothing to do with it. Billy, too. He was in Jamaica with me. We were cleared, out of the country. You can't kill somebody long-distance."

True enough, but you could arrange for someone else to do the killing. Tacot adamantly denied that he and Billy Doyle knew Manson — they'd never even met the guy. Nor, he said, had they sold drugs to anyone staying at the Tate house.

"We were consultants," he said. "We'd tell them if it was okay or not."

"If the drugs were okay?"

"Yeah." He added, "Billy was fucking a whole bunch of broads up there."

"Did you ever hear about any orgies?" I asked.

"If you want to consider Billy fucking the broads an orgy."

Charlie Tacot wasn't exactly the picture of virtue. I wanted to find other people who'd known him, who could say if he'd known Manson. It wasn't hard. Seemingly everyone in town had partied with Tacot at some point. Corrine Calvet, a French actress who'd worked in Hollywood since the forties, had one of the most alarming stories of them all. Calvet was as famous for her turbulent life as her film roles. She'd starred opposite James Cagney in *What Price Glory?* In the fifties, she married Johnny Fontaine, a mobster-turned-actor who'd been a pallbearer at the gangster Mickey Cohen's funeral. A purported Satanist, she'd been sued in 1967 by a long-time lover who accused her of "controlling" him with voodoo.

I met Calvet at her beach-facing apartment in Santa Monica. Solemn and unsmiling, in heavy makeup, her gray hair swept back, she got right to the point.

"The only thing that I can tell you about this Manson," she said, her accent inflecting the words with glamour and gravity, "is that Charlie Tacot brought him and the girls to a party at our house. Two hours after they were there, I caught Charlie Manson taking a piss in my pool. I told Charlie Tacot to get them out of here and they left. After the tragedy happened, the FBI came by and told me I was next on their list to be killed."

When I expressed shock at this, her eyes narrowed. With genuine malice, she said, "Maybe you are new at this. When I tell you something, don't question it! I don't say it unless it is true."

I explained that Tacot had denied ever having met Manson or anyone in the Family. "Maybe he has good reason to say that,"

Calvet said, letting her words hang in the air. She was certain: "Charlie knew them."

I pressed her again. Was she sure that Tacot brought Manson and the girls to her party?

"Well, I would not put my hand in the fire, saying that Charlie brought them over, but Charlie knew them."

I tried to get more out of Calvet, but the rest of the interview was frosty. When I asked her for specific dates, or even years, she grew exasperated, throwing her hands up in disgust. "I do not know years, do not ask me." Before long, she'd had it with me altogether. "I want you to leave now," she said. And I did.

Thinking I could eventually get Tacot to let his guard down, I began to visit him at the Santa Anita Convalescent Center in Temple City. His health was failing, and he had trouble walking. I found him lying in bed naked, a sheet pulled just above his groin; he was bald, with a silver mustache, bony arms, and a gravelly voice. I noticed a fading tattoo on his forearm. On the wall he'd hung a photo of his granddaughter at her senior prom. Later, when he rose to get exercise using a walker, I saw how tall he was: six foot six and rail thin. Although his faculties were waning, he was sharp. He still commanded enough authority to boss around the short orderly who assisted him.

Tacot shared his room with another patient, and he seemed to resent the enfeebling atmosphere of the place — "too much groaning around here," he said — so I offered to drive him to his favorite restaurant, Coco's, a California chain known for its pies. Taking him out to lunch was an elaborate procedure. People from the rest home wheeled him out to my car, lifted him in, and put the wheelchair in the trunk. Once we were at Coco's, however, I had to lift Tacot into the wheelchair myself — an intimate maneuver for two near strangers. Humiliated, he began to threaten me, albeit ineffectually. "Do you realize who you're dealing with?" he rasped as I attempted to hoist him out of my passenger seat. "I could have you hurt, or killed!"

In Coco's, with food in front of him, he calmed down a bit, and soon we were having a freewheeling if combative conversation about the murders and Hollywood in the sixties. Tacot had lived in Los Angeles since the mid-1950s, when he moved there from Mexico with his wife. He had two daughters, one of whom, Margot, would later confirm a lot of her father's story: he was a drug dealer, she said, who operated on the fringes of the music and acting world. Although he would often get arrested, she said, "nothing ever stuck. Someone always took care of it for him."

Tacot continued to deny ever having known Manson, and he bridled at the insinuation that he had anything to do with the crimes. The Tate murders, he went on, led to "the most fucked-up investigation I've ever seen in my life." He had sued the *Los Angeles Times* for announcing him as a suspect. Any effort to implicate him, he said, was probably just the LAPD covering up for their bad police work.

As he grew more comfortable, Tacot made an unexpected revelation: at the time of the murders, he worked for an intelligence agency—he wouldn't say which—and reported to Hank Fine, a veteran of the army's Military Intelligence Service (MIS). This had been a World War II–era operation so secret that it wasn't even acknowledged by the federal government until 1972. Fine, a Polish émigré whose true name was Hersh Matias Warzechahe, was "an assassin who shot people for the government," Tacot claimed.

Thinking the old guy was fantasizing, I barely followed up on the revelation. But he, and later Billy Doyle, would often reference Fine, only to refuse to answer any questions about him. When I looked into him, I learned neither man had been lying. Tacot also described his friend Doyle—they were still close—as "a dangerous man. He'd kill you in a fucking minute. Both of us are second-generation intelligence.

"Don't write this stuff," he implored me. "You'll get killed. These are very dangerous men, they'll find you and kill you." (That was a warning I'd hear a lot from various parties over the years.) Tacot reminded me that Bugliosi, when he wrote *Helter Skelter,* had given pseudonyms to him and his friends, and not just for the sake of politeness. "He was afraid American intelligence would kill him if he exposed us," Tacot claimed. He added that Bugliosi was "an asshole" who'd never interviewed him or Billy. "Vincent Bugliosi knows to keep his mouth shut. I'd've got him killed. I didn't tell him that—didn't have to."

I tried to get Tacot on the subject of Frykowski, who was, to my mind, the victim with the shadiest cast of characters around him. Frykowski was on drugs all the time, Tacot said. Contradicting what he'd told me on the phone, he said that Frykowski *had* sold MDA, but only to close friends.

I didn't take Tacot out again, but I kept calling and visiting him. I found him evasive, or senile, or a little of both. And the more I asked around about him, the more he seemed to vanish into the mist of the sixties. Some people told me, with certainty, that Tacot had been an assassin for the CIA, that he was a "gun freak" and an incredible marksman. (In his 2006 autobiography, *Since Then: How I Survived Everything and Lived to Tell About it,* the musician David Crosby identified Tacot as a "soldier of fortune" who taught him how to shoot a gun.) Others said that he was an ex-marine who'd served in Korea and used to show off his impressive knife-throwing skills. I heard that he grew pot in Arizona; that he was a child molester; that he was a coke smuggler; that he was an uncredited screenwriter; and that his intelligence ties were all fictitious. And the strange thing was, none of this was entirely implausible. About the only thing everyone could agree on was that Tacot had been involved in a lot of schemes—that he'd been a drug dealer and, even more, a drug user. But then, as one source put it, "Hey, man, aren't you?"

When I looked into Hank Fine, the MIS guy Tacot had said he'd reported to, I learned that, like everything Tacot said, there was at least a kernel of truth to it. Fine, who'd been a movie PR man from the 1940s until his death in 1975, had been in the Office of Strategic Services (OSS), the counterintelligence agency that oversaw the MIS and evolved into the CIA after World War II. His work often seemed to combine Hollywood and spycraft. Eddie Albert, the star of the sixties sitcom *Green Acres,* told me that Fine had sent him on undercover missions to Mexico during the war; from his sailboat, the actor had photographed German landing sites and military training grounds. Though I found no proof, the consensus among Fine's associates was that he'd continued working in espionage operations through the sixties. His only child, Shayla, told me that his public-relations gig was a cover—and, yes, she said, Tacot had reported to her father. What kind of work were they doing? She never knew, except that it was classified.

Whenever I saw Tacot, I returned to the subject of Fine. "Don't mention that name anywhere!" he barked, seeming genuinely disturbed. When I asked why not, he said, "None of your fucking business! You're fucking with the wrong people!"

Or was I fucking with lowlifes who only wanted to present an illusion of importance? I really couldn't say. And when I finally was able to talk to Billy Doyle, things didn't get any clearer.

Tacot gave me Doyle's number. "He's a retired old man just like me," he said, "and he may not want to talk too much. Don't push him if he doesn't."

But Doyle liked an audience, just as he had in 1969. I called him often at his home in Toronto, and he talked for hours, sometimes rambling at such length that I would turn off my recorder to save tape. Just when he was trying my patience, he'd say something provocative and I'd have to switch the recorder back on and try to get him to repeat it. He had a short temper, and when he exploded, usually out of nowhere, it could be hard to calm him down. One time, when he didn't like my line of questioning, he told me, "I was shooting targets at a thousand yards yesterday," implying that I could soon be one of them. Another time, when I'd tried to get some specifics about Hank Fine, Doyle yelled, "Go in the bathroom, swallow the gun, and pull the trigger!" When he wasn't angry, he sometimes got a kick out of teasing me: he would make a major revelation and then retract it the next time we spoke. I got the sense that he sometimes trusted me enough to tell the truth, only to realize later that he shouldn't have done that.

Doyle believed that Polanski and Frykowski were Polish spies, the former subverting American democracy with his decadent films. He suspected that Polanski had something to do with the killings. (It went both ways: I'd heard that Polanski thought Doyle had something to do with the killings.) He denied that he'd ever been a drug dealer. I read him passages from the police report, in which he'd confessed to, even bragged about, having vast amounts of cocaine. But even after that, he denied it to me. He wouldn't be stupid enough to carry two pounds of coke on a plane, he said. When I asked him about MDA, the drug that he and Voytek had allegedly bought in large quantities, he said he'd never even heard of it. He relented when I read him some quotes from the transcript—okay, fine, he'd taken it.

I brought up his and Tacot's alibi for the night of the murders: they'd been in Jamaica, you'll recall, filming "a pot movie." Doyle admitted that the movie was a ruse. He and Tacot had really been doing intelligence work there, he said, as part of some effort to keep Cuba out of Jamaica.

"Dead white men will pull your tongue out if you tell this shit," he said. "You have to understand that the government doesn't want to have any exposure on the Jamaican thing—there never was a Jamaican thing. They don't want to know about it." When I asked why, he said, "How the fuck do I know? I'm a Canadian citizen. I went with Charles on an adventure. I thought we were going to do a movie."

"But that's not what you were really there for, and you knew it."

"That's right."

It's an exchange that illustrates how cryptic Doyle could be—and how he reveled in it. I had to ask about the story behind his alleged rape. He said that never happened, either.

"Charles was spreading the rape story to have fun at my expense," he explained. "Even my mom and dad asked if I was raped." And yet he betrayed the same uncertainty he'd shown to the cops so many decades ago, telling me that he'd had a friend take photos of him naked so he could examine his rear end.

Similarly, he told me that Corrine Calvet was dead wrong when she said that Tacot had brought Manson to her house. "That's a lie," he said, noting that Tacot and Calvet had once dated. "She will say anything to grasp at stardom. Men with badges and guns have raised these questions before," he added, "not police, FBI, sitting in D.C." That in itself was astonishing to me; I hadn't heard that the FBI had investigated the murders, but I would find out later that it was true.

I suggested that I didn't believe him about Calvet. "You are going to come to a horrible truth," he said. "Be nervous that you may have discovered the truth and you won't like it."

As spurious and slimy as he could be, I found him believable when he repeated that there was more to the murders than had been reported. Later, when I'd interviewed so many people that some of them had started to compare notes, he said something really impenetrable. "The community has looked at this as a settled thing until you started talking to us."

"What community?" I asked. "Who?"

"The ties that bind."

Eventually, Doyle became convinced that I was Roman Polanski's private investigator. It was never clear to me how much he actually believed this, but it was enough to make me back away from him. I sunk a lot of hours into cultivating sources like Tacot, Doyle, and the crowd surrounding them. They'd been so close to the Tate murders that they were suspects, and yet they'd assumed no role in the mythology surrounding the events of August 9. Bugliosi, like the LAPD, had summarily acquitted them of any involvement in the killings—they were his book's classic red herring. But I still wasn't convinced. In their sleazy, run-of-the-mill criminality, their motivations seemed much more viable than a lofty idea like Helter Skelter. The more I talked to them, the more I recognized certain inadequacies in Bugliosi's story, which had curtailed so many explanations in favor of the most outlandish one.

A Haircut from Little Joe

I wanted to keep one eye open to the possibility that Tacot, Doyle, and their associates had some link to the Manson group. After all, in *The Family,* Ed Sanders had written that it was likely that Mama Cass Elliot knew Manson through her drug connections—it seemed probable that Doyle and Tacot were pivotal there. Plus, Elliot had been friends with Frykowski and Folger; and Elliot's bandmates were close to Polanski and Tate. In other words, everyone knew everyone else, and nobody wanted to talk about it anymore.

Maybe I could suss out the connections there, but I was less enthusiastic about these supposed ties with intelligence agencies—except that I was about to get another push in that direction. Dominick Dunne, the *Vanity Fair* journalist who'd been friends with Tate, Polanski, and Jay Sebring, had given me a tip: get a haircut from a man named Joe Torrenueva.

Nicknamed Little Joe, Torrenueva had been eighteen, fresh out of barber school, when Jay Sebring took him under his wing as an apprentice hairstylist. That was in 1961. Sebring, not yet thirty, was already one of the biggest names in fashion, having revolutionized men's grooming. He was the first to "style" men's hair rather than simply cut it. He patented a "Sebring method," through which "your hair is shaped and conditioned to stay natural between visits," as promotional materials explained, and he introduced a line of hair-care products. (Sebring wasn't his given name; he was born Thomas Kummer and renamed himself after a racetrack in Florida he liked.)

Sebring saw his clients in a private room with only one chair. When Torrenueva began working for him, he was charging an unheard-of twenty-five dollars for a haircut—the going rate was a buck fifty. But his customers were happy to pay a premium, and in turn, he catered to their whims. Sebring traveled every few weeks to Las Vegas, where his clients included Frank Sinatra and several casino owners. Torrenueva always went with him, and in those quiet rooms, as the scissors snipped and tufts of hair gathered on the floor, he saw the casual intimacy between Sebring and his clients, who confided in him even when Little Joe was within earshot.

Now, like his mentor, to whom he referred in hushed, almost reverential tones, Little Joe was a "barber to the stars." He saw his clients in a private, oak-paneled room in Beverly Hills. His price was a hundred bucks. Dunne had told me that if I bided my time and didn't press him too hard, Joe might open up about the murders. When I showed up, he seemed aware of my ulterior motive. Slight and soft-spoken, he sighed and paused before nearly every sentence.

Joe was convinced that Sebring's murder had to do with something more than hippies trying to ignite a race war. Sebring, he told me, had been involved with mob guys from Chicago and Las Vegas. He cut their hair, partied with them in Vegas. Then, after the murders, Little Joe got a call from General Charlie Baron, a casino executive and mobster, who told him, "Don't worry, Little Joe, you're going to be all right." He presumed that the murders had been a drug deal gone wrong, and that Jay and Frykowski had been targeted.

That was all I got. I needed more information. I'd have to get another haircut.

I let a month go by, so I really needed one, and soon enough I settled into Little Joe's leather chair again.

Charlie Baron's call haunted him to this day. It came "right after" the murders, Torrenueva said, before anyone had any notion of who'd committed them. "You didn't do anything to anybody," he said Baron told him. "Nobody's going to do anything to you." The implication was that Baron and his associates were well aware of who committed the crimes, and why.

But then Joe was done snipping. So I went back for a third haircut.

"Charlie Baron was *very* close to Jay," Joe told me in our third conversation. He added: "Charlie killed people." When Baron was a young man during Prohibition in Chicago, he "shot two guys who were going to kill him for fixing a fight." He later went to Havana to run casinos for Meyer Lansky, another mob figure. When he returned to the United States, he was Lansky's eyes and ears at the new Sands Casino in Vegas.

Baron was hardly an outlier in Sebring's shop, which was a "nest of mobsters and criminals," Torrenueva said. But it was Baron who scared Little Joe the most, even before his phone call. Despite Baron's known mob ties, he had some type of security-intelligence clearance with the federal government. He always packed a gun, and he was close with a cabal of right-wing military intelligence and Hollywood figures, many of whom had been Sebring's clients. Little Joe alleged that they "did terrible things to black people," and that "it was Charlie who did the worst things."

I couldn't get him to elaborate on that. But I did ask him why, if he was following the Tate murder investigation and knew that the police had no leads, he didn't tell the cops about his call from Baron. Because he was too close to higher-ups in law enforcement and intelligence, Joe said.

He added yet another intriguing name to the list of Baron's associates: General Curtis E. LeMay, a legendary fighter pilot who'd implemented the carpet bombing of Japan during World War II. A notorious hawk, LeMay had served as chief of staff of the U.S. Air Force under Presidents Kennedy and Johnson. In 1962, during the Cuban Missile Crisis, he'd tried to organize a coup against Kennedy among the Joint Chiefs of Staff; he wanted to force the military to flout the president's orders and bomb the Soviet missile bases they'd found in Cuba.

It was a lot of names to process, and the implications were dizzying. I had one question that Torrenueva was especially reluctant to answer. Why would Sebring—at the time, arguably the best-known men's hairstylist in the world—involve himself in crime? He had so much to lose, and clearly he was thriving.

But he hadn't been, Torrenueva was pained to say. "The deals kept falling through. He was a bad businessman."

"Do you think he sold drugs?" I asked, aware that Frykowski had possibly been doing the same.

"It wouldn't surprise me."

Sebring's problems had multiplied throughout the sixties. He'd clash with other barbers who wanted to unionize. In 1963, a group of his stylists had defected, en masse, to start their own business. At other times, he'd had to hire bodyguards because some guys had come into the shop and "roughed up" several employees, Torrenueva said, for reasons that were never shared with him. Sebring carried a gun, and "he shot someone once who came to his house and was giving his father a rough time at the door."

The bottom line: Sebring, like Frykowski, had a lot more going on at the time of his murder than had ever been revealed. Whatever it was, Little Joe thought it had more to do with his death than any hippie/race-war motive did. Which meant that, in addition to drug dealers and Hollywood's seedier hangers-on, I had to account for mobsters, ex-military figures, and intelligence agents in my reporting. I was already worried about wandering into the weeds—now I risked veering off the map entirely.

Coda: Down the Rabbit Hole

I was writing a story about Charles Manson that had, so far, very little of Manson in it. It was more about the way that events, in all their messy reality, boiled down to canonical fact; the way that *a* narrative becomes *the* narrative.

I had to decide if stories like Little Joe's, Charlie Tacot's, and Billy Doyle's were worth looking into, and, as a responsible journalist, if I was justified in dragging my magazine into it. It definitely meant asking for an extension from *Premiere* and risking, in the final publication, looking like a fool. No matter how you viewed them, these were conspiracy theories. But I was riveted by the stuff I'd turned up that contravened the Manson story as we knew it. For better or worse, it felt like there was something covered up all these years, ripe for exposure. Maybe with the passage of time, people who knew about these things might divulge them at last.

I was starting to figure out that Bugliosi had sifted so many stories out of *Helter Skelter*—to make his narrative about the conviction of the mad hippie guru and his zombielike followers easier and cleaner. If that were merely an editorial choice, so be it. But if he'd changed things to protect people, or to shore up holes in the investigation, then I felt justified in digging deeper. It seemed impossible that a story like Little Joe's, heavy with intelligence agencies and organized crime, could coexist alongside the Helter Skelter motive. I knew that, in the late sixties, intelligence agencies regarded dissident youth movements as the greatest threat to the nation's security, and they'd marshaled their efforts accordingly. Insofar as hippies, musicians, and movie stars played a role in those movements, I could see how the broadest outline of Little Joe's story could have some truth to it. But even a hardened national-security reporter would have trouble verifying his claims, and that I was not.

These were the concerns I faced by the summer of 1999. The obvious answer would be: keep pushing. The only problem was, my deadline was fast approaching. I owed *Premiere* five thousand words, and I'd written zero.

3

The Golden Penetrators

Instilling Fear

Maybe I was naive to think I could discover what was going on at the Tate house in the months before the murders. People had been trying to untangle that rats' nest of rumors for thirty years, and not with a magazine deadline looming in front of them. Now I'd determined to my satisfaction that Frykowski and Polanski appeared to have a lot to hide, and that Frykowski's connections to the drug trade could've put him plausibly in Manson's orbit. Beyond that, my sense of Manson's link to Hollywood was still too tenuous for my liking. And if I felt that Bugliosi's Helter Skelter motive was only a high-profile contrivance, I needed to find the bald truth it concealed. Hoping for a better angle, I focused on one figure who was among the most perplexing in the case: Terry Melcher.

Without Melcher, there would have been no murders at 10050 Cielo Drive. He was the clearest link between Manson and the Hollywood elite. A music-industry bigwig, he'd promised Manson a record deal only to renege on it. The official story was that Manson, reeling from the rejection, wanted to "instill fear" in Melcher—so he chose Melcher's old house on Cielo Drive as the site for the first night of murders. He knew that Melcher didn't live there anymore. He just wanted to give the guy a good scare.

This was a vital point in the case. According to Bugliosi, Manson never went to the house the night of the murders—he just sent his followers there and told them to kill anyone they found. To convict Manson of criminal conspiracy, then, and get him a death sentence, Bugliosi had to establish a compelling, premeditated reason that Manson had picked the Cielo Drive home. Terry Melcher was that reason.

Melcher testified that he'd met Manson exactly three times, the last of which was around May 20, 1969, more than two months before the murders. After Manson's arrest, Melcher became so frightened of the Family that Bugliosi had to give him a tranquilizer to relax him before he testified. "Ten, fifteen years after the murders I'd speak to him and he was still convinced that the Manson Family was after him that night," Bugliosi had told me.

If Manson had wanted to kill Melcher, he could have. He had Melcher's new address in Malibu. Gregg Jakobson, a musician and a friend of the Beach Boys, had testified at the trial that Manson called him before the murders, asking him if Melcher had a "green spyglass."

"Yes, why?" Jakobson answered.

"Well, he doesn't anymore," Manson said. The Family had "creepy-crawled" Melcher's Malibu home—that's what they called it when they dressed up in black and sneaked around rich people's places—and stolen the spyglass. When Melcher himself testified, he confirmed that he'd noticed it missing around "late July or early August." Candice Bergen, his girlfriend, had noted the disappearance, too.

Over the years, Manson researchers have generally agreed that Melcher was stretching the truth. Karina Longworth, whose podcast *You Must Remember This* devoted a whole season to Manson, said in one episode that Melcher "was vague about the details of his meetings with Manson, and probably shaved a couple of visits to the ranch off the official record."

It would be one thing to fudge the numbers a bit—it's easy to see why someone would want to understate their relationship with Charles Manson. But I became convinced that this was graver than that. I found proof that Melcher was much closer to Manson, Tex Watson, and the girls than he'd suggested. A year before the murders, he'd even lived with a member of the Family at the house on Cielo Drive.

There was a strong likelihood that Melcher knew, immediately after the crimes, that Manson was involved—but he never told the police. I found evidence that Melcher lied on the stand, under oath. And Bugliosi definitely knew about it. Maybe he'd even put him up to it, suborning witness perjury.

Just like the omissions about the tape from the Polanski house loft and Frykowski's episode with Billy Doyle, this raised questions about Bugliosi's motives. Did he change the story to protect Melcher, a powerful record producer and the only child of one of Hollywood's most beloved stars? Had he streamlined certain elements for the jury's sake, in the interest of getting an easy conviction? Or was this part of a broader pattern of deception, of bending the facts to support a narrative that was otherwise too shaky to stand? Helter Skelter (the motive) and *Helter Skelter* (the book) seemed more illusory by the day.

Chasing the Melcher angle further imperiled any chance of hitting my deadline. It soured my relationship with Bugliosi; it brought on the first of many lawsuit threats; and it turned my fascination with the case into a full-blown obsession. But it convinced me more than anything that I was onto something—that the full story behind the Manson murders had never been properly told.

"I Live with 17 Girls"

The story of Manson and Melcher starts with Dennis Wilson. By the summer of 1968, Wilson, then twenty-three, had reached an impasse. He'd become world famous as the drummer for the Beach Boys, helmed by his brother Brian; now the band was in decline, edged out by more subversive acts. He and his wife, Carole, had recently divorced for the second time. She wrote in court filings that he had a violent temper, inflicting "severe bodily injury" on her during his "rampages."

The couple had two young children, but Dennis decided to rusticate as a bachelor. He moved into a lavish, Spanish-style mansion in Pacific Palisades, once a hunting lodge owned by the humorist Will Rogers. The home boasted thirty-one rooms and a swimming pool in the shape of California. He redecorated in the spirit of the times — zebra-print carpet, abundant bunk beds — and hosted decadent parties, hoping to have as much sex as possible.

One day, Wilson was driving his custom red Ferrari down the Pacific Coast Highway when two hitchhikers, the Family's Ella Jo Bailey and Patricia Krenwinkel, caught his eye. He gave them a quick lift. When he saw them again soon afterward, he picked them up a second time, taking them back to his place for "milk and cookies." History hasn't recorded what kind of cookies they enjoyed, or whether those cookies were in fact sex, but whatever the case, the girls told Manson about the encounter. They weren't aware of Wilson's clout in the music industry — but Manson was, and he insisted on going back to the house with them.

After a late recording session, Wilson returned to his estate to find the Family's big black bus parked outside. His living room was populated with topless girls. Whatever alarm he felt was eased when their short, intense, unwashed leader, Manson, sunk to his knees and kissed Wilson's feet.

This night ushered in a summer of ceaseless partying for Wilson.

Manson and the Family set up shop in his home, and soon Manson recruited one of the group's deadliest members, Tex Watson, who picked him up hitchhiking. The Family spent their days smoking dope and listening to Charlie strum the guitar. The girls made the meals, did the laundry, and slept with the men on command. Manson prescribed sex seven times a day: before and after all three meals and once in the middle of the night. "It was as if we were kings, just because we were men," Watson later wrote. Soon Wilson was bragging so much that he landed a headline in *Record Mirror:* "I Live with 17 Girls."

Talking to Britain's *Rave* magazine, Wilson offered disjointed remarks about his new friend, whom he called "the Wizard." "I was only frightened as a child because I didn't understand the fear," he said. "Sometimes 'the Wizard' frightens me. The Wizard is Charles Manson, who is a friend of mine who thinks he is God and the devil. He sings, plays and writes poetry and may be another artist for Brother Records," the Beach Boys' label.

This last bit excited Manson, who was desperate to leverage his connection with Wilson into a music career. The two cowrote a song, "Cease to Exist," whose lyrics claimed that "submission is a gift." (Later that year, the Beach Boys recorded it as a B side, changing the title, finessing the lyrics, and dropping Manson's songwriting credit—a snub that fueled his anger toward the establishment.) Manson fraternized with some of the biggest names in music. Neil Young remembered meeting him and the girls at Wilson's place. "A lot of pretty well-known musicians around L.A. knew Manson," Young later said, "though they'd probably deny it now."

Among these was Terry Melcher. He and Wilson had pledged allegiance to the "Golden Penetrators," a horny triumvirate they'd formed with their friend Gregg Jakobson. The Penetrators, who'd painted a car gold to celebrate themselves, aimed to sleep with as many women as they could. Wilson's ex-wife referred to them as "roving cocksmen." Obviously, then, Melcher would want to rove over to Wilson's house—it was full of promiscuous young women. Sometime in that summer of '68, at one of Wilson's marathon parties, he crossed paths with Manson for the first time. After another such party, Melcher rode back to Cielo Drive with Wilson, and Manson came along in the back seat. As Melcher later testified, Manson got a good look at the house from the driveway.

When the end of summer came, things went south with Wilson, who'd finally grown tired of footing the bill for the endless party: upward of $100,000 in food, clothes, and car repairs, plus gonorrhea treatments. According to Bugliosi, Wilson was too frightened of Manson to throw him out. Instead, he simply up and left in the middle of the night, leaving the messy business of eviction to his landlord.

But it must've been more complicated than that. Wilson gave three interviews in which he raved about Manson and the girls—and all of those interviews date to the winter and summer of 1969, nearly a year *after* he and the Family had supposedly parted ways. Why would Wilson brag about his connections to a man he'd just schemed to escape?

The only sure fact is that Manson and his group decamped to the Spahn Ranch in late August 1968. Wilson moved into a Malibu beach house with Gregg Jakobson, who'd also recently split from his marriage.

Having drifted from Wilson—his best shot at a record deal—Manson knew he had to hitch his wagon to Terry Melcher's star. As his chances at fame dwindled, his mood darkened. He became obsessed with the Beatles' *White Album,* released in late November 1968, and started to preach about the prophecies of a race war embedded in its lyrics. Things only got worse in the winter of '69, when he arranged for Melcher to come out and hear his music. Manson prepared meticulously for the prospective meeting, but Melcher stood him up.

On March 23, a desperate Manson went searching for Melcher, thinking he'd goad the producer into a record deal. He found his way back to the house at Cielo Drive, having remembered that Melcher lived there. Instead, Sharon Tate's personal photographer, Shahrokh Hatami, intercepted him. Hatami had never heard of a Terry Melcher. He told Manson to go to the guesthouse and ask the owner of the property, Rudolph Altobelli, who explained curtly that Melcher no longer lived there and hadn't left a forwarding address.

Manson prevailed on Gregg Jakobson — still a friend, and still a fan of the girls — to book another session with Melcher. This time, it worked. That May, Melcher made the winding drive to the Spahn Ranch and auditioned Manson in person, visiting twice over four days.

Manson had rounded out a dozen or so of his best songs with backup singing from the girls. Performing in a gully in the woods, the girls sprawled on the ground and gazed up at their leader, who sat astride a rock with his guitar. "I wasn't too impressed by the songs," Melcher would later testify. "I was impressed by the whole scene...by Charlie's strength, and his obvious leadership." As a courtesy, the producer complimented Manson, saying that one or two of his songs were "nice." He had no intention of offering a recording contract, but he saw how the Family's rustic, cultish lifestyle would lend itself to a TV documentary. Melcher suggested that his friend Mike Deasy, whose van was outfitted to make field recordings, could come out to the ranch and capture another performance.

Before Melcher could get out of there, a foreman at the ranch came stumbling out of a pickup truck. Drunk and belligerent, he was dressed like a cowboy, fingering a holstered gun — the same one that would later be used at the Tate murders. Manson stepped up to him and shouted, "Don't draw on me, motherfucker!" socking him in the gut, taking his gun, and continuing to pummel him.

It spooked Melcher. Here was a peace-and-love cult with naked girls roaming the old Western sets, and yet the constant threat of violence loomed over the place. It needed to be documented in all its oddity. A few days later, Melcher returned with Deasy and Jakobson, and the Family repeated their audition. But what had seemed spontaneous now felt rehearsed. Deasy returned a few more times, until he had a frightening LSD trip with Manson and vowed never to go back.

It was all getting too toxic. Melcher conveyed his rejection through Jakobson, and that was the end of that. Manson's last brush with greatness was gone, and he became full-on apocalyptic. Melcher never went back to the ranch or saw anyone from the Family again. Or so he said under oath, anyway.

After the murders, as Hollywood panicked and the LAPD chased down leads, the Golden Penetrators realized that they hadn't quite washed their hands of Manson. This is where their story began to feel unbelievable to me. Manson wasn't charged with murder until late November. But Wilson, Jakobson, and Melcher had good cause to suspect him back in August, right after the killings. By then, they were frightened of Manson, though *Helter Skelter* does little to indicate their terror. When I saw how much they knew—and how quiet they'd kept, when their information would've helped police solve the case—I realized just how flimsy the Helter Skelter motive was. Its unforgettable grandiosity may have hidden a more prosaic truth: that a few rich guys had gotten in over their heads with an unstable ex-con.

First, Wilson and Jakobson knew that Manson had shot a black man named Bernard Crowe about five weeks before the Tate murders. And Jakobson, who testified that he'd talked to Manson "upward of a hundred times," was well acquainted with his friend's bizarre race-war predictions. Manson warned him that "whiteys" in the affluent homes of Bel Air would be "cut up and dismembered," and that the murderers would smear the victims' blood on the walls, "scatter [their] limbs, and hang them from the ceiling." And yet, when a group of affluent whites really *was* cut up, and Sharon Tate was hanged from the ceiling of her home in Bel Air, Jakobson apparently didn't make the connection. Under cross-examination, Jakobson claimed that he never suspected the connection between Manson and the Cielo murders until the police told him about it.

Nor did it occur to him in mid-August, when he witnessed Manson's violence firsthand. Manson broke into Jakobson's home in the middle of the night, shook him awake, and produced a bullet. "Tell Dennis there are more where this came from," he said. On the witness stand, Jakobson compared Manson that night to a caged bobcat: "The electricity was almost pouring out of him. His hair was on end. His eyes were wild."

A few days earlier, Manson had shown up at Wilson's house, too, demanding fifteen hundred dollars. When Wilson refused to give him the money, Manson threatened him: "Don't be surprised if you never see your kid again."

After Manson's arrest, Wilson fell into a deep depression, spurring his problems with drugs and alcohol. Later, he told the Beach Boys' authorized biographer, David Leaf, "I know why Charles Manson did what he did. Someday I'll tell the world. I'll write a book and explain why he did it." He never got the chance. In 1983, three weeks after his thirty-ninth birthday, an acutely drunk Wilson dove from the deck of his boat into the chilly waters of Marina del Rey and accidentally drowned. Within days, a rock journalist wrote in the *San Francisco Chronicle* about a jarring exchange he'd had with Wilson. "Me and Charlie, we founded the Family," Dennis had said, apropos of nothing.

The Golden Penetrators, then, had an abundance of reasons to accuse Manson of the Tate–LaBianca murders—immediately. They believed he'd shot someone dead. He'd threatened two of them with violence. They knew he stockpiled guns and knives at the ranch. And the slaughter at Melcher's old house was exactly the kind he'd predicted, down to the most chilling detail. Shouldn't they have connected the dots? Was it possible that there was a conspiracy of silence among them?

"Asshole Buddies"

Rudi Altobelli, the owner of the house on Cielo Drive—Tate and Polanski's landlord, and Terry Melcher's before that—became one of my best sources. It was thanks to him that I started looking into Melcher's story in the first place.

When I met up with Altobelli in the spring of 1999, he'd never publicly spoken about the murders that had occurred at his house, except in trial testimony. I wasn't sure why he'd agreed to talk now, and to me, of all people; I'd heard it would be a waste of time even to bother asking. But Altobelli had always been unpredictable. One of the first openly gay men in Hollywood, he'd made a living as a manager, his clients including Henry Fonda and Katharine Hepburn. In November 1969—three months after the murders, before the killers had been found—he shocked the community by filing a lawsuit against Polanski and Sharon Tate's father to recover the damages his property had sustained during the murders. It was an appallingly callous response: to seek money from a victim's family because she'd bled on Altobelli's carpet as she lay dying.

I knew, then, that I'd have to tread carefully with Altobelli. True to old Hollywood form, he suggested we meet at Musso and Frank Grill, a legendary outpost that looked right out of a film noir. Many of its red-jacketed waiters seemed so old that they could've been working there when it opened in 1919. One of them led me through the wood-paneled room past red banquettes to Altobelli, at a corner table, already treating himself to the first in a succession of Gibsons (with extra onions). Compact and nattily dressed, he was a few weeks shy of his seventieth birthday, but he had no lines on his face and no gray in his hair. Admittedly vain, he'd begin all our meetings by asking "How do I look?"—it came before hello. His glasses were always tinted: on some days blue, on others pink, orange, or light purple.

After dinner that night, he kept calling to chat, and I took him out for years to come. The restaurants were always fancy; the bills were always mine. And I always felt, through hundreds of hours of conversation, that I wasn't getting the whole story. His go-to defense was unchanging: "I may not tell you everything, but I have never lied to you." (Robert Towne, who wrote the screenplay for *Chinatown,* called Altobelli "the most honest man in Hollywood"—a low bar to clear, maybe, but I'd take what I could get.) If I printed anything without his permission, he said, "I'll find ya and cut your balls off and feed 'em to you." Fortunately, he later decided it was all on the record.

Altobelli had bought the Cielo house in 1963. In May 1966, he rented to Terry Melcher, who was known at the time for having produced the Byrds' "Mr. Tambourine Man" and "Turn, Turn, Turn." Altobelli liked to befriend his tenants—he'd live in the guesthouse and rent out the main property—and soon the two became what he called "asshole buddies." (An affectionate term, he assured me.)

Not only was Altobelli one of the few people who'd befriended both Melcher and Tate—he was one of the few who'd seen Manson on the property before the murders. He provided critical testimony for the state, identifying Manson as the man who'd barged into his guesthouse looking for Terry Melcher on March 23, 1969. His ID was reliable; he'd already met Manson at Dennis Wilson's house the summer before. He'd sat on Dennis's bed atop a "dirty satin sheet with cum spots on it," Rudi told me, "while Manson sat on the floor" playing music. "I didn't like the vibe from him," Rudi added. "I even told Terry to keep those people off the property."

It sounded like Altobelli, and others in his circle, had suspected Manson from the start. And that was true, Altobelli said. When he heard about the murders, he thought of Manson right away. Altobelli was in Rome at the time, and his memories troubled him enough that within hours of the murders, before he'd even boarded a flight home, he called his lawyer who told him he should mind his own business.

Altobelli returned to Los Angeles hoping to move back into his house right away. The LAPD forbade him. Instead, he crashed with Melcher and Candice Bergen at their place in Malibu. That house belonged to Doris Day, Melcher's mother, but she seldom used it. During Altobelli's stay, Gregg Jakobson stopped by and invited him for a walk on the beach. As they strolled along the surf, past beautiful oceanfront homes fortified in recent weeks with fences, guard dogs, and security systems, Jakobson told him "about the musician that Manson was supposed to have killed."

Altobelli didn't remember the musician's name. I wondered if he was thinking of Gary Hinman, a musician who'd been killed by the Family thirteen days before the Tate–LaBianca murders. If Jakobson knew about that murder, would he not have connected the Tate–LaBianca deaths to Manson, too?

That day on the beach, Jakobson reached into his pocket and pulled out a bullet. "He said, 'This one's for Terry.' It was from Manson."

This strained credulity. As mentioned above, during the trial, Jakobson had said that after the murders, Manson broke into his house, gave him a bullet, and told him to show it to Dennis Wilson. The message: "There are more where this came from." Maybe Altobelli was getting all of it mixed up? But he was insistent. "No, he said it was for *Terry!*"

Then why didn't he tell Terry about it?

"Because when I'm told to mind my own business by my attorney, I mind my own business. In fact, I should be minding my own business now and shut up."

How could Altobelli have spent so much time with Melcher,

doing nothing but discussing the tragedy and speculating on possible culprits, without sharing this crucial information—without telling his friend that there was a bullet with his name on it? He knew it would've helped solve the case. Altobelli did say that he called his attorney one more time to fill him in. He was told, again, to mind his own business. (His lawyer declined to comment.)

If Altobelli was telling the truth, then wouldn't all four of these men—him, Melcher, Wilson, and Jakobson, the main links between Manson, Hollywood, and the house on Cielo Drive—have known that Manson was behind the murders? And yet all they wanted to do was forget about it. Three weeks after the crimes, Altobelli moved back into the house on Cielo Drive, with Melcher as his new roommate—an arrangement that's never been reported before. Remember, during the trial, Jakobson said he never connected the murders to Manson.

Altobelli returned out of a desire to reclaim his home from the evil that had infested it. He hoped to restore some order to the place. By then it had become a morbid mecca for Hollywood's elite, who came by wanting a glimpse at the scene of the crimes. Even Elvis Presley came to pay his respects. Altobelli turned most of these visitors away—but he welcomed Melcher, who'd expressed a bizarre yearning to stay in his old place again. With Altobelli's blessing, Melcher lived there for a month, maybe longer. He hardly left the property.

"He probably figured it was safe there," Altobelli said. "That lightning wouldn't strike twice." Melcher came alone—he seemed to have split up with Bergen. Settling back into the house, he became morose, as Altobelli remembered, wandering around in a daze and drinking heavily. Another friend, the screenwriter Charles Eastman, who lived several doors down on Cielo Drive, said that Melcher showed up at his place wearing Voytek Frykowski's clothing. "I said, This is too gruesome, this is ugly, I don't like this."

Melcher was living out his attachment to the place in macabre ways. "He felt, as everybody did, that the house was sacred," Eastman said. He loved it so much that he'd even tried to talk Altobelli into selling it to him. Which made me wonder: Why had he and Bergen ever moved out? Bugliosi hinted in *Helter Skelter* that their departure was abrupt, but he never said why.

They left in the middle of the night, with no warning and four months left on the lease, Altobelli told me. "Terry blamed it on Ruth [Simmons], their housekeeper...He said they were frightened of her. That she was domineering and a drunk. That it was the only way they knew to get rid of her."

Melcher and Bergen, both privileged children of Hollywood royalty, were so frightened of a housekeeper that they'd sooner move out of a house they loved than fire her? A power couple, scared of the maid.

Eastman was convinced that something else was to blame: Melcher "knew that Manson was after him." Altobelli and Melcher were always being pestered by strange visitors, girls with funny names, he said. "My feeling was that Rudi and Terry both had reason to be uncomfortable about Manson and his people." Eastman had even written about it in his journal in March 1969. He read the entry to me:

> Rudi criticizes Terry for leaving behind so many cats when he moved. When I ask him why Terry moved, he tells me it was money, that Terry became peeved at the rent...remembering Terry's love of the house and how many times, according to Rudi, that Terry offered to buy the house from him, it seems odd to me that he moved away so suddenly, so abruptly.

None of this had ever come out before. Other friends of Melcher agreed that he and Bergen had "snuck out in the middle of the night" because of threats from the Family. "Melcher was afraid of them," one source told me. "They said, 'If you don't produce our album, we'll kill you.' " After the murders, Melcher seemed "really guilty." He "probably felt he should have said to [the new tenants, Tate and Polanski]: Don't rent the house, there are these people who have been harassing me there."

Altobelli gave me the number for Carole Wilson, Dennis Wilson's ex-wife. It was after their second separation that Dennis had taken up with Manson and the girls, much to Carole's chagrin. The two shared custody of their two kids. Later, I would hear from a reliable source that Carole had had photos taken at Dennis's house, capturing him cavorting naked around the pool with women from the Family. She used them to pressure Dennis, getting him to agree to her terms in the divorce.

Carole kept careful tabs on her ex's goings-on. "She kept a diary from the day Dennis first met Tex Watson," Altobelli told me. "It has everything in it, everything on Terry—she hates him." Meanwhile, she pursued a romance with Jay Sebring, which I'd never seen reported before. It felt significant, in light of the fact that her ex-husband had been intertwined with Sebring's killers.

It was just before the weekend when I reached Wilson. I told her that I was exploring the possibility that her former husband and his friends had been more involved with the Manson Family than previously reported, and I wondered if Manson's reach in Hollywood was further than had been known. "Yes, it sure was," she replied. She asked that I call her back on Monday—we could meet for coffee.

When Monday came, though, she'd changed her mind. "I thought long and hard over the weekend," she said, "and I can't talk to you." There were a lot of people involved, she explained—too many. "It's a scary thing," she said, "and anyone who knows anything will never talk."

I couldn't draw her out on that. She suggested that I talk to Melcher and Jakobson, but she wouldn't put me in touch.

Meanwhile, I'd started to hear more sordid stuff about Melcher's affiliation with the Family. Bob April, a retired carpenter who'd been a fringe member of the Family, told me with confidence that Manson "would supply girls" for "executive parties" that Melcher threw, giving well-heeled business types unfettered access to Manson's girls. But what would Manson get in return?

"That's why everyone got killed," April said. "He didn't get what he wanted." Melcher had promised Manson a record deal "on Day Labels," his mother's imprint. But Doris Day took one look at Manson "and laughed at him and said, 'You're out of your mind if you think I'm going to produce a fucking record for you.' Said it to Charlie's face." Melcher and Manson "knew each other very well," April said. "I've tried to get this out for years."

The Paper Trail Begins

I was doing shoe-leather reporting on a thirty-year-old story. The memories I heard were rife with the omissions, contradictions, and embroidery that come with the passage of time. I would interview people and then rush to the library to fact-check, as best I could, what they'd told me—in books about the case, histories of Los Angeles, biographies of organized crime figures, old news clippings, and more. But if I wanted to report this story with veracity, I needed contemporaneous, documentary evidence: the paperwork. When sources like Charles Eastman would mention having journals, I would beg them to find them, often calling back repeatedly until they did. But first and foremost, I wanted police reports and trial transcripts. The case had been the longest and costliest in California history, and Bugliosi said that the transcript numbered more than a million pages. Where was that? Could I have access to it?

The LAPD told me they'd destroyed all their investigative reports; they'd retained some files, but they weren't about to release them to me. How could they have trashed their records of the most infamous case in the history of the city? I didn't believe it. I asked them to put it in writing, and they did, stating in an official letter that "a thorough and proper search" produced "no records"; all the evidence had been "destroyed."

I turned to unofficial channels. I'd heard about a "researcher" named Bill Nelson, an older man who was obsessed with the murders. He'd self-published several books about the case and had a lot of original police reports. Nelson was purportedly a pretty strange guy: he stalked former members of the Family and relatives of the victims, trying to befriend them so he could interview them. He'd become close to Sharon Tate's mother, Doris, even traveling with her to Paris to visit Roman Polanski, but they'd had some falling-out before her death in 1992.

I looked at Nelson's website, Mansonmurders.com. The fact that he had one at all was still something of a novelty in 1999. Regularly updated with accounts of his crusades, his page included an index of crime-scene photos, police documents, and interviews, most of which were for sale.

There was also plenty to suggest his instability. A retired evangelical minister, Nelson boasted of "a close and personal relationship" with Jesus Christ. He bragged about having attended the "United States Secret Service Academy," where his design for the annual class ring was still in use. His exposés of former Family members were vitriolic and often ad hominem. He'd published photographs of some of their children, having stalked them at their homes and schools.

But I had to admit that he was a thorough researcher—and I was at a loss as to how I could come by these documents otherwise. I swallowed my pride and sent him an email.

We met for coffee at a Denny's in Costa Mesa one afternoon. Across the table, Nelson looked like a retired accountant: midsixties, balding, his silver hair neatly combed on the sides. He dressed conservatively, in a button-down shirt and khakis. I paid him forty bucks for copies of the homicide investigation reports, unredacted and numbering almost a hundred pages.

He'd gotten these from Earl Deemer, the cop whose interview with Billy Doyle I discussed earlier. Deemer conducted most of the polygraphs for the Tate investigation, and had copied all the police reports, photos, and audiotapes related to the case. How Nelson persuaded him to part with this stuff was a mystery: some said he bought the files, others that he stole them. He didn't want to tell me, that much was clear.

Deemer had since died, and what was left of his records went to Mike McGann, a retired homicide detective who'd been the lead investigator on the Tate team. McGann lived in Idaho now. Nelson gave me his number.

Like Ed Sanders and others, Nelson believed that certain elements of law enforcement knew that the Tate–LaBianca murders were planned, or they knew who was behind them. They'd been unable to act because it would've exposed their secret intelligence-gathering operations. Nelson had watched nearly every televised interview Manson had ever given; he felt that Manson "never lies," he just "withholds information." But Manson would never tell the truth about the murders—it would involve snitching, and there was no greater transgression in a criminal's mind.

Hearing all this at Denny's made my head hurt, but I felt I had to indulge Nelson. In spite of how far-fetched his theories sounded, some of them resonated with me long after I pulled away from the restaurant that day.

Back home, I put on some coffee and pulled out the sheaf of papers I'd just bought, feeling somewhere between eager and anxious. As explained in *Helter Skelter,* the Homicide Investigation Progress Reports were essentially internal summaries. They outlined the detectives' various leads and efforts to break the case, presenting the investigation in all its disarray, without Bugliosi's streamlining.

The thirty-three pages on the Tate murders — "First Homicide Investigation Progress Report" — dated to the end of August 1969. Much of them was workmanlike, describing the activities of the victims in the days leading to their deaths, the chronology of the discovery of the bodies, the recovery of evidence, and so on. When the investigators speculated on the hows and whys, I sat up a bit. They focused on the possibility that Billy Doyle, Charles Tacot, and others had initiated a vengeful massacre after Frykowski welshed on a drug deal. The "Second Homicide Investigation Progress Report" came six weeks later, describing the battery of polygraphs and interrogations through which investigators concluded they hadn't found the killers yet.

I'd expected to see names like Altobelli's and Melcher's everywhere in the two Tate reports, but I was wrong. Melcher wasn't mentioned once, and Altobelli was only referenced in passing. If investigators had looked into the possibility that the man who owned the house, or its most recent previous occupant, had anything to do with the murders, there was no sign of their efforts here.

As intriguing as these reports were, they were kind of a letdown — and other reporters had already gotten them. If I wanted something new, really new, I'd have to keep pressing. I decided to call Mike McGann, the retired cop who lived in Idaho. If Nelson was right, he'd have a stockpile of documents that dwarfed the collection in my hands.

"Everything in Vince Bugliosi's book is wrong," McGann told me on the phone. "I was the lead investigator on the case. Bugliosi didn't solve it. Nobody trusted him." McGann spoke in gruff sentences, sometimes no more than a word or two — always a breath away from hanging up on me.

I wanted to know more, but McGann, like others close to the case, expected to be compensated for his time. And even more so for his papers—he had the records, he told me, but they were available only for a price. That effectively shut down the conversation.

I kept calling McGann, who was willing to tolerate my curiosity, to a point. I wanted to know about Melcher, Wilson, Jakobson, and Altobelli—what had they told the cops, and when? What about Carole Wilson, and Carole Jakobson, Gregg's wife? McGann said he hadn't gone through the files in years, but he'd look, if he had a chance.

Two months later, during our sixth conversation—he still hadn't agreed to show me anything for free—McGann said that he had 190 written summaries of the interviews by the Tate detectives—some were only half a page long; most were a page or two; a few were longer. There were no interviews of Melcher, Jakobson, Wilson, or Altobelli, but there *were* interviews with Carole Jakobson and Carole Wilson. He pulled out the latter, dated August 15, 1969, and started to read a portion over the phone, but soon he stopped and raised his voice. "Are you taping this? I'm not gonna go for that." I turned off the tape, but he refused to read any more. Before he totally lost patience, I asked if he could tell me one last thing: the date of the Carole Jakobson interview.

He leafed through the pages. "August 10," he said. The day after the bodies were discovered. That meant that both wives, Jakobson's and Wilson's—"the two Caroles," as Altobelli called them—had spoken to police within a week of the murders. Why not their husbands? And why not Melcher or Altobelli, given their close ties to the Cielo home? Where were *those* interviews?

Revisiting Cielo Drive

One night, after taking Altobelli out to dinner, I drove him home, as I always did. He'd totaled his car after our first meeting—he was certain someone had run him off the road as a warning to stop speaking to me—and since then I'd become his de facto chauffeur.

("What, the good car in the shop?" he'd always say.) Our evenings together usually ran to six or eight hours, with Altobelli requesting impromptu stops at the supermarket or at a bar for a nightcap. We were close to Benedict Canyon that night, so I took us back to the Valley that way.

"I used to drive this way back to Cielo," he said, beginning to reminisce about "the happiest period of my life." When I asked if he'd mind if we drove up to the house, he said, "Sure, why not?" I sensed some reluctance in his answer. Cresting the final hill, we proceeded in silence down the narrow road, stopping at the gated entrance to what had once been 10050 Cielo Drive. The house had been razed in 1994; erected in its place was "Villa Bella," an Italianate mansion of concrete and marble behind a tall, ostentatious gate that concealed most of it from the street.

"I want to see what number they put on my mailbox," Rudi said, suddenly irritated. "Where is my mailbox?" I maneuvered the car beside it. "10066," Altobelli said, reading the numbers. "They had it changed." His voice cracked. "We had such a great view," he said, gazing from my passenger seat at the sliver of space beyond the gate. "It's all so cold looking now. My house was so warm and cozy." His voice broke again and his breathing was shallow, like he was gasping for air.

"Let's go," he said after a long pause. "Back up, back up — *now!*" he said. When we were already halfway down Cielo, he shouted again, "Just go!" We drove back to his apartment in silence.

At home, with about a half dozen stray cats greeting him outside, Altobelli perked up, kneeling down to pet each one and calling them all by name. Inviting me in, he apologized for what had happened back at Cielo. It was the first time he'd returned since he left ten years before. "I lived in that house twenty-five years, four months, and thirty-eight hours," he said. Now he lived in a converted garage in a neighborhood known for its gang activity.

Hanging over his desk was a framed photo of the house from the midsixties and a watercolor painting of the front gate. Also framed was a letter from Bugliosi, commending him for his testimony at the trial. Riffling through old snapshots on his desk, he handed me fading photographs of celebrities, all taken at 10050 Cielo Drive. The last one was of Terry Melcher passed out on top of the same desk Altobelli was presently seated at. Melcher's hand gripped an empty bottle of liquor. "Booze and pills," Altobelli said. The photo was taken when Melcher was staying with him at the house after the murders.

In November of that year, when the police told Altobelli that Manson was responsible for the murders, the first thing he did was call "the two Caroles." "I said because of their husbands I was stuck with all of this. I was left in the lurch. Didn't their husbands know what was happening at the house? Terry was the instigator of the whole thing."

Altobelli seemed to be toying with the idea of letting me in on something bigger. He did this a lot—a seemingly offhand remark would complicate his entire portrait of the period. "Terry talked about Manson all the time," he said. "He thought he was wonderful. He asked me to manage him." But hadn't Terry said he wanted nothing to do with him? "Terry *stalked* Manson. They thought they had *Jesus Christ*."

Later, when I got transcripts of the trials, I'd see that Altobelli wasn't just embroidering. On the stand, he'd said that Melcher, along with Wilson and Jakobson, had "talked to me on many occasions about Mr. Manson and his philosophy...his way of living and how groovy it was." Tellingly, in his own testimony, Melcher acted as if he hardly knew the man behind this groovy philosophy. Presented with a photo of Manson, he told a grand jury, "I don't know him but I think I have seen him at Dennis Wilson's house." Later, he revised this story, still stressing that he'd met Manson no more than three times. In other words, even at the time, Melcher's and Altobelli's stories weren't straight.

Thinking of my talk with Mike McGann, I asked Altobelli if detectives had interviewed him after the murders. Of course they had, he said. He even remembered when: it had been on the day of the Tate and Sebring funerals, at his lawyer's office. (At the trial, he'd testified to the same thing.) Following his lawyer's instructions, he reminded me, he hadn't said anything to the police about Manson. I told Altobelli that McGann had said there was no record of his interview. He was as baffled as I was.

"It Might Surprise You"

With McGann stonewalling me, I paid a visit to Stephen Kay, of the Los Angeles DA's office, thinking he might be able to point me toward more documents. Kay had helped Bugliosi prosecute the case in 1970, joining the trial midway through—a career-making turn for the young lawyer. In the ensuing decades, Kay had served as the government's most prominent voice against Manson and the Family, appearing at their parole hearings to argue against their release. He was, after Bugliosi, the legal world's leading expert on the Family.

I met Kay at his office in Long Beach. When I turned the subject to Melcher, he volunteered something else I'd never heard.

"Manson and Watson attended a party at the Cielo house when Terry and Candy Bergen lived there," he said. He was confident about this: the information first came out during the trial for Tex Watson, who'd been tried separately from the other Family members. Kay had confirmed it with Gregg Jakobson. He thought it was another reason that Manson had chosen the Cielo house for the murders; when he sent Watson and the girls there, he noted that "Tex knows the layout of the place." And yet Melcher, in his testimony, had said that he never once saw Watson inside his house. "Melcher doesn't want to have anything to do with this. You'll never get to talk to Melcher or Candice Bergen," Kay told me.

Kay didn't believe that the LAPD had really destroyed their files on the case. For one thing, he said Bugliosi had borrowed what he needed to write *Helter Skelter* and then, conveniently, never returned anything. Bugliosi had seen earlier than anyone that the Manson trial "was going to be his meal ticket," Kay said. He took the ethically dubious step of installing his writing partner, Curt Gentry, in the courtroom every day to watch the proceedings in real time. Gentry was working on the book that would become *Helter Skelter* before anyone was even convicted. The sensationalism only inflamed Bugliosi's hubris. At one point, he grabbed Kay's arm in the courtroom and said to him, "Steve, aren't I great? Do you know anyone as great as me?"

And Bugliosi was still dining out, literally, on his Manson stories. The case continued to earn him a handsome income in royalties and public-speaking appearances. I was curious about those who hadn't made out so well—people still living in the shadow of these crimes, who'd been broken by the tumult of the late sixties. They'd have no vested interest in preserving the official narrative.

Through a series of Los Angeles attorneys, I tracked down Irving A. Kanarek, Manson's defense attorney. I'd been warned that his was a sad story, but I wasn't prepared for the dire straits I'd find him in.

Kanarek comes across as a ridiculous figure in *Helter Skelter*. Bugliosi portrays him as an erratic, bombastic blowhard whose "obstructionist tactics" earned him opprobrium from every corner of the legal world. The book devotes many pages to his history of indiscretions in the courtroom. By the available evidence, Bugliosi wasn't exaggerating here. Kanarek really *was* a reviled, difficult lawyer, and his conduct in the Manson case bore this out. (According to legend, Manson wanted the worst trial lawyer in Los Angeles; someone told him that Kanarek was his man.) He objected nine times during Bugliosi's opening statement alone. By day three he'd racked up an impressive two hundred objections. The judge jailed him twice for contempt. Bugliosi conceded that Kanarek could be effective, even eloquent at moments, but this didn't stop him from calling Kanarek, in court and in *Helter Skelter*, "the Toscanini of Tedium."

I met this Toscanini standing on the sidewalk in tony Newport Beach. It was eighty degrees out, but he shuffled up in an oversized winter coat and threadbare sneakers, lugging a battered briefcase held together with twine. Newspapers and plastic bags were poking out. Short and stooped, Kanarek had an unkempt, patchy gray beard; his hands and face were streaked with dirt, as if he hadn't bathed for weeks. There were sores on his body. He was missing most of his teeth.

Once Kanarek learned I had a car, he asked me to drive him to a Barnes & Noble, where the cashier handed him a copy of the *Los Angeles Times* and sent him on his way. It was the previous day's paper, he told me—that's why he didn't have to pay for it.

Then we got lunch outside at Santa Monica Seafood, a relatively upscale chain. Kanarek struck me as sharp, but eccentric. His explosive volume led diners at two other tables to relocate indoors. He'd shout things like "Manson didn't kill anyone! He's the one who should've gotten immunity!" or "All Charlie wanted to do was screw girls! He didn't know they were going to murder those people!" Most of his diatribes took on Bugliosi, for whom he had endless epithets: Liar! Cheat! Crook! Con man! Adulterer! Stalker! Woman beater! Son of a bitch! "And worse," he shouted, causing another table to flee, "an indicted perjurer who used his influence to be acquitted during his trial!"

When I asked if Kanarek was paid to defend Manson, he smiled wryly and said that he was, but that confidentiality prevented him from revealing by whom.

"It would be big news," he said. "It might surprise you." (If Kanarek had a benefactor, another lawyer later told me, that white knight wasn't generous—Kanarek apparently spent most of the trial living out of his car and sleeping in the press room at the courthouse.)

Over the ten years prior to our meeting, Kanarek had discovered his wife was cheating on him; he'd wandered into traffic and been struck by a car; he'd suffered a nervous breakdown and spent time in a mental institution. He'd lost his law firm, his license to practice, and his life's savings. Now he was living on social security at a motel in Costa Mesa, the next town over. After lunch, I offered to drive him back. He took me up on it. But could I take him on "a few more stops" before we parted ways?

"A few more stops" turned into two harrowing hours in my 1988 Acura. Kanarek screamed at me for missing turns that he'd told me to take just as we were passing them. We drove in circles around Orange County until, to my horror, he announced that he'd decided to accompany me back to L.A.—which meant two *more* hours in the car with him, during rush-hour traffic. Almost as soon as we pulled onto the freeway, he was ranting again. When he said again that Bugliosi was an "indicted perjurer," I asked him to explain.

Belittling me for not having done my homework, Kanarek said that during the Manson trial someone had leaked the rumor about Manson's celebrity "hit list" to a journalist named Bill Farr, who'd published it in violation of the court's gag order. The hit-list scoop must've come from one of the lawyers on the case—they were the only ones with access to it. With the jury out of the courtroom, the judge made the attorneys swear under oath that they hadn't slipped the information to Farr, who'd refused to reveal his source. All six attorneys denied having done it. After the trial, the judge, still suspicious, empaneled a grand jury to investigate the incident. They indicted two of the attorneys for lying. One was Daye Shinn, Susan Atkins's defense attorney. The other was Bugliosi.

"Read the grand jury transcript!" Kanarek shouted. The state decided to prosecute the case. But if Bugliosi was convicted of perjury, it would jeopardize the verdicts in the Manson trial, and the DA's office couldn't stand for that. They got the judge to dismiss the charges on a technicality—they colluded, that is, to protect the convictions from the longest, most expensive criminal trial in U.S. history. "It was a sweetheart deal, don't you see?" Kanarek shouted, his spittle spraying my face.

It wasn't mentioned in *Helter Skelter*, I said. Of course it wasn't, Kanarek scoffed. Neither was the fact that Bugliosi "stalked his milkman" and "beat up his mistress." I should look up those cases, too, both of which, he said, had been "taken care of" because of Bugliosi's political clout. "He's a criminal," he shouted, "and dangerous, too!"

I thought Kanarek was unstable, so I didn't put much stock in his stories. I was relieved when we got to Hollywood; I wouldn't have to endure any more of his delusions. As he gathered his things and got out, I started to worry about him. It'd occurred to me that he might've been homeless. I offered him some cash, but he waved it away, asking me instead to promise that I'd look into his claims about Bugliosi. I watched him disappear into the crowd on the low-rent end of Hollywood Boulevard. Later that year, when my relationship with Bugliosi began to sour, I'd find that everything he said was true.

Coda: I'm Not the Oracle

I'd been sending progress reports to *Premiere*. The magazine's editor in chief, Jim Meigs, was hooked on the story—he was as invested as I was. In the middle of May 1999, the editors agreed to extend my deadline a second time. That meant the piece would be too late for the anniversary of the murders, but it didn't matter, they told me, as long as I could deliver something big. I was relieved, at least in the short term. In the long term, I was starting to feel the pressure of having to produce something mind-blowing. I had to get it right—and to do that, I had to push harder on my sources, find new ones, and, most critically, find more of the documents generated during the investigation.

Having heard so often that Terry Melcher would never talk to me, I knew one thing I could do to set my story apart: get Terry Melcher to talk to me. I'd gotten his number, but I didn't want to use it until I was sure I had some good questions to ask him. I figured I'd only get one shot. I finally called him in early June. He was articulate and, from the start, irritable and distrustful.

"I get so many goddamned calls about this crap from all over the world," he said. "I don't know anything about this shit. Rudi [Altobelli] called me for the first time in ten or fifteen years a few days ago and told me the story of the bullets. I don't know if that's real but, you know, so what? What are you gonna do?"

"At the time of the murders," I asked, "did you suspect Manson?"

"I had no idea. No idea whatsoever. I used to audition three or four bands a week. They all looked the same. They all looked like the cast of *Hair*."

"How many times did you meet Manson?"

"Once, very briefly, at Dennis Wilson's house, and the second time at the ranch."

"But I've spoken to people who claim that you knew them a lot better."

"I really didn't," Melcher said.

Why had he moved out of the Cielo house so suddenly? It was "totally ridiculous" to pin that on his fear of Manson, he said. He still blamed his housekeeper, Ruth Simmons.

"It's just hard to believe that someone as powerful as you would move out of his house rather than fire the maid," I said.

"It's really true. I just couldn't figure out what else to do." Plus, his mom had vacated their Malibu beach house, and he thought it was a good idea to live there to prevent it from falling into disrepair.

Next I probed his friendship with Dennis Wilson. How could he dodge the fact that both of them, plus Gregg Jakobson, should've suspected Manson as soon as they learned of the murders?

Melcher said his friendship with Wilson had dissolved around that time, as Wilson became increasingly reticent. The rumor was that Wilson "knew that they were killing people," Melcher said. "He was so freaked out he just didn't want to live anymore. He was afraid, and he thought he should have gone to the authorities, but he didn't, and then the rest of it happened. So he was in some way just tremendously guilty—now I don't know that that's true..."

"And that guilt doesn't apply to you, too?" I asked.

"I don't think so! Christ, if they wanted to get me, all my doors were wide open that whole summer." After the murders, he'd heard that Wilson met with Bugliosi and "all the DAs in the state of California in one great big room," and that Wilson had managed to eke out only one sentence about the Family: "'Well, we hung around and smoked a little pot and sang some songs.' Period. That was it. That was his entire statement."

"Why would Vince settle for that?" I asked.

"I dunno, he thought he'd just put him on the stand."

"But he didn't put him on the stand," I said. This was something I'd been thinking about a lot. Dennis Wilson would've been a star witness, since he'd known Manson so well and had seen his violent tendencies. If he didn't want to testify, Bugliosi could have subpoenaed him; he did it to force testimony from plenty of others. Why not Wilson?

"Well, they thought he was nuts, and by that time he was," Melcher said. "He had a hard time separating reality from fantasy, seriously. He had inventions. He tried to sell me once a new invention that was the size of a cigarette box, an antigravity device. You kept it in your glove compartment, but when you get into a traffic jam, you just turn it on and fly right over the other cars. He really thought it worked."

I had more questions, but I could feel him growing impatient. "I'm not the oracle about this thing," Melcher said. "I just know that it was an incredible pain in the ass."

That pain would continue. Listening back to my tape of the call, I'd realize that I'd caught Melcher in a lie, one that implicated Bugliosi—and gave me my best shot yet at proving that both of them were involved in a cover-up.

4

The Holes in *Helter Skelter*

Moorehouse Moves In

As my trust in Bugliosi faltered, I kept revisiting *Helter Skelter*, turning its pages in search of some detail that felt forced or wrong—especially where Terry Melcher was concerned. One day, a few sentences jumped out at me:

> After Terry Melcher had moved out of the [Cielo Drive] residence, but before the Polanskis had moved in, Gregg Jakobson had arranged for *a Dean Moorehouse* to stay there for a brief period. During this time Tex Watson had visited Moorehouse at least three, and possibly as many as six, times.

Emphasis mine. Something about that offhand phrasing—"a Dean Moorehouse"—raised a red flag for me.

This was the only time Moorehouse was mentioned in the book. He had been a peripheral member of the Family. A wavering Protestant minister, insurance salesman, and married father of three, he was living in San Jose when he first encountered Manson, in 1967, when the ex-con was fresh out of federal prison and hitch-hiking. Moorehouse pulled over to give him a lift, which turned into an invitation to dinner, which blossomed into a friendship of sorts. Moorehouse, who'd strayed from his ministry and was himself on probation for a forgery charge, was searching for something new and was eager to discuss spirituality; Manson was eager to ogle Moorehouse's fifteen-year-old daughter, Ruth Ann.

Before long, Manson absconded with Ruth Ann on a trip up the California coast, prompting her mother to report her to the police as a runaway. Dean Moorehouse had left the marriage by then—he'd fallen under the spell of the sixties and grown a long white beard. By March 1968, he was in trouble with the law again, facing an arrest for contributing to the delinquency of a minor; police had found him when they raided a home in search of mari-juana. Soon afterward, he was arrested again, this time for selling LSD. The legend is that Manson persuaded him to try it for the first time, after which he renounced his earthly possessions.

Moorehouse kept chasing his daughter, who'd remained with the Family; Manson had rechristened her "Ouisch." When Moore-house followed them to Dennis Wilson's house in Pacific Palisades, Manson kneeled and kissed his feet, launching a charm offensive that effectively ended the conflict. Increasingly sympathetic to the Family's philosophies, Moorehouse moved into the back cabin and lived there rent-free in exchange for maintaining the landscaping. Manson had converted a onetime Christian minister.

But when had Moorehouse taken up residence in the Cielo home? Melcher had told me he had no memory of it. Bugliosi wrote that it was after Melcher moved out, meaning in January 1969.

I found Moorehouse in the phone book and gave him a call. He was friendly, though spacey. Now seventy-nine, he was living in northern California under the name "Baba," which Manson had given him. He'd had more than four hundred LSD trips between 1967 and 1972. "When I talk to you, I'm talking to myself," he explained. "When you talk to me, you're talking to yourself."

Be that as it may, he had a sharp recall for his time with Manson, and what he told me didn't vindicate Melcher or Bugliosi in the slightest. It was impossible that he'd moved into the Cielo house in January 1969, for one simple reason: he'd gone to prison then.

Moorehouse had been arrested on a drug charge in Ukiah, California. In the midst of his time with the Family, he had to head back north for his trial. "They convicted me in December of '68," he said. "I was due back there at the end of December for sentencing, and then on January 3 they hauled me off to Vacaville," a correctional facility.

Moorehouse said he'd really lived at Cielo "off and on" throughout the summer of '68, when Melcher lived there. "Terry was a good friend," he explained, "and when I first met him at Dennis's, he said, 'If it's okay with you I'll send my chauffeur down one of these days and have you come up to my house.'" Melcher "took me in and showed me a bedroom and said, 'This is your bedroom, you can stay here anytime that you want.' So I was staying there off and on, whenever I felt like it." He also confirmed a detail from Ed Sanders's *The Family:* that Melcher had let him borrow his Jaguar for the long drive to Ukiah. "I drove the Jaguar up there with Tex Watson," he said. Melcher "gave it to me to use on this trip and he gave me his credit card to use for gas and anything that happened to the car."

I asked Moorehouse for written proof of his time in prison. With his permission, I got a copy of his parole record from the state of California. It showed that he entered the prison system on January 2, 1969.

So Bugliosi's timeline was wrong, and Melcher had lied to me. I felt I had to talk to Melcher about this, though I knew it'd anger him—he might cut me off afterward. Still, I called him up and laid out the evidence as gingerly as I could. Melcher wasn't having it. He stuck to the story as Bugliosi had told it in *Helter Skelter* and promptly got rid of me.

Not long after, I got a disturbing call from Rudi Altobelli, sounding more upset and angry than I'd ever heard him. He'd been in touch with Melcher for the first time in many years. Their conversations had left him feeling out of the loop. In Altobelli's eyes, the Golden Penetrators—Jakobson, Wilson, Melcher—had always known that Manson had spent time up at the house. But in his view they were too scared to say it on the stand. That task fell to Altobelli, who now felt he'd been pressured into talking about it under oath without understanding the full story.

Once they'd started talking again, Altobelli asked Melcher about Dean Moorehouse, with my reporting in mind. Melcher had snapped, saying he was going to call Bugliosi. "Vince was supposed to take care of all that," he said, "and now it's all resurfacing."

Melcher's Lies

Stephen Kay of the Los Angeles DA's office told me to call another longtime employee there, Sandi Gibbons. She might be sympathetic to my aims. Before she worked for the DA, Gibbons had been a journalist, and her coverage of the Manson trial left her deeply skeptical of Bugliosi and his motives. She became one of several reporters who believed that Bugliosi was corrupt, arrogant, vain, even crazy; later, when he pursued elected office, she wrote a number of stories detailing his misconduct as a prosecutor.

I took Gibbons out to lunch and found her impressively forthright. Soft-spoken and direct, she was certain that Bugliosi had covered up for Terry Melcher during the trial. The two must have made some kind of deal: you testify to this and I'll keep you out of that. She also confirmed that Bugliosi had stolen a bunch of the

DA's files for his book, knowing full well that it was illegal to remove them. It bothered her that he was always portrayed as upstanding and aboveboard—he was a snake. She could still recall the sight of a vein throbbing in his temple—if I ever saw that vein, she warned me, it meant that Bugliosi was about to blow his stack.

Once I'd earned her trust, she agreed to show me the DA's Manson file. I could make photocopies of anything I wanted, though she would have to supervise me as I went through everything. She was under no obligation to show me any of these documents—and, though she never said it, I was under the impression that my visits weren't exactly authorized.

Gibbons led me through the labyrinth of the DA's office and unlocked a storage room. Long, narrow, and windowless, the room accommodated a row of cabinets with barely enough space for the two chairs that Gibbons and I carried in. I leafed through endless folders containing police reports, interview notes, investigation summaries, chronologies, photographs, rap sheets, mug shots, suspect lists—and, best of all, a half dozen or more faded legal pads of Bugliosi's interviews with his most prized witnesses. I made notes and set aside any documents I wanted to copy—Gibbons had to clear them, but she approved everything at a glance. Several times she called my attention to folders that had nothing in them, telling me that Bugliosi or Bill Nelson had removed their contents. I spent hours in that room, returning four times in the next few weeks and several more times in the ensuing years.

On my third visit I struck gold: a long yellow legal pad with pages of notes scrawled in black ink, much of it crossed through but still legible. It was an interview of one of Bugliosi's key witnesses, Danny DeCarlo, who testified for eight consecutive days, often under blistering cross-examination. A biker from Venice in a gang called the Straight Satans, DeCarlo began staying at the Spahn Ranch in the spring of '69. He and his associates provided a degree of security that endeared him to Manson, who'd grown paranoid and embattled. DeCarlo's father was in the firearms business and, although Danny was never a full-fledged member of the Family, he soon ran their arsenal, a cache of weapons that grew to include a submachine gun. In exchange, he and the other bikers got access to drugs and the Family's girls. His testimony did a lot of heavy lifting for Bugliosi. He detailed Manson's plan to ignite the Helter Skelter race war; he outlined the ways Manson dominated his followers; and he identified the weapons used in the murders.

In the crossed-out sections of Bugliosi's notes, to my astonishment, DeCarlo described three visits by Terry Melcher to the Manson Family—*after* the murders.

I read them, reread them, and reread them again. I couldn't quite believe what I was seeing. I took scrupulous, word-for-word notes, in case Gibbons looked too closely at the flagged pages and realized that they completely upended one of the most important cases in her office's history. Luckily, she let me photocopy them without a second glance.

At home, I looked again. I hadn't imagined it. In an interview on February 11, 1970, DeCarlo described Melcher's two visits to the Spahn Ranch in late August and early September, 1969, and his third visit to the Barker Ranch—more than two hundred miles away—in mid-September.

According to Bugliosi's notes, DeCarlo didn't approach Melcher on any of these occasions, so he didn't know what Melcher and Manson discussed—but he was certain, each time, that it was Melcher he saw. Bugliosi's notes on the two visits to the Spahn Ranch read:

[DeCarlo] released 72 hours after the bust on 8-16-69. Went back to Venice for a few days & then went back to [Spahn] ranch. Week or week & a half later, went up to Barker with Tex & Bruce Davis in a flatbed truck. Manson & 4 or 5 girls left at same time in a car. Rest of family stayed at Spahn. Between time that Danny returned to the Ranch

& time he left for Barker, definitely saw Melcher out at [Spahn] ranch. Heard girls say, "Terry's coming, Terry's coming." Melcher drove up in a Metro truck...by himself. Melcher stayed for 3 or 4 hours.

3 or 4 days later, saw Melcher in his same truck.

Then he writes of the third visit, which occurred in the canyon passageway to the Family's hideouts in Death Valley:

1½ weeks later saw Melcher with Gypsy & Brenda at bottom of Golar Wash near Ballarat, sitting in a car with the girls. DeCarlo was with Sadie, Tex, Manson, Bruce & Dennis (w[itness]'s child) on foot. All of them got in Melcher's car, everyone in the car. (Brenda had been the driver. Melcher only a passenger. Everyone called Melcher "Terry[.]") Charlie took over the driver's seat & drove to Ridgecrest & picked up a 1959 Buick. DeCarlo & rest then drove off leaving Melcher, Manson & Brenda in the car they had. That's the last time W[itness] saw Melcher.

I cross-referenced this with the trial transcripts, which I'd photocopied at the California Court of Appeals. Pulling Melcher's testimony from my filing cabinet, I saw that at the grand jury hearing in December 1969, Bugliosi had asked him whether he ever saw Manson after his May 1969 visit to the Spahn Ranch. "No, I didn't," Melcher replied under oath.

During the trial, Bugliosi asked him again: "After this second occasion that you went to the Spahn Ranch, which was a couple of days after May 18, 1969, did you ever see Mr. Manson thereafter?"

"No," Melcher said—again under oath.

Next he was cross-examined by the defense's Paul Fitzgerald: "Do you recall the last time you saw Charles Manson?"

"Yeah, just a few days after May 18...at the ranch."

Three different times on the stand, always as a witness for Bugliosi, Melcher lied about not seeing Manson after May 1969. Next, I pulled out Danny DeCarlo's testimony to see if Bugliosi had ever asked him about Melcher. It never happened.

This was a stunner, never before revealed. Without DeCarlo's testimony, Bugliosi said he might never have gotten his convictions. Only Linda Kasabian, the member of the Family who testified in exchange for immunity, spent more time on the stand.

Clearly, this was information Bugliosi didn't want before the jury. But why? Was it simply because any postmurder visits by Melcher undermined the Helter Skelter motive? Bugliosi argued that Manson chose the Cielo house to "instill fear" in Melcher, as Susan Atkins said. But if Melcher were with Manson *after* the murders, where was the fear? And, most important: What were these additional meetings about? Maybe Melcher knew that the Family was behind the murders but, for some reason, believed he was safe. Was this the secret Bugliosi was hiding, and, if so, to whose benefit?

As I read the DA's file more carefully, I found that every single thing DeCarlo and Bugliosi had discussed that day was later repeated by DeCarlo on the witness stand—*except* the descriptions of Melcher's visits after the murders. In his notes, Bugliosi had crossed out all of these references.

The defense should have received a copy of the DeCarlo interview. Bugliosi was legally required to turn over all his evidence to the other side.

As soon as I could, I scheduled a lunch with the defense's Paul Fitzgerald, to see if he knew anything about this. We met at his favorite dim sum restaurant downtown, near the courthouse. Fitzgerald, an ex-boxer who was legendary in L.A. legal circles, was his usual animated self: loud, vulgar, slapping the table to make his points, already into his second martini before the first course arrived.

Wasting no time, I showed him the documents I'd copied at the DA's, trying not to sway his reaction. His mouth dropped open. "This is Vince Bugliosi's handwriting," he said. "I never saw this before! Obviously [they] didn't want to put on this evidence." Fitzgerald and the defense team had paid a lot of attention to DeCarlo, thinking he might be an asset to them. "He was not a member of the Family, had a good relationship with truth, lived at the ranch, was an outsider—pretty straightforward guy in most ways, credible. I liked him. He didn't embellish anything, told it the way it was."

That made this document all the more legitimate, in Fitzgerald's eyes, and more sensational. "I'm very shocked." He argued that Bugliosi, who was "extremely deceitful" and "the robot he claimed his defendants were," had written "a script for the entire trial," getting witnesses to agree to his narrative in advance.

I was relieved by Fitzgerald's astonishment—it convinced me that I wasn't overreacting here. Wanting to eliminate any possible doubt, I tried for months to find Danny DeCarlo himself, but he seemed to have vanished. I did eventually track down a girlfriend of his, who told me that she'd gotten my interview request to him—he lived mainly in Mexico these days, she said. I never heard back from him.

I felt it was becoming nearly impossible to deny that Bugliosi had manipulated some of his witnesses—or that he'd conspired with at least two of his principals to conceal the facts of the case and shore up his motive. If Melcher and DeCarlo were tainted—and if Melcher had committed outright perjury, suborned by Bugliosi—then the veracity of the prosecutor's entire case, including the extraordinary hippie/race-war motive that made him a bestselling author, was called into question.

"The Guy Is Psychotic"

As one of the biggest bands in the world, the Beach Boys employed a retinue of managers, roadies, engineers, and gofers—I wondered if any of them had any thoughts on Wilson and Melcher, or if they could fill in some blanks for me. (The band's surviving members had all declined to speak to me.) I got in touch with John Parks, who'd been the band's tour manager when Manson and the Family lived at Wilson's place. He recalled that Melcher had not only met Manson but recorded him, too.

"Terry recorded him while we were on a fairly long tour," Parks told me. That was something else Melcher had expressly denied on the stand, something hidden for all these decades. Bugliosi repeated it in his closing statement: "He did not record Manson."

When Melcher moved to end his professional relationship with Manson, things took a dark turn. As Parks remembered it, Manson began calling Melcher and unloading on him, making death threats against him "to everybody he saw"; he was "yelling about it and stuff." Parks could certainly understand, he said, how those threats could've influenced Melcher's decision to move out of the Cielo house so suddenly.

After the murders, I asked, did Parks or any of his colleagues suspect Manson? Of course, he said. "I knew that Terry had kind of fired Charlie and stopped recording him, so my first thought was that Charlie had made a mistake and actually got Sharon Tate instead of Terry." One of Manson's girls, he explained, had already told him that the Family had murdered one of the caretakers at the Spahn Ranch—Donald "Shorty" Shea, whose body wasn't found until 1977.

"You could look at these folks and see that they were totally drugged out," Parks said. "After one of the girls told me that they killed the caretaker, then it got real serious for me." Everyone in their scene suspected Manson right away, he said, even though it took the LAPD nearly four months to bring him to justice. "I have no idea why they didn't arrest him right away because to me it was pretty obvious." The Hollywood community knew that the Beach

Boys had been wrapped up in Manson's world, and it turned them into pariahs, for a time; nightclubs where they'd once been welcomed were suddenly turning them away. "We couldn't go out because people didn't want us at their place," Parks said.

"So you're saying a huge community of people knew before the world did that Charles Manson committed these murders?"

"Yeah."

Parks went on to say something even more dizzying: he was positive that the FBI had sent agents to the Beach Boys' office soon after the murders. "They were monitoring our phones, because they thought there was some connection with those guys," he said. "They were sitting in my office picking up my telephone...I'm sure they had the phones tapped, but they weren't sharing information with us." He told the FBI about Manson "early on," but they didn't seem to act on his tip. "I didn't know why they weren't doing anything, and everybody else was just trying to stay out of the situation. For the Beach Boys, we didn't want that kind of publicity. And neither did anybody else."

Steve Despar, the Beach Boys' recording engineer, remembered the ordeal that Manson had put him through during the recording sessions, when he'd show up with "about twelve girls, many underage, quiet, in a stupor." The group smelled so foul that the studio's management, at the behest of Brian Wilson's wife, soon "installed a sanitary bathroom seat." In the control room, Manson, reeking, would "pull out a knife and clean his fingernails, wave it around and gesture." After three sessions, Despar was fed up. He called the Beach Boys manager and said, "I refuse to be alone with him. The guy is psychotic and scares the hell out of me." Despar emphasized, "He was after Melcher...Melcher was *not* out of the picture at this point. He was part of the project. When I was recording Charles Manson, it was for Dennis *and Terry Melcher.*"

"For a Layperson"

Melcher would never admit that, and I didn't want to talk to him again until I'd done my due diligence. Fortunately, in the archives of the L.A. County Sheriff's Office (LASO), I soon stumbled on further proof that Melcher had visited Manson after the murders.

LASO had records of an interview with Paul Watkins, another key member of the Family who'd testified against Manson. He, too, saw Melcher at the Spahn Ranch, around the same time as Danny DeCarlo had—the first week of September 1969. What he told the unnamed interviewer was shocking to me:

> Melcher was on acid. Was on his knees. Asked Manson to forgive him. Terry Melcher failed to keep an appointment. Called him a pig. They are all little piggies. Helter Skelter meant for everyone to die. Charlie gave Gregg [Jakobson] a 45 slug and said give Dennis [Wilson] this and tell him I have another one for him.

This was even more explosive than the files from the DA, I realized. Not only did it suggest that Melcher had some bizarre debt to Manson—it opened up Watkins to accusations of perjury. Just like DeCarlo, Watkins had omitted these details from his testimony. He made no mention of having seen Melcher at the Spahn Ranch in early September 1969—much less having seen him on acid, begging for forgiveness.

As much as the Watkins interview buttressed my case for a cover-up, it brought a host of new questions. Why did Melcher need Manson's forgiveness? Did he know that it was he who was supposed to die that night—had Manson instilled much more fear in him than anyone had ever known? And what had compelled Bugliosi to believe that he could hide the true extent of their relationship? I wondered how many other stories like this had been kept secret. Now I felt I had a stronger shot at grabbing Melcher's attention, maybe even at getting him to concede that he'd lied.

First, though, I had to contend with Bugliosi. As the summer faded into autumn in the first year of my reporting, I had a hunch that Vince was keeping close tabs on me, even monitoring my progress, in a way. Altobelli had suggested that Vince was always asking about me, trying to undermine my credibility; he thought I was only masquerading as a magazine journalist. When I heard about Melcher's puzzling remark — "Vince was supposed to take care of all that" — I'd made a conscious decision to distance myself from Bugliosi. Although we'd once spoken on an almost weekly basis, I hadn't been in touch with him since June. One day in October I came home to find that he'd left a message on my machine. "I need to talk to you about something," he said, sounding unusually serious. This was it, I thought. I set up my tape recorder and called him back.

"How you doing, buddy?" he answered, sounding manic. "Listen, are you still working on this thing?" Then he added: "Someone, I don't remember who, called me . . . If there's something about my handling of the case — anything at all — that you had a question about, I would appreciate if you would call me to get my view on it . . . I think I did a fairly good job, and I can't think of things that I would do differently. But for a layperson, they may look at it and say, He should not have done this, this is improper or what have you — and I'd like to at least be heard."

I told him I would absolutely give him a chance to be heard, and that I did, in fact, have some questions — but I didn't have them ready yet.

"Okay," he said. "Yeah, call me, because there may be a justification or reason why I did something that, as a layperson, you would not know."

Now I was positive that he had some notion of what I'd been

researching, whom I'd been talking to. I mentioned that I'd made halting progress on the piece, which was still expected for *Premiere,* even if it was running behind schedule. The Melcher angle, I said—wondering if he'd take the bait—had been so impossible to get.

"Were you ever able to get in touch with Terry?" he asked.

I said I was.

"Oh, you *have* talked to him? You got him on the phone?" Vince's surprise was evident, but I couldn't tell if it was feigned or not. I felt like he was hoping to keep me talking, to feel out my progress. I got off the phone as soon as I could.

I didn't hear from him again until December, just a few days before Christmas, when he left a phone message asking for my address. He said he wanted to send me a CD of some songs by Manson that "a guy playing Manson in a movie" had given him. When I didn't return the call, he left another message the next day to make sure I understood that the music was "very rare and not otherwise available." I didn't return that call, either, but the same night I got a call from Altobelli, who said that Vince had called him twice that day "wanting to know what you're doing." Their second conversation ended in "a shouting match," Altobelli said, after he started asking Bugliosi about some of the information I'd shared over the previous months.

That was enough for me. I wouldn't speak to Vince again for seven years.

On Melcher's Roof

When my piece for *Premiere* was more than a year late, I knew I had to talk to Melcher again, and to put my full weight on him. I wanted this conversation to bring my reporting to a close. Then I could file my piece, finally.

Months of constant interviewing had honed my strategy. If I

could get someone on the phone in a talkative mood, I'd suggest an in-person meeting that same day, which would minimize the chance that they'd get cold feet. I'd be ready to go at a moment's notice: showered and dressed, with notes, questions, documents, and tape recorders in my bag by the door. Such was the case on the day I phoned Melcher—July 3, 2000. Surprisingly, he picked up; even more surprisingly, I caught him in a lively frame of mind; most surprising of all, he said he'd meet me on the roof of his apartment building in fifteen minutes.

I bolted out the door and drove over to his high-rise on Ocean Avenue, in Santa Monica, dwelling all the while on his choice of venue: his *rooftop?* I imagined some kind of bleak, desolate place, the sun beating down on us as ventilation fans whirred. Instead, I bounded into his lobby and took the elevator up to find a rooftop lounge with a bar, a pool, and a kingly view of the Santa Monica Bay.

Melcher lived in one of the penthouse suites, and there he was, sitting on a couch with a drink in his hand. Though it was a gorgeous day and anyone in these luxury suites could access the roof lounge, we were alone up there. He was wearing a gold shirt and aviator glasses that he didn't take off until midway through our conversation. When I arrived, he disappeared into his kitchen to leave his drink there. I got the sense it wasn't the first he'd had.

Considering how much time and energy I'd devoted to Melcher, I couldn't believe I'd never laid eyes on him before. He had a pronounced abdomen but skinny legs. His long, wispy, blond-gray hair fell over his ears and across his forehead. His face was swollen and wet, with high cheekbones; his eyes, when the sunglasses came off, were puffy, and he stared at me unsmilingly. Around the mouth and chin, he resembled his mother, Doris Day. And he spoke in a kind of high-pitched, halting half-whisper.

We sat in the shade, where I took my papers out and told him I had reason to believe he'd visited the Spahn *and* Barker Ranches after the murders, and had spent time with Manson.

"The only reason I know the Barker Ranch name is because that's where they arrested them and caught all those people," he said. "Isn't that right? Someplace out in the middle of the Mojave Desert?"

"Dennis and Gregg had been there," I said.

"Well, I hadn't. I had no idea where the Barker Ranch was. None."

I started to read from Bugliosi's interview with Danny DeCarlo, the one I'd gotten from the DA's office. " 'Definitely saw Melcher out at ranch. Heard girls say, "Terry's coming, Terry's coming." Melcher drove up in a Metro truck similar to a bread or milk truck…' "

"It was actually a Mercedes Benz convertible."

"This is *after the murders*," I emphasized. "Between August 16 and the second week of September. Do you recall that?" I watched the frustration come over him as I explained.

"Look," he said, rubbing the bridge of his nose. "Obviously this is something that continues to haunt me whether I'd like it to or not, and I'm not exactly like a convicted felon running around doing bad things. But the only guy to talk to and ask questions about for me is Bugliosi. Vince Bugliosi knows everything that I had to do with this, everything!"

"I wanted to hear it from you first before I went to him," I said.

"Well, you know, if you want to fuck with us and get something from him and something from me, you can do that, too, in which case I'll put four law firms on *Premiere* magazine."

I was floored. We'd barely begun, and already he was threatening to sue. The threats, as I was beginning to understand by then, were almost always a good thing. They didn't happen unless you were onto something. "I just want the truth, Terry," I said. "Can I just finish reading from this?"

"You certainly may, Tom. I have never misrepresented once what happened in this situation. I had nothing to do with this situation other than the fact that I was a great big, famous record producer at the time, period."

Pressing ahead, I pulled out the LASO files, and soon reached the most damning lines: "Melcher was on acid, on his knees."

"Not true!" he shouted. "Not real! Hey, I was a Columbia Records producer! I was the *biggest* Columbia Records producer on the West Coast! I had the Byrds, Paul Revere and the Raiders, all right? I was selling tonnage of product. I was simply looking at acts...I went out there to the Spahn Ranch, met them, I am awfully goddamned lucky to have gotten out of there alive." He adamantly refuted the idea that he'd been to the Spahn Ranch more than the two times he'd testified to at trial, both in May 1969.

"Rudi [Altobelli] is one of my sources," I said. "He called you and you said, 'Vince was supposed to take care of all that and now it's all resurfacing.'"

"No, I never told Rudi that...I like Rudi, we were friends, I hope there's no rancor." He scoffed and crossed his arms. "And Christ, what are you doing a thing like this for?"

"I'm just trying to get the truth about this story, and when I see this stuff from the DA's files and combined with that comment from Rudi, which implies that Vince protected you—"

"Vince never protected me. Vince never protected anybody. Rudi was the guy—" But he cut himself off and sighed. "I got to use the men's room," he said, walking back toward his place.

He came back having collected himself. "I'm going to digress for a while," he said, removing his sunglasses. "First of all, if you want my record as it relates to this, it is so squeaky clean—all I did was audition people for Columbia Records. Some of them I signed. Some of them I didn't sign. I never once spent one second with these girls, although at one point, when they were in jail, like twenty-five of them said that I was the father of all their children, and that put me in bed for about three weeks. I mean, they were *so* ugly. To get the DA's department off my ass in that one, I took Michelle Phillips"—his girlfriend at the time, during the trial—"down to headquarters and I said, 'This is my girlfriend, do you think I'd want to be with any of these…'" He gestured, implying Manson's "ugly" girls. "And they said, probably not."

I reminded him of what Altobelli had said: "On the stand, he said that you wanted him to manage Manson."

"That is total insanity…This is really my book, okay?…You know what? If I'm going to do this with you, then we should write this book together." It was almost a bargaining chip, an under-the-table deal. I thought Melcher wanted me to read between the lines—why say all these nasty things about me in a silly little magazine piece when I can cut you in on the earnings from my book? He proposed that I coauthor his memoirs. People had been begging him for years to write a book. He was the "only American to produce the Beatles!" He seemed to suggest that I'd be a fool not to jump at his offer, even though I was the same writer who believed he'd been lying about one of the most transformative events of his life.

"I need to do *this* story, and I need the truth," I said. "You were a powerful guy—"

"Was? *Am*." He asked, "Is your interest in this purely journalistic or is it just to fuck someone over?"

I stressed, again, that I had no desire to smear him; I just wanted to know why these files told such a strikingly different story from the one Bugliosi had pursued.

"Dennis Wilson was the only one that really knew what was going on," Melcher said. "He's talked about it in various ways that sounds like he knew all about it, he was there." Melcher seemed put upon by the effort of discussing Manson, as if it were a minor nuisance that he'd long ago put behind him. "After a while you get used to it, it's a terrible thing to say, but you kind of get used to it." And then, once more, he acted like he was ready to cut a deal. "So what's the best thing that you and I can do about it?"

The interview suddenly had the air of a tense negotiation. "There has to be an explanation for this," I said, turning the conversation back to the papers from the DA and LASO. "Why was this in the files? How was it suppressed, why? If they were lying"—DeCarlo and Watkins, I meant—"how did they testify to other significant factors?"

"I have no idea where that second ranch is," Melcher said. "I have no idea in the world! It could be in Kuwait." He rose to get a bottle of white wine, half-full, and poured himself a drink. "You're welcome to share that, by the way," he said. He'd brought only one glass.

"If it is true that you were at the ranch after the murders, it undermines the entire Helter Skelter motive for the prosecution," I said.

"I'm curious why you would want to talk to me about this," he said, almost muttering: "out to crucify me..."

"Because nobody's ever had this information that I have, about you at the ranch afterward."

At that point, Melcher dropped his lawyer's name. "Joe Lavely. Do you know who he is? He can shut down everything. Networks, magazines. Anything." He asked me to fax him a draft of my story. I told him I couldn't do that.

Melcher leaned forward. "You know I like you," he said, looking me in the eye. "If I didn't like you, I'd take your briefcase and throw it off the balcony. Okay? I happen to like you, so I hope you'll be fair."

"That sounds like a threat," I said. "But I will be fair with you."

"That's not a threat, it's the truth."

It was the truth, of course, that Melcher had the means to follow through. He could try to sue me or *Premiere*. He could leap up and toss my papers—all photocopies—off his rooftop. But I wondered what he would really do. As unnerving as it was to sit across from him, getting no admissions from him whatsoever, I stayed calm by wondering what form his antagonism could possibly take, considering I was confident I had solid reporting on him.

"I know you have money, resources, powerful lawyers," I said, aware that the interview was next to over. "But that's not going to stop me from writing my story, and there is no way you can shut it down with all of that, because it is the truth, and you can't shut down the truth, Terry."

And soon I was in the elevator and on the ground again, looking up at his building in the sun. I felt the mix of exhilaration and frustration that often followed my biggest interviews, when I felt I'd made headway in some unpredictable direction. No, I hadn't cracked Melcher, but I had his bizarre behavior to report, his threats, his offer that I coauthor his life story, and, perhaps most important, the first on-the-record answers about Charles Manson he'd given since 1974. What I still didn't know was when, or how, all of this was going to end.

Coda: "They Used to Call Me an Angel"

I never saw or spoke to Melcher again. He died in 2004, at age sixty-two, of cancer. To my knowledge, he never gave another interview about Manson or wrote his memoirs.

His death foreclosed the possibility of learning so much about the Family: about their true motivations for the murders, their ties to the Hollywood elite, and their ability to go undiscovered for so many months after their grisly crimes. I remain convinced that Melcher had more of the answers than he let on, and that he cast himself as a bit player in Manson's world when his role was much larger. I don't think I'll ever be able to explain the discrepancies in his story to my satisfaction.

After my confrontation with him that day, I turned my attention elsewhere—though even from a remove, Melcher and his cohort continued to pop up in my reporting. And because of how tantalizingly close I felt I'd been to unearthing something, I couldn't stop from ruminating on some of the questions I'd had about him.

Why had he moved out of 10050 Cielo Drive? Did he ever record Manson? What was his true relationship with Tex Watson and Dean Moorehouse? Most of all, was it possible he could have prevented the murders at the house through some kind of intervention with Manson, or by warning the victims — or just by calling the police?

With Melcher and Dennis Wilson both deceased, you might be wondering: Why not get some answers from that third and final Golden Penetrator, Gregg Jakobson? I did end up finding him. Actually, we spoke well before I ever got to Melcher, in the first months of my reporting — before I knew my way around the story well enough to push back on some of his claims.

In a sense, Jakobson is more mysterious than Melcher or Wilson. Unlike Melcher, he didn't come from privilege or ever know the wealth Wilson would obtain at an early age. An orphan, he was adopted by the chief of police in St. Paul, Minnesota; when he was twelve, his adoptive father died, and he moved with his mother to Los Angeles, where he was soon rubbing elbows with the sons and daughters of celebrities. He parlayed these connections into a career on the periphery of Hollywood, taking gigs as a stuntman, an actor, and a talent scout, and racking up a few arrests along the way (which he maintains were for traffic violations). But it was his past that attracted Manson to him. As an orphan, Jakobson held a special place in the Family's mythology. Manson loathed the influence of parents, and Jakobson, despite his adopted family, was held up as a parentless icon. "They used to call me an angel," Jakobson told me, "because I came into the world without parents."

Dennis Wilson's biographer John Stebbins believed Jakobson "testified to protect Wilson from having to do the same." Wilson gave Jakobson cowriting credits — and therefore a steady stream of royalties — on many of his songs, even though Jakobson "had no idea what he was doing" in the studio, where it seemed he "didn't know a guitar string from a piano key."

In 1999, Jakobson wanted one hundred bucks an hour to talk to me. When I made it clear that I wouldn't pay him, he claimed that the passage of thirty years had fogged up his memory. Jakobson contradicted himself with nonchalance. Consider the theft of the green spyglass, for instance. This was a huge point in the trial: Jakobson testified that Manson had called him before the murders, asking him if Melcher had a "green spyglass" at his new address in Malibu. When Jakobson said yes, Manson responded, "He doesn't anymore." This proved that Manson knew that Melcher had moved out of the Cielo house. And yet, speaking to me, Jakobson dismissed the whole episode. "I don't know how much of that is legend and how much of it is true," he said about something he'd testified to under oath. "I think there was a good chance that [Manson] didn't know that Melcher had even moved." I've found dozens of discrepancies between his statements on the stand and his statements to me.

Sometimes, sorting through old news items, I'll chance upon something that reminds me of how much remains unsaid here. I found a November 1970 bulletin from the Associated Press, headlined, "Defendant in Tate Trial Well Liked." It noted the curious affection that Melcher and Jakobson held for the man who'd brought so much scrutiny on them. "Jakobson frequently smiled at Manson," the report noted, "who, upon leaving the courtroom one day, said to Jakobson, 'Come see me.'" What are we supposed to make of that friendliness, and of the insider knowledge it augurs? Why would Manson have wanted to commune with someone who'd just testified against him in a case that carried the death penalty? Manson's lawyer Irving Kanarek chose not to cross-examine Terry Melcher. He infuriated the judge by saying that Manson and Melcher were "still good friends," and that he wanted to "thank Mr. Melcher for his presence" — comments that earned him admonishment from the court, and were ordered stricken from the record.

Jakobson told me that he never really took Manson all that seriously. "There was so much bullshit," he said. "I never tried to make sense out of it. I didn't care." He left open the possibility that there'd been some scheming to make the story more presentable at trial. "I wonder if Bugliosi was doing Melcher a favor," he said to me, "or there was some reciprocity there…honest to God, I have no knowledge of it." He was a little more willing to talk about Melcher's attraction to the girls in the Family. "He might have been carrying on with one of the girls," he told me, though Melcher had fiercely denied exactly that. "I had a soft spot for little Ruth Ann Moorehouse. He might have, too. She was the little gem of the group. Little sweet fifteen, sixteen." Likewise, Jeff Guinn's 2013 book *Manson* includes several references to Melcher's having sex with Ruth Ann Moorehouse, all sourced to Jakobson.

Melcher always policed his image in regards to Manson, especially when others implied or wrote outright that he'd slept with the girls. Nothing made him more litigious. And he often subjected writers to the same kinds of legal threats he'd made to me. Barney Hoskyns, the author of the aforementioned *Waiting for the Sun,* told me that Melcher's lawyers had ordered his publisher to pulp all existing copies of the first edition, and to delete "all and any references to Terry Melcher in connection with 'Manson's girls' from any future editions." His publisher complied.

But the most glaring example of Melcher's interventions came from Stephen Kay, the attorney in the Los Angeles DA's office who'd helped Bugliosi prosecute the case. He told me that Melcher's lawyer approached him in the mid-1990s, requesting that he sign an official document certifying that Melcher's connections with the Family didn't extend beyond his three occasions in Manson's presence: once at Wilson's house, twice at the Spahn Ranch. Kay signed it, though he said he hadn't retained a copy. At the time, he hadn't seen the documents I had detailing Melcher's relationship with the Family.

One of the most bewildering parts of reporting on a case like this is figuring out how much weight to give your findings. I spent years wondering if I was crazy to think that Terry Melcher was so important, indicative of some hollowness in Bugliosi's motive.

Years later, in 2005, it was Kay who gave me a semblance of vindication. I met with him again and showed him the notes I'd found in Bugliosi's hand. By that point, my obsession with the case had become a full-blown mania: my reporting had taken over my entire life, and I often wondered if there would be any end to it, any form of closure or consequence. I can still remember sitting in Kay's Compton office and watching him shake his head as he looked over my photocopies.

"I do not believe that Terry Melcher was at the Spahn Ranch after the murders. I just don't believe that," he said. "If he was there at the Spahn Ranch, Manson would have harmed him, because Manson was very upset."

But with the sheaf of papers in front of him, and the handwriting undeniably belonging to Bugliosi, Kay slumped in his chair. "I am shocked," he said. "I am just shocked." He was planning his retirement then, having boasted that he was leaving office "sixty and zero": sixty court appearances opposite Family members, without a single one of them earning parole. With the evidence of Bugliosi's corruption in his hands, Kay said, "This throws a different light on everything...I just don't know what to believe now." He went on: "This is egregious conduct if this happened. All of this should have been turned over to the defense."

The fact that Paul Watkins and Danny DeCarlo told similar stories seemed to indicate that both men were telling the truth, impeaching Melcher's testimony and, with it, much of the basis for the Helter Skelter motive. Looking at the heavy lines that Vince had drawn through the most damning parts of the interviews, Kay said, "I just don't understand the cross-outs...it just doesn't make any sense."

His voice trailing off, he asked the question I'd so often asked myself. "If Vince was covering this stuff up," he said, "if he changed this, what else did he change?"

I asked Kay whether this evidence would be enough to overturn the verdicts against Manson and the Family. Yes, he conceded—it could get them new trials, and it would mean big trouble for Bugliosi. If he were found guilty of suborning perjury, he would technically be eligible for the death penalty, since that was the maximum possible sentence in the Manson case.

I wasn't on some crusade to prove Manson innocent, or to impugn Bugliosi's name. I just wanted to find out what really happened. Kay, sitting across from me that day, seemed to be struggling with the same thing. Neither of us could grasp why Bugliosi had covered this up, or how Melcher and his friends had, for so many years, consigned the truth to the realm of rumor and hearsay.

I felt a familiar conflict welling up inside me. Part of me was convinced that if I kept pushing, if I were more tenacious and vigilant and hard-nosed than ever before, I could crack this case and figure it all out. The other part of me feared that I was too late. Powerful interests had aligned themselves against the truth.

5

Amnesia at the L.A. County Sheriff's Office

"Keep Going"

The thirtieth anniversary of the Tate–LaBianca murders passed with no story, at least not in *Premiere*. That didn't worry me—not at first, anyway. I knew that Jim Meigs, the magazine's editor in chief, shared my obsession. He started leaving the due date blank on the contracts I had to sign every month: a reporter's dream come true, until it wasn't.

Within a year, I'd interviewed more than five hundred people: movie-industry players, friends and relatives of the victims, witnesses, journalists, cops, attorneys, judges, suspects, and hangers-on. My one-bedroom apartment in Venice had become a hoarder's nest of Manson ephemera. I installed shelves above my desk to house a growing collection of books and binders—I bought the thickest ones I could find—with labels like "News Clips—1967–1969," "Time-lines," "Trial Transcripts," "Questions—Witnesses," and so on. They multiplied as if they were breeding. When my friends visited, they'd stop in their tracks upon entering my apartment and cast worried glances my way. Above my computer was a whiteboard with "MANSON" circled in the center. Springing from his name like a psychedelic spiderweb were lines in erasable ink, leading to associates of the Family who'd never been publicly identified before, Hollywood drug dealers, and other names that had seldom been uttered in three decades.

I tried to interview as many people as I could in a day, so my workdays became endless. I was always behind, needing to hop in my battered Acura to drive to the Valley or San Diego or Santa Barbara for an interview at a moment's notice. When I wasn't interviewing, I was researching, arranging my binders, or working the phones to set up more interviews. I'd basically adopted my neighbor's German shepherd, Bully, who spent day and night at my house; I sometimes worried my files could be stolen, and I felt safer with the dog by my side.

My magazine assignment was coming to feel like a vocation. Manson and the theories surrounding him were always on my mind, whether I was alone or with friends—though, in the hopes of wrapping up the story, I was alone much of the time. Since Meigs was authorizing my extensions, he would visit me on trips to L.A. We'd sit on the floor as I spread out documents for him to examine, kicking around various explanations for the discrepancies in the case. He was a reassuring presence; the things that seemed suspicious to me bothered him, too. As long as I had his confidence, I could keep putting in long hours. At that point, the end—the break, the big scoop—seemed just around the corner. Looking from a document to a name on my whiteboard, Jim would nod and say, "Yes, yes—I see. Good. Keep going." And I did.

"Political Piggy"

The Tate–LaBianca murders are etched into the public imagination. They are, in casual conversation, what people mean when they say "the Manson murders": two nights of unhinged blood-shed that came out of nowhere.

It's too often forgotten that the Family had taken another life by then. Gary Hinman, thirty-four, lived in a secluded house in Topanga Canyon, a hippie community about fifteen miles south of the Spahn Ranch. A soft-spoken Buddhist and music teacher, Hinman had treated Manson and his followers with a dignity that few afforded them. He hosted members of the Family for long stays in his home, and he was generous when they needed food or money.

In July 1969, the increasingly agitated Manson was convinced that Hinman had just come into an inheritance of some twenty thousand dollars. Seeing green, he ordered three of his followers—Bobby Beausoleil, Mary Brunner, and Susan Atkins, the last of whom would later participate in the Tate–LaBianca murders—to seize Hinman's money by any means necessary.

The three showed up at Hinman's on July 25. Manson was wrong, he said, there was no inheritance, but they refused to take him at his word. They tied him up and ransacked the place, but there was no cash to be found. Manson decided to see for himself, coming over with Bruce Davis, another Family member. But even Manson couldn't extract anything from Hinman. Finally, incensed, Manson drew a saber from a sheath on his belt and cut Hinman's ear in half. He and Davis left the house, but he told Beausoleil and the girls to stay until they found the money.

For two days, they battered and tortured Hinman, who insisted he had no inheritance. (They also sewed up his severed ear using dental floss.) By day three, Manson had had enough—he wanted Hinman dead. Over the phone, he ordered his followers to take care of it. Beausoleil tied Hinman up and stabbed him at least four times. As Hinman incanted a Buddhist prayer, Atkins and Brunner took turns holding a pillow over his face until he stopped breathing. Just as Manson would do in the Tate–LaBianca murders, he told his followers to leave signs implicating the Black Panthers.

They dipped a rag in Hinman's blood and smeared the words "political piggy" on the living room wall, surrounding it with bloody paw prints.

Some of Hinman's friends grew concerned. On July 31, not having heard from him in six days, they drove over to check on him. They found his body and called the cops.

Charles Guenther and Paul Whiteley, homicide detectives from the Los Angeles County Sheriff's Office, went to investigate. They spent five days searching the crime scene for evidence and conducting interviews. Although no one had seen or spoken to Hinman in the days before his body was discovered, it seemed that a woman had been in his house answering the phone during his captivity. At one point, when a friend of Hinman stopped by, she'd even answered his front door, holding a candle and explaining in a flimsy British accent that Hinman had gone to Colorado to see his parents.

The detectives issued an all-points bulletin for two vehicles missing from Hinman's driveway: a Fiat station wagon and a VW microbus. Seven days after the body was discovered, the Fiat turned up on the side of a highway in San Luis Obispo, 189 miles north of L.A. Inside was Bobby Beausoleil, fast asleep. A state trooper took him into custody, and Guenther and Whiteley hurried to question him.

Beausoleil had concocted a story that blamed the Black Panthers for the murder, but he kept muddling the details. First he said that he hadn't known Hinman at all; he'd bought the Fiat from a Black Panther a few days earlier. When the police told him they'd found the murder weapon in the Fiat's tire well, he half-confessed: sure, he'd been in Hinman's home, but he hadn't killed the man. He and two women, neither of whom he would identify, had arrived at the house to find Hinman bloodied and beaten, complaining that a group of Black Panthers had robbed him. They'd stayed and nursed Hinman back to health. As a sign of gratitude,

Hinman gave them the Fiat. The murder, Beausoleil speculated, must have occurred after he and the girls left the house—maybe the Panthers had returned seeking more money. So why was the knife in his car? He couldn't explain. Nor could he say why he'd suddenly changed his story.

Guenther and Whiteley were confident they'd found their man. They charged Beausoleil with first-degree murder and booked him into the Los Angeles County jail on August 7. But they knew he had at least one accomplice: the girl who answered the phone and front door during Hinman's captivity.

The next day, according to Bugliosi's narrative, Manson decided it was time to kick off Helter Skelter, his all-out race war. He ordered the Tate–LaBianca murders, making sure, again, that his followers left signs at the crime scenes implicating the Black Panthers.

Anyone might wonder: How could the police fail to connect Hinman's murder to the Tate–LaBianca killings, given their macabre similarities? It's a good question—and the official answer, even when I first read it in *Helter Skelter,* stretched credulity. Part of the problem was a simple matter of jurisdiction. The Hinman murder occurred outside the city limits of Los Angeles, so it was an L.A. County Sheriff's (LASO) case; the Tate–LaBianca murders were handled by the LAPD. The two police forces didn't talk as much as you might expect. In fact, as Bugliosi tells it, it was their failure to communicate that led them to overlook Manson in the first place.

By August 10, the day after the LaBiancas had been murdered, Guenther and Whiteley *had* connected Hinman's murder to Manson. They knew Bobby Beausoleil had spent time at the Spahn Ranch, living with a strange group under the control of an ex-con named Charlie. And, according to Bugliosi, the two detectives did the right thing: they rushed to the county morgue, where autopsies of the Cielo Drive murder victims were under way, and they reported their suspicions to the LAPD. A sergeant named Jess Buckles heard them out. Wasn't it curious, they said, that both the

Hinman and Tate murders involved brutal stabbings, plus some iteration of the word "Pig" smeared in the victims' blood near their bodies? They explained that their suspect, Beausoleil, had been living out at a disused movie ranch with a band of hippies led by a guy who claimed to be Jesus Christ.

Their theory fell on deaf ears. Sergeant Buckles didn't see the connection—especially not if hippies were involved. He told the LASO detectives that they were barking up the wrong tree; the LAPD was already pretty sure that the Tate murders were a drug deal gone awry.

And so, Bugliosi argued, the LASO lead withered on the vine, and shoddy police work kept the Manson Family at large for months longer than they otherwise would've been. They weren't taken into custody until a pair of raids nabbed them on October 10 and 12. Even then, their arrest was for stolen vehicles: the police wouldn't connect them to Tate–LaBianca for more than another month. While they were at large, Manson and the Family may have killed dozens more people, Bugliosi speculated.

In the official narrative, Manson had a lot of sheer dumb luck. Not only did he evade these early suspicions against him—he also survived, ostensibly on a technicality, the largest police raid in the history of California.

On August 16, 1969, LASO descended on the Spahn Ranch en masse. Just past six in the morning, as the sun was creeping up and most everyone was still asleep, more than one hundred officers swarmed the property, led by the organization's elite SWAT team. Armed with handguns, AR-15 rifles, and tear gas, they were assisted by two helicopters, numerous ATVs, and a fleet of some thirty-five squad cars. Surrounding the ranch's two hundred acres, they descended from five prearranged outposts with a show of force the likes of which no one in LASO had ever seen before. They arrested everyone in the Family—twenty-seven adults and seven juveniles. They confiscated seven stolen cars and a vast cache of weapons, including an automatic pistol and a submachine gun. One officer praised the raid's military precision, telling me, "It was the most flawlessly executed operation I'd ever been involved in."

The raid had nothing to do with the murders. In the preceding weeks, deputies had been keeping the ranch under close surveillance, perhaps even sending undercover agents to investigate. They suspected that Manson was running an auto-theft ring out of Spahn, stealing Volkswagens and converting them into dune buggies.

It would seem like a coup, wouldn't it? Even if they had no knowledge of the murders, sheriffs had just picked up Manson and everyone involved with him on suspicion of crimes that were damning in their own right. Had the Family been formally charged, they would've been sitting in jail already when the cops realized they were behind the killings.

But the Family wasn't charged. Despite the preponderance of evidence—the cars, the guns, the numerous sightings of Manson and his followers with stolen vehicles—the entire group was released three days after the raid, no questions asked. Bugliosi explained it in *Helter Skelter:* "They had been arrested on a misdated warrant."

His book downplayed the size of the raid; you'd never know it was the biggest in the history of Los Angeles law enforcement at that time. He also took it as a given that Guenther and Whiteley, seasoned and widely respected detectives, would back away from a lead to the most prominent unsolved murder case in California history. It seemed to me that they wouldn't do that unless they were told to.

I wanted to get the story straight from Guenther and Whiteley. What they told me was, at the very least, the story of an agonizing series of coincidences and near misses, a comedy of errors that had never been given a proper airing. At most, it was the germ of an extensive cover-up by LASO, which moved to conceal either its own ineptitude or something more sinister: the hand of a higher authority, warning that pursuing Manson would come with steep consequences.

"Leave a Sign"

Paul Fitzgerald, the defense attorney, gave me Charlie Guenther's number. Guenther was the most honest cop he knew; when he'd taken the liberty of telling the retired detective about my research, Guenther had said he might be able to help me.

When I got Guenther on the phone, he already knew what he wanted to tell me—but he refused to say it. I had to come to his house, he said, more than a hundred miles away in Victorville, California. I tried to wrestle a hint out of him. Sounding exasperated, he said it had something to do with Bobby Beausoleil and "maybe a call that had been made." After a pause, he added, "and the destruction of evidence."

The very next day, I made the two-hour drive to Victorville. If you're driving from L.A. to Vegas, it's just about the last place to fill up your tank before you're surrounded by the endless vastness of the Mojave Desert. The town is an oasis of man-made lakes and sprawling golf clubs, all catering to the community's many retirees—among them, Charlie Guenther, who welcomed me into his new condo dressed in a white T-shirt and shorts. I sat on an overstuffed couch beneath a framed painting of a forlorn Jesus in prayer at Gethsemane. Guenther sank into a large recliner, though he was seldom relaxed enough to stay in it for long.

Guenther was famous among true-crime devotees—he'd become something of a staple in the genre, his skilled investigative work having solved a number of notable murders. His better-known cases included the Cotton Club murders and the 1958 killing of the author James Ellroy's mother. Guenther never solved that crime, but Ellroy still hailed him, in *My Dark Places,* as one of the best homicide detectives ever to work in L.A. Most everyone who wrote about Guenther noted his penetrating blue eyes, his unruly mop of hair—now gone white—and his stocky build.

Listening to him talk, I could see why Guenther was so highly regarded—but that day he was also nervous, jumpy. He wouldn't let me tape our conversation, saying that "smart cops" never allow themselves to be recorded. As the words came spilling out of him, I tried to get his every utterance on paper while appearing nonchalant, lest he become even more inhibited.

He remembered going to the Tate autopsies with his partner, Whiteley, to tell the investigators about the similarities between the Hinman murder and the Tate murders. The coroner, Thomas Noguchi, had already reached the same conclusion: they must be connected. "I know Charlie, I know," Noguchi told him. "Same knife. Same wound. Same blood on the wall." But the LAPD detectives weren't nearly as receptive. They were "convinced it had something to do with narcotics," Guenther said.

I turned the conversation to Bobby Beausoleil. The mere mention of his name launched Guenther out of his recliner: "He lies, and I can't tell you how I know that."

Of course he lies, I said. Didn't all murderers?

"He called the ranch after he was arrested," Guenther said, pacing in front of me. To his mind, it was this phone call that had initiated the Tate–LaBianca murders. "The sole motive for those murders was to get Bobby out of jail."

I'd heard this before—the copycat theory of the murders. Bugliosi had discredited it, I reminded him. That name didn't sit well with him, either.

"Arrogant son of a bitch!" he shouted. "Vince didn't want anything to do with the Hinman case. Hinman was a nothing case. Vince didn't want to prosecute it."

So Guenther didn't buy into the Helter Skelter motive? He absolutely didn't, he said, sinking back into his recliner. He thought

Bugliosi "made up" the motive to sell books. No one in law enforcement believed it, either, he added. As soon as the Family's Linda Kasabian flipped and became a prosecution witness, the entire motive for the murders changed. Guenther slouched in his chair, his great paw of a hand rubbing his forehead.

When Beausoleil called the ranch from jail, according to Guenther "he said, 'Tell Charlie I've been arrested for killing Hinman.'" Guenther was sure about this, because there was a recording of Beausoleil's call. Knowing that he had accomplices in the Hinman murder, police had tapped the phone at the men's jail and recorded the calls he made. On August 8, the day after he was booked, Beausoleil called the Spahn Ranch and told the person on the other end, allegedly Linda Kasabian, that he'd been arrested for Hinman's murder. "I need help," he was heard telling her. "Leave a sign."

That night, Sharon Tate and her friends were killed, and Susan Atkins scrawled the word "Pig" in blood on the front door of the Cielo house, just as she'd done on the wall at Hinman's. Guenther believed this was the "sign" Beausoleil referred to—Atkins hoped to exonerate Beausoleil, since he was in jail when the Tate–LaBianca murders had taken place. Manson's followers were, in effect, imitating themselves on a more devastating scale just to free one of their own. After that, they could escape to the desert.

Essentially, the wiretap was the best evidence yet for the copycat theory of the murders, and Guenther had never told anyone about it. He was visibly anxious to get it off his chest after thirty years, sometimes shaking in his seat. But he worried that it would overturn the verdicts against the convicted killers. "I don't want this reversed after all these years!" he said, pounding his fist on the arm of his chair.

Guenther's intensity moved me—he seemed on the verge of tears. But I couldn't figure out why he'd decided to reveal the recordings *now*, after all these decades. And why to me? Surely other journalists had sniffed around before. I asked if he had a copy of the tape. No such luck. Because the wiretap was illegal, his commanding officer, Captain George Walsh, had ordered him and Whiteley to turn over the recording; Walsh apparently destroyed it, or made sure that someone else did.

But if any of this was going into my *Premiere* story, Guenther didn't want to go on the record alone about it. He needed someone else to say it with him, someone who could verify the tape's authenticity—ideally, someone from the other side of law enforcement. He named Aaron Stovitz, who'd been Bugliosi's coprosecutor for part of the trial. Stovitz had heard the tape. Guenther was sure of that—the detective had brought it to him before it was destroyed.

"Get Stovitz to say it," he urged me, tears welling in his eyes again. "Say, Charlie Guenther gave me this reluctantly. Say I owned up after a long conversation and did it reluctantly. Ask him, how can it hurt? Promise me, promise me! I don't want them all back out on the street, and I'm worried this will do it!"

I promised him. But I still didn't understand why Walsh had destroyed the tape. Even if it were illegal, it so clearly solved the Tate–LaBianca murders—the day after they occurred, at that. "He said it would eliminate the narcotics angle," Guenther told me.

That startled me. Why would Walsh, who wasn't involved in the LAPD investigation, want them to pursue what he now knew was a false lead?

Talking to Guenther reminded me of something in an old issue of *Rolling Stone*. Aaron Stovitz had given an interview to the magazine in June 1970, right before the trial started. He mentioned exactly the phone call that Guenther had just told me about, though he'd couched it in more uncertain terms. Using the pseudonym "Porfiry," and speaking in the present tense, Stovitz told *Rolling Stone* that Bobby Beausoleil "puts a phone call in at the ranch telling them that he was arrested there and telling them he hasn't said anything":

Now—this is only a supposition on my part, I don't have any proof to support it—I suppose he, meaning Manson, said to himself, "How am I going to help my friend Beausoleil out? By showing that the actual murderer of Hinman is still at large. So I know that Melcher used to live in this house on Cielo Drive. 'Go out there, Watson, with these girls and commit robbery and kill anyone that you see there. Don't forget to leave'"—and this is very important because in the Hinman case they wrote POLITICAL PIGGY in blood. He said "Don't forget to leave a sign."

Given that Guenther had used that exact phrase—"leave a sign"—I was almost sure that none of this was a mere "supposition" on Stovitz's part. But he'd never divulged *how* he knew about Beausoleil's phone call. Would he admit to having heard the tape?

I doubted it. I'd interviewed Stovitz once already, and he was cagey. He'd said he was always convinced that the Tate–LaBianca murders were copycat crimes, but he wouldn't say why. When I'd asked him why the case wasn't prosecuted that way, he said it was because Bugliosi called the shots.

And sure enough, when I paid him a second visit, Stovitz was even more aloof. He denied ever having heard the Beausoleil tape. He'd heard "rumors" of it, he conceded, but never from Guenther. He dismissed me with a message: "Tell Charlie Guenther, Mr. Stovitz has a great deal of faith in you but unless you have some notes [it didn't happen]."

I called Guenther, and I could hear him wilt on the other end of the line. "Is that how he wants it? Then let's just drop it." I was deflated, too. Just as easily as he'd given me the scoop, Guenther was prepared to take it back. "You're just not going to be able to use it," he said. "That's all."

As if to prove how thoroughly he'd given up, Guenther began to change his story. When I talked to him again two weeks later, he said that he'd neither seen nor heard the tape—he only knew of its existence. Exactly Stovitz's position.

This was going to be a lot more difficult than I thought.

I drove all the way to Vegas to speak to Guenther's former partner, Paul Whiteley, whose demeanor was the polar opposite. Where Guenther would bound about the room, pacing and shaking and pleading, Whiteley barely moved. We sat among graceful Chinese porcelain pieces—his wife was a collector—and he was as serene and contemplative as the figures depicted in the china.

He remembered the Beausoleil tape clearly. "I heard it, yes," he told me. "Something about leaving a sign." And he corroborated the story of Captain Walsh's infuriated response. "Walsh was a by-the-book captain. He hit the roof!"

Like Guenther, his investigation had made him overwhelmingly confident of one thing: "Helter Skelter *didn't* happen." So many veterans of this case, I noticed, were willing to say that the prosecutor had basically fabricated a motive, using Manson's ramblings to button up his case. Helter Skelter was "not a motive," Whiteley said, "but a philosophy." Bugliosi was well aware of this; he just didn't care. And that meant he didn't care about the subtleties of the Hinman case, either, or about how LASO might go about prosecuting it.

The Beausoleil wiretap was maybe the single biggest break I'd gotten at that point, but the stories around it had begun to multiply. Guenther would eventually allow me to use him as an on-the-record source, but his account muddied the waters more than it cleared them. Despite their bombshell evidence of a copycat motive, both he and Whiteley insisted that they simply gave up after the LAPD told them to. Although they knew Beausoleil had an accomplice, and that he'd called someone at the Spahn Ranch, they never even drove out there to question anybody. That didn't track. Not with these guys.

"The Biggest Circus"

Around the time I reached an impasse with Guenther, I began to research another figure from the county sheriff's office, one whose scintillating claims about LASO and Manson had circulated for decades among counterculture enthusiasts and conspiracy theorists. Preston Guillory, once a LASO detective, had left the police force under a cloud of suspicion in December 1969, immediately after the LAPD had announced Manson's apprehension.

A couple of years later, in 1971, Guillory gave an interview to Mae Brussell, a cult-favorite radio host whose show trafficked in conspiracies—some plausible, others outright loony. Reading through the transcript, I found myself more intrigued by Guillory than I wanted to be, especially in light of what I'd gone through with Guenther and Whiteley.

Guillory's thesis was this: Manson had gotten away with far too much at the Spahn Ranch in the months before the murders. Even though he was a federal parolee, Manson had no job; he had ready access to drugs, alcohol, and underage girls; he had a cache of firearms. And LASO officers knew all about it. At LASO's Malibu station—Spahn was in its jurisdiction—Manson's lawlessness was something of an open secret, Guillory said. Firemen patrolling the ranch's fire trails had even encountered Manson and the Family toting machine guns. And yet Manson never paid a price. The cops always looked the other way. According to Guillory, that was because his station had a policy handed down from on high: "Make no arrests, take no police action toward Manson or his followers."

And so, despite the raft of crimes that Manson and the Family were committing, they were never apprehended, and Manson never had his parole revoked. There was even an occasion where Manson was picked up by LASO police for statutory rape, but they ended up cutting him loose.

Even as the station instituted this hands-off policy, they kept a close watch over Manson. Guillory was sure that LASO's intelligence unit, or some other intelligence unit, was running surveillance on the Spahn Ranch. He alluded to memos about Manson—with cover sheets to protect against prying eyes—that went straight to the station captain, and who knows where after that. Guillory didn't think the surveillance "was just a local thing."

Then came the murder of Gary Hinman, and soon after it the Tate–LaBianca murders. How had LASO failed to see this coming? They'd been monitoring Manson constantly. Guillory theorized that the massive August 16 raid on the Spahn Ranch was LASO's effort to cover its tracks after the murders. Calling it "the biggest circus I've ever been involved in," he marveled at the fact that all the charges had been dropped seventy-two hours later. Something didn't add up about the raid—all that force, all those arrests, for nothing? It was "like we were doing something perhaps a week late to show that we had really been watching," he said on the radio.

But that raised a bunch of problems. If the sheriff's office was surveilling Manson before the raid, it would've known enough to bring him in for the murders. If it *wasn't* watching him, then how had it amassed enough evidence to get the search warrant authorizing the raid?

When the LAPD held a self-congratulatory press conference to announce that Manson and his group were suspects in the Tate–LaBianca murders, Guillory decided to become a whistle-blower. He went to a news station, KCAL, and told them everything he knew, thinking the press would be all over this story. They hardly touched it. Worse, the leak cost him his job: LASO's internal affairs department got wind of his remarks and sent him packing.

After his departure, Guillory described how LASO did all it could to discredit him. An internal memo said that no one should discuss his previous employment there. It implied that he was a drug addict and an unrepentant leftist bent on smearing the office's reputation.

Listening to Guillory's radio interview, I couldn't say if he was a crackpot or not. He was airing a version of events that, a year before, I would've dismissed as sheer lunacy—and he was doing it on a radio show that traded in unadulterated paranoia. But his message resonated with me, especially now that I knew how much had been covered up. Guenther had convinced me that the tape of Beausoleil's phone call was real, and I never would've believed that, either. It seemed possible, if not entirely plausible, that there was still more to the story of the sheriff's office, especially its bungled raid on the Spahn Ranch.

I added Guillory's name to my whiteboard: one more in the jumble of cops and Hollywood has-beens, witnesses reliable and unreliable, with fading memories and ulterior motives. Then I picked up the phone. He wasn't hard to find—he ran a private detective agency, paired, somewhat oddly, with a traffic school, out of a strip mall off the highway in Riverside.

When I drove out to visit him, I was relieved to find him calm, confident, even fearless. Portly and white-haired, his mustache still flecked with red, he had a strong recollection of what he'd told Mae Brussell back in '71, and he stood by all of it. As we spoke, I noticed he had a weapon in a pouch on his desk, along with some model police cars; his diploma and graduation photo from the sheriff's academy were hanging on the wall behind him. Despite his contentious end with LASO, he remained a proud cop.

"We were told not to bother these people," he told me, referring to the Family. The order came in a memo from his captain. "Tell him whatever we saw or heard, that was one of the first things that I was told when I got to Malibu." Peter Pitchess, the sheriff of Los Angeles County at the time, was "memo-minded," Guillory explained. He exerted immense authority—and that authority extended to his officers' conduct with Manson. "We were asked to generate memos every time we had contact with any member of the Family," Guillory said.

Despite this intense period of information gathering, Manson was never charged when he was arrested. Why was a law-breaking parolee allowed to go free? "A lot of times we arrest people and the DA would say, We can't keep this person in custody, he's too valuable, we want him on the streets. My suspicion is that Manson was left alone for a while for some reason—I don't know." It was "very unusual" that someone with a record like Manson's would be left on the streets.

The shock of the Tate–LaBianca murders, Guillory thought, forced the sheriff's office to hide its own intelligence-gathering efforts. If Manson were guilty of homicide, "How could anybody possibly say we let him on the streets?" There would've been civil liability issues. Careers would have been destroyed. And, of course, it would've cost Pitchess the next election.

But that didn't explain why the police allowed Manson to go free for another three months after the Tate murders, knowing he could have killed more people. Why not just arrest him right away, and keep their surveillance program quiet?

Guillory had no idea—he'd been asking himself the same question. All he knew was "that Manson was under some kind of loose surveillance by our department or somebody else. We know he's being watched by somebody, but we don't know who. The thing is this—if he was under surveillance, those people left the ranch on two occasions, committed the seven homicides...why was there no intervention?" He added that there was no legal obligation for LASO to intervene; they could've chosen to let the murders pass without action, if Manson were so important that they didn't want to risk interrupting their surveillance.

Guillory was fairly confident that someone from LASO knew right away that the Family had committed those murders. "Probably someone saw them come and go and there's a log entry someplace and then, of course, later they found where they went and all hell would've broken loose."

Plus, he reiterated, LASO never could have launched such an extraordinary raid without sound intelligence—enough to persuade a judge to grant a search warrant. "You don't mount a raid without surveillance like this!" he said. More infuriating still: none of it stuck. The sheriff's office went to all that effort for nothing. And it didn't have to be that way, Guillory was sure. "We did find evidence of enough criminal activity—stolen property, narcotics—to violate [Manson's] parole in the first place. It was astounding! I never could figure out why he was released." Guillory had been part of the operation that day, and he remembered finding stolen purses, wallets, and pocketbooks with IDs—all damning evidence, and all seemingly ignored. After the raid, he said, the surveillance ended, as mysteriously as it had started.

In another interview, with the writer Paul Krassner, Guillory explained, "It appeared to me that the raid was more or less staged as an afterthought... There was some kind of a grand plan that we were participating in, but I never had the feeling the raid was necessary." He speculated that Manson was never arrested "because our department thought he was going to attack the Black Panthers." Their intelligence had revealed that Manson had shot Bernard Crowe, whom he mistakenly believed to be a Black Panther, in July, and this apparently convinced LASO that Manson "was going to launch an attack" on the whole organization.

Of Guillory's many outrageous claims, this one was maybe the hardest to swallow—but, again, he stuck by it when I asked him. "I believe there was something bigger Manson was working on," he said. "Cause a stir, blame it on the Panthers... I've got to believe he was involved, based on all info we have. Maybe a witting player in someone else's game."

When Manson was finally brought to justice for the murders, LASO took dramatic precautions to hide its surveillance of the ranch. "I thought what they were doing was illegal," Guillory told me. "All the crime reports disappeared from the station. Everything was gone, all of our reports were gone. Normally you had access to your own reports; they were all gone, disappeared. The whole file was gone, and the memo went up that no one involved in the Spahn Ranch raid was to talk to anyone outside the department." That convinced Guillory to go to a reporter—the move that cost him his job.

I found Guillory credible, if overheated. I knew I *wanted* to believe him—and that put me at risk of falling into the great trap of conspiracy theorists, who come to believe in grand plots simply because they make the world a more fascinating place. Certainly I'd have a more interesting magazine story on my hands if Guillory were correct. But that was a big *if*.

I was in touch with a number of former LASO deputies at this point, and I collected their opinions on Guillory. One described him as "kind of an off-the-wall guy." Another said he had "a gigantic chip on his shoulder," and "hard feelings for the sheriff's department—always feeling that he was being beset upon."

According to the most pejorative story I heard, Guillory had once tried to kill himself in the most dramatic way possible: "He had barricaded himself in a motel room in Malibu, I believe, and one of the inspectors was trying to talk him out of the room. He was threatening suicide and he had an automatic weapon." I asked the officer if he'd witnessed this firsthand. "I wasn't actually there," he said, "I just heard about it in the station. John Graham was the inspector who talked him out of the room."

Guillory called this allegation "bullshit," reminding me that LASO had embarked on a campaign to discredit him after he left. "They tried to put me out of business, basically ... It was goodbye, we'll see you, never darken our door again. I was crazy, malcontent, a loose cannon." If he'd really barricaded himself in a motel room, he said, "produce a report." Neither LASO files nor the media would have any record of it, because it never happened. "Ask Captain Graham: where was the hotel, what was the date? Tell him to put up or shut up."

In so many words, I did. I called Graham, who, like his colleagues, had a negative opinion of Guillory. But had the man really barricaded himself in a motel room? "Not that I know of," Graham said. Once I told him the story, he changed his mind. "Now that I recall, I did hear that there was probably a phony attempt at suicide." But he hadn't been there.

However reliable Guillory was—and I came to feel he was largely reliable, in the end—I was in a familiar predicament. I needed documentary evidence to back up his claims. My best shot was leering at me from the pages of *Helter Skelter:* the search warrant for LASO's massive raid. If Bugliosi had found it, couldn't I?

On the Paper Trail (Again)

Charlie Guenther was wary of appearing in my story, but we still talked a lot. When I told him I wanted LASO's files on the Hinman case, he made a phone call. Next thing I knew, I had backdoor access to the office's closed-case archives. With some directions and the name of another retired deputy sheriff scrawled on a piece of paper, I parked at the sheriff's training academy in East L.A. and knocked on the door of a windowless, barrackslike building.

The deputy let me in and walked me through rows of dusty filing cabinets, stopping in front of two and leaving me alone with them. I pulled up a folding chair and opened the top drawer. It was crammed with disorganized documents that appeared not to have been handled for decades. In the silence of the large, dim shed, broken only by the occasional sound of gunshots from a nearby firing range, I began my search.

The crux of the reports, to my delight, covered sheriffs' activities at the Spahn Ranch over the roughly sixteen months the Manson Family had lived there. Over the next few months, I made half a dozen visits to the hangar at the sheriff's academy. The retired detective was always happy to see me—I suspected I was the only other person he saw all day. When I had questions about language or codes in the reports, or even LASO procedure, he'd patiently explain them to me as I took notes. And he let me photocopy documents, but only after reviewing them first. After a while he barely glanced at what I brought him, instead reminding me how he preferred his coffee—I'd always return with a cup when I ventured out to a Kinko's nearby. I wasn't entirely surprised when I learned, several years later, that these visits of mine were completely unsanctioned—and unknown to LASO top brass.

In one of my earliest visits, with great relief, I found a copy of the search warrant for the August 16 raid. Although other researchers have since uncovered it, at that time it had never been seen by anyone outside law enforcement. Once I read it, I could understand why: it revealed that LASO had a far broader understanding of Manson's criminal activities—and his gurulike control over his followers—than had ever been shared with the public.

Running to sixteen pages, the warrant was rooted in the testimony of Deputy Sheriff William C. Gleason, who sought permission for LASO to recover "stolen automobile parts...and rifles, automatic pistols, and revolvers" from the Spahn Ranch. Charles Manson was the only suspect identified by name in the document, which stated that he was the unchallenged "leader" of the crime ring and also "on Federal Parole for Grand Theft Auto."

That last bit is crucial: it means that LASO was officially aware of Manson's parole status. If the police turned up any stolen vehicles or weapons—and they did, of course—he would be in violation of the terms of his release agreement, and would have to go back to federal prison.

If Manson was aware of that fact, he didn't act like it. And the police had already shown a willingness to look the other way. The search warrant related an incident from an Officer Williams of the LAPD. He told Deputy Gleason

that within the last two weeks he and his partner were on duty at the Spahn Ranch...Mr. Manson was bragging to

161

the officers about the weapons available to him and his friends at the Ranch. Mr. Manson told the officers that while he was talking to the officers that his friends had rifles trained on the officers...this is standard procedure whenever officers approach the Ranch.

Manson had flouted the law and bragged about it to LAPD officers as he had his followers train rifles on them—something else, incidentally, not reported in *Helter Skelter.*

Manson's cavalier, taunting behavior continued. Elsewhere in the warrant, the LAPD's Ted Leigh said he had found three loaded ammunition clips for a carbine that "fell from a dune buggy while on the highway" sometime on or around July 29. Leigh soon heard from Manson himself, who said the ammunition was his and that he would stop by and pick it up.

So Manson, a paroled ex-con with a known history of violence, had simply called up the cops and asked them if he could come collect the ammunition he'd lost? And he'd done this a little more than a week before the Tate–LaBianca murders. Manson, the warrant noted, had been "mentioned in prior memos," which fit with Guillory's insistence that police knew how dangerous he was.

Whether that awareness was the result of surveillance was an open question. The warrant explained that LASO deputies had cultivated an informant at the ranch, someone who "has seen guns in practically every building on the property. The informant was also threatened by Charles Manson." And there was extensive reconnaissance by the same Officer Leigh, who "flew over the Spahn Movie Ranch approximately August 1, 1969, and...observed a 1969 Volkswagen laying [*sic*] in a ditch." How often did the LAPD use planes to investigate car theft? Why were they flying over the ranch, which was out of their jurisdiction?

Manson was prepared to match their vigilance. Per the warrant, someone in the Family had bragged that "we have a guard at each road in [to the ranch] with a rifle and a telephone so if anyone comes in, we'll know they're coming." Another memo quoted Manson telling a fire inspector, "Don't try to play the 'man,' because the next time you try it, you'll find yourself hanging from a tree, upside down, dead."

And two days before the murders, an informant told an LAPD sergeant that Manson was on his way back from San Francisco with a young runaway girl and "a large amount of narcotics." The memo was partly correct. Manson had been in northern California then with a young runaway, but he'd been in Big Sur, not San Francisco. Who knows if Manson had that "large amount of narcotics," or if they played a role in the bloodshed to come. In any case, the document shook me—it suggested that authorities had tracked Manson with plenty of diligence, and with the help of an informant, in the days before the murders. They had a reliable sense of his comings and goings from the ranch mere hours before he dispatched his killers to the Tate house. And yet, somehow, it took them months to pin the murders on him.

Given the abundance of evidence, it came as no surprise that the raid had been authorized. Manson was practically begging for the strong arm of justice to come swooping in. When it did, the police got more than they bargained for. I found a one-page arrest report for Manson dated August 16, the day of the raid. In addition to the stolen cars and weapons, the arresting officer wrote that Manson had four stolen credit cards in his possession that day: they "fell out of his shirt pocket" when he was taken into custody. This had never been reported before.

In summary: Manson, the known federal parolee, walked away from an arrest that caught him with stolen cars and credit cards, an arsenal of weapons, and underage runaways. And meanwhile, two of the LASO's best homicide detectives failed to realize that the biggest raid in California history was going down at the very same ranch that their murder suspect had called.

Hundreds of Man-hours and Zero Indictments

Bugliosi, you may recall, had chalked up the failure to a simple mistake—the search warrant was "misdated." But now that I had it in my hands, I saw no evidence of any misdating. The warrant was clearly dated August 13, 1969. According to the California penal code, a warrant is good for ten days after its date. The raid was completely legal on August 16, a fact I verified with many police and attorneys.

Was there another potential explanation? Ed Sanders went a bit further in *The Family*—in addition to the "misdated" warrant, he wrote that the Family was let go because of insufficient evidence.

To figure it out, I talked to Bill Gleason, the sergeant who'd written the search warrant and spent two weeks organizing the raid. We spoke often. I always found him quick to smile and patient with my questions, even when I implied that he'd been negligent.

Gleason was still furious at Bugliosi and Sanders for impugning his reputation with their talk of "misdating." They'd led millions of readers to assume that a clerical slipup had invalidated the hundreds of man-hours that went into the raid.

The "insufficient evidence" excuse, Gleason told me, was closer to the mark. The problem was that none of the evidence—stolen vehicles, guns—could be linked to any of the suspects, most especially Manson himself. It was all scattered around the ranch. What seemed, in the warrant, like an airtight case turned into more of a fishing expedition.

"It's pretty hard when you got twenty-seven adults there to prove who actually stole a car," Gleason told me. They'd tried to dust one of the vehicles for fingerprints, but it had been sitting out in the dirt for so long that they got nothing.

"The warrant specified Manson's body to be searched for car keys and small parts, because he was said to be the leader," Gleason said.

"But do you sleep with your car keys?" I asked, thinking it was ridiculous to expect to find them on Manson's person at the crack of dawn.

"No," Gleason said, laughing. "At six a.m. we didn't know what they were going to be doing."

What about the stolen credit cards? They *were* found on Manson's person, having fallen out of his shirt pocket. Couldn't they have prosecuted Manson for those?

"Yeah, we could," Gleason said. "But we didn't know he was going to have credit cards when we were doing the search warrant. It was the DA's call, and if he says we're not going to prosecute him there's not a whole lot I can do."

Robert Schirn, the DA who'd signed the warrant for the raid and then dismissed the charges a few days later, was still working at the Los Angeles District Attorney's office, so I set up an interview with him. Surrounded by plaques and awards, Schirn greeted me with a warm hello and told me to take a seat opposite his desk. Like Gleason, he said that it was hard to bring charges in a case where the thefts couldn't be linked to anyone. But what about the credit cards?

"It's been so many years," Schirn replied. "I don't know if I was told about the credit cards. If they're in a report, I assume I would have been shown the report—and I would have been able to determine that there were in fact some stolen credit cards attributable to him." Maybe Manson was never caught attempting to use the cards. He couldn't recall.

"So you just don't remember what went into the decision?" I asked.

"I really don't."

He looked a little sheepish, and the silence lasted a beat too long. "All I did was just fill out the card and went on to my next case."

My inner skeptic had trouble taking Gleason and Schirn at face value. But let's say they were right, that the colossal raid of the Spahn Ranch had failed to yield any arrests worthy of prosecution, and that it was only a freak coincidence that it brought them so close to the group responsible for so many murders. Even if you believe that, LASO isn't free and clear. Because a week after their botched raid, the sheriff's deputies arrested Manson *again,* on totally different charges. And again, he was allowed to go free.

On August 24, the owner of a property adjacent to the Spahn Ranch alerted LASO sheriffs that someone was trespassing. Deputies drove out to find Manson and a seventeen-year-old girl, Stephanie Schram, in an abandoned cabin, where they'd just had sex. On a bedside table were several joints. And the LASO brought in Manson once more, this time on a felony pot possession charge and for contributing to the delinquency of a minor.

As with the raid, published accounts of this incident are thin at best. Bugliosi kept it out of *Helter Skelter* altogether, and Ed Sanders makes only passing mention of it in *The Family,* writing that Manson and Schram were released because there was no pot in the cigarettes, only tobacco.

However, according to an arrest report I found in the LASO files, the joints *did* contain pot—and on August 26 the sheriffs released Manson anyway, instead charging Schram with felony possession, even though she was a minor with no criminal record. No reason was given for the decision.

The day after Manson's release on August 26, a judge signed *another* warrant, this time for Manson's arrest, on the strength of his having been found with drugs and a juvenile. This time, LASO detectives never even bothered going to arrest him, something else none of the forty-plus LASO officers I interviewed could explain to me, and something again left out of *Helter Skelter*. Manson stayed at the Spahn Ranch until he moved to Death Valley around September 10.

The DA's order rejecting the pot charges against Manson was signed by Monte Fligsten, the deputy district attorney of Van Nuys. Incredibly enough, like Schirn, Fligsten was still working in the DA's office. When I called him, though, I found him much warier than Schirn had been. I gave him a quick rundown of the files I'd found: Manson, Schram, marijuana, delinquency of a minor...ring any bells?

"I have no recollection," he said.

"Do you recall investigating Manson at the time of August of '69?"

"I didn't participate in any of the Manson issues at all," he said. I offered to fax him the documents so he could verify his signature. He said he didn't want to be involved and hung up.

The LASO deputies who'd arrested Manson were flabbergasted when he wasn't charged at any point after the raid—especially given the effort of the raid itself. It was "a bunch of bullshit."

The deputies and the DAs had numerous chances to get Manson behind bars, or to keep him there, and they failed.

Even if none of Manson's charges were prosecutable, they were egregious enough to send the parolee back to prison. Bugliosi said as much in *Helter Skelter:* "During the first six months of 1969 alone, [Manson] had been charged, among other things, with grand theft auto, narcotics possession, rape, contributing to the delinquency of a minor. There was more than ample reason for a parole revocation."

If LASO officers did try to get Manson's parole officer to send him back to prison, I found no written record of such a request in the files. No one I spoke to could even agree on whose job it was to report a federal parole violation. The DAs said it was the detectives' job. The detectives said it was the DA's job. And, at the end of the day, everyone said, Wasn't it the parole officer's job? "It's always been a problem," Bill Gleason told me, "that guys would get arrested and released before the P.O. could place a hold." Then again, I had it on good authority that it was precisely Bill Gleason's duty to have told the parole office, and he didn't.

I felt like I was trapped in the swirling eddies of some forgotten bureaucracy. Maybe Manson was just the beneficiary of a simpler time, when police had fewer forces at their disposal and cruder methods of communication.

Samuel Barrett, who was Manson's parole officer at the time of the murders, told me he'd never been informed of the August 1969 arrests. If a parolee was involved in a crime at the local level, he said, it was "paramount" for the DA to file the charges. Otherwise, it would be hard to send anyone back to federal prison.

"But sheriffs, the DA," I said, "they all said it was up to you."

"They pass the buck," Barrett said. "It's all hearsay without filing charges."

Chasing Kitty Lutesinger

While Bobby Beausoleil was busy torturing Gary Hinman, he left his girlfriend behind at the ranch. Kitty Lutesinger, sixteen, was pregnant with his child, and in his absence, she set off a chain of events that gave the sheriff's office another chance to nab Manson.

Lutesinger had moved out to the Spahn Ranch to be with Beausoleil, but she'd never been a perfect fit for the Family. Now that she was pregnant, Manson mistrusted her, fearing that she'd compel Beausoleil to leave the group and raise their child. Lutesinger, in turn, was uneasy around Manson. He was always speechifying about the end of the world, fooling around with guns, and heaping abuse on anyone who crossed him. So, with her boyfriend showing no signs of returning anytime soon, Lutesinger ran away from the ranch.

LASO sheriffs found her on July 30 and took her in for questioning, since she was a teen runaway. She told them everything she knew about Manson: that he was an ex-con who'd threatened her life and her relatives' if she left the Family, that there were drugs and guns stockpiled at the ranch, and that many of the Family were runaway girls. Police sent her home to her parents in the San Fernando Valley. But she'd proven so informative that Bill Gleason drove out there to interview her again eleven days later, in preparation for the big raid. This would've been on August 10—just a day after the bodies had been found at Cielo Drive.

I couldn't find his full report in the LASO files, but Ed Sanders wrote about it in *The Family,* and he included an eye-opening detail: Lutesinger asked Gleason if the Black Panthers were behind the Tate murders. "I had been programmed to believe it was the Panthers who did it," she told him.

That remark should have raised a red flag. The timeline is the key. This conversation took place when the bodies at Cielo Drive were barely cold. As Gleason knew, Lutesinger had been away from the Manson Family since August 1, when she fled the ranch. So if she had, in fact, been "programmed to believe" that the Panthers killed Tate, the programming must've occurred *before* the murders, by someone who was responsible for them. Gleason should've suspected that Manson, or at least someone at the Spahn Ranch, knew more. (He told me he had no memory of discussing the Tate murders with Lutesinger, and found it unlikely that he had. The murders "had only occurred a few hours before. There probably wouldn't have been anything much on the news at that time." In fact, the bodies had been discovered more than twenty-four hours before he interviewed her; they'd dominated the news.)

Even though Lutesinger had cooperated with police, she

apparently couldn't decide where her allegiances were. On August 15, she ran away again, fleeing her parents' home and returning to the Spahn Ranch.

That same day, Guenther and Whiteley, still searching for accomplices in the Hinman murder—though, for some reason, they never checked the Spahn Ranch—learned that Lutesinger was Beausoleil's girlfriend and immediately deemed her a person of interest, issuing an all-points bulletin for her arrest. On August 17, the day after their colleagues raided the Spahn Ranch, Guenther and Whiteley visited her parents. I found Whiteley's interview notes in the LASO files. Lutesinger's parents confirmed that she was pregnant by their main suspect, that she'd been living at the Spahn Ranch until August 1, and that she'd run away again the night before, though they didn't know where. Whiteley did note that Manson had personally phoned the Lutesinger home the preceding week, and that Kitty had spoken to him.

In fact, at the very moment of that interview, Kitty Lutesinger was in LASO custody. She'd been picked up with the rest of the Family in the raid.

And here, to my mind, the credibility of the LASO deputies stretches to its breaking point. Guenther and Whiteley had just posted the bulletin for Lutesinger's arrest. They'd just learned that she'd been living at the Spahn Ranch—along with their primary murder suspect. And yet they didn't go to the ranch to look for her. They did nothing.

All they had to do was stop by, and they would have learned that everyone from the ranch was in jail at the Malibu station; they could've gone there, interviewed Lutesinger, and potentially cracked the Hinman *and* the Tate–LaBianca murders four months earlier than those crimes were.

Why didn't they go? For two reasons, Guenther told me. First, he and Whiteley never heard about the August 16 raid, even though their colleagues conducted it, and it was the largest in state history.

Bill Gleason backed them up on this. "We were two independent units," he told me. "We really had no reason to contact each other or even knew about the investigations going on."

Gleason said he "purposely kept everything quiet" about the raid. But he'd also said that a few stray LAPD squad cars had found out about it somehow and came along uninvited. Plus, as Bugliosi reported in *Helter Skelter,* the raid was on the front page of the local section of the next day's *Los Angeles Times,* beside a story about the still unsolved Tate murders.

Guenther's second reason was that Kitty Lutesinger's parents told him they'd already been to the ranch to look for her, and they'd been told that she wasn't there. But did he really expect a runaway's friends to turn her over to her parents, especially when everyone knew the cops were sniffing around for a murder suspect? He didn't even attempt an answer; we just sat in silence for a while.

Gleason had organized the raid. It would seem that it was only a matter of time until he realized that Lutesinger, whom he'd interviewed just six days earlier, was sitting in one of his jail cells while homicide detectives sought her out. He'd given me copies of his files on the case—one of them, a timeline of the investigation, had an entry dated August 17, 1969: "Whitely [*sic*] & Guenther tell Gleason that Lutesinger is wanted for questioning in Hinman murder."

But Gleason told me that he didn't even know Lutesinger was arrested during his own raid. She'd been booked under a fake name, because everyone in the Family used aliases. I reminded him that he'd already known that. It was in the search warrant affidavit he wrote before the raid, and Lutesinger herself had told him. Plus, one of the arrest reports in the LASO files said that he'd taken it on himself to learn the true identities of each suspect. He was unmoved. "She was just another face," he said. "I had a lot of things going on that day. I doubt if I would have recognized her." Lutesinger was released with the rest of the Family on August 18, and remained with them at the Spahn Ranch until mid-September, when they all moved to Death Valley. No one ever went to the ranch to look for her, despite the all-points bulletin out for her arrest.

The last time I saw Guenther was in January 2005, when I visited him to go through a timeline I'd made of his investigation of the Hinman murder. I told him that I couldn't believe he never went to the Spahn Ranch to solve the case. The police had Bobby Beausoleil in custody, and they knew he'd called the ranch asking for help. They knew his girlfriend lived there. They knew he'd stolen two of Hinman's cars. If nothing else, surely they would've gotten a warrant to search his last known residence—the ranch—for evidence of the theft.

But Guenther stuck to his story. He looked at the floor and said, "Maybe we just made a mistake."

I wasn't a seasoned crime reporter. Most of what I knew about the criminal justice system I'd gleaned from the news, police procedurals, and legal thrillers. So I went to Kimberly Kupferer, the chairman of the criminal law section for the California State Bar, and asked her to walk me through the standard operating procedure in murder investigations.

Kupferer contradicted Guenther on every point. She said it was standard practice to go to a murder suspect's last residence—whether "it's a ranch, motel room, or rat hole"—to search for evidence, especially in a robbery-homicide, like the Hinman case was. The fact that the detectives didn't go was "highly unusual," in her estimation.

Though I knew I was really pushing my luck, I made another call to Guenther in February 2005. "I know you've always told me, 'You'll never hear an untrue word from Guenther or Whiteley,'" I said, "but is there anything you haven't told me that would make me better understand your actions in this case?"

"No," he said faintly.

"Okay," I said. "One last question: Were you ever told by anyone to back off the Manson Family or the Spahn Ranch in your investigation of the Hinman murder?"

"No," he said again, this time almost inaudibly. "I was not."

I couldn't ask Whiteley the same questions. After my first meeting with him, he refused to speak with me again.

"Chicken Shit"

Sometimes, seemingly ancillary people would completely refocus my reporting. Such was the case with Lewis Watnick, the former head deputy DA of Van Nuys. I wanted to talk to Watnick precisely because he had nothing to do with the Manson case: he worked in the same office as the DAs who had, so he could offer some valuable perspective without feeling boxed in.

I went to visit him at his house in Thousand Oaks. I can still picture him shuffling to the door: a frail, thin man in his sixties, with wispy brown hair, a nice smile, and sad eyes. Suffering from an illness, he spoke in a labored, rasping whisper. His home was air-conditioned to frigidity.

He spent a while reading my documents in silence, and then he sighed. "Chicken shit!" he croaked. "This is all a bunch of chicken shit." The size of the raid; the fact that the DA's office kept releasing Manson when they had enough evidence to charge him, or at least violate his parole... "It dovetails right in," he said. "Manson was an informant."

It was only a guess, he conceded, but an educated one, based on his thirty years in the job. It wasn't the first time I'd heard the theory. One of my LASO sources had wondered if Manson "had his finger in a bigger pie." Having been in the office's intelligence division, he'd seen stuff like this before. "What happens in those situations is either he's giving up somebody bigger than himself or he's on somebody else's list as far as a snitch, or he's ratting out other people." And if he were informing for someone else, the DEA or the feds, no one in the LASO would know about it, necessarily. Robert Schirn, the DA who authorized the raid only to dismiss the charges, had made the same suggestion: "Another possibility, sheer speculation, is that [Manson] may have been an informant for somebody." But LASO deputies had all denied it.

"Of course," Watnick said when I told him that. "Confidential informant means they're *confidential*."

Neither of us could say what or who it was that Manson would have any decent information about. Drug dealers? Watnick wondered if it had a political dimension, given Manson's antagonistic relationship to the Black Panthers. "Maybe," he continued, muttering more to himself than to me, it was someone "big...possibly the FBI."

True, the search warrant was littered with references to Manson's fear of the Black Panthers. He thought the group was about to attack the ranch. One memo I'd found even said that Manson claimed to have seen "carloads" of "negroes" on the property photographing the Family. A fire patrolman reported that Family members had told him they'd moved into the canyons because they'd "killed a member of the Black Panthers."

"You know there's an old saying: an enemy of my enemy is my friend," Watnick said. "So, if Manson figured out this black-white confrontation, he may have been giving out information to the FBI," who had a vendetta against the Panthers.

Hearing this from Watnick—someone from the DA's office, but unaffiliated with the case—boosted my confidence. Looking at the lengthy search warrant again, he kept grumbling. "Helicopters, agents carrying automatic weapons, three different departments, four weeks of official surveillance...They had this massive raid and everybody's released *two days* later!" He shook his head. "The more that he's released, the more I feel that he was released because they'd get more out of him by having him released," he said. "They'd been watching this guy for something large...The thing that I wonder about is *who* was watching."

Watnick urged me to go back to Gleason—he knew the detective well, he said, and he trusted him. Why did Gleason just roll over when the DA's office undid all his hard work? As for this notion that Manson's parole officer couldn't find him in violation without charges from the DA, "That's bullshit, too," Watnick said.

As promised, I went back to Gleason, who calmly but adamantly denied that Manson was an informant. He didn't even see a glimmer of a possibility. "I'm sure that I would have heard something like that," he told me. "I never heard anything. Even if he was an LAPD informant, I'm sure I would have been contacted by LAPD...I never heard a word." He added, "The guy was a jerk... Every cop I talked to wanted to get him buried."

Then why had all of them failed? I couldn't stop turning it over in my mind: the image of Watnick, hunched over my files in his chilly home, grumbling with such certainty, "Manson was an informant."

Coda: "A Huge No-no"

I did most of my reporting on LASO in 2000. As with all aspects of my investigation, I kept thinking that I'd return to the key subjects someday and try them again, seeing if the passage of time had loosened them up somehow. I imagined a cascade effect—once I got somebody—say, Vince Bugliosi or Terry Melcher—to admit to a major cover-up, other areas of the case would begin to open up, too, or I could brandish an incriminating document that would change people's minds.

But you can guess what happened. I kept reporting and reporting, and time had other plans. In my obsession, I began to think of the story as a puzzle I could solve, if only I recovered all the pieces. I listened again and again to my interview tapes; I wrote out intricate timelines listing my subjects' every move, day by day and sometimes hour by hour, trying to discern who knew what, and when they knew it. I kept lists of possible explanations, about gun laws and parole laws and car-theft laws, and, most critically, about how those laws were written and enforced in 1969.

By 2005, I'd moved away from the LASO angle of the story, but I found myself constantly thinking about it. I knew I had to take another look at the archive to fill in some blanks. I was under the impression that I could go back anytime. I'd interviewed more than forty deputies over the years, making no effort to hide my reporting. One of them had told me that the sheriff himself, Leroy Baca, wanted to learn about what I was doing and "offer the sheriff department's cooperation."

But no one—except, evidently, the pair of retired deputies who got me into the archive in the first place—had any idea that I'd accessed the LASO files on the case. When I called the main office and asked to go back in, they were, to put it mildly, enraged. From the first officer I spoke to, all the way up to Sheriff Baca, the response to my request was a resounding no.

I argued that they'd set a precedent by letting me in before, unauthorized or not. For accuracy's sake, they owed it to me—and to the public, assuming I ever reached the end of my reporting—to let me in to recheck my notes. But because I'd never signed in anywhere, there was no record of my visits, they said, so it was like I'd never been there at all—even though I could show them the many files I'd photocopied.

When I persisted, they allowed me to make my case in person with the sheriff's captain of homicide. I arrived to find not one but three deputies, who'd found a new reason to keep me out. I couldn't go back in, they said, because there was an "open case" against unnamed Family members involving "stolen credit cards."

That couldn't be, I said. The statute of limitations on any type of theft by the Family would have long run out. They didn't care.

Sergeant Paul Delhauer, who had more or less seized control of the meeting, told me there was "stuff you can never be told, will never know about" regarding the case. Then he showed me the door.

When I'd been in the LASO archive all those years ago, it had been Delhauer's job to decide who got access and who didn't. For that reason, the sheriff's office had decided he was the guy who had to take my calls now. So I did call him—again and again, and again after that. We got on each other's nerves, and our conversations devolved into intense acrimony. "What happened as far as you getting access to those materials," he said with the air of a martinet, "was a huge no-no."

Delhauer accepted that this no-no wasn't my fault, and in his more charitable moments he allowed that it put me in a tricky position. But he didn't see what he could do to help.

"I don't really care, Tom," he said. "I see absolutely no significance to those questions. They have nothing to do with the resolution of the case. They have nothing to do with the scope of the investigation."

I told him about Watnick's theory—that Manson might've been an informant. "This is rank speculation," he said. "I honestly find this appalling." Well, of course it was speculation. That was one reason I'd tried to get back into the files—to see if there was any validity to it.

"I don't get paid to do your research," Delhauer said. "Everybody seems to be jumping to conclusions about some big grandiose thing," he said.

Worn down by my persistence, Delhauer finally agreed to remind Sheriff Baca of his long-ago offer of "the sheriff department's cooperation." If I wrote a letter to Baca, Delhauer would make sure he received it.

When Baca didn't respond to my letter, I was unrelenting, following up constantly. At last, I was granted an interview with the sheriff himself, who, it became apparent, had been thoroughly briefed on the angle I was pursuing.

Elected to his post in 1998, Baca had become a major figure in California law enforcement. Heading the nation's largest sheriff's office, he oversaw eighteen thousand employees with a jurisdiction covering more than four thousand square miles. Known as a strict enforcer with a no-nonsense style, he was at the peak of his power in November 2005, when we met at his headquarters.

I followed the tall, lean lawman as he marched down a hall to his office: large and comfortably furnished, with ceramic sculptures from Asia and three dramatically lit, floor-to-ceiling trophy cases. Hanging on a wall was a framed quote of Baca's from the *Los Angeles Times:* "We need to carefully concern ourselves with the feelings of other individuals and not engage in rhetoric that just inflames divisiveness."

We sat at a coffee table; I was on a couch, he in an easy chair, tan and slightly stooped, wearing his uniform. Making it clear the meeting was going to be brief, he suggested I get right to my point. I wanted to get back into the files, I said, to learn why his department had been so lenient on Manson.

Baca fixed me with an unblinking, unnerving stare, and said, "The reality is that Charlie Manson as an individual was a dope-head, a weirdo, a cultist, and a control freak . . . Charlie's not a guy who is going to get pimped by a cop."

"He seemed pretty fearless of them," I said. "When they went to the ranch, he told them he had men in the hills with guns on them."

"It further exemplifies that he doesn't need anyone to help him . . . You know, look at the obvious here, he's not reliable even in terms of his own conditions. Now, if he's not reliable in defining himself, how is he going to be reliable in defining something useful for the cops?"

Most of what he said followed this line of thinking: Manson was too unstable to be of use to law enforcement. As for Guenther and Whiteley's backing away from the case, he didn't want to touch it.

"Every sheriff I interviewed," I told him, "said they couldn't get around the fact that Guenther and Whiteley didn't go to the ranch."

"I think that only they can account for why they didn't go," he said. "It's interesting, in the pursuit of criminals, even when you're on the hot trail, and something distracts the effort that you're into, you'll say I'll do that tomorrow, and then tomorrow is going to interfere with some other damn thing…and then before you know it a whole week has gone by."

I reminded him that this wasn't any old murder case. Guenther and Whiteley believed, *truly* believed, that their case was tied into the biggest unsolved murders in Los Angeles history, a crime that had the city living in fear.

"I can assure you that they aren't part of a larger deal-making person with a guy like Charles Manson. You can't hide something like that."

"If I present it this way," I said, implying that he was leaving me no other option, "they're going to look like bad cops."

"Incompetent. Not bad."

Our meeting ended almost as quickly as it started. Baca, who'd kept me waiting more than an hour, had to get to a dinner in Pasadena. We walked out together, trailed by his driver. Out in the dusk, he turned to me before we parted ways. "If you'd like a little more assistance, I will get you in touch with someone who does run informants and let you throw that hypothetical at them," he said. Thinking of Manson, he added, "He's a weirdo. What kind of cop is going to rely on a weirdo for anything?"

I didn't say anything. I knew it was useless. The sheriff had his mind made up before he met me. As his driver pulled up in his sedan, Baca gave me a final once-over, as if still not certain what to make of me. Then he shook his head and, getting into his car, said, "You got Hollywood fluff, like Marilyn Monroe was murdered, that's what you got. But that's good. That's what sells books."

Baca retired in 2014. In 2017, a jury found him guilty of obstructing an FBI investigation into inmate abuse in Los Angeles County jails. He was sentenced to three years in federal prison. Before a packed courtroom, a U.S. district judge told him: "Your actions embarrass the thousands of men and women who put their lives on the line every day. They were a gross abuse of the trust the public placed in you...Blind obedience to a corrupt culture has serious consequences."

I found Baca contemptuous and condescending that day in 2005. He did, however, make good on his offer to me, putting me in touch with the head of his detective division, Commander Robert Osborne, who was the closest thing LASO had to an expert on informants. I gave him my song and dance—well rehearsed, by then—and, while he found it unlikely that Manson had ever informed for his office, he said it was possible for a federal agency to call and ask for one of its informants to be released from LASO custody. In such cases, they'd call the investigator; the captain would be uninvolved.

"It's possible that a phone call was made, yes. [But] what benefit would be gained by keeping it a secret forever? The theory that somebody asked them to do something different than the norm is not implausible," he admitted, "though I don't know why they wouldn't tell you. I can't imagine why they would want to keep it a secret. I don't see anything to be gained—if, in fact, there was some other agency involved in 1969 or 2005—to keep that quiet."

Unless, I thought, it resulted in the murders of innocent people.

I sensed this was the closest thing to a concession I'd ever get from the L.A. County Sheriff's Office. I thanked Osborne for his time and went on my way.

This is what desperation does to a writer. I knew that Guenther would be enraged if he learned that Baca had called him and Whiteley "incompetent." I wondered if this might be what would finally get him to break the code of silence—the fact that he, one of the most legendary detectives in LASO history, had been denigrated by the head of his former office. I didn't have the heart to tell him, but I did tell one of his friends, who was understandably outraged. I had a hunch he'd share it with others, including Guenther. But it still took me six years to call him.

When I did, he sounded tired and defeated, not like the Charlie Guenther I remembered. He still had a funny way of calling me by my full name in conversation.

"I want to close the door on that, Tom O'Neill," Guenther said. "I want to end it with you. Lee Baca kind of upset me. Our conversation is over."

I apologized and explained why I didn't think he was incompetent, and why I was sure that anyone who knew his record didn't, either. But it didn't break the wall. "Twenty years I did this," he said quietly, referring to his time in homicide, "and Baca said I'm incompetent...I just want it to finish. Hell, I'm eighty-three years old."

"I just want to write the truth about why those murders happened," I said.

"I know what you're saying, Tom, and I'd ask you to accommodate me. This is over forty years ago and I'd like to be out of it... please, Tom O'Neill. I have no squabbles with you...I'm totally done."

Guenther died in 2014. I was heartbroken by the frailty I heard in his voice that day. And I was confused. In the throes of my obsession with the case, I couldn't understand how such a celebrated detective would want to shut the door on it, to lose his drive to get to the bottom of it. But that was when I assumed I'd soon shut the door myself. Now many more years have passed, and that door is still open, and I understand Guenther perfectly.

6

Who Was Reeve Whitson?

Fairly early in my reporting, I knew I could have wrapped up my *Premiere* story if I really wanted to. I had the guts of a great piece, even if it was too late for the milestone thirtieth anniversary of the murders. I'd spoken to duplicitous celebrities, seedy drug dealers, bumbling cops, and spurious prosecutors. I'd been threatened and cajoled and warned off my investigation. But I didn't have a smoking gun. There were only mountains of circumstantial evidence. The thrust of my story was still mired in ambiguity. I worried that my reporting could be too easily dismissed, Lee Baca–style, as "Hollywood fluff."

So I kept going, although in many ways I've come to regret it. A few of my interviews were especially tormenting—the ones that convinced me I couldn't call it quits yet. I thought of Little Joe, Jay Sebring's barber, who'd received an elliptical phone call from a mobster after the murders. And of the first suspects, Charles Tacot and Billy Doyle, who claimed to have intelligence connections. And of Preston Guillory, who alleged that police allowed Manson to remain free because they knew he planned to attack the Black

Panthers. I thought most of all about the possibility that Manson, of all people, had some type of protection from law enforcement or was even an informant. It boggled the mind even to speculate that someone like Manson could be plugged into something bigger, and presumably even darker, than he was. But this is where the reporting took me.

I started reading up on the use of informants. Perusing old editions of the two major Los Angeles papers of the era, the *Times* and the *Herald Examiner,* I learned that in the midsixties both the LAPD and LASO had infiltrated groups they considered a threat to the status quo: antiwar leftists, the Black Panther party, and other black militant groups like the US Organization, a fierce rival of the Panthers in Los Angeles. Posing as leftists, agents provocateurs would gain the trust of these groups from the inside, provoking them to commit crimes or do violence against rivals.

Even from a distance, this line of inquiry gave me pause. I'd never been interested in conspiracies. I wasn't one to speculate about a second shooter in JFK's assassination or faking the moon landing. For the first time, though, I saw the appeal of trafficking in murky secrets—it was an attractive option, as long as people believed you. If I found the plot, I could change the way people understood one of the seminal crimes, and criminals, of the twentieth century. If I got it wrong, or took too much on faith, I'd become someone who made people glaze over at parties, politely excusing themselves as I droned on about "the big picture."

Even if it made me look crazy, I wanted to see whether the informant theory held water: if Manson had any credible connections to the government or law enforcement, and if I could link him to the police infiltrations of leftist groups I'd read about. Then, as if I'd conjured him from thin air, someone emerged who fit into the puzzle. He seemed to have wandered into Southern California from the pages of a spy novel, and not a very well written one, at that. His name was Reeve Whitson, and his intersections with the

Charles Manson sitting opposite his lawyer, Irving Kanarek, at the 1970 trial for the Tate–LaBianca murders. (Bettmann Archive)

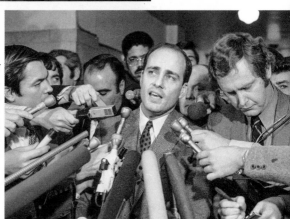

Vincent Bugliosi, chief prosecutor in the Tate–LaBianca trial, speaking with reporters outside the courtroom in 1971. (Associated Press)

Four of Manson's followers (from left: Cathy Gillies, Kitty Lutesinger, Sandy Good, and Brenda McCann) kneel on the sidewalk outside the Los Angeles Hall of Justice, March 1971. (Associated Press)

Roman Polanski, Sharon Tate's husband, at the house on Cielo Drive mere days after the murders in August 1969. (Courtesy Julian Wasser)

Jay Sebring (far left), Roman Polanski, and Sharon Tate at a party in London. (Bill Ray / The *Life* Picture Collection)

Terry Melcher with Candice Bergen at the Whisky a Go Go in the summer of 1967. During Manson's trial, Melcher would become one of the prosecution's most important—and most suspicious—witnesses. (Phil Roach/ipol/Globe Photos, Inc.)

Rudi Altobelli, standing and speaking to Candice Bergen during a gathering at the guest house on Cielo Drive. Altobelli, who owned the house, suggested that the true story behind the murders has never been told. (Courtesy Dominic Pescarino)

Altobelli in 1999, with one of his many adopted cats. (Courtesy Dominic Pescarino)

One of several memos in Bugliosi's handwriting suggesting that Melcher continued to see Manson after the Tate–LaBianca murders. (Public archive)

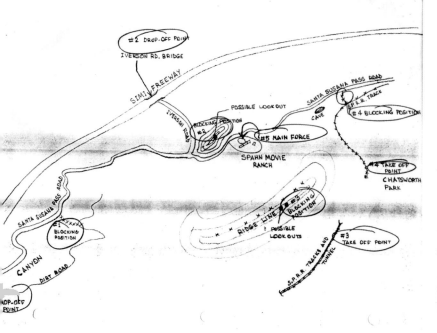

A police drawing of the Spahn Movie Ranch, the Family's hideout. Deputies from the Los Angeles County Sheriff's Office raided the ranch on August 16, 1969, but they apparently failed to connect the Family to the rash of murders it had recently committed. (Courtesy John A. Kolman)

A mug shot of the Family's Bobby Beausoleil, who participated in the murder of Gary Hinman. (Courtesy Lee Koury)

Reeve Whitson with his wife, Ellen, in the winter of 1961–62. Whitson claimed to have been at the house on Cielo Drive in the hours after the Tate murders. (Courtesy Liza Josefson)

Whitson disguised as a hippie. His friends and family believed he was an intelligence agent with ties to the Manson case. (Courtesy Liza Josefson)

At work in my home office in Venice Beach, around 1999 (top) and 2014 (center, below). (Top: author collection; center and bottom: courtesy Errol Morris)

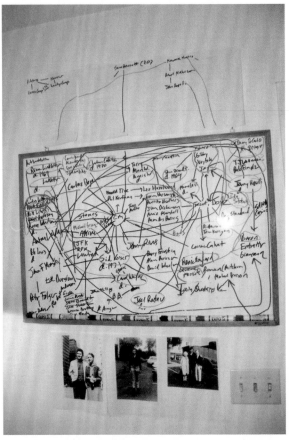

The whiteboard on which, to the concern and amusement of my friends, I tried to keep track of all the connections I'd made in the case. (Author collection)

Manson investigation suggested a dimension to the Tate–LaBianca murders that had been wiped from the official record.

"I Had to Save My Ass"

It started with Shahrokh Hatami, Sharon Tate's friend and personal photographer. When I spoke with Hatami over the phone in 1999, he'd never given an interview about the murders. Sorting through his memories, he recalled something he'd never been able to explain.

At seven in the morning on August 9, 1969, Hatami got a frantic phone call from a friend. Rubbing sleep from his eyes, he listened as the caller delivered the terrible news: Sharon Tate and four others had been murdered in her home on Cielo Drive. Afterward, in numb terror, he and his girlfriend switched on the radio and listened all morning for further reports. They had to wait a while. As Hatami later learned, that call came ninety minutes before the Polanskis' maid had arrived at the house, discovered the bodies, and ran screaming to the neighbors, who called the police. Unwittingly, Hatami had become one of the first people in the world to hear about the murders—all because of his friend.

That "friend" was Reeve Whitson, whom Hatami characterized as "a mystery man"—a phrase I'd hear a lot as I researched him in earnest. A close friend of Tate and Polanski, Whitson had a talent for discretion. When people remembered him at all, he was usually on the periphery, coming and going, his purpose unknown, his motives inscrutable.

If Whitson's involvement had been limited to that early phone call, I don't know whether I'd have given him a second thought. It seemed entirely possible that Hatami had gotten the time wrong. To get some sense of Whitson's role in the case, I looked his name up in the trial transcript. It appeared four times, all during Hatami's testimony. It was Whitson, he confirmed on the stand, who brought him to Bugliosi during the investigation. And yet Whitson never appeared in *Helter Skelter,* which gave an otherwise detailed account of Hatami's story.

As well it should. Hatami's testimony was a dramatic high point. Before the packed courtroom, he explained that five months before the murders, he'd been visiting Sharon Tate when he noticed someone on the property. Hustling toward the front door, he found short, scraggly Manson standing there. Manson asked if Terry Melcher was around. Hatami, wanting to be rid of him, sent Manson around back. He knew that Rudi Altobelli lived in the guest-house and could tell him where to find Melcher.

Hatami's story proved that Manson knew where the house on Cielo Drive was, and how to get there. And it added some tragic foreshadowing: since Tate, Sebring, Folger, and Frykowski were in the room behind Hatami, this would be the one and only time Manson laid eyes on his future victims.

The problem, Hatami revealed to me, was that he'd never been confident that it was Manson he saw that day. His uncertainty meant nothing to Bugliosi and Reeve Whitson, who coerced his testimony anyway. "The circumstances I was put through to become a witness," Hatami said, "I didn't like at all." Whitson told him, "'Hatami, you saw that guy, Altobelli said so, we need another person to corroborate it.'" (Presumably, Bugliosi felt he needed two accounts of Manson's visit to the house that day; it was such an important part of tying Manson to the murder scene.)

Hatami demurred, and Whitson turned the screws, effectively threatening him with deportation—he said he'd ensure that Hatami, an Iranian without U.S. citizenship, wouldn't be able to get another visa. If he wanted to stay in America, all he had to do was say he'd seen Manson that day at Tate's house. Not long after, Whitson brought Hatami to his car and showed him his gun. Although Hatami didn't know Whitson too well, he took the threat seriously—he believed that Whitson really had the means to deport him.

"I was framed by Mr. Whitson," Hatami told me. "I was never sure it happened that way. I had to save my ass." Bugliosi and I were still speaking then, so I asked him if he knew Whitson at all. He didn't recall the name, he claimed. Hatami thought that was "rubbish." "Bugliosi knows him very well," he said. "I could not have been a witness without Reeve."

He was right. Because the defense suspected that Bugliosi and Whitson had, indeed, coerced Hatami's story, they called on Bugliosi to explain himself at the trial. Under oath, but out of the presence of the jury, Bugliosi tried to answer for the fact that he'd interviewed Hatami without a tape recorder or a stenographer. Who was in the room when Hatami talked? "Just Reeve Whitson, myself, and Mr. Hatami," Bugliosi replied. The judge decided that Hatami couldn't testify to having seen Manson. The jury heard only that he was at the house when a man came to the door, and that he sent the man to the guesthouse.

But of course Bugliosi had forgotten that he'd supplied Whitson's name under oath. Whitson wanted it that way. He served his purpose and then disappeared, Hatami said, like "a piece in a chess game."

A Photographic Memory

If Whitson was a chess piece, who was moving him around? He'd died in 1994, so I couldn't ask him. Hatami gave me the names of people who might've known him. Almost invariably they told me the same thing: that Whitson had been an undercover agent of some kind. Some said he was in the FBI, others the Secret Service. The rough consensus, though, was that he was part of the CIA, or an offshoot special-operations group connected to it.

It seemed absurd, the first time I heard it: an undercover agent wrangling witnesses for the Manson trial. It seemed absurd the second and third times, too. But then I kept hearing it, dozens of times—Reeve Whitson belonged to an intelligence agency. As I talked to his confidants, a portrait emerged. Whitson had been serious, secretive, compartmentalized. He lived "about eight lives simultaneously," as one friend put it. He had eccentric habits and an eidetic memory. What he did with that memory, and whom he did it for, remained the subject of feverish speculation.

Bill Sharman, a former NBA player and general manager of the Lakers, had known Whitson since 1980. He recalled his friend's "photographic mind." Sharman met me with his wife, Joyce. Both believed Whitson was connected to the Manson case. "He said he worked for the CIA...He told us he was involved in the investigation, but gave us no details," Joyce said. "Reeve would tell us the most preposterous things and eventually we'd find out that they were true...we learned to start believing him. We loved him very much, but he was always a mystery to us."

That word cropped up whenever I asked anyone about Reeve. Even those who'd known him well described him as a complete enigma, with a penchant for telling unbelievable stories that turned out to be true. Another friend, Frank Rosenfelt, the former president and chief executive of MGM, who'd known Whitson since '75, called him "the strangest guy in the world."

"He didn't lie," Rosenfelt told me. "He did not put himself in a position where he told you something and you could disprove it." He was confident that Whitson "had some intel connection, no doubt about it." Rosenfelt was one of a few people who remarked on Whitson's odd tendency to call from pay phones. He "would call me for hours...I always wondered, who the hell is paying the bills? And always from a phone booth on the street!" And "Reeve knew a lot about the Manson situation," Rosenfelt said. "He indicated that if they had listened to him that a lot of people may have not been killed. He was heavily involved."

"If who had listened to him?" I asked.

"I think he meant whoever was looking into it. The federal people, law enforcement people. He implied he gave a lot of suggestions, he was involved and they didn't listen to him...He was bitter about it."

That implied Whitson had some advance knowledge of the Family's plans. I wrote it off as a faulty memory until I heard it again. Richard and Rita Edlund, who met Whitson through Rosenfelt, described a "very cryptic" figure who took pains to avoid detection. "I knew he helped in the Manson investigation," Richard, a special-effects cinematographer, said. "Reeve was among those, if not *the* one, who broke the Tate case." But, like the others I'd spoken to, Richard couldn't offer too many specifics, only beguiling memories: "He operated in the CIA—I believe he was on their payroll...Reeve was the kind of guy who, because of his background, he still would turn the inside light of his car out, so when he opened his door the light wouldn't go on. Because he had it that you never know who's looking." He "used his thumbnail to tear the top-right-hand corner of every piece of paper he handled, to mark it. Can't shake old ways, he used to say."

With his "gift of gab," Whitson had "anything *but* a military bearing." A man who couldn't be stereotyped, he "was infiltrating the town in his incredibly charming way. He was friends with Jay Sebring and Polanski was a buddy of his, and the Beach Boys—and he met Manson through all this."

"Before the murders?" I asked.

"Oh, yeah!" Their encounter had come through Dennis Wilson, Edlund recalled, in the period when Manson was trying to break into the music business through the Beach Boys. "Reeve was the kind of guy who would meet everybody. He would create the infrastructure of the town in his mind—there was hardly anybody that he didn't know."

The likeliest story, I'd thought, was that Whitson was some kind of con man, or at least a slick liar—and that Shahrokh Hatami had simply misremembered or exaggerated the incidents culminating in his testimony. But Whitson's friends had me more and more convinced that he'd been involved with Manson. Maybe the most compelling evidence came from Neil Cummings, a lawyer who'd known Whitson since '84. Several people had told me he was among Reeve's closest confidants, so I took him to lunch. I hadn't told him about Hatami's claim—that Whitson had called him before the bodies were even identified—but he corroborated it independently.

According to Cummings, Whitson was in a top-secret arm of the CIA, even more secretive than most of the agency. He talked a lot about his training in killing people, implying that he'd done it at least a few times. And when it came to Manson, he "was closer to it than anybody," Cummings avowed:

He was actively involved with some sort of investigation when it happened. He worked closely with a law enforcement person and talked quite a bit about events leading up to the murders, but I don't remember what they were. He had regrets for not stopping them, for doing something about it.

He had a reason to believe something weird was about to happen at the [Tate] house. He might have been there when it happened, right before or after—the regret was maybe that he wasn't there when it happened. He told me he was there after the murders, but before the police got there. He said there were screw-ups before and after. I believe he said he knew who did it, and it took him a long time to lead police to who did it.

Whitson had the Tate house under surveillance, Cummings added, which is how he knew something was going to happen. On the night of the murders, he'd been there and left. As outlandish as it sounded, Cummings was confident about all of this. "He knew more than anyone else."

I was flummoxed. For a year, I'd been hearing a rumor from people inside and outside the case: that Manson had visited the Cielo house after the murders, that he'd gone back with someone unknown to rearrange the scene. This would've accounted for discrepancies in the positions of the bodies: the killers left them one way, and the police found them in another. There were pools of Tate's and Sebring's blood on the front porch, splatters on the walkway and the bushes. But according to the killers, neither Tate nor Sebring had ever left the living room, where they died. The coroner described blood smears on Tate's body, as if she'd been dragged—again, never mentioned by the killers. Those in the area, including a private security officer, had heard gunshots and arguing hours after the killers said they'd left. And Manson himself had claimed on a few occasions that he'd gone back to the house with an unnamed individual to "see what my children did."

The mere mention of this claim made Bugliosi apoplectic. I'd seen a video in which another researcher had raised the possibility. An indignant Bugliosi asked: Why would Manson put himself at risk like that? He may have been crazy, but he wasn't stupid. And when I asked Bugliosi about it at our first meeting, he refused even to consider the possibility, despite all the discrepancies.

Now, though, here was Cummings, along with others, saying that Whitson had been at the Tate house after the murders but before the police. Here was Hatami, saying Whitson had called him that morning. Cummings said it was Whitson's "biggest regret" that he hadn't been able to prevent the slaughter. Maybe these were the words of a self-important liar, or maybe Manson was telling the truth about this return visit, and Whitson had been there, too. That seemed delusional to me. But Cummings and Hatami weren't crazy. They were two independent, credible sources with the same story.

It seemed possible to me that Whitson was the fulcrum, the man who could connect everything. The strange omissions at the trial and in *Helter Skelter;* the blatant failures of LASO to follow up on good leads; the suspicion that Manson could be an informant; the murmurs about a narcotics deal gone south: if I wanted to construct a unified field theory, Whitson, linked to intelligence work by no fewer than a dozen sources, would have to be at the center. Knowing that a lot of what I had was circumstantial and speculative, I contained myself—I had a ton of work ahead of me. But, looking back, when I wonder how I let this case consume me for the better part of twenty years, I can point to Whitson as a major cause.

"He Did Not Exist"

The vital records on Whitson were thin. Born in Chicago on March 25, 1931, he'd grown up in Kendallville, Indiana, and even his childhood had a whiff of the fanciful to it. His mother was a dancer, and his father was a world-renowned acrobat, part of a traveling family act. An only child, he developed a flair for the dramatic. At Indiana University, he was the lead in school plays, and he so enjoyed acting that he transferred to the Pasadena Playhouse, moving to L.A. and hoping, like so many before him, to become an actor or a singer. As a friend put it: "His great strength was his natural affinity for people...He could play all these roles. His life really was a series of theatrical productions."

It's not clear when that life swerved into espionage. According to a few people I spoke with, Whitson said that he'd had a mentor, Pete Lewis, who'd inducted him into undercover work. Lewis apparently met a tragic and deeply improbable end, like something out of a James Bond movie: he was killed by a poison dart hidden in an umbrella. Richard Edlund, one of several to mention the poison-dart story, saw it as a vital part of Whitson's origin story; it was almost like Whitson thought he could avenge his friend's death by working as a spy. Who could say how much of it was true? My hope was that Whitson's family could separate fact from fiction.

A few of the people I'd met in California told me that he had a Swedish ex-wife, as well as a daughter. Their very existence was speculative, because he was so reluctant to disclose anything about them. The family had lived together in America briefly, until, in 1962, after the Cuban Missile Crisis came to a head, he'd sent them back to Sweden, certain that the United States was on the brink of nuclear war. All of this sounded far-fetched to me, too, but what didn't, with Whitson?

Sure enough, I reached his ex-wife, Ellen Josefson (née Nylund), by phone in Sweden. Josefson didn't beat around the bush.

"He was working for the CIA," she said. "That is why I am worried to talk to you."

Was she sure about that?

"Yes, I am sure." She and Reeve had met in Sweden in '61, she explained. They fell in love in an instant. Before the end of the year they'd married and moved to New York. In those days he was undercover as a journalist, producing pro-Communist pieces as a ploy to meet radicals. This, he seems to have hoped, would lead to more contacts in Russia. It was a scheme so elaborate that someone from the Polish embassy was involved, she remembered, and in due time Whitson was bringing Russians to their place.

"I got furious with him," she said. "I was very anti-Communist." How could she have married a pinko? That's when Whitson felt he had to pull the curtain back. He explained that it was just part of his work for the agency—something he was otherwise ill inclined to discuss.

In October 1962, Josefson said, she gave birth to their daughter,

Liza. By then, she had misgivings about her marriage; the bloom was off the rose. Reeve's job jeopardized her life, and now her daughter's, too. And it made him hard to love. He would be dispatched to remote areas of the world for months at a time, returning with no explanation for where he'd been or what he'd been doing. In 1962, he was always going off to Cuba, and after the missile crisis he decided it would be best to send his family back to Sweden. They returned to Ellen's homeland sometime before JFK died, as she recalled. And then—radio silence.

"I didn't hear anything from him," Ellen said. When he did resurface, it was to demand a divorce. The legalities dragged on for two or three years. "I had to be nice," she said. "He said that things could happen to me if I didn't divorce him."

After the divorce was finalized, neither she nor Liza heard from Whitson for some fifteen years. He reappeared in the late seventies or early eighties, saying that he'd retired and that he wanted to atone in some way for his absence. Although they spoke only a few more times, Ellen did remember his bringing up Manson and the Family.

"He said that his mother and Sharon Tate's mother were close," she said, "and that's why he had to go back to it, to help . . . I never wanted to have any details. I was scared. He said, 'It's best for you to not know.'"

On Ellen's advice, I got ahold of Liza, her daughter, who'd met Whitson for the first time since her infancy when she was eighteen. In several long phone calls, she filled in more biographical blanks about him. Now a married nurse living in Sweden, she had trouble reconciling her father's intense secrecy with his role in her life. She found him inexplicable, opaque.

"I could never understand how he got to know all these important people," she told me. "He told me that he worked within the Central Intelligence Agency. And he was in a part of the agency that was absolutely nonexistent. He did not exist."

"Did you believe him?"

"Yes," she said. "My existence was kept a secret to all his friends." When she made a trip to California to see him, he told some friends that she was coming. They "were absolutely convinced that he was just making a practical joke, like he always did. When I came through the door, I had two people just staring at me! They were so stunned." Whitson told her that he'd kept her at arm's length for so long because "he lived his life in complete control over other people, and I was the only one that he could not control." If people wanted to hurt him, "they could get me," she said. "My mother and my grandparents in Sweden feared that I was going to be kidnapped because I was his daughter." Even after her father retired, they had a difficult relationship. He still wouldn't discuss his past, and his politics bothered her—he was an archconservative with a rabid disdain for leftists.

When Whitson died, Liza flew to Los Angeles to attend his funeral and was astonished to see how many powerful friends he had, and how few of them knew much about him beyond his or her personal experience. "He kept his friends apart," she said. Hoping to recover any mementos, she went to his sparsely furnished apartment, finding nothing of any sentimental value. He did leave behind a few photos, which surprised her—Whitson had always refused to be photographed. One of them caught her off guard. It was a black-and-white picture of her father with long, flowing hair—not a wig, by all appearances—and bell-bottoms. "He looks like he could've been one of the Manson Family members," she told me.

She sent me the photograph, which, sure enough, showed a grimacing Whitson dressed as a hippie, not flamboyantly, but plausibly, in blue jeans and a wide belt, his shirt open at the neck. Liza was convinced that it was from one of his undercover operations. My impression was that the photo dated to about the mid-1960s; the cars in the background were from that period. I wondered if the disguise could have been related to Manson at all. She couldn't say. Although he'd told her that he played some role in the case, "I never figured out why he was involved," she said. "He was a master of telling you things but not really spelling it out."

Whitson had a large extended family. Many of his "cousins" weren't even related by blood, but they'd bonded with him anyway. As Frank Rosenfelt told me, "He had a strange habit of getting in touch with people named Whitson and saying they were his cousins."

Linda Ruby, however, was a real cousin of his—Liza had put me in touch—and she presented another side of Whitson's activities during and after the Tate murders.

In August 1969, Ruby told me, Whitson was living with his parents in L.A. On the day the bodies were discovered at the Tate house, she said, he went missing. His father, her uncle Buddy, had told her this story. The morning after the murders—around the same time Whitson would've placed his call to Hatami—Buddy woke up and discovered that Reeve hadn't come home that night. When news of the murders flashed on the radio, Buddy got nervous. He knew that Reeve had planned to visit the Cielo house the night before, and early reports said that one of the bodies there had yet to be identified. (It was Steven Parent, who wasn't IDed until eight that night.)

Fearing that his son had been murdered, Buddy Whitson called the cops, who sprang into action. "The police set up a nerve center at their house," Ruby said. They remained there, manning the telephones, until Reeve finally returned home late that night, at which point they eagerly debriefed him.

Ruby couldn't understand why the police would set up a command center at the home of an anonymous Los Angeles resident. Why not just check to see if the unidentified body was his? Making things weirder still, Whitson himself was present when his father told her the story—he was sitting right there, she remembered, quietly refusing to clarify or contribute. He never even said where he was during the hours he was missing.

Another friend summed it up nicely: "He always wanted to go to restaurants that no one went to. He said, 'I have to keep a low profile.' It was so low that there was no profile."

"Mr. Anonymous"

As usual, I was anxious to find some way to verify everything I'd heard. With Whitson, especially, my reporting had crossed the line into conspiratorial territory, and I would be hard-pressed to convert skeptics on the merits of my interviews alone. Of course, clandestine intelligence agents are exactly the sort of people who don't leave a lot of paper behind, and Whitson, by all accounts, was so savvy that he didn't need to take notes. I'd filed a Freedom of Information Act request (FOIA) with the CIA, asking for any information on him. Their response said that they could "neither confirm nor deny" Whitson's connection to the agency. FOIA specialists told me that this is the closest one can get to confirmation that someone worked for the CIA.

I did, eventually, find corroboration in print, but it came in a strange form: a manuscript for an unpublished book called *Five Down on Cielo Drive*. Written around 1974 or '75 — before *Helter Skelter*, and thus before Bugliosi's telling of the Manson story had ossified into the "official" narrative — the book had a tortured history, not least because it involved at least three authors. The most prominent was Lieutenant Robert Helder, who'd headed the LAPD's investigation into the Tate murders. Another contributor was Sharon Tate's father, Colonel Paul Tate. The third author was Roger "Frenchie" LaJeunesse, an FBI agent who'd "unofficially" assisted the LAPD.

It's not hard to see the appeal of the book, especially before *Helter Skelter*. Here were three authorities on the case who could give a rich account of it when no such account existed. They secured a contract with a publisher. When too much time passed without a viable book, a ghostwriter came on board, but by the time the manuscript was ready, Bugliosi had beaten them to the punch, and *Helter Skelter* had claimed the mantle of "official" Manson book. The deal fell through. In the ensuing years, the *Five Down* manuscript gained a reputation among researchers and obsessives. It was exceptionally rare—hardly anyone other than its authors had read it—and even though it was apparently tedious, it was rumored to have the most complete account of the LAPD's investigation, false leads and all.

Another journalist passed me a copy. I read the parts about Colonel Tate especially closely. A retired military intelligence officer, Tate had mounted his own inquiry into his daughter's death, separate from but parallel to the LAPD's. Many had told me that Whitson was under his wing. You wouldn't think that LAPD detectives would have been so keen on two outsiders helping them, especially given those outsiders' connections to intelligence—but a LASO detective told me that Colonel Tate "appeared to be running the LAPD."

Then in his midforties, Tate had only recently left the army. To mount his "independent" investigation, he tried to masquerade as a laid-back Californian, growing a beard and long hair. But he retained the upright carriage of a military officer as he wandered into hippie clubs and drug dens in search of his daughter's murderer, offering a lavish reward to anyone who would help.

How did Whitson play into this? The *Five Down* manuscript refers to a Walter Kern, "a somewhat shady character who can best be described as a 'police groupie.' Apparently he had been a friend of Jay Sebring . . . and wanted to help in any way he could." "Kern" was always one step ahead of the other investigators. Helder wrote, "In this business, as you might imagine, a policeman gets to meet many strange people. Kern was among the strangest. No one knew what he did for a living, yet he always seemed to have money and knew just about everyone on the wrong side of the tracks. I didn't like him but he was useful."

And he kept popping up. When Helder arrived to interview Roman Polanski at the Paramount lot where he was sequestered with Witold Kaczanowski, Kern was there, "lurking in the shadows. He sure did get around." Believing that Voytek Frykowski was involved with drug dealers who may have murdered him, Helder instructed Kern to cozy up to anyone who might know them, especially those in Mama Cass's circle.

In another section of the manuscript, a "Hollywood hooker" is said to have spoken to Kern, "who by now was well-known as an amateur sleuth on the case." Kern shared leads and took orders, and yet the man was so shrouded in mystery that Helder referred to him as "Mr. Anonymous."

It seemed likely to me that there was more to "Mr. Anonymous" than Helder had shared. By that point, Helder had died, but I'd already spoken to Frenchie LaJeunesse, the FBI agent who'd contributed to *Five Down*. I called him again to ask whether Walter Kern was really Reeve Whitson.

His answer: "Yes." In fact, the publishing deal couldn't have happened without Whitson, LaJeunesse said. "Reeve Whitson was a part of putting the book together, the linchpin between all of us."

It was Lieutenant Helder, the lead investigator for the LAPD, who'd assigned Whitson the pseudonym of Walter Kern, to protect his undercover status—hardly a step one would take with an ordinary "amateur sleuth." "Reeve didn't want his name associated with a book," LaJeunesse said, even long after the Manson case had been solved. "Not on the jacket, not even in contracts—he didn't even want money."

In effect, I now had written proof from the LAPD's head investigator, and from Sharon Tate's own father, that Reeve Whitson was smack in the middle of the Manson investigation from the start.

LaJeunesse didn't know who Whitson worked for, just that he was an "astounding fellow" who'd been an informant of some kind. He "wanted to project an aura of mystery," LaJeunesse said. But the heart of his motivation was an antidrug conservatism. He was "interested in keeping young people away from the curse of narcotics."

Mike McGann, the LAPD detective whom I'd interviewed about the early days of the investigation, remembered Whitson's involvement, too.

"He was heavily involved," McGann said. "And he had no need for money." McGann was nearly certain that Whitson was in the CIA, and found him "very credible." Still, when I said that Whitson had reportedly believed he could've stopped the murders, McGann laughed. "Bullshit. He'd talk for three hours and never say anything. Typical government employee—a real good line of bullshit."

If I could prove once and for all that Whitson was working for the CIA, even McGann might admit I had a story on my hands. The CIA wasn't even supposed to operate on domestic soil. What could they have been doing messing around with an acid-soaked cult in Los Angeles? And if Whitson had been close enough to the murders to stop them, why didn't he?

Everyone agreed that Paul Tate was the key to understanding Whitson. I knew that Tate was still alive, but getting him to open up would be a long shot.

His wife and Sharon's mother, Doris, had been comfortable discussing the murder. She'd formed a national victims' rights advocacy group and mobilized it whenever anyone from the Family was eligible for parole. Her friends said she believed there was something deeper than Helter Skelter behind the murders. Like her husband, she'd conducted her own investigation through the years, becoming convinced that the Cielo house was under surveillance by some type of law enforcement at the time of the murders.

(Whether she knew that Reeve Whitson had claimed to be watching the house, we'll never know.) She was also sure that her daughter wasn't supposed to be home when the killers arrived that night. Whoever was watching the house, she believed, had noticed that Sharon's red Ferrari wasn't in the driveway—it was in the repair shop—and concluded that she wasn't there. She'd planned to write a book about her theories, but she never got to: she was diagnosed with cancer and died in 1992.

Paul Tate, rumor had it, had never discussed the case with his wife. Before she died, they'd barely spoken to each other, having taken up in separate parts of their house. He hadn't spoken publicly about Sharon's death since Manson had been captured, and he'd already declined an interview with me once. But I phoned him again in May 2000, telling him I'd gotten a copy of *Five Down on Cielo Drive* and planned to quote it.

That got him to agree to meet with me. But as the date approached, he canceled on me; we rescheduled, and he canceled again. When he called to cancel yet another meeting, I tried to butt in with a question about Reeve Whitson before he could get off the phone. He was receptive—at first, anyway.

"Reeve was my main person to help me," Tate said. "He's been a friend of Roman Polanski and Sharon and mine and Jay Sebring... He was very, very helpful."

Even so, Tate found it ridiculous that Whitson's friends were going around saying that he could have prevented the murders. That simply wasn't true, he said. Could he help me clear it up, having contributed so much to the investigation?

"I contributed, just—put in there I contributed nothing."

"But you *were* involved in the investigation," I said. "You wrote a book about it!"

"Yeah, well..."

"Did you ask Reeve to do the undercover work or did someone else?"

"I'm not gonna answer those questions," he said, impatience creeping into his voice.

Could he at least tell me who Whitson worked for? He refused. "Why not?"

"I don't have to tell you that!" he nearly shouted.

Out of desperation, I made a foolish mistake. Sometimes, when I sensed that someone was withholding something sensitive, I'd remind the person that, in all the speculation about Manson himself, the basic, brutal loss of human life was too often the first thing people stopped thinking about. So I said, "Just out of respect to the victims, don't you think—"

Paul Tate sounded a million miles away to me, and he had a gruff, emotionally detached tone befitting his military background. But he was, first and foremost, Sharon Tate's father: a man who'd lost a child to an unimaginable horror, who'd seen her death become a kind of shorthand for tabloid atrocities. I'd forgotten that truth, and my comment understandably upset him. I regretted it right away.

"Out of respect for the victims!" he shouted. "What kind of fuck do you think I am?" He laughed bitterly. "You go ahead and do whatever you want to do, but...if any son of a bitch ever had respect for the victims, it was me."

"I apologize," I said. "I didn't mean it to sound the way it came out."

"Okay," he said. "Bye, bye." And that was the end of my relationship with Paul Tate, the man who knew better than anyone what Reeve Whitson was up to. He died in 2005.

The Spy Who Came in from the Cold

Helder had written that Whitson "knew just about everyone on the wrong side of the tracks." The opposite was true, too—he knew how to pull the levers of power. Colonel Tate was just one of his friends in high places. Usually, in the same breath, Whitson's friends named another military bigwig: General Curtis LeMay.

As discussed earlier, LeMay was part of the unsettling story I'd heard from Jay Sebring's barber, Little Joe. One of Sebring's clients, the mobster Charlie Baron, had called Joe after Sebring's murder, pledging that no harm would come to the barber. Charlie Baron was a friend of Curtis LeMay, too. Meetings between the two were noted by the FBI, who surveilled Baron for decades. LeMay, a former air-force officer nicknamed "Bombs Away LeMay," had retired in '65 and turned to defense contracting, where one critic feared that he "could be more dangerous than when he was air force chief of staff." He moved to L.A. to become the vice president of a missile-parts manufacturer, but it fizzled, as did LeMay's brief political career. After that, Mr. Bombs Away had spent his retirement roaming the city with Mr. Anonymous.

I added a few more connective arrows to the big whiteboard on my wall, realizing more than ever that its tangle of lines and circles made sense only to me. Though I never figured out what LeMay and Whitson got up to together, it was plausible that they were tied up in Charlie Baron's cabal of right-wing Hollywood friends, the ones who, Little Joe told me, had "done terrible things to black people." (George Wallace, who'd chosen LeMay as his running mate in his '68 presidential bid, was among the nation's most notorious racists.)

"I'm sure he knew Baron," Whitson's friend John Irvin told me. A British film director who himself claimed to have ties to MI5, Irvin said that Whitson got meetings "within minutes" at "the highest levels of the defense industry—it was amazing." He was "on the fringes of very far-out research" for the government, "not discussed openly because it verges on the occult." He added that Whitson "had very good connections with the Los Angeles Sheriff's Office" and pull with immigration officials, as Shahrokh Hatami had said. But Irvin couldn't elaborate on any of this.

Then came Otto and Ilse Skorzeny, the most sinister of Whitson's friends. They were Nazis—genuine, German, dyed-in-the-wool Nazis. The United Nations listed Otto Skorzeny as a war criminal. He'd been one of Hitler's most trusted operatives, leading the manhunt of one of the Führer's would-be assassins and spearheading a secret mission to rescue Mussolini. After the Third Reich fell, Skorzeny safeguarded the wealth of countless Nazis and helped disgraced war criminals settle into new lives around the world. Brought to trial before a U.S. military court, Skorzeny was alleged to be "the most dangerous man in Europe"—but he was acquitted, having made himself an asset to U.S. intelligence. His wife, the Countess Ilse von Finkelstein, was once a member of the Hitler Youth; a shrewd businesswoman known for her beauty and charm, she negotiated arms deals and contracts for German engineering companies. Irvin had met Ilse many times through Whitson. When she got drunk, he said, "she was always doing Heil Hitler salutes!"

Whitson could look past any ideology, no matter how abhorrent, if someone proved useful to him. His friends construed him as the purest form of Cold Warrior, lifted from *The Spy Who Came in from the Cold*. He carried an outmoded fifties-era politics into the future, masquerading as a hippie, infiltrating an LSD cult, and befriending Nazis to eliminate the scourge of communism and narcotics—the latter being, to his mind, a direct extension of the former.

"He believed there was an operation to destabilize American youth," one friend told me. "Russians were bringing drugs in to battle the American system from within."

Having worked in South America, Whitson believed "we should kill the drug lords in Bolivia and their whole families...If there's a baby, you kill the baby. I don't think he would say something like that and not be capable of doing it. He didn't believe in the individual, but in the larger picture." Another acquaintance recalled,

"The entire Manson situation, the Black Panther movement, and probably similar other movements . . . people like that were discredited by certain things that, according to Reeve, may have been staged or done by government authorities in order to make them look bad."

If I could find out where Whitson's money came from, I might be closer to understanding what he actually did. His résumé was scant from the fifties through the seventies, after which it covered more ground than seemed possible for a single life. He was the special advisor to the chairman of the board of Thyssen, among the largest corporations in Germany. He sank years into a scheme to construct a maglev monorail train stretching from Las Vegas to Pasadena. He wanted to build a *Brigadoon* theme park in Scotland. He was involved in weapons manufacturing, early iterations of the Miss Universe pageant, and a new variety of childproof medicine bottle. And he had a passion for race cars—building them, selling them, driving them—which may explain how he befriended Jay Sebring, another racing enthusiast.

These ventures had one thing in common: they fell through. The easiest explanation, of course, was that they were covers, and sometimes Whitson told his friends as much. So where did his money come from? No one knew. He always paid in cash—he stowed it in his freezer—and when he had it, he was quick to settle a tab. Whitson dressed in gabardine suits, but for much of his adult life, an ex-girlfriend recalled, he lived "like a hermit," sleeping "on a cot in his parents' kitchen." The man who loved fast cars drove an economical Ford Pinto.

In his final years, Whitson was destitute and disgruntled, telling rueful stories of the "Quarry"—his term for the section of the CIA he worked for—and trash-talking the agency. Once you're in, he told one friend, "You really are a pawn." In his dying days, the government had said, "You didn't even exist to us." Even the movies were no reprieve, offering reminders of his glory days.

About a year before he died, seeing the thriller *The Pelican Brief,* Whitson leaned over in the dark of the cinema and told a friend, "*I* wrote the yellow papers on everything that happened." With a hint of nostalgia, he explained that "yellow papers" detailed interrogation techniques, including a procedure in which a man had a plastic tube inserted in his rectum, peanut butter smeared on his scrotum, and a rat dropped in the tube.

Whitson died at the relatively young age of sixty-three. With no health insurance, he left behind an enormous unpaid hospital bill, something to the tune of half a million dollars. A few of my sources felt there may have been foul play. He'd given conflicting explanations for his health problems: a heart attack, or a spider bite, or a brain tumor, or lymphoma. "I think he committed suicide," his daughter told me. "His greatest fear was to be a vegetable."

Coda: Neither Confirm nor Deny

Reeve Whitson "was a walk-in," as one of my sources put it, "an extraterrestrial." Once he consumed me, I found myself fixating on possibilities that I would've dismissed as insane only months before. His life opened onto a vantage of intrigue, where Manson and the sixties counterculture were just one element in a political struggle that encompassed Nazis, Cuba, Vietnam, South America, military intelligence, and byzantine matters of national security.

But Whitson was too much the mystery man he was said to be. He brought my reporting to a standstill. At a certain point, I felt I'd learned everything I could about him without tapping official sources. I'd attempted to find his tax records and asked reporters with stronger connections at Langley if they could look him up. They never found anything. FOIAs to the FBI, the Secret Service, the DEA, the ATF, the IRS, and the military all got responses that said they'd had nothing to do with him. It was only the CIA that gave me the "neither confirm nor deny" response. Later, responding to my appeal, it wrote that Whitson had "no open or officially acknowledged relationship with the Central Intelligence Agency."

I worry that I'll never know the truth about Reeve Whitson. There is, of course, the possibility that he was little more than an effective con artist, someone who weaseled his way into a minor role in the Manson investigation by sweet-talking people in power. Someone who's constantly implying to his friends that he's in the CIA might not be very effective as an undercover agent. If Whitson were truly a high-functioning member of the intelligence community, would anyone have had any idea?

On the other hand, maybe the stories I heard are fundamentally correct—Whitson was an intelligence agent who led a storied international career, and he wasn't exaggerating when he said that he could've stopped the Manson murders. If that was true—what then? Why would the CIA, or any intelligence group, have had Whitson infiltrate the Family, and what did Manson know about it? The bottom line was that I'd learned just enough about Whitson to dwell on him. It was as his daughter said: "He gives a little and then he goes away."

7

Neutralizing the Left

Dawn of the "Campus Malcontents"

I couldn't expect to report on the likes of Reeve Whitson, or on outrageous claims about intelligence connections and military figures, until I learned more about the politics and pressures of California in the sixties. My research was pushing me toward broader connections and social implications, and I didn't always know what to do with them. If Preston Guillory was correct, for instance, then LASO knew about Manson's plan to attack the Black Panthers. How could the police have known, and why would they have wanted that attack to happen? I had vague notions of the tension between the Panthers and the government, but I couldn't say how it fit in the larger context of protest in the sixties, when the nation's unrest had crystallized in California. The state was the epicenter of the summer of love, but it had also seen the ascent of Reagan and Nixon. It had seen the Watts riots, the birth of the antiwar movement, and the Altamont concert disaster, the Free Speech movement and the Hells Angels. Here, defense contractors, Cold

Warriors, and nascent tech companies lived just down the road from hippie communes, love-ins, and surf shops.

If there was any truth to Reeve Whitson's story, I needed a crash course in the government's involvement in antileft action in California, and solid sources to tell me how Manson could have been swept up in it. I focused on two secret intelligence operations that were under way in Los Angeles in 1969: the FBI's COINTEL-PRO and the CIA's CHAOS. Their primary objective, according to three congressional committees that investigated them in the midseventies, was to discredit the left-wing movement by any means necessary—an aim that, coincidentally or not, described exactly the effect of the Manson murders.

The sixties youth movement was born on May 13, 1960, when hundreds of demonstrators, most of them UC Berkeley students, began a two-day protest at San Francisco's City Hall. The House Committee on Un-American Activities (HCUA) had convened a series of hearings there, and students were chagrined to learn that they were barred from the proceedings. A riot broke out as police turned firehoses on the protesters, the intense pressure forcing them down the building's imposing marble stairway. Police clubbed protesters and made sixty-one arrests, including more than thirty students.

"Black Friday," as it came to be known, marked the end of the fifties, the dawn of a new age of dissent. The following day, the demonstrators returned undeterred, this time totaling more than five thousand. The HCUA was cowed—never again did it conduct hearings beyond the Capitol. J. Edgar Hoover, the director of the FBI, couldn't believe the left had such strength in numbers. He was convinced that foreign Communists sponsored the movement. Thus began a pitched battle between federal law enforcement and young "subversives."

In the midsixties, with the war in Vietnam escalating, Berkeley became a hotbed of antiwar activity. Sit-ins were staged on campus; rallies were held throughout the Bay Area, each growing in size and fervor. Late in 1964, some fifteen hundred students crowded into Berkeley's Sproul Hall to protest the university's mistreatment of campus activists. More than seven hundred of them were arrested that day.

On January 28, 1965, a distraught Hoover met with the director of the CIA, John McCone, hatching a plan to take "corrective action" at Berkeley. The CIA's charter prohibited the agency from domestic operations, but McCone collaborated with Hoover nonetheless, hoping to quash the protests. One of their targets was Clark Kerr, the president of UC Berkeley, who was widely perceived as sympathetic to the protesters. McCone and Hoover circulated false information claiming that he had Communist ties. They also targeted faculty supporters of the demonstrators and the student leaders themselves.

A few months later, McCone resigned from the CIA, having felt unappreciated by President Lyndon Johnson. His next job brought him back to California: he took a post on Ronald Reagan's gubernatorial campaign, shoring up the candidate's credibility with right-leaning voters. Reagan campaigned fervently against "the so-called New Left," vowing a swift end to California's burgeoning antiwar movement. Without citing evidence, he claimed that Berkeley had suffered reduced enrollment as a result of the protesters' "destructive conduct." If elected, he said, he would appoint McCone to lead a formal investigation of the university's "campus malcontents and filthy speech advocates." Reagan won by a landslide. As he cemented his power, antiwar sentiment continued to flower at Berkeley. In April 1970, soon to win a second term, Reagan famously declared war against the movement. "If it takes a bloodbath, let's get it over with," he announced. "No more appeasement."

The Oval Office was similarly disturbed by the rise of student activism. By 1967, Lyndon Johnson believed that the country was on the verge of a political revolution that could topple him from power. Having mired the nation even further in the Vietnam War, he faced constant jeers at rallies: "Hey, hey, LBJ, how many kids did you kill today?" As antiwar demonstrations spilled from campuses into the streets, Johnson ordered the FBI and the CIA to take action. That August, with the president's approval, CIA director Richard Helms authorized an illegal domestic surveillance program, code-named CHAOS. Meanwhile, J. Edgar Hoover revived the FBI's dormant counterinsurgency program, COINTELPRO. Both agencies opened the first offices of their respective operations in San Francisco—still considered ground zero for the revolution, especially since the founding of the Black Panther party in nearby Oakland the previous summer.

Thanks to these two secret programs and their network of well-placed informants, there was an all-out war raging in California by the summer of '69. The FBI and CIA had induced the left to feed on itself; among competing factions, what had been sectarian strife had devolved into outright violence. The more I read about it, the more I saw how someone like Charles Manson could fit into a scheme like this. I was only speculating, but I knew that he'd spent a lot of time in Berkeley, San Francisco, and Los Angeles, often inveighing against the Black Panthers; and I had reliable sources suggesting that he was an informant, or at least hanging around with others who could've been.

It struck me that the Tate–LaBianca murders had been so often invoked as the death knell of the sixties. Arguably, they did more than any other event to turn the public opinion against hippies, recasting the peace-and-love flower-power ethos as a thing of latent, drug-addled criminality. As the writer Todd Gitlin noted, "For the mass media, the acid-head Charles Manson was readymade as the monster lurking in the heart of every longhair." Wasn't this the goal of CHAOS and COINTELPRO?

It was a sound connection in theory. To report it, to take it out of the realm of the hypothetical, seemed an impossible task for someone with no background in national security. But I had to try. And so, feeling the line between "researcher" and "conspiracy theorist" blurring before me, I hunkered down in the library to read about the many ways our government has deceived us.

"Fomenting Violence and Unrest"

The FBI and the CIA launched their counterintelligence programs in the same month. On August 25, 1967, J. Edgar Hoover issued a memorandum to the chiefs of each of his FBI field offices in the United States, outlining the objective of COINTELPRO. (The name was an abridgment of *Co*unter *Intel*ligence *Pro*gram.) First launched in 1956 to "increase factionalism" among Communists in the United States, COINTELPRO had been activated on and off throughout the early sixties, often to vilify civil rights leaders— Martin Luther King Jr. most prominent among them. In his '67 memo, Hoover formed a new branch of the operation, aiming

> to expose, disrupt, misdirect, discredit, or otherwise neutralize
> the activities of black nationalist, hate-type organizations...
> The activities of all such groups of intelligence interest to this
> Bureau must be followed on a continuous basis...Efforts of
> various groups to consolidate their forces or to recruit new or
> youthful adherents must be frustrated. No opportunity should
> be missed to exploit...the organizational and personal con-
> flicts of the leaderships of the groups...[and] to capitalize
> upon existing conflicts between competing black nationalist
> organizations.

Hoover specified more than twenty cities where COINTELPRO methods could be put to effective use, Los Angeles among them. In a later memo, he ordered the Bureau to "pinpoint potential troublemakers and neutralize them before they exercised their potential for violence."

Informants were COINTELPRO's lifeblood, providing the only effective way for the FBI to learn about, and exert influence on, the groups it hoped to discredit. The Bureau went to extreme lengths to cultivate solid informants; if it found a convict willing to infiltrate a political group, it would commute his prison sentence. In Quantico, Virginia, at the sprawling marine corps base where the FBI would soon open its own academy, a less-formal "Hoover University" trained agents in the delicate art of passing as leftists. They grew unkempt beards, refrained from bathing for days at a time, parroted radical talking points, got stoned, and tripped on acid.

In the Black Panther party and, in Los Angeles, the US Organization, informants were instrumental in fomenting violence. They would spread disinformation to catalyze an intergroup rivalry, or they'd simply arrange for the bloodshed themselves.

Founded by Huey Newton and Bobby Seale in Oakland in 1966, the Black Panther Party for Self Defense (commonly known as the Black Panther party) had become the bête noire of federal law enforcement. From Hoover on down, the FBI's ranks saw the group as a threat to the national order rivaled only by communism and nuclear holocaust. Originally, the Panthers served to safeguard Oakland's black residents from overzealous policing. They promoted lawful, armed self-defense in inner-city neighborhoods, and their social outreach programs brought meals and health care to those who couldn't afford them. Their Ten-Point Program demanded "power to determine the destiny of our Black Community."

But as the party grew in size and prominence, opening chapters in nearly every major city in the United States and abroad, it embraced more militant action against the long arm of law enforcement, starting in Oakland. In 1967, Newton shot and killed a cop during a traffic stop. In '68, Eldridge Cleaver, who headed the Panthers' Ministry of Information, was in a firefight during which he and two cops suffered gunshot wounds and a seventeen-year-old Panther was killed. That same year, the violence found its way to Los Angeles, as gunfights led to four Panther deaths.

By 1969, the Panthers had been involved in more than a dozen shoot-outs with police, some the result of ambushes. Fearing infiltration by informants, the party began to implode, purging members and, in one notorious case, torturing and killing a nineteen-year-old member suspected of being a snitch. Their paranoia was far from unfounded. Hoover's FBI chalked up the internal strife, not to mention the rash of deaths, as a victory.

COINTELPRO promised the violent repudiation of what Hoover had dubbed a "hate-type organization." The Bureau's strategy was merciless, its results disastrous but effective. In Chicago, famously, the FBI recruited William O'Neal, recently charged with impersonating a federal officer and driving a stolen car across state lines, to infiltrate the Panthers' Illinois chapter, forgiving those charges in exchange for his services. Soon O'Neal became the personal bodyguard for Fred Hampton, the chapter's chairman. O'Neal's post allowed him to provide the Bureau with a steady stream of intelligence, including detailed floor plans of Hampton's apartment. Although he found no evidence that Hampton or the group posed a threat to anyone's safety, O'Neal continued to inform. In December 1969—days, coincidentally, after Manson was charged in the Tate–LaBianca murders—O'Neal slipped a barbiturate into Hampton's drink over dinner. By the end of the night, the police had raided Hampton's apartment and shot him twice in the head at point-blank range.

O'Neal was one of many such informants around the country,

and Hampton's death one of many such deaths. The FBI's role may never have come to light if not for the Citizens' Committee to Investigate the FBI, an audacious crew of activist-burglars who took it upon themselves to break into a small FBI field office in Media, Pennsylvania, just west of Philadelphia. One night in March 1971, the group took a crowbar to that office's dead-bolted door, stuffing suitcases with papers revealing the FBI's domestic spying, which they soon parceled out to the press.

Hoover was in high dudgeon: the group's methods were straight out of the FBI playbook. They'd cased the office for months, sending in a woman disguised as a college student to get a sense of the building's security. In his fury, Hoover allocated some two hundred agents to track down the burglars, but they were never found; only in 2014 did they reveal themselves. They were motivated, they said, by a sense that the government had lied to them about Vietnam, and that conventional protests had proven useless.

The existence of COINTELPRO was the single most earth-shaking revelation in the stolen documents, among which was Hoover's incendiary '67 COINTELPRO memo, the one in which he pledged to "discredit" and "neutralize" leftist organizations. With his pet project exposed, Hoover took steps to end COIN-TELPRO. But the burglary inaugurated a spate of whistle-blowing that undermined the FBI's credibility over the next few years. Congressman Hale Boggs, the House Majority Leader, compared the FBI to the "secret police," conceding that even Congress lived in fear of them, and that they'd "hastened the growth of a vine of tyranny." Lawsuits brought under the Freedom of Information Act forced the attorney general to reveal more incriminating FBI files. By 1975, anti-intelligence sentiment was so high that Congress formed a committee to scrutinize the Bureau.

Led by Senator Frank Church, of Idaho, the committee's investigation exposed FBI duplicity on a scale that had been unthinkable even after the Pennsylvania burglary. The Church Committee's findings, published in '76, gave the nation its first glimpse of the astonishing success that Hoover's counterintelligence operation had seen. As reported in the *New York Times* that May, the committee's final report determined that "FBI headquarters approved more than 2,300 actions in a campaign to disrupt and discredit American organizations ranging from the Black Panthers to Antioch College," and that the Bureau "may have violated specific criminal statutes" in pursuing actions that "involved risk of serious bodily injury or death to targets."

The Church Committee noted that COINTELPRO encompassed "a staggering range of targets," and that the FBI's deployment of "dangerous, degrading, or blatantly unconstitutional techniques appears to have become less restrained with each subsequent program." Hoover had specifically requested that these techniques be "imaginative and hard-hitting," and they were—the FBI tried seemingly everything, from gossip to gunfights. The Bureau mailed pejorative articles and newspaper clippings to college administrators. Its agents tried to destroy marriages by writing unsigned, malicious, rumor-mongering letters. They smeared leftists as informants when they weren't, and they stoked the flames of internecine conflicts until they grew into feuds.

The committee detailed several of the FBI's exploits in Los Angeles, and by now I wasn't surprised by the scope of the mayhem. The operations described, especially the deadly ones, were equal parts sophisticated and reckless, with the Bureau taking great pains to install informants and incite violence with no care for the consequences. I looked for any signs of Manson, no matter how tangential—any pattern among law enforcement, any familiar name.

The most conspiratorial possibility, of course, would be that the FBI had carefully groomed Manson and pressed him into service as a COINTELPRO informant—but I knew that was the longest of long shots, and if the facts didn't lead me there, I had no desire to force the connection. Given the FBI's sloppiness, I wondered if Manson could have been implicated in other, more indirect ways, willingly or not. Maybe he wasn't an informant but had been close to someone who was; maybe someone like Reeve Whitson had influenced his actions from two or three degrees of removal; maybe someone at the sheriff's office had assisted the FBI.

I was encouraged by one simple fact: the FBI had behaved conspiratorially with COINTELPRO, early and often. One of its greatest coups came in January 1969, when G-men had incited the murders of two Black Panthers on the UCLA campus. FBI infiltrators had lied to the Panthers' rivals, the US Organization, telling them that the Panthers were meeting on the campus to plan their assassinations. US responded by ambushing two Panthers at a Black Student Union meeting and shooting them dead.

LASO knew that the Panthers were murdered because of the FBI's meddling. They didn't care. In fact, they hid the FBI's role in the violence. In their eyes, the most desirable outcome had been achieved: two Panthers were dead, three US gang members were in jail, and the American public was more fearful of black militants. The FBI used the incident to spur more violence between US and the Panthers, according to a 1970 memo from the Los Angeles Field Office:

> The Los Angeles Division is aware of mutually hostile feelings harbored between the organizations and the first opportunity to capitalize on the situation will be maximized. It is intended that the US Inc. will be appropriately and discreetly advised of the time and location of BPP [Black Panther party] activities *in order that the two organizations might be brought together and thus grant nature the opportunity to take her due course.*

That emphasis comes from the Church Committee, who noted that "due course," in this case, meant nothing less than first-degree murder. The committee's final report blasted the FBI for its complicity in the deaths of the Panthers. "The chief investigative branch of the Federal Government engaged in lawless tactics and responded to deep-seated social problems by fomenting violence and unrest," it wrote. "Equally disturbing is the pride which those officials took in claiming credit for the bloodshed that occurred."

Indeed, it seemed that whenever the FBI made headway with its tactics, it doubled down. Rather than halt its provocations as the Panthers and the US Organization claimed each other's lives, the FBI escalated the campaign, spreading propaganda, including political cartoons, designed to inflame the violence. "The FBI viewed this carnage as a positive development," the Church Committee wrote.

Maybe the most lacerating testimony came from William Sullivan, a high-ranking FBI official who'd helped implement COINTELPRO before Hoover fired him in 1971. Sullivan had masterminded an episode in which Coretta Scott King, Martin Luther King Jr.'s wife, received a recording in which her husband could be heard flirting with other women. Sullivan had deemed King "a fraud, demagogue, and scoundrel." Now, before the Church Committee, he allowed that the FBI's ruthless pragmatism had obscured any sense of morality he and his colleagues might've had. "Never once," he said, "did I hear anybody, including myself, raise the question: 'Is this course of action which we have agreed upon lawful? Is it legal? Is it ethical or moral?' ... The one thing we were concerned about was this: 'Will this course of action work? Will it get us what we want?'"

COINTELPRO's excesses were well documented, but the FBI's director—Clarence M. Kelley, who'd succeeded Hoover—refused to admit wrongdoing, defending the operations as a necessary precaution against violent extremists who hoped to "bring America to its knees." He added, "For the FBI to have done less under the circumstances would have been an abdication of its responsibilities to the American people."

"Lined Up Against the Wall with the Rest of the Whites"

When Hoover reconstituted COINTELPRO, he was already worried that America's black militants would be embraced by liberal whites, especially in a left-leaning place like Hollywood. In the August 1967 memo reanimating the counterintelligence program, he'd noted the importance of "prevent[ing] militant Black Nationalist groups and leaders from gaining respectability": "they must be discredited to the white community, both the responsible community and to the 'liberals' who have vestiges of sympathy for militant black nationalists simply because they are Negroes."

Two years later, the Panthers had become almost synonymous with Hollywood's liberal elite. Actresses such as Jane Fonda and Jean Seberg appeared at their rallies. Hoover felt he had to widen the chasm between blacks and whites in Los Angeles. In a November 1968 memo, an L.A. field agent discussed new efforts to spread disinformation to Hollywood's liberal whites.

In the context of the Tate–LaBianca murders, the memo is chilling. Remember, the Tate house by then had become a high-profile gathering place for liberal Hollywood—among others, for Fonda, Cass Elliot, and Warren Beatty, all three of whom were reportedly under FBI surveillance. Abigail Folger, who would die at the hands of the Family, was an outspoken civil rights activist. That year she campaigned for Tom Bradley, the first African American candidate for mayor of Los Angeles. Many in the Polanski–Tate crowd belonged to the White Panther party, explicit allies of the

Black Panthers, or to the Peace and Freedom Party of California, which also voiced its support. The FBI, according to the memo, planned to generate distrust through disinformation:

> The Peace and Freedom Party (PFP) has been furnishing the BPP with financial assistance. An anonymous letter is being prepared for Bureau approval to be sent to a leader of PFP in which it is set forth that the BPP has made statements in closed meetings that *when the armed rebellion comes the whites in the PFP will be lined up against the wall with the rest of the whites.*

Emphasis mine. The FBI would make it seem as if even sympathetic leftists were in the Panthers' crosshairs. Less than a year after this memo was written, Manson's followers lined up four denizens of liberal Hollywood in Roman Polanski's home and cut them to pieces, leaving slogans in blood to implicate the Black Panthers.

Of course, the FBI couldn't have done this work alone. They needed local law enforcement on their side, and, according to the Church Committee, they got it.

The committee looked into one of the most notorious COIN-TELPRO actions in L.A., the framing of Gerard "Geronimo" Pratt, a Black Panther and a decorated Vietnam vet. Pratt would be imprisoned for twenty-seven years for a murder the FBI knew he didn't commit. He was in Oakland at the time of the crime, four hundred miles away, at a Black Panther house that the Bureau had wiretapped. It had transcripts of a call he'd made to the Panther headquarters in Los Angeles just hours before the murder. Still, Bureau agents enlisted a federal informant to lie on the stand about Pratt's involvement. Even before the frame-up, FBI gunmen had attempted to kill Pratt by shooting at him through the window of his apartment; he survived only because a spine injury he'd sustained in the war made it more comfortable to sleep on the floor.

Pratt was serving a life sentence when the Church Committee released its landmark findings, confirming what he'd long suspected: LASO and the LAPD were complicit in the COINTELPRO operation. The committee quoted a report that the FBI's Los Angeles outpost had sent to Hoover himself, advising that "the Los Angeles [Field] Office [of the FBI] is furnishing on a daily basis information to the Los Angeles County Sheriff's Office Intelligence Division and the Los Angeles Police Department Intelligence and Criminal Conspiracy Divisions concerning the activities of black nationalist groups in the anticipation that such information might lead to the arrest of the militants." This meant that Los Angeles law enforcement may have been guilty of obstructing justice and hindering prosecution.

Manson the Race Warrior

If there was a bridge between the Family and COINTELPRO, I thought it probably stemmed from this basic fact: Charles Manson was a racist. According to Gregg Jakobson, Manson sincerely believed that "the black man's sole purpose on earth was to serve the white man." Another member of the Family recalled that Manson looked forward to the day when, having survived the apocalyptic race war, he could "scratch blackie's fuzzy head and kick him in the butt and tell him to go pick the cotton."

And at the start of '69, as COINTELPRO provoked black militants in L.A., Manson's bigotry reached a delusional fever pitch. He became convinced, seemingly without a shred of evidence, that the Black Panthers were spying on the Family at the Spahn Ranch, planning an attack on him. His paranoia mounting, Manson placed armed guards at every entrance to the ranch, sending lookouts to the mountains with powerful telescopes.

His fear was self-fulfilling, in a way. On July 1, 1969, during a dispute over drug money in a Hollywood apartment, Manson shot Bernard "Lotsapoppa" Crowe, a black drug dealer. According to *Helter Skelter,* the dealer had told Manson that he was a Panther, and that his "brothers" would "come and get" Manson at the ranch if he didn't pay up. Manson shot Crowe in the chest and fled the scene, believing he'd killed the dealer. Back at the ranch, Manson was sure that Crowe's friends were readying their attack. In Bugliosi's account, this contributed to Manson's decision a month later to "speed along the race war" by inciting "Helter Skelter": the Tate–LaBianca murders would sow racial discord.

But Bernard Crowe wasn't a Black Panther. And he survived after Manson shot him—Bugliosi even called him to the stand during the trial. Bugliosi chalked it up to a misunderstanding on Manson's part, but the more I thought about it, especially in light of what I'd learned about COINTELPRO, the more I wondered if there was more to the story. The prosecutor reported that Manson was already frightened of the Black Panthers before the Crowe shooting. If Manson were truly scared of the Panthers, the last thing he would have done is shoot a man whom he believed to be a Panther—a man who'd already told his "brothers" where Manson lived, and made a threat to kill him. True, Manson hoped to launch a race war, but he didn't want to be caught in its crossfire. That was a fate he wished on other whites, but never on himself.

Furthermore, Tex Watson's girlfriend and three of Crowe's friends had witnessed the shooting; they called an ambulance after Manson made his getaway. At the hospital, Crowe refused to tell the police who'd shot him. Wouldn't the police have questioned the four witnesses? Did Crowe even say who they were? Why didn't the police pursue a near fatal shooting with plenty of witnesses, especially when the alleged shooter was a paroled ex-con?

We might never know—Bugliosi doesn't clarify any of it in *Helter Skelter.*

I'd always considered the Crowe shooting an inexplicable sideshow in the Manson circus. It took on grander proportions after I'd learned about the FBI's disinformation campaign against the Panthers—at this same time, this same place. Less than a week after the Tate murders, further COINTELPRO provocations led to the shootings of three more Panthers, one of them fatal.

The CIA on Domestic Soil

In August 1967, the same month Hoover launched COINTEL-PRO, CIA director Richard Helms inaugurated the agency's aforementioned illegal domestic surveillance program, CHAOS, which also employed agents and informants to infiltrate "subversive" groups and then "neutralize" them.

CHAOS was born of Lyndon Johnson's neurosis. In the summer of '67, the president was convinced that the divided, disorderly America he led couldn't possibly be the product of his own policies. Foreign agents, and presumably foreign money, must be to blame. He ordered the CIA to prove that the nation's dissidents, and especially its antiwar movement, had their origins abroad.

Richard Helms complied without hesitation. In the six years that followed, the CIA tracked thousands of Americans, insulating its information gathering so thoroughly that even those at the top of its counterintelligence division were clueless about its domestic surveillance. CHAOS kept tabs on three hundred thousand people, more than seven thousand of them American citizens. The agency shared information with the FBI, the White House, and the Justice Department. At its peak, CHAOS had fifty-two dedicated agents, most of whom served to infiltrate antiwar groups, like their counterparts in the FBI. Undercover, they hoped to identify Russian instigators, although they never found any. With the Interdivision

Intelligence Unit (IDIU), a new branch of the Justice Department outfitted with sophisticated computerized databases, they collaborated on a list of more than ten thousand names, all thought to be dangerous activists; the IDIU produced regular reports on these people, hoping to predict their activities.

The journalist Seymour Hersh got wind of CHAOS late in 1974. He told James Jesus Angleton, the head of CIA counterintelligence, and William Colby, the director of the CIA, that he had a story "bigger than My Lai" about CIA domestic activities. Colby was forced to admit that Hersh's findings were accurate, and Angleton resigned from the agency. The story broke on December 22, on the front page of the *New York Times:* "Huge CIA Operation Reported in U.S. Against Anti-War Forces, Other Dissidents in Nixon Years."

The Church Committee probed the CIA's illegal activities, as did a separate government investigation, the Rockefeller Commission—but neither was able to penetrate the agency's veil of secrecy. Since the CIA has no right to operate on American soil, the program should have brought even more censure than COINTELPRO; instead, it drew only a muted response. CIA leadership stonewalled at every opportunity. Even if they hadn't, investigators were crippled by the dearth of information. When Richard Helms had disbanded CHAOS before leaving office in 1973, he ordered the destruction of every file pertaining to it, and since the seventies, almost nothing has come out. The operation hardly left a footprint.

Even if reams of paperwork had survived, the Rockefeller Commission was hardly willing to press the agency. While the commission made some shocking findings—evidence of wiretaps, bugging, and hidden burglaries, in addition to the extensive record keeping mentioned above—by the end of the seventies, well after it had disbanded, allegations arose that it had suppressed information. (Its chairman, Vice President Nelson Rockefeller, had worked with the CIA in the late fifties.) In a memoir, former CIA director Colby later claimed that President Gerald Ford fired him for refusing to help Rockefeller sabotage his own investigation. According to Colby, CHAOS was so highly classified that even he, the director of the CIA, didn't have access to it. "I found it impossible to do much about whatever was wrong with [CHAOS]," he wrote. "Its super-secrecy and extreme compartmentalization kept me very much on its periphery."

In the spring of '78, the *New York Times* revealed that the investigations into CHAOS had been woefully inadequate. When one agent was asked why he hadn't been more forthcoming, he said simply, "They didn't ask." The true extent of the agency's domestic activities against dissidents would probably never be known, the *Times* declared—but the paper had been able to uncover CHAOS activities from the late sixties that had targeted the Black Panther party. Rockefeller's commission failed to reveal that "between 150 and 200 CIA domestic files on Black dissidents had been destroyed," the *Times* reported. "The CIA conducted at least two major programs involving the use of American blacks, when the Panthers, organized by young blacks in the mid-60s, were publicly advocating revolutionary change...Just how successful the CIA was in those alleged activities could not be determined."

Winning Hearts and Minds

Knowing more about CHAOS and COINTELPRO, I felt that men like Reeve Whitson were potentially much more common than I'd anticipated, always in peripheral, undefined roles. Part of the reason that Whitson seemed like such a wild card to me was that he appeared to have walked on the scene from nowhere: an outré, worldly man suddenly hobnobbing with the LAPD's top brass. I wanted others who fit that profile. To cover up an operation like

CHAOS, the agency needed friends in law enforcement—insiders who could make arrests or, just as important, not make arrests.

The most promising but frustrating of my inquiries concerned an LAPD officer named William W. Herrmann. I could never connect him to Whitson or Manson, but he certainly fit the profile of someone who'd helped with counterintelligence actions. When I was deep in the weeds of my CHAOS research, split between feeling that I was onto something or that I was risking my credibility, Herrmann's was a name that came up several times—usually from sources I didn't quite trust, or in arcane articles from the alternative press. What I heard about him was just plausible enough to get me to look closer. I'm glad I did. Herrmann's story hints at how intelligence agencies may have collaborated with police in Los Angeles.

A longtime lieutenant with the LAPD, Herrmann had an unusual background for law enforcement. He had a doctorate in psychology; he specialized in quelling insurgencies; he'd developed one of the first computer systems to track criminals and predict violent outbreaks in cities. Daryl Gates, the head of the LAPD from 1978 to 1992, hailed him as a "genius," praising his technical aptitude in particular.

But Herrmann's work wasn't limited to Los Angeles, or even to the United States. My FOIA request to the FBI yielded a collection of redacted documents detailing his extensive employment history. Concurrent with his time in the LAPD, he'd worked under contract for a dizzying list of American intelligence and military agencies: the air force, the Secret Service, the Treasury Department, the President's Office of Science and Technology, the Institute for Defense Analysis, the Defense Industrial Security Clearance Office, and the Defense Department's Advanced Research Projects Agency. Most of his work for these groups remains classified.

You'd think these projects wouldn't have left much free time, but Herrmann piled on even more work, taking leaves of absence from the LAPD to pursue side gigs with defense firms. These had opaque, generic names like Electro-Dash Optical Systems, System Development Corp., and Control Data Corp. This last, a super-computer development firm with military contracts in Minneapolis, relied on Herrmann's services for ten years, from 1961 to '71 — or so Herrmann told the FBI. When the Bureau went to Control Data Corp. for a background check, the company claimed that Herrmann never worked for them.

You might have guessed: given Herrmann's long list of government employers, I wondered if his work for these defense contractors could have been a front for the CIA, one of the few agencies that *didn't* appear on his résumé. As usual, official channels were useless. My FOIA request to the CIA for Herrmann's records yielded the same "neither confirm or deny" response that Reeve Whitson's had.

I did find, however, a record of Herrmann's overseas work, much of which he conducted while still employed with the LAPD. Having spent four months in 1967 training Thai police in counter-insurgency tactics, Herrmann returned to Asia in September 1968 to join the U.S. effort in South Vietnam. Documents from the National Archives in College Park, Maryland, listed him as a sci-entific "advisor" to the army. His responsibility was to train South Vietnamese police in "paramilitary techniques" to deploy against Viet Cong insurgents. None of the records described those tech-niques in any detail, but the mere mention of them was enough to make me put a few things together. The dates of Herrmann's stint in Vietnam, his job description, his professional affiliations, and his training made it abundantly likely that he was working for a CIA project called Phoenix, one of the most controversial elements in the agency's history.

Lyndon Johnson had secretly authorized Phoenix in 1968; it was discontinued in early '71. The agency described it as "a set of pro-grams that sought to attack and destroy the political infrastructure of the Viet Cong." Inside Vietnam, Phoenix operatives waged a campaign of terror against the Viet Cong guerrillas, with tactics including the assassination and torture of noncombatant civilians. According to a 1971 congressional investigation, the program violated the codes of the Geneva Conventions and rivaled the Viet Cong's own terrorism in its mercilessness.

During the Senate hearings, a number of Phoenix operatives admitted to massacring civilians and making it appear that the atrocities were the work of the Viet Cong. Their hope was to "win the hearts and minds" of neutral Vietnamese citizens, compelling them to turn away from the insurgency in revulsion. A Special Forces soldier, Anthony Herbert, the single most decorated combat veteran of Vietnam, published a bestselling book, *Soldier,* that detailed typical orders from his Phoenix superiors: "They wanted me to take charge of execution teams that wiped out entire families and tried to make it appear as though the Viet Cong had done it themselves. The rationale was that the Viet Cong would see that other Viet Cong had killed their own and . . . make allegiance with us. The good guys."

Their attempts were sometimes even more unhinged. In 1968, CIA scientists at the Bien Hoa Prison outside Saigon surgically opened the skulls of three prisoners, implanted electrodes on their brains, gave them daggers, and left them alone in a room. They wanted to shock the prisoners into killing one another. When the effort failed, the prisoners were shot and their bodies burned.

According to Seymour Hersh's 1972 book, *Cover-Up,* Phoenix had "committees" set up across all forty-four provinces in South Vietnam. They kept blacklists of Viet Cong fighters and had strict orders to meet weekly or monthly quotas of "neutralizations." The whole operation relied on computerized indexes. The identity of its CIA leader never came to light—but whoever he was, he was there ostensibly as part of the Agency for International Development (AID), later revealed as a CIA front.

Herrmann, of course, was known for his aptitude with computers, and his time in Vietnam coincided almost exactly with Phoenix's operations. The papers I found at the National Archives confirmed that he was a part of AID.

I had no way to press him about any of this; he'd died in 1993. As I had with Whitson, I wondered whether his family could tell me more about him. I found one of his daughters, Cindy, a dog breeder in Spokane, Washington; she invited me to see her. Only a teenager in the sixties, she didn't have many memories of her father's work, but she was confident that much of it had been top-secret, and that he'd worked for the CIA. He never discussed his work with the family, not even her mother; she was instructed never to talk about her father with anyone, including extended family. She knew he did undercover work, both while he was with the LAPD and afterward. She showed me his passport. Visa stamps chronicled at least four trips to Vietnam between 1968 and '70. Among his ID cards was one for "The Xuat Nhap Vietnam Cong HOA."

She also shared several documents confirming Herrmann's participation in Phoenix. A framed memo from the U.S. Military Assistance Command, Vietnam, dated September 9, 1968, advised all personnel that Herrmann was a "member of the Pacification Task Force working for Ambassador Komer." Komer, first name Robert, was nicknamed "Blowtorch Bob" for his take-no-prisoners approach to warfare. He served fifteen years in the CIA before arriving in Vietnam to work on Phoenix; according to Senate testimony, he was behind the program's notorious kill quotas. Even Herrmann's ephemera captivated me. Cindy had held on to a photo of dozens of men on an airplane, captioned, " 'Bad guys' leaving a bad spot after having been bad."

Once he returned from Vietnam, Herrmann retired from the LAPD after more than twenty years on the force, embarking on a series of "research" gigs for various federal agencies—again, all top-secret. With information from Cindy, a growing pile of press clippings, and the government documents I'd amassed, I tried to piece together Herrmann's postretirement projects. Whatever he'd learned in Southeast Asia, he brought it back to L.A.—his work in California bore disturbing resemblances to the techniques he'd honed as part of the Phoenix project. In 1968, Governor Reagan appointed him to head a new Riots and Disorders Task Force, dedicated to studying urban unrest and devising ways to prevent future outbreaks of violence. But in a 1970 interview, Herrmann revealed, maybe by accident, that the task force was hardly the research-based enterprise it claimed to be.

Herrmann didn't give many interviews, but when he spoke to the *London Observer*'s Charles Foley in May 1970, he was apparently in a voluble mood. Discussing his work for the task force, he described a program of spying and infiltration far exceeding the "studies" that the group was committed to—his words sounded as if they'd been lifted from COINTELPRO and CHAOS manuals. (Both of those operations, of course, were well under way in Los Angeles.)

Like Governor Reagan and President Johnson, Herrmann believed that California's student dissidents were funded by foreign Communists. He told the *Observer* that he had a "secret plan" for "forestalling revolution in America." The key was "to split off those bent on destroying the system from the mass of dissenters; then following classic guerilla warfare 'theory' to find means which will win their hearts and minds." He called this plan, simply, "Saving America," and it included strategies for "deeper penetration by undercover agents into dissenting groups," such as "army agents pos[ing] as students and news reporters." In a turn worthy of *Minority Report,* he wanted to use mathematical probability models to predict when and where violence would erupt. He also called for the use of long-range electronic surveillance devices; if informants had already penetrated any "dissenting groups," they would "secretly record speeches and conversations."

What that information would be used for, and how, Herrmann didn't say. He spoke of the task force in the future tense, making it hard to discern how operational its "Saving America" tactics were. Whatever the case, his brazen claims generated backlash from the left. His daughter showed me a flyer from the Students for a Democratic Society depicting him as a pig. Maybe he felt he'd said too much—or maybe his superiors told him so—but a few months later, he gave another, more circumspect interview. Talking this time to the *Sacramento Bee*, he walked back some of his more chilling claims about "Saving America." "Herrmann bridles at an article in the *London Observer*," the reporter wrote, quoting Herrmann: "The council could not set up a plan like that...We have a nonoperational role. All we can do is review and fund projects suggested by local authorities."

"Saving America" sounded a lot like COINTELPRO, which sounded a lot like CHAOS—they all ran together, in part, it seemed, because they'd all shared notes. In June 2002, the *San Francisco Chronicle* published an investigative series detailing Governor Reagan's secret dealings with the CIA and the FBI, all part of his effort to halt what he construed as a Communist-sponsored antiwar movement in California. The *Chronicle* revealed an internal FBI memo from July 1969, when Herbert Ellingwood, one of the governor's top advisors, visited FBI headquarters to discuss Reagan's plans for the "destruction of disruptive elements on California campuses." As the *Chronicle* reported, "Ellingwood asked the FBI for 'intelligence' information against protest groups...the FBI had secretly given the Reagan administration such assistance in the past."

J. Edgar Hoover himself approved the request. The FBI suggested that the California state government might attack dissidents through "a psychological warfare campaign." If that's what Reagan wanted, he didn't have to look far. In his own circle of advisors was Herrmann, the chairman of the Riots and Disorders Task Force, a veteran of Phoenix, and a man whose antileftist ideas jibed perfectly with the Reagan's administration in Sacramento, to say nothing of the FBI's and the CIA's.

In 1978, a congressional committee uncovered evidence that the CIA had "operatives" in at least one city's district attorney's office in the late sixties. I wondered if a similar situation existed in Los Angeles and, if so, who those operatives might have been.

It wouldn't have been too difficult an agency to penetrate. At the time of the Manson murders, in 1969, the district attorney of Los Angeles was Evelle Younger, whose résumé linked him to tons of intelligence work. Decades earlier, he'd been "one of the top agents" of Hoover's FBI. In 1942, he left the Bureau to join the Office of Strategic Services. Trained in espionage and counterintelligence techniques, he opted to enroll in law school after the war.

In the fifties, Younger was elected to the bench before becoming Los Angeles district attorney in 1964. A staunch Republican and a friend of Governor Reagan, he was appointed head of a federal law-and-order task force in January 1969, organized by incoming president Richard Nixon to crack down on crime and internal threats to the nation's security. According to the 1974 book *Big Brother and the Holding Company: The World Behind Watergate*, the "politically ambitious" Younger advised Nixon to "appoint tougher judges, use more wiretaps, encourage 'space age techniques and hardware,' and support local police with better training and equipment."

Younger's subordinates in the DA's office referred to him as "the General." In his obituary, the *Los Angeles Times* in 1989 noted

that he was "the first prosecutor in America to undertake mass felony prosecutions of college campus demonstrators in the 1960s";
he'd prosecuted students who'd protested the absence of a black
studies program at San Fernando Valley State College. The November 1969 trial resulted in twenty convictions, a coup for the up-
and-coming deputy DA who tried the case: Vincent Bugliosi.

If the CIA wanted a presence in the Los Angeles DA's office,
Younger didn't strike me as someone who'd put his foot down.
Nor did his second in command, Lynn "Buck" Compton, who'd
been an LAPD detective before getting his law degree and joining
the DA's office. Compton was the lead prosecutor in the trial of
Sirhan B. Sirhan for the assassination of Senator Robert F. Kennedy. And he'd been a World War II hero—his exploits with the
parachute infantry regiment, the Easy Company, were chronicled
in the HBO miniseries *Band of Brothers*.

I found a letter that Compton wrote to Herrmann on March 14,
1969, five months before the Tate–LaBianca murders, thanking him
for "obtaining good advance intelligence…on subversives and militants." The two had served together on the LAPD in the fifties, so I
wasn't surprised that they knew each other. I *was* surprised that
Compton had written a note that all but proved that he and Herrmann were operating beyond their remit for the State of California.
Neither man had any business gathering "advance intelligence" on
"subversives and militants"—or on anyone else, for that matter. The
DA's office was supposed to prosecute crimes, not prevent them. And
Herrmann, in his strenuous correction to the *London Observer* article,
had stressed that his role was "nonoperational."

Coda: Front-Page News

I read about CHAOS and COINTELPRO until I must've sounded,
to all my friends, like a tinfoil-hat-wearing conspiracy theorist,

someone who might go off on a long-winded tangent about the threats of the deep state. But the fact that the CIA has become an all-purpose scapegoat—the preeminent symbol of global power run amok—doesn't change the fact that its abuses of power in the 1960s were legitimate and myriad. If anything, these abuses were so gross that they've lent authority to any and every claim against federal intelligence agencies: if the CIA and the FBI are capable of killing American citizens in cold blood, often in elaborate schemes, what *aren't* they capable of?

There had been a day in the summer of '69 when the major elements from my reporting collided on a single page of the *Los Angeles Times*. An August 12 article about the DA's argument in the UCLA Panther murder trial ("Panther Killings Result of Power Play, Jury Told") ran next to a piece on the LAPD's theory that the LaBianca killers were imitating the people who'd murdered the Tate victims the night before ("Police See 'Copycat Killer' in Slaying of Los Feliz Couple"). The irony was that both of these stories were wrong. The LaBianca murders weren't the work of a "copycat killer," and the police should've known by then; the real "power play" at UCLA was perpetrated by the FBI. I was tantalized by the juxtaposition of the two items: by how much of the "news" in them was flawed when it was first reported, and by how much of it might be flawed still.

Manson's race-war motive dovetailed almost too perfectly with the goals of these federal agencies and the DA's office. In programs like CHAOS and COINTELPRO—and in people like Reeve Whitson, William Herrmann, and Buck Compton—I saw the potential for a major turn in my reporting, even as I tried to accept that so much of what they did would always be untraceable.

Still, if nefarious plots from the CIA and FBI had eventually exploded into public view, I thought I should at least try to see where my hunches led me. What I wanted to answer was this: How did a body like the Los Angeles DA's office exert its political force?

If it wanted to be of service to a higher agency, like the FBI or the CIA, would that be easily accomplished, or was I veering too much into the realm of the paranoiac?

I didn't have to look very far to see how the DA's office wielded its power. One glaring example came at the start of the Manson trial, when, without anyone being the wiser, the DA's office conspired to make sure that its narrative for the Tate–LaBianca murders was the only one that anyone ever heard.

8

The Lawyer Swap

"My Hands Were Tied"

When it came to prosecuting the Manson Family, the Los Angeles DA's office left nothing to chance. I'd already seen that Vincent Bugliosi had no problem getting his witnesses to lie on the stand, and that Deputy DA Buck Compton gathered intelligence on "subversives and militants." What I found next was evidence of more pervasive, top-down interference by the DA's office, which took extraordinary measures to control, and likely in part to fabricate, the story of the Manson murders.

The first signs of misconduct came during the trial of Bobby Beausoleil. He was accused of murdering Gary Hinman, the musician who'd been found stabbed to death just days before the Tate–LaBianca murders.

For reasons never disclosed by Bugliosi, the DA's office tried Beausoleil separately from the rest of the Family. As I suggested earlier, it made sense to try all three of the murder cases together—Hinman, Tate, and LaBianca. Law enforcement had connected the crimes. Uniting them under a single trial would've made it easier to convict Manson of conspiracy, since he'd helped torture Hinman and had ordered all three sets of slaughters.

And yet they kept the cases separate. I thought I knew why. If they'd thrown Hinman in with Tate–LaBianca, the resulting testimony would have revealed that the Los Angeles County Sheriff's Office (LASO) knew as early as August 10 that the Manson Family was responsible for all the murders. Remember, LASO detectives Charlie Guenther and Paul Whiteley broke the Tate case when a recorded phone call from one of Hinman's murderers, Beausoleil, clued them in to a link with the Tate murders. The only way to hide this early break was to try the Hinman murder case separately.

Beausoleil went to trial on November 12, 1969. The prosecutor was Ronald Ross, the deputy DA in Santa Monica, who confirmed to me that the case had been tried separately under very suspicious circumstances. He had orders, he said, to keep Charles Manson and the Family out of the trial. That meant that scoring a conviction against Beausoleil would be an uphill battle — since, after all, without Manson's instructions, he may never have murdered Hinman.

Still, Ross felt he had no choice but to obey. "My hands were tied," he told me. When we first spoke, in 2000, he'd recently retired after thirty years in the DA's office, and the case sounded fresh in his mind. He remembered "the orders from on high: don't mention the name of Manson or these other people."

Ross later learned that his superiors at the DA's office, and his own investigating detectives, Guenther and Whiteley, had withheld all evidence related to the Manson Family from him to keep their secret. "I was pissed when I learned later that they had other evidence," Ross said. "I [was] closed out of the thing. I really don't know why they did that."

He could still recall the day the case first landed on his desk, in early September 1969. He was just back from a vacation. The horrors of the Tate–LaBianca murders, then only a month old, still dominated the news. The killers remained at large, and no one even knew who they were. Ross was struck by reports that they'd left the bloody word "Pig" in conspicuous areas of both the Tate and LaBianca homes. His Hinman murder scene featured such writing, too. He took one look at the case and immediately connected it to the unsolved Tate–LaBianca murders. "You'd have to be deaf, dumb, and blind not to," he said.

He called in Guenther and Whiteley to ask them about it. "And they said, 'Oh, no, no, it's not related. No, [we] can't find any connection between the two.'" He still sounded bruised when he added, "Now I think they were lying through their teeth."

Guenther denied the allegation to me, but I found it believable, given what he'd told me about his investigation. And if it's true, it shows that by September 1969, he and Whiteley were conspiring to hide what they'd learned about the Manson Family's role in the murders.

Since Ross wasn't allowed to link Beausoleil to the Family, his case was mostly circumstantial and, by his own admission, weak. After just two days of testimony, the trial was more or less wrapped up. Beausoleil's defense attorney, Leon Salter, didn't call a single witness. When the defense rested, Ross's superiors feared they might lose the trial; they needed more evidence. At the last minute, they decided to take a gamble.

Just before the attorneys delivered their closing arguments, David Fitts—the head deputy DA of Santa Monica, and Ross's supervisor—went into a closed meeting with the judge, who emerged ten minutes later to announce that the trial would be delayed for five days to accommodate a new witness for the prosecution: Danny DeCarlo, the Straight Satans bike-gang member who'd moved to the Spahn Ranch that spring of 1969.

The judge's action here was unprecedented, or close to it. For one thing, the two lawyers who'd just rested their cases, Ross and

Salter, had no say in it. Plus, as a matter of course, trials are almost never reopened after the defense has rested; it risks prejudicing the jury.

When I reached Salter on the phone, he was still incensed by the choice. "For the judge to discuss the case without the opposing attorney being present is just unheard of," he told me. "There was just something rotten about it...I never reported it to [the] state bar, which I'll always regret." In the trial transcript, Salter made his objections plain. "It is shocking," he told the judge, "that when you are in the middle of a trial, where this young man can end up with a life imprisonment, that the District Attorney...has the audacity to talk about this case without my being present."

You might think that Ross wouldn't have minded the intervention so much — Fitts was his boss, after all, and they were both angling for Beausoleil's conviction. But Ross bristled at having been excluded, too. In his thirty years as a DA, he told me, he'd never been left out of a meeting about his own witness lineup.

Ross felt he had no choice but to put DeCarlo on the stand. "That was the first time in my whole career where I was actually *ordered* to use a witness," Ross said. The decision came from the highest levels of the DA's office. Fitts was taking orders from someone. "My best estimate," Ross said, "would be Buck Compton."

Ross thought DeCarlo lacked credibility. The biker, already a convicted felon, had decided to testify only because he was facing new charges for marijuana possession and having stolen a motorcycle engine. He was, to use Ross's word, a snitch, and it was impossible to say if he was telling the truth or not. "DeCarlo was simply amoral," Ross said. "He could have said whatever he wanted to say." And getting something useful out of DeCarlo on the stand would be no mean feat, because Ross still wasn't allowed to introduce anything about Manson or the Family, even though his new witness was a known associate of theirs.

Once he was sworn in, DeCarlo relayed the story of the Hinman stabbing. He claimed he was telling it exactly as he'd heard it from Beausoleil himself. He even included the parts where a man named Charlie, who lived at the Spahn Ranch, cut Hinman's ear off with "a long sword," and later ordered Beausoleil to kill Hinman, telling him, "You know what to do." But he never gave Charlie's full name.

Then came Salter's cross-examination.

"This person Charlie that you referred to in your testimony," he said to DeCarlo. "Were you aware of this person Charlie's full name?"

"Charles Manson," DeCarlo said. It was the first time the name had been uttered in the whole trial—on the last day of testimony.

That was November 24. Outside the courtroom, police and district attorneys were finally making headway on the Tate–LaBianca crimes. Like Ross, Salter knew enough to suspect a link. The prosecution's sudden addition of DeCarlo only encouraged those suspicions. Salter knew that police had questioned DeCarlo about the Tate murders, and he intended to let the jury know it, too.

Manuel Gutierrez, an LAPD officer who'd been the first to hear DeCarlo's story, took the stand to lend the biker some credibility. Salter tried to get the information out of him. "Sir," he asked, "you were investigating the Tate murder case at that time, were you not?"

Ross objected; the court sustained.

"Your Honor, may I be heard on this?" Salter said. At the bench, out of earshot from the jury, Salter argued that the jurors should know that DeCarlo was connected to the unsolved Tate murders. "I think we can prove [Gutierrez] was interviewing [DeCarlo] with regard to the Tate murder case," he said. "If it was a small case, fine, but he is investigating a case in which there has been so much publicity, and they are rather anxious, I imagine, to find out who did it."

But the judge allowed no further questions on the topic, and that was the last anyone heard of a potential connection to the Tate murders.

Ironically, the addition of DeCarlo did nothing to help the prosecution. The jurors didn't trust him any more than Ross did. The trial ended in a hung jury. Thanks to Ross's candor, it is clear that the lack of evidence could be blamed squarely on the higher-ups in the DA's office: they needed to cover up Guenther and Whiteley's early knowledge of the Manson Family as the Tate–LaBianca murderers.

"Warm and Sticky and Nice"

As they tailored the Hinman trial to suit the needs of the state, Buck Compton and Vincent Bugliosi were also behind the scenes of the Tate–LaBianca case. The DA's office knew it needed a momentous conviction, a sense of justice befitting the crime of the century. And Bugliosi, who aspired to power and celebrity, saw how much he could gain from some good publicity here. His office needed to control the narrative from the start, whether they had the evidence to back it up or not.

Even in clear-cut circumstances, a criminal trial is a messy, protracted affair—and once the verdict comes in, all the particularities fade from the public mind. In the fifty years since Manson and his followers were convicted, the details have become largely irrelevant. If people recall any aspect of the trial, it's usually the testimony of Linda Kasabian, the state's star witness. She'd served as a lookout and a driver for the Family during both nights of murders. Granted immunity, Kasabian was able to describe the crimes and the inner workings of the Family in nauseating detail, clinching the case against Manson. And while many observers weren't pleased that an accomplice to the murders would walk free, Kasabian took pains to appear more honorable than the others. She showed remorse; she emphasized that she hadn't participated in any of the violence.

What hardly anyone remembers is that Kasabian wasn't the first one in the Family to get a deal from the prosecutors. Before her was Susan Atkins, the woman who'd led the police to break the case—and who was eventually convicted along with the other killers, spending the rest of her life in prison before her death in 2009. Before Kasabian flipped, Atkins, an unrepentant killer, was the foundation for the LAPD's case, and for the prosecution that followed.

To pursue the conviction of Manson, the prosecution first had to bring their charges before a grand jury. They relied strongly on Atkins's testimony there—it was instrumental in securing the first-degree murder indictments against Manson and five others, including herself. In short, it was her story that made Bugliosi's famous trial possible.

But I found two memos indicating that Atkins was improperly obtained as a witness. Before she or any other Manson followers had been charged, prosecutors colluded with a Superior Court judge to have her legally appointed defense attorney replaced by a former deputy DA who would do their bidding. Her story, sanctioned and tweaked by the DA's office and her planted defense attorney, was based on lies. The entire narrative put before that grand jury should be reconsidered.

It started with the end of the Family. About a month after the Tate–LaBianca murders that would bring them to infamy, they fled the Spahn Ranch; Manson believed the police were closing in on them. (He also feared retaliation from the Black Panthers, having mistakenly believed, as discussed in the last chapter, that he'd murdered one—Bernard Crowe, who was neither a Panther nor dead.) He resettled his clan deep in Death Valley, at an adjoining pair of remote, barren ranches called Myers and Barker. There they sustained themselves through petty crimes and an auto-theft ring. It was this last that brought them to the attention of Inyo County law enforcement, who tracked them to their compound and captured them in raids over two nights in mid-October 1969.

In Independence, California, the group of twenty-some bedraggled hippies sat in the cramped county jail. LASO detectives Guenther and Whiteley drove 225 miles to the dusty desert town to seek out a possible witness in the Hinman murder. You may remember her name: Kitty Lutesinger, Bobby Beausoleil's girlfriend, the same witness the detectives had seemingly deliberately failed to track down months earlier.

Lutesinger's parents had called the detectives to say that their daughter was in custody in Independence. When Guenther and Whiteley found her, she told them that Susan Atkins had boasted of torturing and finally killing Hinman with Beausoleil over two nights. The story aligned with what they'd already heard. They asked the Inyo County sheriff to take them to Atkins herself.

Atkins agreed to speak to the detectives without an attorney present. They told her that her fingerprints had been found at the Hinman crime scene and that Beausoleil had already ratted on her—both lies, but they got her talking about the crime. Atkins admitted to having held Hinman while Beausoleil stabbed him, but she claimed she never hurt him. She was booked on a first-degree-murder charge and transferred to the Sybil Brand Institute for Women, in downtown Los Angeles.

Atkins's cellmate was a longtime con artist and call girl who went by Ronnie Howard. The two became fast friends. Almost immediately, Atkins was telling Howard and another inmate, Virginia Graham, all about her role in the Tate–LaBianca murders. She had personally stabbed Sharon Tate to death, she bragged, as Tate begged for the life of her unborn baby. After Tate died, Atkins said she'd tasted the dead actress's blood; it was "warm and sticky and nice."

Howard was shocked. Here was a woman casually crowing about the biggest unsolved murder in Los Angeles history. On November 17, she made a hushed call from a pay phone to the Hollywood station of the LAPD, telling a detective that she knew who was responsible for the Tate–LaBianca murders.

That night, the LAPD sent two detectives to interview Howard at Sybil Brand. She convinced them easily of the veracity of her claims. Fearing for her safety, detectives had her moved to an isolated unit. The next morning, more detectives interviewed her, and that same day they brought their information to the district attorney, Evelle Younger. He assigned Aaron Stovitz and Vincent Bugliosi to prosecute the case. The Tate–LaBianca murders had been solved.

"Strong Client Control"

On the evening of November 19, Bugliosi attended a hastily convened meeting at the district attorney's office. In attendance were his immediate superior, Assistant District Attorney Joseph Busch; Aaron Stovitz, also from the DA's office; and, from the LAPD, Lieutenant Paul LePage and Sergeant Mike McGann, of the LaBianca and Tate investigative teams, respectively.

With the consent of the DA's office, the LAPD wanted to cut a deal with Susan Atkins: she'd share what she knew about the murders in exchange for immunity. Bugliosi thought this was a grave error. Atkins, he reminded his colleagues, had described personally stabbing Sharon Tate to death and tasting her blood. She'd admitted stabbing other victims at the Tate house. She'd participated in the murder of Gary Hinman. And that was only what they'd heard so far—who knows what else she'd done? "We don't give that gal anything!" he claimed to have said.

But the LAPD was adamant. For months, they'd been under enormous pressure to solve the case. The press had derided them constantly for their failure. Now they could announce their success with a splashy press conference and rush the case to a grand jury. Bugliosi countered that they were getting ahead of themselves. They didn't have a case yet, only a solid lead.

The group reached a compromise: instead of total immunity, Atkins would be offered a second-degree-murder plea, sparing her the death penalty while ensuring she wouldn't walk free. But, as Bugliosi acknowledged in *Helter Skelter,* they didn't work out "the precise terms" of this offer. One of the most pressing concerns went unaddressed: Would Atkins have to testify at the trial—before the public, and Manson himself—or only for the grand jury?

However Bugliosi claimed to have felt about Atkins, the district attorney's office was desperate to secure her cooperation; without it, they weren't sure they could indict Manson and the other killers. A lot depended on her reliability and consistency. What if she changed her story, which, so far, they'd only heard from her cellmate? And even more was riding on her defense attorney—if he didn't like the deal, he could prove to be a major obstacle. Rather than risk that, the DA's office decided they'd do better to replace him with someone guaranteed to play by their rules—and someone who could make sure Atkins said the right thing at the right time.

Atkins's attorney was Gerald Condon, a lawyer in private practice who'd been legally appointed by a judge to represent her in the Hinman murder. Normally, the court would've assigned her someone from the public defender's office, but they couldn't do that here—Beausoleil, her accomplice in the Hinman killing, was already represented by a public defender, and in such cases the court had to avoid a potential conflict of interest. So Condon it was.

Condon was appointed on November 12. Two weeks later, on November 26, he was out.

What happened? In the LASO archives, I found a seven-page memo that gave me a good lead. In an entry for November 20—the day after the DA's office and the LAPD had agreed to attempt a deal with Atkins—the document notes a never-before-reported meeting between LASO officers, the LAPD, and "Mr. Compton and Mr. Stovitz of the DA's office." The men discussed the fact that "the Atkins woman would be in court on 11-26-69 for the Superior Court arraignment, *at which time it was stated that there would be a change of her counsel and Mr. Caballero would be designated as her counsel*" (emphasis added). There's no mention of Condon's or Atkins's consent to this change. And it was presented as a fait accompli. This meeting came six days *before* the hearing in question—and yet all parties involved were already certain of the outcome. How?

A second, less ambiguous document turned up in the files of LAPD lieutenant Paul LePage. It was a three-page summary of his investigative work on the LaBianca murders. A section on Susan Atkins's court appearances described the same November 20 meeting in more detail: "It was decided that because of the gravity of the case and the importance of Atkins's information and cooperation, that her attorney be the type who had 'strong client control.' Deputy District Attorney Fitts made several inquiries and it was decided that Condon might not have the necessary control."

So, behind Atkins's and Condon's backs, Fitts "recommended Dick Caballero as an attorney who had good client control and would properly represent his client." Fitts got in touch with Judge Mario Clinco, who was overseeing the case, "and arrangements were made for Caballero to be appointed as Atkins's attorney of record at her felony arraignment. This was accomplished."

"This was accomplished"—yes, it was, with no small contribution from Fitts, the same DA who'd inserted himself in the Beausoleil trial.

According to the minutes of Atkins's November 26 arraignment, the judge assigned Caballero to the case right then and there. No mention was made of Condon's removal—or how or why it occurred. The full transcript of the hearing has vanished from the archives of the Los Angeles Superior Court. The court's spokesperson told me that a thorough search of the archive produced no results.

I called Condon to ask him about his removal from the case. He confirmed that he'd been replaced against his wishes—and his client's—and that Judge Clinco had never given him a reason.

"Whatever was going through Clinco's mind, I don't know," Condon told me. "Atkins did ask that I stay on." He remembered being "temporarily distressed" by Clinco's action, but he never complained to the court about it. Once the news came that Atkins was involved in the Tate–LaBianca murders, his wife told him she'd leave him if he tried to represent her again.

That was that. The LAPD and the district attorney's office had quietly decided that their star witness needed a certain lawyer. Whether she or her attorney wanted it or not, they "accomplished" it.

"Improper and Unethical"

In addition to his much vaunted "client control," the replacement lawyer, Richard Caballero, had another quality that endeared him to the DA's office: he'd worked there himself for eight years. As a prosecutor, Caballero had won five death-penalty convictions, and he was still close with his former colleagues. Bugliosi, Compton, and the others could trust him. Now all he had to do was get Atkins to take the deal. She didn't have to stay under his thumb forever, just long enough to make it through the grand jury and bring on the indictments they needed.

We'll never know exactly what Caballero promised Atkins, or how he laid out the terms of the deal: unlike most agreements of this nature, hers was never formalized in writing, never marked by her signature. Whatever he said, it was enough to satisfy the higher-ups at the LAPD and the DA's office. On December 1, they were finally ready to tell the public: they'd solved the case of the century.

That was the day Police Chief Edward Davis got his big press conference: sturdy podium, cameras rolling, hundreds of stunned and eager reporters jostling for space. Reading from prepared remarks, Davis doled out the details sparingly. He didn't even provide Manson's name, announcing that "legal restrictions prohibit the revelation of further information at this time." Pressed for more information about the suspects, he said only that they were part of a "roving band of hippies" that called itself "The Family" and were led by a man they called "Jesus."

Davis had to be judicious, or at least appear to be. A thorough account of the murders could taint the jury pool. The next day, however, an endless trough of specifics came flooding out, provided by two unassailable, on-the-record sources: Atkins's new attorney, Richard Caballero, and his law partner, Paul Caruso.

Acting as no less than a bullhorn for the DA's office, Caballero and Caruso—the latter a well-known mob lawyer and a longtime friend of Los Angeles DA Evelle Younger—outlined what would become, in essence, the prosecution's case for murder against the Manson Family.

Standing on the steps of the Santa Monica Courthouse, Caballero told gathered reporters that Atkins was a follower of Charles Manson, and that she'd been "at the scene of the Tate slayings, the Hinman murder, and the killings of the LaBiancas." Atkins was under Manson's "hypnotic spell," but she had "nothing to do with the murders"—seemingly his only effort at exonerating her amid the onslaught of grim particulars. He added that Manson called himself "both God and the Devil," and that the police had told him "that Atkins and the others were directed by Manson to go to both the Hinman house and the Tate house." Atkins would "tell her complete story" to the grand jury later that week.

In *Helter Skelter,* Bugliosi claimed that he'd come across Caballero's comments in the evening paper, and that was the only way his office learned that Atkins had accepted their deal. He never even tried to explain why it wasn't in writing or why Caballero wouldn't have alerted him more formally.

Over the next few days, Caballero and Caruso kept talking to the press—and talking, and talking. In case there was lingering ambiguity, they described Manson's dictatorial methods. They offered a timeline of events for the nights of the murders, including the order of the deaths. They tossed in sordid details, describing the killers' dress code and noting that, after killing the LaBiancas, they'd helped themselves "to a snack from the icebox."

It was a four-day fusillade of specificity. Finally, on December 4, the president of the Los Angeles County Bar had had enough. "Bar Chief Scores Atkins Attorney over Tate Comments," read the Santa Monica *Evening Outlook*'s front page, quoting him as he accused Caballero and Caruso of "entirely improper and unethical" conduct by "revealing vital facts about the Sharon Tate murder case from the viewpoint of Miss Atkins."

But the scrutiny didn't last. Amid the swell of coverage on the murders, no one seemed to mind the lawyers' leaking. In a passing remark to the *Los Angeles Times* on the day before Atkins's grand jury testimony, Caballero more or less admitted that he wasn't acting in his client's best interest, saying he was "gambling that her voluntary testimony might save her from the gas chamber"—"gambling" and "might" being the operative words.

Bugliosi and his team had essentially arranged for the defense lawyers to taint the jury on the prosecution's behalf: everyone in Los Angeles was suddenly an expert on the Manson Family. Meanwhile, on December 4, as they continued their press tour, Caballero and Caruso met with the DAs to finalize their "deal." Bugliosi described it as "excellent"; it was, in fact, nonexistent. As all the parties present would later admit during the death-penalty phase of the trial, nothing was ever formalized or signed.

The next day, Atkins testified before the grand jury, as promised. The papers reported that Manson, Atkins, Linda Kasabian,

Patricia Krenwinkel, Leslie Van Houten, and Tex Watson had been indicted on seven counts of murder after only twenty minutes of deliberation.

Soon after, Caballero and Caruso walked away from the case, richer and more famous, with no apparent regrets. A reporter asked Bugliosi if he would have gotten the indictments without Atkins's cooperation. He answered, "Do the French drink wine?"

The Shape-Shifting Deal

When Bugliosi made his "deal" with Caballero, he knew full well that Atkins was an unstable witness and a murderer. He needed her to get indictments for the other members of the Family, but he also needed a pretext to back away from her after she'd served her purpose. It wouldn't look good if he could only score convictions by easing up on one of the killers. His reversal would be a lot easier since the deal wasn't on paper, but even so, he'd have to provide some explanation if and when the prosecution parted ways with her.

Before Bugliosi put Atkins in front of the grand jury, he approved an odd request from her lawyers: to have her removed from jail and brought to their offices in Beverly Hills for a taped interview. In *Helter Skelter,* calling the arrangement "unusual" but "not unprecedented," Bugliosi claimed that his team went along with it because they thought Atkins would speak more freely away from her fellow inmates. But it also set up a chain of events that allowed the prosecutor to rid himself of her.

In the comfort of Caballero's office, Atkins spoke on tape for two and a half hours about her role in the murders. Listening the next day, Bugliosi noticed that she'd changed her story. At first, she'd told her cellmates that she'd stabbed Sharon Tate. Now she claimed that she couldn't bring herself to do it, and instead held Tate by the arms while Watson stabbed her. That's what she told the grand jury, too: that she didn't kill Sharon Tate. But the discrepancy wasn't a problem for Bugliosi as long as he got his indictments.

Throughout *Helter Skelter,* Bugliosi inadvertently proved how malleable the Atkins deal was, describing it in different terms at different times. Early in the narrative, he said that all she had to do was testify truthfully to the grand jury and cooperate with authorities; she'd never have to testify against her codefendants at the actual trial. In exchange, the prosecution would *consider* not asking for the death penalty.

But after the grand jury, the deal changed. Suddenly, she *did* have to testify against the others. Without her, "we still didn't have a case," Bugliosi wrote. Later still, he said that the prosecution was "stuck" with Atkins on the stand because of the deal, bemoaning the fact that he'd made an agreement with a killer.

I tend to think this is all rhetorical hand-wringing—a way of upping the stakes in his book when really he knew that Atkins was never going to take the stand.

Caballero, in fact, was doing everything in his power to lead his client away from testifying. He allowed Atkins to take visits from her former friends in the Family, who came bearing messages from Manson. The lawyer knew full well that, given enough exposure to her former lifestyle, Atkins was likely to return to Manson's fold and refute her grand jury testimony. It worked. One day, she called Caballero and told him that she refused to testify at the trial. It was her first step toward formally undoing everything—except the indictments, which couldn't be undone. Bugliosi fretted that he'd lost his "star witness."

But inwardly, he must have been pleased. Although he omitted it from his book, he was already in negotiations with the attorney of Linda Kasabian, a far more sympathetic witness, to cut a deal and take Atkins's place at the trial. Of course, had Atkins's attorneys been independently appointed, they would've reminded the prosecution of the terms of *her* deal, which precluded her testimony at the trial. Now Bugliosi could claim that she'd violated the deal and would lose her security against the death penalty.

Atkins kept unraveling. On March 5, 1970, in the attorney's room at the Central County Jail, Caballero presided over an hour-long reunion between his client and Manson. He described it as "joyous," adding that Atkins and Manson "both burst into laughter when their eyes met for the first time in five months." The meeting was only possible because Judge William Keene had granted Manson the right to represent himself—an allowance that shocked the courtroom. As his own attorney, Manson was entitled to meet with his jailed codefendants on the pretext of interviewing them as possible witnesses in the case against him. Among his first requested interviews was the woman responsible for his indictment: Susan Atkins.

After their meeting, a reporter asked Atkins if Manson had ordered her to "change the story she related to the grand jury." Atkins responded just as Caballero and the prosecution always knew she would: "Charlie doesn't give orders. Charlie doesn't command"—contradicting the thrust of her grand jury testimony, of course.

The day after the meeting, Atkins fired Caballero and Caruso. She announced that she was recanting her grand jury testimony and formally declined to testify for the state. That same day, Judge Keene revoked Manson's right to represent himself, arguing that he had filed too many "outlandish" and "nonsensical" motions.

Caballero later testified that, after he was fired, he didn't check in with the prosecution about the status of Atkins's deal. But in an interview with the *Hollywood Citizen News* several weeks after his firing, he made the status of the deal crystal clear: it didn't exist. "Susan Atkins' former attorney, Richard Caballero, said that no deal had been made which caused her to testify before the grand jury," the paper reported.

The "excellent deal" that Bugliosi had written of was no deal at all. Its nonexistence has gone unnoticed all these years. Who cares about the legal vagaries of a confessed killer like Susan Atkins? But without this hoax of a deal—and the lawyer swap that enabled it—Manson and his followers may never have been indicted, and the reigning narrative of Manson as an all-controlling cult leader may never have come out.

Gary Fleischman, Linda Kasabian's attorney—he now goes by Gary Fields—told me that he was convinced the DA was "instrumental in getting Dick Caballero appointed," and that Bugliosi never had any intention of keeping his deal with Atkins. "They used [her] to get an indictment," he said, "and then they dumped her because they couldn't use her at trial because she was dirty." The whole thing "smelled to high heaven," he continued. "Caballero and Caruso got away with fucking murder. They sold her down the river." It was a stunning assessment from Fields. No one had benefited more from Caballero and Caruso's dirty dealings than his client.

Ice Cream for Atkins

Caballero had another coup during his tenure as Atkins's lawyer: he made sure that her story was heard around the world, in all its gory, self-incriminating detail.

A few days before Atkins's grand jury testimony, her attorneys met with a self-described "Hollywood journalist and communicator" named Lawrence Schiller to negotiate the publication of her firsthand account of the murders. Essentially, the text would be an edited transcription of the recording she'd made in Caballero's office, with her byline slapped on it. Caballero and Caruso later claimed that they intended for the story to appear only overseas, far from the eyes of any potential jurors in Los Angeles. But such was not the case. On Sunday, December 14, Atkins's byline landed on the front page of the *Los Angeles Times*. "Her" piece ran to 6,500 words, spilling across three full pages.

The piece was an immediate sensation, far and away the most robust account of the Manson murders available to the public. Readers in Los Angeles—and within twenty-four hours, in nearly every place on the planet with a printing press—now had all the lurid details, including those that had been kept from the public by both the prosecution and the other killers' defense attorneys. The piece spiked a vulgar account of the bloodshed with hints of Atkins's naive girlishness. "My lawyer is coming soon," it ended, "and he's bringing me a dish of vanilla ice cream. Vanilla ice cream really blows my mind." As *Rolling Stone* put it later, "Any doubts about Manson's power to cloud men's minds were buried that morning between *Dick Tracy* and one of the world's great real estate sections."

And that, it seemed, was the real purpose of the piece—to eliminate any doubts about Manson the public might've had. In just the first column of the article, Atkins used the word "instructed" five times in reference to Manson's role in the killings. Everything she and the Family did was on Manson's orders, she said. He was a criminal mastermind, a cult leader, a conspiring lunatic.

The task of assembling an unbiased jury was suddenly a lot harder. A spokesperson for the Southern California branch of the American Civil Liberties Union told *Newsweek,* "The interview makes it all but impossible for [the defendants] to get a fair trial in Los Angeles." Bugliosi, craving convictions and the deluge of publicity from a high-profile trial, was presumably unbothered by this.

But Caballero should've been bothered. Even though this piece was in effect a continuation of the many detailed press conferences he'd given, he went through the motions of outrage. Claiming to be "shocked and surprised," he told the press that Schiller had double-crossed him, breaking a promise that the story wouldn't appear in the United States. Although Caballero threatened lawsuits, they never materialized. (Schiller later testified that he had nothing to do with planting the story.)

Nor did Caballero make any effort to halt the dissemination of the story, which continued apace. One week later, Schiller released an expanded version in a "quickie" paperback called *The Killing of Sharon Tate: Exclusive Story by Susan Atkins, Confessed Participant in the Murder.* In the acknowledgments, he thanked "several attorneys involved in this case" and "two journalists," writing, "Without their help this book could not have been produced."

Bugliosi maintained that his office had no idea the story was coming until that fateful issue of the *Times* landed on his doorstep. He hadn't learned a thing about the sale of Atkins's story, he claimed in *Helter Skelter,* until the death-penalty phase of the trial. At that point, since Atkins was eligible for the death penalty, her (third) new attorney, Daye Shinn, made an attempt to save her life by arguing that Caballero had misrepresented her. He called on everyone involved in the publication of her story to explain themselves. Reading the transcript, I learned that the DA's office not only was aware of the planned publication, but may have facilitated it. And, of course, *Helter Skelter* left all of this out.

The key to the scheme was Lawrence Schiller, the so-called communicator who'd brokered the publication deal. This wasn't Schiller's first high-profile article. Among other pieces, he'd arranged to publish the "deathbed confession" of Lee Harvey Oswald's murderer, Jack Ruby; nude photos of Marilyn Monroe; and photos of the comedian Lenny Bruce lying dead on his bathroom floor. He finished the Atkins deal on December 8, when the contract was signed—just in the nick of time. Two days later, Judge Keene issued a gag order, making it illegal for anyone involved to talk to the press.

That should've brought a decisive end to the publication. But in violation of the gag order, Caballero drove Jerry Cohen, a *Los Angeles Times* reporter and a friend of Schiller, to interview his client in jail. Cohen had been tapped to ghostwrite the piece. His main source was the taped account that Atkins had made in Caballero's office. But apparently he needed more material, and the lawyer was happy to accommodate him.

In the car that evening, besides Caballero and Cohen, were Schiller and a stenographer, Carmella Ambrosini. At the jail, Cohen and Ambrosini went inside to interview Atkins. The purpose of the visit, as recorded in the visitors' log at Sybil Brand, was to discuss a "future psychiatric evaluation."

Remember, Caballero had earlier claimed that Atkins could speak safely only at his Beverly Hills offices. Now a journalist and a stenographer were talking with her right there in jail. They spoke for about an hour. When they got back in the car, Caballero made an unusual demand of Ambrosini: he told the stenographer to pull out a small section of the tape from her machine, maybe about three minutes' worth, and give it to him. Caballero "ripped the tape into tiny pieces," Ambrosini later testified, "and then threw them on the floor of the car. Then he picked them up from the floor and put them into his pocket."

On the stand, Caballero finally admitted that the taped section contained comments from Atkins suggesting that she'd lied to the grand jury at his direction. She'd said something to the effect of "Okay, I played your game. I testified. I said what you wanted me to say, I don't want to do it anymore"—at which point he told her to stop talking. Under more persistent questioning, Caballero conceded that Atkins "used the word 'lie'" and "appeared" to be "repudiating" her grand jury testimony.

It was the closest thing to an admission that Caballero had manipulated Atkins—that her testimony, and all the indictments that stemmed from it, were unreliable. But again, because Atkins was a confessed murderer, this hardly seemed remarkable to the media. And, of course, the story of *how* Caballero and Caruso became Atkins's attorneys was locked in police vaults until I found it.

"Something Very Smelly"

Jerry Cohen was a ghostwriter in the purest sense of the word. No one was supposed to know that he'd finessed Atkins's words, let alone that he'd interviewed her in jail. To that end, Lawrence Schiller had presented himself unambiguously as Atkins's interlocutor. "I will be the first and the last newsman with whom Susan Atkins can speak freely until her fate is decided," he wrote in the paperback version of the Atkins story.

In fact, Schiller had been sitting outside in the car while Cohen talked to Atkins in jail. After that interview, Cohen ripped through his ghostwriting in two days at Schiller's house. Schiller made three carbon copies of the finished piece: one for Caballero; one for a German editor who'd bought the translation rights; and one to be flown overseas to the London *News of the World,* which had paid $40,000 for exclusive English rights. Or so said Bugliosi, who wrote in *Helter Skelter,* "How the *Los Angeles Times* obtained the story remains unknown."

Bugliosi did not write that Cohen, a reporter for the *Times,* was also a friend and collaborator of his. That relationship came out only when Bugliosi himself appeared as a witness during the trial's penalty phase. Under cross-examination, he admitted that he'd known Cohen for the "last two or three years." As he later confirmed to me, he was collaborating with Cohen on a book of his own: not *Helter Skelter,* but *Till Death Do Us Part,* another true-crime chronicle (it eventually appeared in 1978 with another coauthor). The two men had begun work on the book before Sharon Tate was even murdered; Bugliosi set it aside when he realized that the Manson murders would be the more sensational story.

The defense alleged that Bugliosi had helped broker the publication of Atkins's story. They never proved it, in part because Jerry

Cohen had dodged subpoena servers and never testified. But certainly it was a point in their favor that Bugliosi had omitted his working relationship with the reporter who ghostwrote the story—and that said reporter worked for the same newspaper where the story eventually appeared.

As for Schiller: in his turn on the stand, he did finally admit that he never met Susan Atkins. But afterward he claimed in interviews with *Vanity Fair, Playboy,* and the *New York Times,* and even in his Pulitzer Prize–winning collaboration with Norman Mailer, *The Executioner's Song,* that he'd interviewed Atkins in her cell.

Cohen's ghostwriting would've remained a secret if not for Pete Miller, an investigative reporter for Los Angeles's KTTV. In January 1970, as preliminary hearings continued in the Manson case, he decided to look into the Atkins sale. He wanted to see if Lawrence Schiller had actually interviewed Atkins in her jail cell, as he'd claimed he had.

Miller checked the jail's visitors' log and saw that Schiller had never been in to see Atkins. But he did notice a name he recognized: Jerry Cohen's, appearing alongside Caballero's. On the phone, Caballero admitted that he'd brought Cohen "in case he wanted to prepare a psychiatric defense" for Atkins. Miller pointed out that Cohen was a reporter, not a psychiatrist, and Caballero abruptly ended the conversation.

Miller tried to bring this to light, but he couldn't get very far. After his initial reports aired in January 1970, Bugliosi requested a meeting with him. The two sat down at KTTV's headquarters, along with Caballero, a second DA, Miller's bosses, and attorneys for the station.

This meeting came up during the penalty phase of the trial, when the defense called Miller to testify. He tried to say what they'd discussed and why no more stories aired after his first one, but Bugliosi objected every step of the way. All he could get out was that they'd talked about "some of the reports I had been doing...concerning Susan Atkins."

"As a result of this meeting, was something done regarding your further broadcasts of this case?" asked Daye Shinn, Atkins's attorney.

"Objection!" cried Bugliosi. "Irrelevant."

"Sustained," responded the court.

Shinn tried again later. "As a result of this meeting did you further terminate—"

"Objection!" Bugliosi said again. "Irrelevant."

"Will you complete the question?" the judge asked Shinn.

"As a result of this meeting did you further terminate the broadcasts concerning this case?"

"Objection! Irrelevant."

"Sustained."

Out of earshot of the jury, Bugliosi told the judge, "Miller's testimony has nothing to do with death as opposed to life. It is my contention that [the defense attorneys] are going to use this death-penalty hearing as a forum to sling dirt at various people." Including, of course, him. The judge said he wouldn't allow any mention of what happened at the meeting. It constituted hearsay.

Thus the prosecutor kept much of Miller's investigation under wraps. Most of the media covering the trial never even mentioned the Miller appearance. The *Los Angeles Times* omitted him entirely, focusing instead, as they always had, on the litany of bizarre behavior from the defendants and their supporters outside the courthouse.

Under oath, both Bugliosi and his coprosecutor, Aaron Stovitz, denied that they knew about the sale of Atkins's story before it was published. Maybe inadvertently, Richard Caballero impeached their testimony.

Under questioning by the defense's Irving Kanarek, Caballero said, "I did state to someone at the district attorney's office—I believe it was Mr. Stovitz, I may be wrong—that I had entered into the arrangement for the sale of the story . . . And they were upset."

"Who is 'they'?" Kanarek asked.

"I believe Mr. Stovitz was there, and I am almost positive someone else was there . . . but I cannot recall who."

Kanarek did his best to bring out the implication that this "someone else" was Bugliosi. Caballero, in a response worthy of the CIA, neither confirmed nor denied it.

After the Atkins story came out, Lawrence Schiller spoke to *Newsweek,* which asked how he'd been able to penetrate the security surrounding the state's "star" witness, risking a mistrial by publishing her story. He answered "with a grin": "Let's say this, the prosecution didn't put up any obstacles."

I was more than ready to believe him on that count. But what about the judge, William Keene—why didn't *he* put up any obstacles? The worldwide publication of Atkins's story was about as blatant a violation of his gag order as one can imagine, but he never held Caballero and Caruso in contempt. In a story for the *Los Angeles Free Press,* Ed Sanders, who would go on to write *The Family,* argued that Judge Keene must've known in advance about the publication, letting it slide because he, like Bugliosi, wanted the publicity from the case. Keene was considering a run for district attorney.

After Atkins's story was published, Linda Kasabian's attorney, Gary Fields, filed a motion to dismiss the case because of unfair pretrial publicity. Judge Keene denied the motion, despite abundant evidence of publicity. "*That's* where the story is," Fields told me thirty years later. "Something very smelly there."

"A Strange Little Guy"

Richard Caballero refused to discuss the case with me. "The answer is no thank you," he said on the phone. I asked him why not. "The answer is no thank you," he said. I tried one more time, saying I wanted to discuss the sale of the Atkins story. "The answer is no thank you!" he shouted, hanging up the phone.

Lawrence Schiller wouldn't talk to me, either, and Jerry Cohen had died by his own hand, in 1993. Looking into those two men, I found that throughout the sixties, their journalism had often gotten them mixed up in furtive arrangements. In '67, Schiller had published the first book to attack the conspiracy theorists around John F. Kennedy's assassination, staunchly supporting the official explanation for JFK's death. That same year, foreshadowing his feat at Sybil Brand, Schiller wormed his way into the Dallas hospital room of Jack Ruby, who'd killed Kennedy's assassin, Lee Harvey Oswald. The reporter emerged with the only recording ever made of Ruby's confessing to the murder. Schiller released it on vinyl that year. Notably, he'd taped Ruby saying that he *hadn't* killed Oswald as part of a conspiracy, thus shoring up the government's official line.

During a congressional investigation of the CIA's illegal domestic operations, the agency admitted that it had more than 250 "assets" in the American media in the 1960s. Their identities were never revealed. Mark Lane, who'd written the first book questioning the findings of the Warren Commission—the investigative committee appointed by President Lyndon Johnson, which concluded that Kennedy was killed by a lone assassin—told me he couldn't prove it but that he believed Schiller was one of those assets, and Jerry Cohen, too. Lane believed they'd been tasked with disrupting investigations of the Kennedy assassination. In testimony before Congress, Lane charged that the CIA had paid Cohen to "smear" him in the press.

I could never prove that, but I did find a trove of documents in the National Archives showing that Schiller had been acting as an informant for the FBI in 1967 and 1968, sharing confidential information with the Bureau about Mark Lane's sources. His work as an informant continued under the cloak of his "reporting" for *Life* magazine, which was later named in a 1977 *Rolling Stone* story as one of the publications that provided CIA employees with cover. Schiller tracked down authorities who were investigating potential malfeasance in the Kennedy assassination, using his press credentials to obtain interviews and then sharing his findings with the FBI. He'd written to J. Edgar Hoover to say that he was "in possession of the names and whereabouts of [the] confidential informant whom Mr. [Mark] Lane refused to identify" in his testimony to the Warren Commission. Schiller dug up information about officials looking into the CIA's involvement in the Kennedy assassination. According to memos, the FBI eagerly awaited Schiller's information.

Others had made similar claims about Cohen and Schiller. Pete Noyes, a TV investigative reporter who'd written a book on the assassinations of President Kennedy and his brother Robert, said that Cohen, a friend, had pressured him to abandon the project. If Noyes dropped the publication of the book, Cohen promised him a plum job at the *Los Angeles Times*. Noyes declined the offer, but he was disturbed by how much Cohen knew about his unpublished work. A few weeks later, he was fired from his job at CBS News. Cohen was "a strange little guy," Noyes told me. He wondered why his onetime friend tried to quash his book, and he suspected that Cohen had played a role in his firing, too. Although he could never prove it, Noyes was fairly certain that Cohen was a CIA asset.

Coda: What Did Atkins Really Say?

Susan Atkins's testimony was the blueprint for the official narrative of the murders. But if it was shaped to serve the prosecution, how much of it should we believe?

If there's an unvarnished account—a sense of what Atkins said about the crimes before she came under the "control" of her attorneys and the DA's office—it's the one she shared with her cellmate Ronnie Howard. We'll never get to hear that account verbatim, but there's something that comes close. In the files of LAPD lieutenant Paul LePage, I found notes from detectives' November 18, 1969, interview with Howard; they contained several inconsistencies with what would become Atkins's official story. And by the time Howard was reinterviewed seven days later—after Caballero's insertion in the case—she changed what she said, and all of these discrepancies were gone. To my knowledge, they've never been reported.

First: Atkins told Howard that Sharon Tate died in her bedroom, on the bed. (Later, she was said to have died in the living room.)

Second: she said the killers were tripping on LSD the night of the Tate murders. If that were true, the defense could've argued that they had "diminished capacity," thus sparing them the gas chamber. Bugliosi, wanting to eliminate that possibility, made Linda Kasabian testify on multiple occasions that no one took any drugs on the nights of the murders. (In a 2009 documentary, Kasabian contradicted her testimony, saying that all the killers had taken speed on the night of the Tate murders.)

Third: Atkins said that they killed the LaBianca couple because of something to do with "blackmail," although she couldn't elaborate. She said she'd participated in those murders, too—she was the one who left the kitchen fork protruding from Leno LaBianca's belly. (In the official narrative, Atkins was in the car that brought the killers to the LaBiancas', but she never went inside the house.)

What's just as remarkable is everything that Howard *didn't* mention in that first interview. She said nothing about Helter Skelter, Manson's race war, except to note that those words were left in blood on the LaBianca refrigerator. She made no mention, in other words, of a racist motive, black people, holes in the desert, Armageddon, or the Beatles, all of which became central to Bugliosi's prosecution.

And, as you might expect by now, she made no mention of

Manson's "instructing" anyone to go anywhere or kill anyone—all of which would be repeated incessantly in Atkins's later accounts.

As for Atkins's most heinous act—the stabbing of Sharon Tate as she begged for the life of her baby—Howard was much more equivocal about it than we've been led to believe. She said that Atkins "didn't admit she did the stabbing on the Tate deal." And yet, the next time Howard talked, after Caballero had arrived, she said without reservation that Atkins had boasted about stabbing Tate in nauseating detail.

Think of all the unanswered questions that have swirled around the Manson case for fifty years now. Just a few: Why did the killers target strangers for murder? Why would previously nonviolent kids—except for Atkins, none of them had a criminal record—kill for Manson, on command, and with such abandon and lack of remorse? And if Manson hoped to ignite a world-ending race war, why didn't he order more killings, since the two nights of murder didn't trigger that war?

Bugliosi made a fortune and achieved worldwide fame from his prosecution of the Manson Family and *Helter Skelter*. Over the years, many people in law enforcement have told me that they never believed the Helter Skelter motive. Their theories were always more mundane—they would've made thinner gruel for Bugliosi's book.

Eventually, all the killers settled on a story similar to the one that Atkins told after her attorney swap. And all of them have sought parole releases based on that story's thesis: that they were not responsible for their actions because they were under Manson's control. Many of the psychiatrists who testified said that the defendants' minds had been so decimated by LSD that they likely had no way of discerning real memories from false ones. They may not even have known if they were *at* either house on the nights of the killings, let alone whether they participated in the murders.

The only person who never endorsed Atkins's final story, and the Helter Skelter motive along with it, was Manson. After his conviction, he said little about the crimes, except that he didn't know what his "children" were going to do before they did it, and that he had no explanation for why they'd done it. Curiously, Bugliosi admitted in one of his last interviews that he was pretty certain Manson never believed in Helter Skelter. "I think everyone who participated in the murders bought the Helter Skelter theory hook, line, and sinker," he told *Rolling Stone*. "But did Manson himself believe in all this ridiculous, preposterous stuff about all of them living in a bottomless pit in the desert while a worldwide war went on outside? I think, without knowing, that he did not." Unfortunately, the reporter didn't follow up with the obvious rejoinder: If the murders *weren't* committed to incite a race war, what was the reason?

As I've mentioned before, there was a persistent rumor among followers of the case, including the detectives who'd investigated it, that Manson had visited the Tate house after the murders, arriving with some unknown companion to restage the crime scene. If it's true that Susan Atkins's story was the product of careful sculpting by the DA's office, the prospect of Manson's visitation isn't nearly as far-fetched as it would be otherwise.

One of the more perplexing clues to that end is a pair of eyeglasses recovered from Tate's living room after the murders. They didn't belong to any of the victims; they didn't belong to any of the murderers; they didn't seem to belong to anyone, period. Detectives never explained them to anyone's satisfaction. In a 1986 book called *Manson in His Own Words,* ostensibly cowritten by Manson and an ex-con named Nuel Emmons, Manson mentioned these glasses, saying he went to the Cielo house with an unnamed conspirator and took elaborate measures to rearrange the crime scene. "My partner had an old pair of eyeglasses which we often used as a magnifying glass or a device to start a fire when matches weren't available," he wrote. "We carefully wiped the glasses free of prints and dropped them on the floor, so that, when discovered, they would be a misleading clue for the police."

To be clear, *Manson in His Own Words* is a far from unimpeachable source. Emmons wrote the book years after a series of prison interviews with Manson, but he wasn't allowed to record these or take notes at the time. Manson himself vaguely disavowed the book, although not before appearing with Emmons in several televised interviews to promote it.

I was inclined to take a kinder view toward it when I found, in the LASO files, a "kite," or prison note, from Manson to Linda Kasabian. His coded language is hard to decipher, but he may have been admitting that he left the glasses at the Cielo house after the murders. The note seems to have been delivered in an effort to persuade Kasabian not to make a deal with the prosecution:

So what if I did make you do it I don't care if you're a snitch...you been a lien bitch...I did what I did because I felt it was to be done & I even put the eye glasses to where I could show you all are blind & give them Shorty...each time you skiw down you think of Sharon Tate & know that's you if I can't get to my Nancy's love...

The next lines had been underlined by police: "tell Gold to hold the bone yard and no bones outside the yard."

While it's always difficult to decode anything Manson said or wrote, this note isn't as impenetrable as others. "Gold" was Manson's nickname for one of his Family favorites, Nancy Pitman, whom he had referred to as "Nancy" a few lines earlier. In early 1970, Pitman paid frequent visits to all the defendants in jail, doing Manson's bidding. She told Linda Kasabian not to turn state's evidence; she told Atkins to stop cooperating with the prosecution. "Shorty" refers to Shorty Shea, the Spahn Ranch caretaker whom the Family had killed and buried in a remote part of the property; as mentioned earlier, his remains weren't recovered until 1977.

To hazard a guess: Manson was warning Kasabian not to flip, and instructing her to tell "Gold," when next she visited, that Shorty Shea's "bones" were not to be removed from "the bone yard" at the Spahn Ranch where he was buried. Manson even may have been referring to other victims' buried remains at the ranch; it's long been suspected that more victims of the Family are buried somewhere. While the implications of the note are sensational, what's more important to me is Manson's apparent admission that he returned to the Tate house after the murders and planted the glasses.

I expected investigators to dismiss the possibility of Manson's meddling at the scene, but some were open to it. Late in my reporting, I spoke with Danny Bowser, a retired lieutenant from the LAPD homicide squad who'd never given an interview about Manson. In 1965 Bowser had been appointed the first commander of the LAPD's new Special Investigations Section (SIS), an elite, high-tech unit that served as "professional witnesses" by running covert surveillance on known criminals. Its goal was to gather such a preponderance of evidence that convictions were all but guaranteed, and plea bargains all but impossible. And the SIS was a furtive bunch: for a decade, the LAPD never even publicly acknowledged its existence. "We weren't even connected to a division," Bowser told the *Los Angeles Times* in 1988. "They carried us [on the roster] at different places, different times."

That was the only time Bowser ever commented about the SIS. A second piece reported that SIS was called the "Death Squad" within the LAPD because its members had killed thirty-four suspects since 1965. The "secretive" twenty-man unit had a controversial policy: it refused to intervene to stop crimes, even those in which people's lives were at stake. The *Times* investigation "documented numerous instances in which well-armed teams of SIS detectives stood by watching as victims were threatened with death and, some-times, physically harmed by criminals who could have been arrested beforehand." The later piece in the *Times* reported that "Even within the LAPD, SIS officers are known as a fearsome and mysterious bunch. Some of their colleagues repeat unsubstantiated—and vigor-ously denied—rumors of SIS officers conspiring to shoot suspects and celebrating gunfights with 'kill parties.'"

I'd heard from other detectives that, after Sharon Tate's mur-der, the LAPD assigned Bowser to serve as Roman Polanski's "bodyguard." Why would such an elite officer get such a low-level task? Polanski confirmed the assignment in his 1984 autobiogra-phy, *Roman by Polanski,* writing that Bowser had been the first detective to interview him and had shadowed his every move. He added somewhat cryptically that "Bowser wasn't, strictly speaking, on the investigative side of the case...One of his responsibilities was to keep in touch with me." Why, then, was his name never mentioned in *Helter Skelter* or at the trial?

I had trouble finding a way to talk to Bowser. Finally, in 2008, I settled on a time-honored reportorial tactic: I showed up at his doorstep unannounced. He lived way out in Inyo County, five hours from L.A., at the end of a quiet suburban street.

Bowser refused to let me in, saying he wouldn't talk to me. Despite his advanced age, he cut an imposing figure—he had a glass eye, and I later learned that his real eye had been shot out—but I kept him standing in his doorway by blurting out ques-tions about the Tate crime scene, hoping to convince him that I'd done my homework. It worked—kind of. Bowser would shut the door on me, only to open it again to say more. Whenever he seemed to have said his piece, he'd find something else to add. For the next thirty minutes, as the sprinklers chirped next door and a TV blared from inside his house, he told me things that he insisted he'd never shared outside the SIS.

Most of our stilted conversation was about the homicide investigation report for the Tate case, a document that was pretty much the basis of the prosecution's physical evidence. Bowser said it was littered with inaccuracies. The detectives in the homicide unit, he claimed, "left things behind, things they missed...an awful lot of evidence didn't get processed."

At least two key pieces of physical evidence weren't, in fact, discovered at the crime scene the morning of the murders, although more than a dozen police officers and forensic investigators had testified that they had been. One was that mysterious pair of eyeglasses. Bowser told me he'd found those himself, five entire days after the murders. That contradicted the homicide report, which said the glasses had been located and taken into custody on August 9, 1969. Gently, I suggested he might be mistaken — that the homicide report suggested otherwise.

"What, you think that's the Bible?" He snorted. "You believe the stuff you read in there?" He made sure I didn't jump to the conclusion that he or any of the SIS agents working under him had done anything improper. He said that his guys didn't write reports, nor did they report to anyone. Nevertheless, if what he said was true, then critical elements of the prosecution's presentation of the crime scene were inaccurate. Included, just for starters, would be the means of entry into the house, the way the victims were bound and by whom. "Everything evil over there kind of connects," he added.

If he was accurate, then all those cops — his colleagues at the LAPD — had lied under oath, I reminded him.

"Did you see any of *my* guys on the stand?" he asked. And he added that I wouldn't find any of his "guys" named in the police reports, either. He was right.

Toward the end, Bowser toyed with giving me a proper interview. "I was going to give you my number," he said before shutting the door again, "to protect you from stumbling over your dick. But I changed my mind." I waited a good ten minutes, but the door remained closed this time, and I finally left. Two years later, in 2010, he died.

As I drove away, my mind was awash with possibilities. I'd always wondered about the crime-scene discrepancies. I wondered if Bowser, just by alleging that the crime scene had been presented incorrectly or possibly even staged, was pointing to other reasons for the murders, or other people, perhaps, involved in covering up what had really happened. I had to think of Reeve Whitson, and his claim of having gone to the crime scene after the murders but before the police had arrived.

All of this is compelling evidence of a different scenario for the crimes, but I'll be the first to admit that it proves nothing for certain. I do believe it's possible that there was another reason for the Tate–LaBianca murders. And I do believe the crime scene suggests that the sequence of events as we know it is wrong. But our best chance to learn the truth vanished in November 1969, when the DA's office put Susan Atkins's testimony on lockdown. The question remaining was: *Why?*

9

Manson's Get-Out-of-Jail-Free Card

No More Extensions

Good reporting takes time—vast and often unreasonable amounts of time. Behind every solid lead, quotable interview, and bomb-shell document, I put in weeks of scut work that led to dozens of dead ends. My Freedom of Information Act requests alone would stretch on for months, as I quibbled with bureaucrats over redactions and minutiae. Since my three-month assignment from *Premiere* had long since evolved into a years-long project, I'd accepted that the Manson case was something akin to a calling, like it or not. Even in the longueurs between my major break-throughs, I worked diligently with the confidence—and, some-times, the hubris—that comes with the hunch that you're onto something big.

That confidence would've been nothing if my editors at *Premiere* didn't share it. The camaraderie and support they offered was critical, but more basically than that, they were keeping me alive.

For almost a year and a half, through one deadline extension after another, they paid me a generous monthly stipend to keep reporting, on top of the standard fee from my original contract. Even then, I knew that these paychecks were a tremendous act of faith, and I didn't take them lightly. I wanted to deliver a news-making piece, unlike the usual stuff printed in entertainment magazines, and I thought I could do it. I just needed time.

But there were limits to *Premiere*'s largesse. In November 2000, Jim Meigs—the editor in chief, who'd sat on the floor of my apartment, examining documents with me—was fired. I heard a rumor, which I could never confirm, that the handsome monthly payments he'd authorized for me were part of the problem. Whatever the case, *Premiere*'s new regime got down to brass tacks right away. In total, including expenses, they'd paid me a king's ransom at that point, and now they demanded the goods. Immediately.

Looking back, maybe I was too full of pride. I still can't decide if what I did next was best for me in the long run. But I did it: I walked away from *Premiere*. I thought I had a historic story, and to publish it in that condition, with loose ends and so much research left to be done, would've been giving too much away. The minute I let it go, I thought, the *Los Angeles Times* or the *Washington Post* would put six reporters on the story to finish what I couldn't. If they got the big scoop that had eluded me—the story of what *really* happened, as opposed to the millions of tiny holes in what was *supposed* to have happened—all the glory would be theirs, and I would be only a footnote.

A writer friend had referred me to her literary agent, who took me on, convinced that I had an important book on my hands. If I could write up a proposal and sell it to a publisher, he said, I'd get the time and the money I needed to put my reporting to bed. He disentangled me from my obligation to *Premiere* and I started right away.

It took more than a year to write the first draft of the proposal. My friends, many of whom were writers, could never understand why it was taking so long. Why not just sit down and crank the thing out? I was constantly on the defensive with them, looking for justifications. The problem, of course, was that I was still reporting. Because that's what I always did. I never stopped.

Without the backing of an institution like *Premiere,* my mindset started to change—it was expanding. I found myself looking into Manson's year in San Francisco. He was there for the summer of love, in 1967. It was where he'd formed the Family. I was flummoxed by the authority figures who'd surrounded Manson at this time: his parole officer and the locally renowned physician who ran the clinic where he and his followers received free health care. Neither of them had spoken much to the press, and neither had testified at the trial, despite the fact that each man had seen Manson almost daily in the critical period when he'd started his cult.

These weren't fringe figures like Reeve Whitson or William Herrmann: they were well-known and respected in the Bay Area, and, even better for me, they were still alive. So when I plunged into their stories with Manson and found what appeared to be evidence of serial dishonesty—again, often connected to federal law enforcement and intelligence agencies—I had to ask myself if I was crazy to be doing all of this.

The question wasn't whether it was "worth it"; I thought it was, assuming the truth could be wrested out of aging scientists, reformed hippies, and dusty government files. The question was how much of myself I was willing to give, irrespective of any consequences to my reputation or well-being. I was haunted by something Paul Krassner, a journalist who'd covered the trial for the legendary counterculture magazine *The Realist,* had told me after a lunch in the first months of my investigation. At a Venice Beach sushi bar, we'd been discussing our belief that the reasons behind the murders had been misrepresented. "Be careful, Tom," he said as we parted ways. "This will take over your life if you let it."

I'd shrugged it off at the time. Now it felt like a prophecy. But if I wanted my book, or even just my proposal for the book, to be more complete than my *Premiere* piece would've been, I had to let the story consume me.

Scot-Free in Mendocino

To understand my fascination with Manson's parole officer, you might pick up where we left off: with Susan Atkins. She was plainly pushed around by the DA's office. Her story was cut and polished until it glimmered for the prosecutors, bringing indictments, convictions, and a raft of publicity.

The more I learned about Atkins's past, though, the stranger her manipulation became to me. In the years before the Family's rise to notoriety, the justice system afforded her a shocking amount of latitude. If anything, she'd gotten away with far too *much* in those years. When she was on probation, she broke the law regularly, but her arrests never put her in any further legal jeopardy. Instead, there was a pattern of catch-and-release. Whenever the police brought her in, she'd find herself cut loose within a few days. Why was law enforcement so lenient with her?

The events of June 4, 1969—about two months before the Tate–LaBianca murders—are as good a starting point as any. At 3:30 that morning, an LAPD patrolman pulled over a '68 Plymouth for speeding in the San Fernando Valley, ordering the driver to step out of the car. A small, long-haired man emerged, staggering toward him, his arms flailing in "wild gyrations." "He appeared under the influence of some unknown intoxicant," the officer later reported.

It was Charles Manson. He was arrested and charged with driving under the influence, being on drugs, and operating a vehicle without a license. He had four passengers in the car, all arrested for being under the influence: Thomas J. Walleman, Nancy Pitman, Leslie Van Houten, and Susan Atkins.

Within twenty-four hours, all of them—including Manson, who'd informed the booking officers that he was on federal parole—were released with no charges. All except Atkins. She was held for more than two weeks.

The police had discovered a warrant for Atkins, not even a week old. On May 29, hundreds of miles away in Mendocino, a judge had ordered her arrest for violating five conditions of her probation. (Atkins had gotten a three-year probation sentence in 1968, after an arrest near Ukiah, California.) Now, notified of her arrest in Los Angeles, two Mendocino County sheriff's deputies drove 1050 miles round-trip to scoop her up and bring her back up north. On June 7, she was booked into the Mendocino County jail.

The state had a strong case against Atkins. She had probation officers in both L.A. and Mendocino, and neither was happy with her. According to their reports, she'd brazenly defied all attempts at supervision since her sentence was imposed. Since she'd received a courtesy transfer of her probation from Mendocino to Los Angeles County, she'd changed her address more than six times without permission. She hadn't sought employment. She'd failed to check in for almost every monthly appointment. And most recently, she'd told the probation office that, although she knew it was forbidden, she was moving to the Mojave Desert with her friends, with no plan to return to L.A.

Describing Atkins's whereabouts as "totally unknown," the probation office's report advised, "The best thing is to revoke the defendant's probation as it appears she has no intentions of abiding by it."

Despite that recommendation, at a hearing that month, Judge Wayne Burke of Mendocino County Superior Court decided that "the defendant has not violated probation. She has complied with the terms. Probation is reinstated and modified to terminate forewith. She is released." Not only did the ruling defy the probation office—it seemed to reward Atkins's bad behavior, "terminating" her probation more than two years before it was scheduled to conclude. And off she went, soon to participate in the murders of at least eight people. The fact that she was nearly sent to prison so soon before the killings has never been reported.

Hoping to shed some light on the deceased Judge Burke's decision, I found the head of the Mendocino County Probation Office in 1969, Thomas Martin, who'd appeared at the hearing. I also spoke to Atkins's L.A. probation officer, Margo Tompkins, who'd written the recommendation for her revocation. Both recalled their shock at the ruling. Calling it "very strange," Tompkins said, "Judges almost always went along with a probation officer's recommendation. Clearly she had not had any employment, no fixed addresses . . . I have no idea why [he] would have done that."

Martin said he'd never experienced anything like it in thirty-two years on the job. He was especially galled because they'd gone to the trouble of sending two police officers on the thousand-mile journey to retrieve Atkins. "That seldom, if ever, happened," he said. Martin remembered Burke well; he felt the ruling must have had some ulterior motive. "Judge Burke was not just somebody in the woods," he said. "There was something in his mind. Something that he knew that he never shared with us."

Whatever that something was, it had worked to Atkins's benefit before. A year and a half earlier, an entirely different set of probation officers—in another state—had tried to have her probation revoked, and they met with an almost identical response from a different judge.

Atkins was living in San Francisco then. She'd fallen in with a strange man who promised to change her life, and her probation officers weren't thrilled about it. Her sudden infatuation with this "Charlie" meant she might backslide into the recklessness that had gotten her arrested in the first place, when she'd been found in a stolen car in Oregon with two ex-cons, one of whom she'd met while working as a stripper. It was the end of a crime spree for the trio. They'd stolen the car in California, driven it across the state line into Oregon, and held up a string of gas stations and convenience stores, with Atkins at the wheel.

When they were apprehended outside Salem, she told the officer she would've shot and killed him if he hadn't caught them by surprise. Then only eighteen, Atkins was convicted of being in possession of stolen goods and a concealed weapon. Her three-year probation sentence was transferred to San Francisco, where she promised to clean up her act. And so she had, until the summer of '67, when she'd fallen under Manson's spell.

According to probation records, Atkins phoned her San Francisco probation officer, Mary Yates, that November 10, saying that she'd joined a communal marriage with seven other women. They were all hitched to a "traveling minister" by the name of Charlie, fresh out of federal prison. Atkins and Charlie's other "wives," many of them pregnant by him, would soon be leaving San Francisco in a "big yellow bus" bound for Southern California, Florida, and ultimately Mexico.

Yates had been supervising Atkins for a year, and she was surprised by her charge's sudden change in character. True, Atkins had always been "flighty," but she'd also been respectful and polite, and she'd never failed to follow the rules. Now she sounded defiant, if also lackadaisical. She didn't seem to understand, or care, that her behavior would land her in prison.

After that disturbing phone call, Yates wrote to the head office in Sacramento to fill them in. "Charlie," she wrote, not knowing his last name, "is in love with all of them and they all love each other." Yates had told Atkins not to leave, but she was "certain she will do as she pleases." She recommended getting Atkins in court to decide whether her probation should be revoked. She closed her letter with chillingly prophetic words: "Hopefully, she won't get into further difficulties with Charlie and the other seven girls."

The phone call had so worried Yates that she got in touch with *another* probation officer, M. E. Madison, of Oregon, where Atkins had originally been sentenced. Madison, who also kept tabs on Atkins, raised an alarm of his own. He'd spoken to Atkins, too, and he didn't like what he heard. "Her speech was quite disorganized," he wrote to his superiors, "and she repeated several times... that 'Love is everything; everything is nothing.'" He told her she couldn't go; she said she was leaving anyway.

The officers tried to track her down, to no avail. November faded into December. Feeling they'd exhausted their options, they wrote to the original sentencing judge, George Jones, of Marion County, Oregon, advising that the court take action. That was on December 12. Afterward, the paper record abruptly stopped. For twenty-three days, there were no more documents, memos, or court filings regarding the truant probationer.

Then, on January 4, 1968, Judge Jones signed an order *terminating* Susan Atkins's probation. Probation officials in two states had gone so far as to warn Atkins that her return to prison was inevitable. Instead, the judge rewarded her by releasing her from all obligations to law enforcement.

As in the later case, there was no record explaining the judge's decision. He knew the nature of her crimes; he knew how serious a threat she could become. Why would he have reversed himself? Why would another judge have followed suit? Atkins hardly seemed the type to win over two separate judges. Only one thing had changed when these reversals occurred: she was with Manson. As long as she stayed on his side, it seemed the rules didn't apply.

Roger Smith, "the Friendly Fed"

The law afforded special privileges to everyone in Manson's orbit. Once I was absorbed in the Family's origin story, I found evidence everywhere of a curious leniency, always helped along by a hand from the outside. Of special note was an incident in June 1968 that earned Atkins her second probation sentence, the one that almost—*almost*—had her off the streets for good before the Tate–LaBianca murders.

It began in the small outpost of Ukiah. As the seat for Mendocino County—one of the Family's favorite getaways—Ukiah by 1968 had become a haven for hippies fleeing San Francisco, which was no longer the untrammeled paradise it had been a few years before. In Haight-Ashbury, speed was now the drug of choice, and with it came violence, con men, bikers, dope peddlers, and runaways. Worst were the tourists, who'd started to congregate in the Haight to admire the psychedelic memorabilia for sale: tie-dyed shirts, MAKE LOVE NOT WAR buttons, beads, baubles, and bell-bottoms.

Mendocino County, 150 miles northwest of the Golden Gate Bridge, was an oasis by comparison. Rolling acres of land and dense forests of centuries-old redwoods stretched all the way to the sea. Small towns speckled the landscape with a patchwork quilt of groves and orchards. Communes had sprouted up as early as 1965, but they increased tenfold after the implosion of the Haight. In early June 1968, Manson sent his girls there to win some recruits for their own commune.

The delegation of five women—Susan Atkins, Ella Jo Bailey, Patricia Krenwinkel, Stephanie Rowe, and Mary Brunner—used a technique that they'd refined into an art form. They sought out impressionable young men, invited them to an all-girl orgy, and offered them a plethora of narcotics, including marijuana quietly spiked with LSD. Unfortunately, that day in Ukiah, they snared three underage boys. More unfortunately, one of them happened to be the son of a Mendocino County deputy sheriff.

The seventeen-year-old awoke in a tangle of limbs, extricated himself, and darted home, telling his parents that his "legs looked like snakes" and that he "saw flashes when he closed his eyes." Soon all five women had been charged with felony drug possession and contributing to the delinquency of minors. They were locked up in the Mendocino County jail.

The outlook was grim for the Manson girls. Two of them were already in the probation office's sights—Atkins had just been released from her sentence, and Brunner's had just begun. But all they had to do was make one phone call and they were as good as gone.

The man they called was Roger Smith, Manson's parole officer in San Francisco. Or rather, his former parole officer. At the time of these arrests, Smith had recently left his job, and you'd think he would have severed ties with his one remaining parolee: Manson. But the two had grown close. Smith, who called Manson "Charlie," ended up becoming one of the most vital figures in my investigation—more than anyone else, he knew how and why Manson had formed the Family, because he'd watched it happen. And legally, he wielded immense power over Manson. He could've sent him back to prison at any time.

Instead, he acted more as Manson's guardian. Their bond was such that, when Manson's disciples called him from Ukiah that day in June, Smith and his wife decided to drive up to Mendocino County to check on them. They had no professional obligation to do this.

Brunner had recently given birth to a son, Michael Valentine, and with the girls in jail, the baby had no one to take care of him. (Manson was the father, of course; Michael Valentine, sometimes known as "Pooh Bear," was the Family's first child.) Smith and his wife took an extraordinary step: they got the court to appoint them as Pooh Bear's temporary foster parents, and they returned to the Bay Area with the baby, looking after him for eight weeks.

In the meantime, a friend of Smith named Alan Rose repaired to Mendocino County to get the girls out of jail. Rose, a college dropout who met the Family through Smith, made a valiant effort. He'd become enamored of the girls. He visited them almost daily, hired lawyers for them, and testified as a character witness at their preliminary hearings. And finally he raised their bail money, winning their freedom until the trial at the end of the summer.

All the while, Manson remained in L.A., ensconced in the comfort of Dennis Wilson's home. He received periodic updates about the girls, but he never seemed terribly concerned. Why should he have been? By that time, he'd been through enough to know that he was golden: it seemed that with Roger Smith watching over him, crimes had no consequences.

In the end, charges were dropped against three of the women for lack of evidence. Atkins and Brunner pleaded guilty to possessing narcotics. In exchange, the charges that they'd furnished drugs to minors were dismissed.

Then the court shocked the community by granting Atkins probation instead of sending her to prison. Brunner was already on probation in L.A., or one assumes she would've gotten it, too. The sixty days they'd already spent in the county jail was apparently punishment enough—they were free.

As we now know, Atkins would violate her probation in June 1969, forcing her to be spirited away from the Family and carted back to Mendocino County by police. And her violation wouldn't matter—the beneficent Judge Burke would return her to the fold, no questions asked.

Once again the pattern held: when it came to women in the orbit of Charles Manson, the court was unusually forgiving, ruling against the wishes of police and prosecutors.

I wanted to find the reasons behind the court's clemency. I

called the Superior Court in Ukiah and bought the entire file for the Mendocino case, including the record of the probation investigations for Atkins and Brunner.

It turned out that both women had received glowing appraisals and impassioned pleas for leniency from none other than Roger Smith. In his petitions, Smith identified himself as a "former federal parole officer," but as far as the court records show, he neglected to mention that his most recent and final parole client was Charles Manson—the very man who'd sent Atkins and Brunner to Mendocino in the first place.

If the court knew about Smith's relationship to Manson, there's no record of it. And the judges weren't the only ones from whom Smith apparently withheld this information. David Mandel, a Mendocino County probation officer who filed the sentencing report for Atkins and Brunner, wrote extensively about Manson and his "guru"-like hold over the women, and he spoke to Roger Smith—without realizing the two were connected. Neither Smith nor his wife, who'd allegedly also advocated for the girls' release, ever saw fit to mention their relationship with Manson. (Smith's wife, Carol, who divorced him in 1981, denied any involvement in the recommendations, suggesting that Smith had used her name without her knowledge.)

Mandel put a lot of stock in Smith's word. He was impressed that a former federal parole officer would put his weight behind a slouch like Atkins, whom he described as "hostile and possibly vengeful." Smith swore that Atkins would "comply willingly with any probationary conditions." And while Mandel saw Brunner as "much influenced and often manipulated by her present group," Smith praised her as an emblem of "traditional Christian values."

Of course, Smith had spent a long time with the Family by then. He knew that Brunner and Atkins had every intention of returning to the man who dictated their lives, often inciting them to criminality. And sure enough, when the court let them go, they fled Mendocino immediately for the Spahn Ranch, where Manson was now situated.

In 2008, I met with David Mandel in Marin County. I was the first to tell him that Roger Smith had been Manson's parole officer.

"Of course it should have been disclosed," said Mandel, poring over the documents I'd brought. "It's a huge conflict of interest!"

Mandel remembered visiting the Smiths at their home in Tiburon, outside San Francisco. He noticed that the couple cared enough for Mary Brunner to have petitioned for temporary custody of her child. The couple was a major factor in his decision to recommend probation, he said, shaking his head. "I should've put two and two together."

One other strange fact bears mentioning, even though I've never known what to make of it. Six months after the Ukiah trial, one of the judges, Robert Winslow, lost his reelection bid to the bench—in no small part, according to one insider, because of his leniency with the Manson girls. Winslow resurfaced in Los Angeles. Remarkably, he'd become the attorney for Doris Day and her son, Terry Melcher. It was Winslow who prepped Melcher for his appearances at the Tate–LaBianca trial, and Winslow who accompanied him in the courtroom as he testified, incorrectly, about the number of times he'd met Manson. Ironically, Winslow was helping Melcher speak out against the same group he'd helped the year before. Neither he nor Melcher ever made a public comment about the sheer unlikeliness of it all.

"A Totally Irresponsible Individual"

Even before I got the probation records, I was convinced that something was off about Roger Smith's relationship with the Family. My interest in the federal officer coincided with my deep dive into COINTELPRO and CHAOS, both of which were active in the Bay Area in 1967.

I wanted to know everything about Smith and Manson. How had Smith become Manson's parole officer? Why were they so close? And what made Smith so inclined to treat Manson like a harmless hippie rather than a dangerous ex-con?

The answers came mainly from a pivotal chapter of Manson's life, one that Bugliosi glossed over in *Helter Skelter*: the summer of love. From the late spring of 1967 to June 1968, Manson lived in Haight-Ashbury, the hotbed of the counterculture. Given how often Manson is characterized as a curdled hippie—a perversion of the principles of free love—you'd think his year in the Haight would attract more attention. It was the crucible in which his identity was forged. He arrived there an ex-con and left a confident, long-haired cult leader. It was in the Haight that he began to use LSD. He learned how to attract weak, susceptible people, and how to use drugs to keep them under his thumb. And he internalized the psychological methods that would make his followers do anything for him.

This might not have been possible without Roger Smith.

The two came together in a roundabout way. Manson had been released from Terminal Island prison in Los Angeles County on March 21, 1967. He'd served seven and a half years for forging a government check. When he stepped out that day, he was thirty-two, and he'd spent nearly half his life in prisons and juvenile detention centers. As Bugliosi would marvel in *Helter Skelter,* prison supervisors had largely assessed Manson as nonviolent. Though he'd faced juvenile convictions of armed robbery and homosexual rape, and had beaten his wife, these didn't add up, in the eyes of the state, to a "sustained history of violence." Nor, as Bugliosi noted, did they fit the profile of a mass murderer in 1969.

Another peculiarity: all of Manson's prison time was at the federal level. Bugliosi found this startling. "Probably ninety-nine out of one-hundred criminals never see the inside of a federal court," he noted. Manson had been described as "criminally sophisticated," but had he been convicted at the state level, he would've faced a fraction of the time behind bars—maybe less than five years, versus seventeen.

Within days of his release, Manson violated his parole. Unless he had explicit permission, he was supposed to stay put; he was forbidden from leaving Los Angeles under penalty of automatic repatriation to prison. But practically immediately, he headed to Berkeley, California.

Years earlier, Manson had had his parole revoked just for failing to report to his supervisor. Now, for some reason, the police bureaucracy of an entirely different city welcomed him with open arms. When he called up the San Francisco Federal Parole Office to announce himself, they simply filed some routine paperwork transferring him to the supervision of Roger Smith, an officer and a student at UC Berkeley's School of Criminology.

Helter Skelter is deeply misleading on this point. Bugliosi writes simply that Manson "requested and received permission to go to San Francisco." The prosecutor had a copy of Manson's parole file, so he knew this wasn't true.

I wanted that file, too. After a FOIA request and months of negotiations and appeals, I received a portion of it in 2000. It contained a letter from the San Francisco parole office to the Los Angeles office, dated April 11, 1967—three weeks after Manson's release. "This man called our San Francisco Federal Parole Office to announce that he had been paroled and was now within the city of Berkeley, California," the letter begins.

> He had no parole documents (he impresses as a totally irresponsible individual)...the institution at Terminal Island tells us that this man was paroled on March 21, 1967, to the

> Central District of California (Los Angeles). Since this man
> indicates his intention to stay within the San Francisco
> Metropolitan area for the indefinite future we now indicate
> our willingness to accept transfer of supervision to this
> Northern District of California.

And so began Manson's assignment to Roger Smith, whom the ex-con came to revere.

As the months passed, Manson granted Smith a special role as "protector" in the abstruse mythology he'd begun to construct around himself. The Haight had introduced him to *Stranger in a Strange Land,* Robert Heinlein's provocative 1961 sci-fi novel. Manson was obsessed with the book. He carried a worn copy with him at all times, and though he was barely literate, he seemed to grasp the nuances of its dense narrative and its invented language.

There's no saying who might have read the book to him or told him about it, but in its hero, Valentine Michael, Manson recognized himself, so much so that he named his first child after him. Roger Smith got a nickname from Manson, too: "Jubal Harshaw," the most important character in the hero's life, his lawyer, teacher, protector, and spiritual guide on Earth.

The plot of *Stranger in a Strange Land* has eerie parallels to Manson's rise, so much so that, after the murders, fans of the novel went out of their way to disavow Manson's connection to it. Valentine Michael, a human raised on Mars, is endowed with hypnotic powers. He descends to Earth to foster a new and perfect race. Guarded by Jubal, he assembles a "nest" with about twenty others, almost all women, whom he initiates through sex. He demands that his followers surrender their egos to him in a spirit of total submission. They worship the innocence of children and yearn to exist in a state of such pure consciousness that they can communicate telepathically. The group sleeps and eats together; one of their most sacred rituals is the act of "sharing water," which takes on vaguely druggy undertones. In Valentine Michael's philosophy, there is no death, only "discorporation"; killing people saves their souls, giving them a second chance through reincarnation. The group begins to discorporate their enemies with impunity. In time, Valentine Michael draws strength from the "nest" and, like Christ, saves the world.

After the Family was caught, *Time* magazine picked up on the bizarre parallels between *Stranger in a Strange Land* and Manson's own "nest." In January 1970, it ran a piece called "A Martian Model?" arguing that Manson had "no powers of invention at all... He may have murdered by the book."

But Roger Smith was amused by Manson's fascination with the novel. He thought it was good that Manson saw his own fantasies in it; there was no harm in his desire to become a savior. If that meant that Smith himself took on the role of Jubal, so be it.

When we spoke, Smith was hazy on the details of how he became Manson's parole officer. Manson had been assigned to him as a part of the so-called San Francisco Project, an experimental parole program funded by the National Institute of Mental Health that monitored the rehabilitative progress of newly released felons. When Manson arrived in the Bay Area in March 1967, he was attached to the program—and to Roger Smith.

Manson's participation in the San Francisco Project has never been reported. In part, it explains why the two men had developed such a powerful bond—because Smith spent much more time with Manson than the average parole officer would. The project studied the relationship between federal parolees and their supervisors; researchers wanted to know how varying degrees of oversight affected recidivism rates. The six participating parole officers, all of whom had advanced degrees in criminology, were assigned one of three caseloads: "normal," averaging about one hundred clients; "ideal," numbering forty clients; or "intensive," twenty clients.

Roger Smith fell into the middle group. He met with his clients once a week, per project guidelines. But at some point, his "ideal" caseload became even more intense than his colleagues' "intensives." By the end of '67, he'd winnowed his set of parolees from forty down to just one: Manson.

I was shocked that Manson had become Smith's one and only client, but I could never figure out why. Hoping to learn more, I interviewed Smith's research assistant from that time, Gail Sadalla. Although Smith had assured me that he'd never met Manson before becoming his parole officer, Sadalla had a different recollection. Smith told her in 1968 that Manson became his charge because he'd already been his probation officer years earlier—in the early sixties, at the Joliet Federal Prison in Illinois. Admittedly, this seemed all but impossible. Manson had never been in the Illinois parole system, and he'd only been incarcerated in the state for a few days in 1956. But Sadalla was convinced that the two had met previously. When I told her that her former boss had no memory of meeting Manson before March 1967, she was stunned.

"He didn't remember that?" she asked. "I'm surprised... It was always my understanding. That's why there was this *connection*."

I didn't know what to believe, but if Sadalla was correct, it might explain how Manson was able to move to San Francisco without being sent back to prison for violating the terms of his parole: he may have been sent there.

"Wipe Your Eyes and See"

As a doctoral student at the Berkeley School of Criminology, Roger Smith studied the link between drug use and violent behavior in Oakland gang members. In April 1967, the study had seen enough success to merit a press conference. As the *New York Times* reported, Smith and his colleagues had found that a gang's drug use, rather than "mellowing them out," more often triggered violent behavior. The students wanted to distinguish between gang members who fell into violence because of inherent sociopathic tendencies and those who became sociopathic because of drugs.

Smith conducted research through his own "immersion." He and the other researchers created "outposts" in the Oakland slums, hanging around at community centers and churches, befriending gang members under less-than-transparent circumstances. They embraced a "participant-observer" approach to social research, which Smith would further incorporate into his methods in the years to come.

By 1967, Smith was regarded as an expert on gangs, collective behavior, violence, and drugs. Manson, his one and only parole supervisee, would go on to control the collective behavior of a gang through violence and drugs.

Smith described himself to me as a "rock-ribbed Republican"— he never struck me as someone with much tolerance for the counterculture. And yet it was his idea, he admitted, to send Manson to live in the Haight. He hoped that Manson could "soak up" some of the "vibes" of the peace and love movement exploding in the district that summer. Maybe it would allay some of Manson's hostility.

So Manson moved from Berkeley to Haight-Ashbury, crashing wherever he could and never paying rent. The hippie movement was nearing its high point. Bohemians were dispensing with boundaries, giving away clothes, drugs, sex, music, and hours of talk about tolerance. Anarchists called for the end of racism, capitalism, and imperialism; the mere act of picking up a guitar had a new ideological voltage. The length of your hair said everything about you. Drawn by the psychedelic aesthetic, teens flocked from around the country to get laid, to try to bring enduring peace to the world, or to try pot and LSD, the latter of which had only recently been made illegal in California.

It was a concerted, grassroots effort to reject middle-class morality. But where some saw earthshaking radicalism, others saw only Dionysian excess. George Harrison, of Manson's life-defining band, the Beatles, stopped by the Haight that summer and came away unimpressed: "The summer of love was just a bunch of spotty kids on drugs," he said. A press release for the Human Be-In, a sprawling gathering a few months before Manson came to town, gives a sense of the era's transformative rhetoric: "A new nation has grown inside the robot flesh of the old...Hang your fear at the door and join the future. If you do not believe, please wipe your eyes and see."

When Manson went to wipe his eyes and see, he wasted no time adopting the folkways and postures of the flower children. Once he landed in the Haight, he dropped acid on a daily basis. It took just one trip to foment the most abrupt change that Roger Smith had ever witnessed in one of his charges. Manson "seemed to accept the world" after LSD, Smith wrote. Seemingly overnight, he transformed himself into an archetypal hippie, his worldview suddenly inflected with spiritualism. He grew out his hair and played guitar in the street, panhandling and scrounging for food. Although only in his early thirties, he presented himself as a father figure, attracting young, down-and-out men and women as they embarked on the spiritual quest that had led them to the Haight.

If Manson was eager to portray himself as Jesus, then Roger Smith would've been John. According to one of my sources, no one knew Manson better than his parole officer did. It would be surprising if Smith didn't know that his ward was breaking the law—a lot. But he had only praise for his sole client. "Mr. Manson has made excellent progress," he wrote in one of several reports he made to the head parole office in Washington, D.C. "He appears to be in better shape personally than he has been in a long time."

Smith wrote those words on July 31, 1967. At the time, Manson was sitting in a jail cell. A few days earlier, in Ukiah, he'd been convicted of interfering with a police officer in the line of duty—a felony. He'd been trying to prevent the arrest of Ruth Ann Moorehouse, aka Ouisch, one of his newly recruited underage girls. Though the charge was reduced to a misdemeanor, Manson was given a thirty-day suspended sentence and three years' probation. (The arrest merited only a footnote in *Helter Skelter*—and Bugliosi didn't say that it resulted in a conviction.) Instead of being sent back to prison, Manson, who'd been out for only four months then, was back on the streets again in a few days.

That incident continued the distressing pattern of amnesty that Roger Smith could never explain. In part, Smith benefited, and continues to benefit, from a veil of secrecy. Manson's complete parole file has never been released. It wasn't even permitted into evidence during the trial. During the death-penalty phase, the defense's Irving Kanarek had subpoenaed the file, hoping he could use some part of it to argue for his client's life. Not only did the United States Attorney General, John Mitchell, refuse to release it, he dispatched David Anderson, an official from the Justice Department, to aid Bugliosi in his effort to quash the subpoena. It was an almost unprecedented action. During death-penalty arguments, when a defendant's life hangs in the balance, anything that could be introduced to save that life is routinely allowed into evidence. In the courtroom, stunned that the government wouldn't allow Manson access to his own file, Kanarek asked Anderson if it contained information that would "incriminate the Attorney General." Bugliosi objected; the judge sustained, and Anderson didn't have to answer. Ultimately, the judge upheld the prosecution's motion to quash the subpoena. The file was never allowed into evidence, and the whole episode was excluded from *Helter Skelter*.

The fifty-five parole documents turned over to me (later sixty-nine, after exhaustive FOIA appeals) by the federal Parole Commission represent only a sliver of Manson's total file, which was described as "four inches thick" at his trial. Still, those pages have enough raw data to show that during Manson's first fourteen months of freedom in San Francisco—months during which he attracted the followers that became the Family—he was given virtual immunity from parole revocation by Roger Smith. Under Smith's supervision, Manson was repeatedly arrested and even convicted without ever being sent back to prison. It was up to Smith to revoke Manson's parole—it was ultimately his decision. But he never even reported any of his client's violations to his supervisors.

In interviews with me, Smith claimed not to have known about Manson's conviction in Ukiah, even though it had occurred under his watch. In fact, in the same July 1967 letter that should have mentioned Manson's conviction—the letter that lauded his "excellent progress"—Smith requested permission for Manson to travel to Mexico, where he would've been totally unsupervised, for a gig with a hotel band. (Smith failed to note the fact that Manson had been arrested in Mexico in 1959, resulting in his deportation to the United States and the revocation of his federal probation.) When I interviewed him, Smith claimed not to know about the Mexico arrest.

"Manson is not to leave the Northern District of California," the parole board responded, noting that Manson's "history does not mention any employment as musician," and that his record was "lengthy and serious."

And yet, two weeks later, Smith tried again—he really wanted to send Manson to Mexico. He told the parole board that Manson had been offered a second job there by "a general distributor for the Perma-Guard Corporation of Phoenix Arizona named Mr. Dean

Moorehouse," who wanted Manson to survey "the market for insecticides, soil additives and mineral food supplements." Smith did not mention that Moorehouse was on probation—regulations barred associations between them—and one of Manson's newest recruits, the father of the fifteen-year-old whose arrest Manson had tried to prevent three weeks earlier.

The parole board rejected this second request, too. Interestingly, at the same time Smith made these requests, he'd launched a criminological study of Mexican drug trafficking for the federal government. He'd attempted to send Manson to Mazatlán, which was the main port city of Sinaloa, the drug trafficking capital of Central America in the 1960s.

"In hindsight," Smith told me when I presented him with the documents, "it was not a good decision." Then he reversed course a bit, saying that he probably made the requests "just to show Manson they wouldn't let him go."

"But, twice?" I asked. "And at the expense of your own credibility?"

He erupted. "If you want to be conspiratorial," he said, "yes, I was doing research on Mexican drug trafficking at the same time I was trying to send him there. So, yes, you could make it look like that, but that wasn't what it was. I wasn't a career PO. I only did it for a couple of years because I needed the money while I did my dissertation. My wife was a teacher, but we had no money. Was I a career, committed parole officer? *No!*"

Committed or not, Smith had official responsibilities—and the paper trail, in its sparseness, suggests that these didn't much weigh on him. After those two Mexico requests, Smith generated only two more documents regarding Manson for another five months. Both were simple form letters authorizing Manson to travel to Florida to meet with "recording agents."

Those interested me for several reasons. First, they violated

Smith's orders from Washington—he was to forbid Manson from leaving the Northern District of California under any circumstances. Second, from my examination of the documents it seemed that Smith had postdated them, suggesting that he wrote them *after* Manson had already left town, safeguarding him from another potential violation. And third, there's no sign that Manson and the Family ever actually went to Florida. If they went anywhere, the only available evidence suggests, it was to Mexico.

Smith's letters are from November 1967. On the very day that Susan Atkins's probation officers were frantically trying to prevent her from traveling, she, Manson, and the others were pulling out of San Francisco in their big yellow bus with permission from Roger Smith.

Manson was required to send postcards to Smith; there's no record that he did. Later, probation reports noted that Atkins and Mary Brunner had said they spent quite a bit of time in Mexico with Manson that winter. Otherwise, their whereabouts for November and December 1967 are entirely unaccounted for.

Fourteen Naked Hippies in a Ditch

After the Florida letters, the record of Manson's supervision stops for another five months—a period during which Manson reported to Smith on a weekly and sometimes daily basis, as he turned his soul-searching followers into programmed killers and planned for a race war.

There should be an avalanche of paperwork on Manson from this time. While certainly Smith wrote reports, the Parole Commission released only twelve documents from his fourteen-month supervision. The Los Angeles portion of Manson's file—covering approximately May 1968 to October 1969—is nearly as incomplete, with sixteen letters from agency officials and Samuel Barrett, who succeeded Smith as Manson's parole officer.

As few as they are, those letters depict an unmanageable parolee at odds with the "excellent progress" described by Smith a year earlier. Barrett once wrote to Manson, "Considering the nature of your last two arrests, and the suspicion you have aroused with law enforcement in this district, the reflection of your status leaves much to be desired."

Despite this admonishment, Barrett was the parole officer Bugliosi singled out for blame at the trial and in *Helter Skelter.* Not Smith, the foster parent to Manson's baby; not Smith, the proud possessor of an affectionate nickname from Manson; not Smith, the parole officer who praised Manson's "progress" allegedly without knowing he had been criminally convicted three days previously. By smearing Barrett, Bugliosi diverted attention from Smith's seemingly far graver sins. After all, where Smith's caseload had dwindled from forty to just one, Barrett had between two hundred fifty and three hundred parole cases between 1967 and 1969. But in *Helter Skelter*'s more than seven hundred pages, Bugliosi could spare only twenty-one words for Roger Smith, whom he never called to testify at trial. Smith told me that he was never questioned about Manson by Bugliosi, the police, or any federal agency—ever.

I knew there had to be more papers from Smith's time as Manson's parole officer. Remember, under oath at the trial, Barrett had described Manson's parole file as "about four inches thick." I asked the Parole Commission spokesperson, Pamela A. Posch, how it could have been reduced to what I'd been told was only 138 pages, and why I could see only 69 of these, extensively redacted. The Bureau of Prisons "apparently did not retain all of the parole documents pertaining to Mr. Manson," Posch wrote, conceding that this was unusual. The bureau had a policy to preserve the files of "notorious felons" for history's sake. Manson was about as notorious as a felon could be.

I thought I'd exhausted my options, but then I remembered that Smith and Manson were part of the San Francisco Project. Since it was a federal study funded by NIMH, it would have required even closer scrutiny of Manson's activities; according to Smith, its clients were to be tracked, analyzed, and recorded in a separate file. But it practically goes without saying: that file was missing, too.

If Smith maintained a close record of Manson, he kept a lot of people in the dark, including his own colleagues. He provided so few details that the parole offices in Los Angeles and San Francisco didn't even know where Manson was living.

In April 1968, Manson was arrested yet again. And there was no covering it up—too many papers had gotten the story. When Smith's colleagues at the parole office read about it, they flipped out and tried to do what Smith hadn't: send Manson back to prison.

The headline in the *Los Angeles Times* read, "Wayward Bus Stuck in Ditch: Deputy Finds Nude Hippies Asleep in Weeds." Other papers picked up the news, too. Their articles were the first to describe what the world would soon know as the Manson Family.

The *Times* staff writer Charles Hillinger described an Oxnard deputy on a late-night patrol who stumbled on a broken-down bus in a ditch by the Pacific Coast Highway. When he saw the bodies scattered in the weeds—nine women, five men—he thought they were dead. Then he realized they were only sleeping. After running a check on the bus's tags, he learned it had been reported stolen from Haight-Ashbury. Waking the group, he told them to get dressed and wait for the county bus he'd ordered, which would take them all to jail. Before they left, one of the women (later identified as Mary Brunner) said, "Wait, my baby's on the bus." She went back to pick up her child, then only a week old. He was sick, with grime and open sores all over his body.

The article identified the "self-proclaimed leader of the band of wanderers" as Charles Manson, adding that he was booked on suspicion of grand theft. Brunner was charged with endangering the life of a child. She was later convicted and received two years' probation.

Within several days, the chief of the San Francisco probation office, Albert Wahl, was alerted to an article about the arrest in the *Oakland Tribune:* "14 Nude Hippies Found Beside Wayward Bus." Of course, one of those hippies was a parolee under his office's supervision.

Wahl flew into a rage, writing to his counterpart in Los Angeles, Angus McEachen, for assistance in finding Manson and sending him back to San Francisco. Wahl had to admit, embarrassingly, that his office's file on Manson was "incomplete," but "apparently" he had been traveling "freely between San Francisco and Los Angeles" for months. Wahl didn't know if Manson had permission to travel, but one thing was clear, he added in a moment of supreme understatement: "regulations weren't followed." Smith's name didn't come up in the letter, but presumably Wahl had him in mind when he wrote, "The officer who was handling the case is no longer attached to this office."

Wahl also wrote of two more arrests in McEachen's district, noting that Manson had failed to report them, as required. For good measure, he sent a copy of his letter to the head of the national office in Washington, adding a copy of the *Tribune* story and a handwritten note: "Be sure to read the clipping—there are people like this."

"You Have Nothing More Important to Do"

So far, the "people like this" had yet to suffer any consequences for their actions. Having been found the legal owner of the bus, Manson spent one day in jail. Then he was released, along with the rest of the group.

McEachen, the chief of the Los Angeles probation office, was not happy about this. He had something of a personal stake in Manson's fate. All the way back in May 1960, he'd been the one to violate Manson's probation for failing to report to his supervisor, sending Manson back to federal prison. He had every intention of following a similar course this time—but he soon learned that, while Manson's probation had been easy to violate in 1960, things were different now.

In a letter to Wahl, McEachen said that Manson had "personally appeared in our office to bring us up-to-date on his adventuresome nature." Claiming to have no interest in money or work—"he has over 3,000 friends who are willing to give him any needed assistance"—Manson said that he owned the school bus and that he and his "girls" had been traveling between San Francisco and Los Angeles in it for months. If anyone from the probation office needed to contact him, he could be reached through a "friend named Gary Hinman of Topanga Canyon"—the same Hinman whom the Family would murder about a year later.

Manson had gall, but McEachen thought he'd gained the upper hand—because Manson had since been arrested *again*, this time on a drug charge. Apparently he was at that moment sitting in the Los Angeles County jail awaiting arraignment.

Sadly, McEachen was wrong: Manson had been released the previous day. For unknown reasons, the DA had declined to file charges. Not to be deterred, McEachen and Wahl tried to rein in their wandering, lawbreaking parolee. As the highest-ranking figures in their offices, they had a lot of clout—but not enough to catch Manson.

Wahl's most vigorous attempt came on June 3, 1968, when he sent a stern ultimatum to Manson's last two known addresses in San Francisco and Los Angeles. (The latter belonged to Dennis Wilson.) Because Wahl didn't know Manson's exact whereabouts, he was forced to give him two options: report to the U.S. probation office in either city immediately. "Failure to follow this direction," he wrote, "will result in my recommending that a warrant for mandatory release violation be issued":

> From this point on, you are not to leave your current residence without written permission from a U.S. Probation Officer. Any permission given you by Mr. Smith, who is no longer connected with this Service, is hereby canceled. Give this matter your immediate attention. You have nothing more important to do.

Manson defied the orders. Rather than showing up in person, he made a phone call to Wahl, who was out of the office—and furious to learn, in a message taken by a subordinate, that Manson had said he was living at Dennis Wilson's place and had been offered a $20,000 annual recording contract by the Beach Boys' label. As Wahl later wrote to McEachen, "It would appear that Mr. Manson is on another LSD trip."

Still, at least they knew where Manson was living now. That was a step in the right direction, wasn't it? On June 6, they sent Samuel Barrett, his new parole officer, to make an unannounced visit. As Barrett reported back, "Manson and some of his hippie followers, mostly female," had "found a haven" at Wilson's home; "apparently [Wilson] has succumbed to Manson's obsequious manner."

Just how deeply had Wilson "succumbed," though? Could it really be true that their delinquent parolee had sweet-talked a Beach Boy into giving him a record deal? McEachen must've been relieved to hear from Nick Grillo, the Beach Boys' manager. Requesting anonymity, Grillo complained that "Manson and his followers are proving to be a threatening factor to the music company." The record label "would have to be idiotic" to have signed him.

The parole office decided they had to order Manson back to

San Francisco, making it clear that he'd return to prison if he failed to comply. On June 12, Barrett sent a letter giving him twelve days to return.

Someone must have intervened. There's no record of what happened between June 12 and the June 24 deadline, but apparently that deadline evaporated. The next letters came in late July and early August. Making no mention of the skipped deadline, McEachen reported to Washington, D.C., that he'd received a phone call from Manson, who had moved on to the Spahn Ranch, where he was "receiving free room and board in exchange for his work as a ranch hand." By then, someone above Wahl, McEachen, and Barrett must've decided that it was best to just let Manson be.

Manson built the Family right under his federal supervisors' noses. From then on, the federal government, as well as local and state law enforcement, only backed further away from the group as they more brazenly broke the law.

The only one who didn't was Roger Smith. Well after his supervision of Manson ended, he was still writing letters to the Mendocino County court about Atkins's and Brunner's sterling characters, and he was caring for Manson's son. Smith and his wife even hosted Manson at their home. With all I'd learned, I still couldn't grasp how a "rock-ribbed Republican" would fall in with an aspirant hippie like Manson—and why their friendship persisted beyond the dissolution of their official relationship.

Coda: The Speed Scene

Smith may have had ulterior motives when he told Manson to move to Haight-Ashbury. As part of his criminology research, he'd been tapped to lead a study on amphetamines and their role in the violent behavior of Haight-Ashbury hippies. The National Institute of Mental Health funded this study, as they had the San Francisco Project. In 1976, a FOIA request forced NIMH to acknowledge that it had allowed itself to be used by the CIA as a funding front in the sixties.

Smith hoped to learn why some people, but not others, became psychotically violent on amphetamines—and to see if this violence could be controlled. The goals of the Amphetamine Research Project (ARP), as he dubbed it, were to "illuminate three major areas" of the "speed scene" in the Haight: the "individual" experience, the "collective or group experience," and the "way in which violence is generated within the speed marketplace." Smith studied hippie collectives by observing them in their daily routines, and he enjoined his researchers to participate, too. He later recalled that when he was appointed to lead the study, "[I] took off my gray-flannel suit and my wing-tip shoes and grew a moustache. Soon the kids on Haight Street were calling me the Friendly Fed and asking me to help them with the law."

There's no indication that his technique proved useful—because there's not much indication that the ARP ever happened at all. Smith never published his research. Two papers about the ARP were scheduled to appear in the *Journal of Psychedelic Drugs,* but they never materialized. The closest thing to a record of the ARP is Smith's unpublished dissertation, submitted to Berkeley a month before the Manson murders. Even this, however, contains no actual "participation–observation" data—it is mainly secondhand anecdotes and statistical analysis.

But the paper, "The Marketplace of Speed: Violence and Compulsive Methamphetamine Abuse," does describe the nature of participant-observation, which, Smith wrote, forced a social scientist to break the law. Hiding in a "deviant group," he had to convince drug users

that they can trust him with information which, in other hands, would place them in jeopardy, and perhaps most important, he must resolve the moral dilemma of being part of something which he may find morally objectionable (at best), probably by association he could himself be arrested... in a very real sense, he becomes a co-conspirator...with information and insight which under normal conditions the average citizen would be obliged to share with law enforcement...he must try to understand what individuals within the group feel, how they view the "straight" world, how they avoid arrest or detection...

To ensure success, Smith argued, researchers had to protect their subjects from criminal prosecution, concealing their activities from the police and granting them anonymity in all reports. The ARP, then, had something resembling police immunity baked into its very mission.

Smith ran the ARP out of the Haight-Ashbury Free Medical Clinic (HAFMC), which had just opened the previous summer. Soon, he was spending so much time there that he made a proposition to his only parole client: instead of meeting with Manson in downtown San Francisco, where Smith had an office, why not just meet at the clinic? It was more convenient for both of them, and anyway, by that time Manson and "his girls" had started to contract sexually transmitted diseases; the clinic could treat those for free.

Soon Manson became a mainstay at the HAFMC. Between visiting Smith and receiving medical care, there were some weeks when he appeared at the clinic every day. He became a familiar presence to a number of the doctors there, including several who, like Smith, had received federal funds to research drug use among hippies.

Smith got the ARP off the ground at the same time he was supervising Manson for the San Francisco Project. It was during this overlap that the record of Manson's parole supervision was either spotty, nonexistent, or later expunged. This funny, scruffy little visitor to the clinic, always with his retinue of girls, was taking a ton of drugs and forming the Family. By the time he and his followers turned up in that ditch by the side of the Pacific Coast Highway in April 1968, the girls had traded the flowers in their hair for steel knives, sheathed in leather and strapped to their thighs beneath long flowing dresses. I was convinced that Roger Smith had facilitated this transformation; now I began to wonder whether the HAFMC, with its emphasis on hippies, drugs, and research, had some role, too.

10

The Haight-Ashbury Free Medical Clinic

Too Many Smiths

To tell the story of Manson properly, as I'd argue Bugliosi never did, you've got to familiarize yourself with a dauntingly large cast, as is clear by now. When I was preparing to turn my aborted *Premiere* story into a book, I realized just how frustrating it was to keep everyone straight, to tell the narrative in a way that gave its major players their due without getting mired in details. Because, in a sense, the details were everything. The lacunae and silences and seemingly irrelevant detours in Manson's life made it clear that he was far more a product of his times, and his surroundings, than something as outrageous as the Helter Skelter motive would have you believe. That motive makes it seem like Manson and the Family lived in a vacuum. But during their formative year in San Francisco, by most accounts, they were part of the zeitgeist. To understand that zeitgeist, I had to deal with the sheer proliferation of names: hundreds and hundreds of names.

It's a confusing story to tell because it involves two Smiths, and they ran in the same circles—both were drug researchers with a sociological interest in the Haight-Ashbury youth scene. On top of Roger Smith, Manson's parole officer, there was David Smith, no relation, the charismatic creator of the Haight-Ashbury Free Medical Clinic.

You wouldn't think that Manson, a chary ex-con who disdained conventional power structures, would spend a lot of time at a government-funded clinic, no matter how groovy its trappings. But Manson and the girls were at the HAFMC a lot. When they moved from the disused school bus into a proper apartment, he chose one right around the corner from the clinic. His involvement with the place, and the extent to which it dovetails with both of the Smiths, has been serially unexplored in popular writing on him. Because Bugliosi seemed to have no use for the Smiths, no one else did, either. But having seen how crucial Roger was to Manson's development, I knew I had to dive into David's history, too.

Dr. Dave

David Elvin Smith grew up in the dusty farm community of Bakersfield, California, at the southern end of the San Joaquin Valley. When he moved to the Bay Area in 1960 to study at UC Berkeley, Smith was, by his own admission, a hick. He'd never traveled much beyond his backwoods town, and he lacked the political and intellectual curiosity that animated Berkeley's sophisticated, international student body. Had it not been for his pushy peers, always scolding him for missing their sit-ins and marches, Smith probably wouldn't have noticed the dawn of the Free Speech movement on his own campus. Later, he liked to remember a teaching assistant who canceled class so he and the other students could head to a protest downtown. Smith refused to join. He wanted to study for an upcoming test. The TA told him he'd never get an A if he didn't go.

Smith has been open about his louche behavior in this period: an inveterate womanizer and a binge drinker, he disappeared for days at a time on benders, nevertheless graduating at the top of his class. At the end of 1965, a debilitating blackout and a messy breakup led him to give up alcohol. By then, Smith, a raffish, good-looking man of twenty-six, was a postdoctoral student at UC San Francisco and the chief of the Alcohol and Drug Abuse Screening Unit at San Francisco General Hospital. Later he remembered his curiosity flaring as his research collided with the city's cultural upheaval. "I was injecting white rats with LSD in the lab," he said, "and then I'd walk home past the Haight, where I'd see kids who were high on the same substance."

He began to experiment with psychedelics himself, and he liked them. The lifestyle brought new friends and new politics. He and his friends tracked the burgeoning counterculture in the Haight, where some were predicting an influx of 100,000 young people in the coming year. Smith, who felt that health care was a right, wondered where the newcomers would receive medical attention, and how they would afford it. He moved to Haight-Ashbury himself with plans to found a free clinic.

When it opened at 558 Clayton Street in June 1967, the Haight-Ashbury Free Medical Clinic (HAFMC) was an immediate sensation. Staffed entirely by volunteers and unauthorized by the city health department, it treated hundreds of patients a day, offering nonjudgmental care for those suffering from bad trips, overdoses, sexually transmitted diseases, and malnourishment, or for those who just needed a kind ear. Lines at the HAFMC sometimes stretched around the block with hippies waiting to ascend the creaky wooden stairs to its second-floor office. Inside, loitering was encouraged. The clinic did everything it could to advertise its psychedelic affinities. Exam rooms were painted in aqua and Day-Glo orange; one of them was wallpapered with a vibrant collage of peace signs, naked bodies, and hypnotic swirls. Even as Smith struggled to pay the rent and keep the cops at bay, he reveled in his creation. Few things so perfectly encapsulated the utopian ideals of the summer of love.

As faces filed in and out of the clinic that summer, Smith and his colleagues befriended the repeat visitors, and the HAFMC became a scene within a scene. It could be hard to tell the hippies apart, with their long, beflowered hair, their upstart communes, their shifting legions of followers and leaders. But decades later, no one at the clinic had any trouble remembering Charlie Manson and his girls.

Negate Your Ego

In 1971, David Smith published *Love Needs Care,* a memoir of the HAFMC's germinal years. I found it rife with details about Manson and the Family, and about the very period that Bugliosi had omitted from *Helter Skelter:* the summer of love, when Manson, apparently at his most charismatic, began to attract followers and ensure their unconditional devotion. Better still, *Love Needs Care* had a few contributions from Roger Smith, offering his own appraisal of Manson.

As invaluable as these portraits are, though, I called them into question when my reporting led me to doubt both of the Smiths. The more I reread certain passages, the more they seemed like gingerly public-relations efforts. The Smiths had to make it clear that they knew Manson well, and that they'd felt some sympathy toward him—there could be no denying that, given how often they'd been seen together. But the book came two years after the murders, when both men had an interest in distancing themselves from *that* Manson, the murderous one, the metaphor for evil. *Love Needs Care* attempts the delicate task of elucidating the Smiths' relationships to Manson while insisting they had no idea that he and his followers would someday erupt into unconscionable violence.

David Smith described the Family's frequent trips to the HAFMC, where "Charlie's girls," as they were known around the halls, were treated for sexually transmitted diseases and unwanted pregnancies. The girls tended to Manson's every need, never speaking unless spoken to. They referred to him as Christ, or "J.C."

When the Family moved to an apartment on Cole Street, Manson began in earnest to "reprogram" his followers. David had an elaborate sense of Manson's tactics, although he never explained where he got it. Using a combination of LSD and mind games, Manson forced his followers to submit to "unconventional sexual practices," Smith wrote; he would invoke mysticism and pop psychology as the acid took hold, saying, "You have to negate your ego." Treating the girls "like objects," he eroded their independence, turning them "into self-acknowledged 'computers,' empty vessels that would accept almost anything he poured in." Before long, they obeyed him unquestioningly.

Acid was unmistakably essential to the process. Manson's insistence on it sometimes put him at odds with trends in the Haight, David thought. Typically, hippies who dropped a lot of acid eventually moved on to speed. A schism grew in the scene. The "acid heads" (a phrase David claims to have coined) favored nonviolence, whereas the "speed freaks" (ditto) caused the rash of violence that destroyed the Haight's live-and-let-live ethos. But Manson had an aversion to needles; he wouldn't use amphetamines. The Family's drug pattern was effectively reversed, with Manson urging his disciples to relinquish speed and embrace acid. Weaning his recruits from amphetamines reduced the chance of interference with his induction process.

Speed became a part of the Family's lifestyle only later, David told me, when it came time to kill in Los Angeles. He'd heard this from Susan Atkins herself, when she asked him to assess her mental health for a parole hearing in 1978. "When they went to the south, they got very deeply involved in speed," he said. They got it from the Hells Angels. "They were trading sex for speed, and [Atkins] thinks that Helter Skelter and the ultimate crime was a paranoid speed delusion."

Bugliosi kept any mention of the Family's speed use out of the trial. David thought he understood why—it risked presenting "mitigating circumstances" for the prosecution. And the defense wouldn't want it coming up, either; no one wants his or her clients to look like addicts.

Both the Smiths have said that Manson's fear of needles made speed a nonissue, but obviously speed can be taken orally or snorted. Over the years, a smattering of evidence and firsthand recollections has suggested that the Family used amphetamines more often than was suggested at the time. In a 2009 documentary, Linda Kasabian claimed that she and her companions each swallowed a "capsule" of speed before leaving for Cielo Drive on the night of Sharon Tate's murder. (At the trial, she testified that she hadn't taken any drugs around the time of the murders.) In books and at parole hearings, Susan Atkins also later copped to taking speed before the Tate murders. Tex Watson wrote that he frequently snorted it with the group, and that he, too, took it on both nights of the murders. Others added that the Family kept an abundance of speed at the Spahn Ranch toward the end of their time there, and that Manson himself wasn't above taking it, especially as he grew more paranoid. He would use it to stay up for days at a time, brooding on his delusions.

Remember, Manson lived in the Haight because Roger Smith sent him there, thinking its "vibes" would assuage the ex-con's hostility. And make no mistake: Roger did believe that Manson was hostile. In a short essay for *Life* magazine published months after the murders, Roger offered his first-ever insights about Manson. ("He speaks of Manson here out of his extensive unofficial contact with him," the magazine noted, without describing the nature of that contact or any potential conflict with Smith's parole duties.) "Charlie was the most hostile parolee I've ever come across," Roger wrote. "He told me right off there was no way he could keep the terms of his parole. He was headed back to the joint and there was no way out of it."

Roger would seldom write or speak about Manson again, wanting to distance himself from his most infamous client; when I first spoke to him, in 2001, I was only the third reporter to do so. But his remark about Manson's hostility always stayed with me. I'd already seen, after all, how he'd characterized Manson in official parole documents as a well-behaved guy making "excellent progress." The disparity suggested that Roger had been willing to sweep Manson's "hostility" under the rug.

In a passage he contributed to *Love Needs Care,* Roger did his best to support the idea that the bizarreries of the Haight suited an ex-con like Manson. Daily LSD trips made him mellower, more thoughtful. He still had the slick duplicitousness of a con man, and he was still a master manipulator, but he was suddenly fond of vacuous self-help bromides like "If you love everything, you don't need to think about what bothers you."

Roger Smith couldn't seem too credulous, so he made sure to note the "messianic" tilt of Manson's acid days—an oblique acknowledgment of Charlie's growing megalomania. David Smith mirrored the sentiment, writing that Manson's LSD trips replaced his "underlying depression with a manic smile" that sometimes betrayed darker philosophies. David admitted that Manson "began to develop a number of delusions as his involvement with LSD progressed." He fantasized about the Beatles ordaining him their musical equal; he imagined a Judgment Day when blacks would slaughter whites.

Some of Roger's familiars, including his wife, couldn't understand his affinity for Manson. Roger was "pretty much in awe of Charlie's ability to draw these women to him," one said. Another thought that he "was always kind of fascinated" with "the charming charismatic sociopath."

After Manson's role in the Tate–LaBianca murders came out, Roger allowed that "he had made an error" in bringing him to the Haight. But at the time, the Family enjoyed a remarkable kinship with Roger. They "swarmed over [Roger] Smith and often filled the [clinic] reception room," David Smith wrote, "bringing operations to a standstill." Roger didn't mind the adulation, in part, David claimed, because "Charlie frequently offered him the services of his harem." (Roger declined this offer.)

Among the HAFMC alumni I spoke to, the understanding was Manson had visited the clinic on many occasions to see Roger for their mandatory parole meetings. Roger himself would later claim that the Family simply came by out of the blue, for no particular reason, and that they didn't begin seeing him there until after his duties as Manson's parole officer had ended. In either case, something about the arrangement didn't sit well with me. One reason the HAFMC was free, after all, was that David, Roger, and their colleagues had received private and federal grants to conduct drug research there. The Smiths were both studying amphetamines and LSD, the latter being the crucial component in Manson's "reprogramming" process. How had an uneducated ex-con—someone who, months ago, had never taken acid and maybe never even heard of it—come to use the drug to such sophisticated ends? And wasn't it suspicious that he was coming to the HAFMC to see two people who were studying that very phenomenon, the use of drugs to control and change behavior?

At least one friend of Roger's had foreseen that it would be "a conflict of interest": "I always thought there would be problems."

Another noted, "Roger had really made a career at that point in trying to help Manson . . . He was going to soothe the savage beast." Instead, the beast grew more savage than ever.

"Frenzied Attacks of Unrelenting Rage"

When he launched the HAFMC, David Smith left a loose end dangling in his past: he'd never actually received his PhD in pharmacology. He'd completed a two-year research project on amphetamines and their effects on groups of confined mice, but he never finished his dissertation. Although he shrugged off the lapse—he'd already completed medical school, after all, and he'd taken quickly to his new life in the Haight—it surprised many of his closest friends, and in our interviews, he was reluctant to admit it. It wasn't like him to leave something undone.

Even in its unpublished form, Smith's research on mice defined him, creating the larger-than-life personality who would eventually be known as "Dr. Dave." In my obsessive way, I found as much of this research as I could. I saw that Smith had published a brief article based on his study in the HAFMC's own house organ, the *Journal of Psychedelic Drugs,* in 1969. It wasn't nearly as robust as his full thesis would've been, but it gave me something to go on.

Before long, I was noticing parallels between Smith's mice and the Family. At first I was inclined to disregard these as the product of my more speculative side—I saw no purpose in linking the behavior of mice in a controlled experiment to the behavior of people in the world at large. But I took another look when I saw that Smith himself had made such a connection. He spoke of his mice as proxies for human beings.

His research started with sixteen albino mice. With the assistance of other researchers, he separated these into two groups of eight in "aggregate" settings—small, closely confined communities intended to simulate crowding. Then he injected the mice with amphetamines. Over the next twenty-four hours, they transformed from docile animals into frantic combatants, fighting one another until they died either from injuries, self-inflicted wounds from overgrooming, or simple exhaustion. The violence was unremitting; Smith described "frenzied attacks of unrelenting rage." Afterward, all that remained in the blood-spattered cages were scattered, dismembered body parts. Simply by confining the animals in close quarters, he'd increased the toxicity of the amphetamines more than four times.

In another attempt, some of the mice were dosed with other chemicals—mescaline, chlorpromazine, or reserpine—before they received amphetamine injections. The extra drugs sometimes had a sorting effect, segregating the mice that would kill from the mice that wouldn't. Or they had a soothing effect, all but eliminating the violent tendencies.

Smith told me he'd started his research having foreseen an influx of amphetamine abusers in San Francisco. He didn't say how he'd predicted that influx, but he was right. In the summer of '67, as he opened his clinic, amphetamines exploded in popularity in the Haight.

"When the speed scene hit, it was a total shock to everybody," he told me. "Suddenly, what I'd learned in pharmacology relative to amphetamines was applicable [to people]."

Throughout *Love Needs Care,* Smith draws parallels between the rodents he'd studied and the speed-addled hippies in the Haight. The mice on speed, he wrote, "become inordinately aggressive and assaultive ... [turning] upon one another with unexpected savagery. Their violent behavior is probably intensified by confinement for it is strikingly similar to that observed in amphetamine abusers who consume the drugs in crowded atmospheres."

In the Haight, Smith watched as people living cheek by jowl took huge doses of speed, inspiring paranoia and hallucinations. Once peaceful and well-adjusted, the "speed freaks" of San Francisco now "lashed out with murderous rage at any real or imagined intrusion," assaulting, raping, or torturing to relieve the paranoid tension. "Cut off from the straight world, crammed together in inhuman conditions, and controlled by chemicals," Smith concluded, "they behaved, quite naturally, like rats in a cage."

But when I spoke to Smith, he was quick to discount these parallels. "I happened to study amphetamines before they hit the Haight," he said. "The Haight didn't give me the idea. It's kind of like a historical accident... I was studying LSD before LSD hit the Haight [too]."

In fact, according to Dr. Eugene Schoenfeld, who participated in a portion of Smith's rat research in 1965, LSD was an integral component of the project. Smith and his colleagues would inject the rats with acid in hopes of making them more suggestible before he gave them amphetamines. Suggestibility was among the most prized effects of LSD from a clinical perspective. And yet Smith kept LSD out of the official documentation of his research. The article he published in the *Journal of Psychedelic Drugs* never mentioned acid.

I asked Smith if LSD was part of his protocol. He denied it— then, a moment later, without provocation, he reversed himself.

"Yeah, I stuck LSD in them," he said.

But he couldn't explain why. "I was sticking all different kinds of drugs in them," he added. In his recollection, LSD "produced disorganized behavior, but not violent behavior." The rats would just wander around in a daze.

If you've noticed that I've used "rats" and "mice" interchangeably, there's a reason for that—Smith used them interchangeably, too, even though the two species have vastly different behavioral patterns, especially in groups. In his *Journal of Psychedelic Drugs* article, he calls them mice; in *Love Needs Care* and another book he published, they're rats. Schoenfeld insisted that he'd worked with rats during his part of the research. But Smith was adamant that they were mice, and he couldn't explain his confusion on the subject.

Like the San Francisco Project and Roger Smith's Amphetamine Research Project (ARP), some of David Smith's research, according to his academic papers, was funded by the National Institute of Mental Health (NIMH), which, as mentioned earlier, later acknowledged that the CIA used it as a front for LSD research. And though David never mentioned it in his writing, his work owed a clear debt to the landmark research of another NIMH psychologist, John B. Calhoun, who'd studied rat populations since 1946.

Calhoun reported that rats in confined groups—even *without* drugs—became uncharacteristically aggressive. They'd erupt in rape, murder, cannibalism, and infanticide. A dominant male rat emerged in the "behavioral sink"—Calhoun's term for his aggregated rat cultures—subjugating other males into a tribe of cowering, enfeebled followers and organizing female rats into a "harem" of sex slaves. The strangest group to emerge was "the probers": "hypersexualized" male rats that stalked and raped both males and females, and often cannibalized their young. The probers would commit "frenzied" and "berserk" attacks against rat families sleeping in their burrows, leaving the remains of half-eaten victims. Again, no drugs were involved here; the probers emerged simply as a result of their confinement. They deferred only to the dominant male rat, fleeing if he caught sight of them.

Calhoun's study was a watershed. In the midsixties, amid growing concerns about population density, social scientists, politicians, and journalists cited him to explain the riots in America's overcrowded ghettos. His term "behavioral sink"—defined as "the outcome of any behavioral process that collects animals together in unusually great numbers...aggravating all forms of pathology that can be found within [the] group"—entered the scientific lexicon almost right away. David Smith used it extensively in his writing and in interviews with me.

Though Smith never mentioned Calhoun by name, his research was essentially a continuation. He sought to control the pathologies of rats (or was it mice?) in crowded environments by aggravating them with amphetamines. He concluded that amphetamines were more toxic to rats in groups than rats alone. Their crowding essentially exacerbated the effects of the stimulant.

And this conclusion, like so much in Smith's research, confused me. I didn't see how it could be objective and unbiased. According to Calhoun, the rats' violence wasn't *intensified* by confinement, but created by it. So what difference did it make if Smith shot them up with amphetamines? It seemed like the equivalent of studying drunk, inexperienced ice skaters to learn about alcohol intoxication. The novice skaters were going to fall down on the ice anyway, regardless of whether they'd been drinking or not. Plus, the more interesting subtleties of Calhoun's research—the emergence of a dominant male, a harem of subservient females, and an underclass of "probers," all of which, it had to be said, sounded a lot like the Family—had gone entirely unnoted in Smith's project. I wondered if amphetamines, with or without LSD, had increased the dominant male's grip on his followers.

Given how eerily Smith's research prefigured the creation of the Family—under David's nose, in the Haight, during the summer of '67—I wondered if he had deliberately underreported it. I've never come close to proving that he did, but I haven't been able to explain the holes in it, either. Why would he use LSD to induce suggestibility in rats before injecting them with amphetamines and making them berserk?

Past a certain point, Smith had little interest in helping me sort it out.

"I was just talking about the parallels to what happened with the Manson Family," I said, "and when I try to describe your research, I just kept getting hung up on—"

"Well, then why don't you just forget about the research, then. Just delete the whole thing from your book."

"It was important," I said.

"You're spending way too much of your and my time on it. Take what you want and reject the rest."

The Psychedelic Syndrome

When Roger Smith joined forces with the HAFMC to begin the ARP, he was picking up where David left off—but this time, the research involved people. This meant that both Smiths, and Manson, were often in the same place, at the same time, with both Smiths having received funding from a federal institute later revealed to be a CIA front.

"It was in a certain sense coincidental," David said of the arrangement. "Roger was the head of the speed project and Charlie came to the Haight and visited Roger. He didn't come to be part of the speed research project. It was just that Roger happened to be his [parole] officer."

Details on the ARP, and on the pharmacological goings-on at the HAFMC more generally, were hard to come by. The reams of record keeping you'd expect from clinical experimentation simply weren't there. Stephen Pittel, a forensic psychologist who'd worked with both Smiths at the HAFMC, volunteered a stunning bit of information that Roger and David had neglected to share with me.

"The only thing I remember about ARP was that it got burglarized one night and Roger lost all of his files," Pittel told me. Their disappearance had been jarring, in part because Roger was "an unusually paranoid guy to begin with." He was especially skittish about Manson. After the murders, Roger refused to discuss him with anyone. Pittel assumed that Smith didn't want to be blamed for "directing" Manson to the Haight. "He felt people were saying that he was the one who put the toxins into the environment."

The HAFMC's original chief psychiatrist, Dr. Ernest Dernburg, remembered the theft of the ARP files, too. As he recalled, they'd gone missing right after the announcement of Manson's arrest for the Tate–LaBianca murders and that "Roger, understandably, was pretty upset." Nothing else was taken from the HAFMC, which led the staff to believe that the police or some federal agency might've removed the files. These were research papers, he reminded me: "It didn't make sense for someone to steal these things when they didn't inherently have any value to the average individual. It seemed to have a more nefarious purpose."

The Smiths both denied that the theft had ever happened. "You're dealing with aging memories," David said. But Dernburg and Pittel—full-time doctors, and credible sources, I thought—stood by their stories. "They were absolutely stolen," Pittel said. Dernburg, perturbed by David's insinuation about his faculties, told me more that he remembered. "It was a considerable amount of research—the premier amphetamine research conducted at a street level. It would have been very important to the clinic... and it disappeared. Call David. Ask Roger if he has the files or knows where they are."

Both men said they had no idea.

What *have* survived are the many issues of the *Journal of Psychedelic Drugs,* the HAFMC's in-house research organ, still active to this day. David Smith founded it in '67, and at various points both he and Roger served on its editorial board. In the late sixties and early seventies, the journal printed a raft of articles by David and other clinicians about the long-term effects of LSD and amphetamines.

One of these articles hoped to find out "whether a dramatic drug-induced experience" would have "a lasting impact on the individual's personality." Another observed that feelings of "frustrated anger" led people to want to try LSD: "The soil from which the 'flower children' arise," the author wrote, "is filled more with anger and aggression, thorns and thistles, rather than passion and petunias." Under "emotional pressure," acid could induce "images and sensations of anger or hate magnified into nightmarish proportions."

David Smith had studied these same phenomena, formulating an idea that he called "the psychedelic syndrome," first articulated in 1967 or early '68. The gist was that acid, when taken by groups of like-minded people, led to a "chronic LSD state" that reinforced "the interpretation of psychedelic reality." The more often the same group of "friends" dropped acid, the more they encouraged one another to adopt the worldview they'd discovered together on LSD, thus producing "dramatic psychological changes."

Usually the psychedelic syndrome was harmless, but regular LSD use could cause "the emergence of a dramatic orientation to mysticism." And in people with "prepsychotic personalities," Smith wrote, LSD precipitated "a long-term psychological disorder, usually a depressive reaction or a schizophrenic process."

Had Smith seen this "syndrome" in the Family? After Manson had been arrested for the murders, David wrote, "Charlie could probably be diagnosed as ambulatory schizophrenic." He said the same thing when I asked about Manson: "I felt that he was schizo." It was Roger Smith who'd had the better diagnosis, and the earlier one, David maintained: "Roger said that he knew from day one that Charlie was a psychopath."

But Roger apparently never thought it was necessary to intervene—to send his parolee back to prison or to get him proper psychiatric care. (Roger maintains he didn't believe Manson was dangerous and couldn't have foreseen what would happen.) Instead, he sent him to the Haight and watched him drop acid every day, accruing suggestible young followers as he went. Meanwhile,

David was studying the exact psychological conditions that gave rise to the Manson Family while he treated them at his clinic. Bugliosi had erased all of these facts from his history of the group.

Roger Smith knew that the stereotype of the addict had a lot of potency in the popular imagination. Casual drug users were regarded as inherently criminal, a tear in the fabric of society. The public's fear of such people was easily manipulated.

In 1966, the year before Manson was released from prison, Smith published a criminology paper called "Status Politics and the Image of the Addict," examining the propaganda that had stigmatized Chinese (or "Oriental," as he put it) opium smokers in San Francisco in the early twentieth century. Citing police files and strategy manuals, Smith described an organized effort to cast opium addicts—who were by and large peaceful—as "insidious" "deviants" who "posed a threat to society."

To this end, some agents "were assigned to pose as drug addicts" and infiltrate the opium scene. Their objective was to "characterize the addict as a dangerous individual likely to rob, rape, or plunder in his crazed state." And it worked: the once invisible opium users of San Francisco's Chinese ghettos were, by 1925, depicted in the media as crazed "dope fiends." The shift in public perception allowed the police to crack down on the Chinese population, deporting or institutionalizing the undesirables. Smith neither valorized nor condemned these efforts, but he noted that they were effective. "The Orientals," he wrote, "were viewed as a threat to the existing structure of life in this country." Tainting their image meant that they could be "differentiated and degraded to the satisfaction of society."

It's not hard to see how such research could be applied to Haight-Ashbury hippies in the late sixties. Most Americans frowned on acid, as they frowned on all drugs, but it took Charles Manson to give LSD new and fearsome dimensions. Suddenly it caused violence, and the hippies who used it were perceived as wild-eyed and dangerous where once they'd been harmless, if vacuous, pleasure seekers.

The HAFMC's goal—free health care for everyone—was an unimpeachable part of the hippie ethic, and there could be no doubting that David Smith and his volunteer doctors had improved the community. But just because the clinic had "Free" in its name didn't mean that it had no cost. The place served as a gateway between the hippie world and the straight world, affording doctors a closer look at the hierarchies and nuances of the counterculture. In exchange for their "free" health care, patients were held up to the light and scrutinized by eager researchers, David Smith chief among them.

Emmett Grogan, the founder of the Diggers, was one of a few observers who saw something amiss behind Smith's idealism. The Diggers were an anarchist group known for providing food, housing, and medical aid to runaways in the Bay Area. Smith liked them, and he worked with them at a free infirmary based out of their Happening House; it inspired his own clinic.

But as Grogan wrote in his 1972 memoir *Ringolevio,* the admiration wasn't mutual, at least not for long. Smith soon "began his own self-aggrandizement." He appeared "more concerned with the pharmacology of the situation than with treating the ailing people who came to him for help." Grogan noticed that he kept detailed records "about drugs and their abuse." These he used to secure funding for the HAFMC, which he opened only six weeks after he'd joined the Diggers' operation. Grogan saw through the HAFMC's mission statement right away: "Just because no one was made to pay a fee when they went there, didn't make it a 'free clinic,'" he wrote. "On the contrary, the patients were treated as 'research subjects' and the facility was used to support whatever medical innovations were new and appropriate to the agency."

Of course, one of these patients was Manson, who became one of David Smith's "research subjects" as well. He was such a special case that Smith tracked him far beyond the walls of the HAFMC, sending his top researcher all the way down to Los Angeles, where Manson and his ranks of followers had set up shop on the time-worn Western sets of the Spahn Ranch.

The Group-Marriage Commune

You might remember the name Alan Rose. It was Rose who dropped everything and went to Mendocino County in '68 when several of Manson's followers wound up in jail there. That trip was only a prelude to his deeper involvement with the Family, which saw him embed with the group to study their sexual dynamics—or just to get laid, depending on whom you ask.

Rose was a friend of Roger Smith—he'd helped set up the ARP—but he was even closer to David Smith, who told me, "Al was like my disciple and I was like his father." A former rabbinical student, Rose had dropped out of college in Ohio to move to the Haight in '66, when he was twenty-one. He became the HAFMC's head administrator and a research assistant, at various times, to both Smiths. Rose and David went on to coauthor three studies of the Haight's drug culture in the *Journal of Psychedelic Drugs*. Like the Smiths, Rose had an intuitive grasp of the population and a clinician's knowledge of the drugs they were taking, even though he had no formal medical training.

While reserved and socially awkward by many accounts, Rose enjoyed the Haight, especially its sexual openness. He felt inexperienced in that regard, and he hoped he could change that when Roger introduced him to Manson and the girls, who were coming by the clinic with increasing frequency. Rose was enamored. He decided, along with David, that they'd make for good research subjects. But already there was the question of his impartiality. The legend around the HAFMC was that the girls had "seduced" Rose, probably on Manson's orders.

When, in June 1968, Manson hand-selected a number of his group to accompany him to Los Angeles, Rose may have feared that the yearlong party was drawing to a close. He invited the remaining women to move into his Haight-Ashbury home, where he could tend to their needs until Manson summoned them.

It was then that some of the girls headed to Ukiah for their ill-fated recruitment effort. When they landed in jail, Rose jumped at the chance to rescue them. As David Smith described the episode in *Love Needs Care,* Rose outdid himself, visiting the girls daily and fetching candy and cigarettes for them. Mary Brunner, the mother of Manson's newborn son, was still lactating. The other girls made a habit of going naked and sucking the milk from her breasts. This rattled the jail staff, but Rose vouched for the girls. Outside the jail, he kept busy by consulting with lawyers on courtroom strategy and preparing his testimony as a character witness. All the while, he was living on money funneled to him by David.

When the case was resolved, the girls made tracks for the Spahn Ranch, not wanting to keep Manson waiting. By now, it seemed, Rose couldn't bear to part with them; he elected to go, too. And then he stayed with them. For four months.

Was this a business trip or a vacation? It's up for debate just how totally Rose succumbed to the Family's power. Judging from the published accounts of his time with them, he was more an enabler than a blind devotee. Somewhat opaquely, David wrote that Rose was "both a sympathetic cousin and . . . a sociologically oriented participant-observer in the strange communal phenomenon." Roger Smith had used that term "participant-observer," too, for his ARP—he endorsed looking the other way when one's subjects broke the law. Did that same laxness apply to Rose at the Spahn Ranch?

David provided varying and sometimes contradictory accounts of Rose's role in the Family, and he lost his temper when I tried to set the record straight. The first time we spoke, he admitted that

"Al became enraptured with their philosophy and he traveled with them." Rose dropped acid with the Family, Smith said, "and then six of the girls just fucked his brains out and he saw God...He borrowed some money from me and he didn't pay it back and it turned out he gave it to Charlie...So it was, like, very weird." Other sources also remembered Rose having some kind of ecstatic sexual encounter with the Family.

But at some point, the appeal of the group faded for him, and he left. "He came back," Smith said. "I can't really say he got kicked out. He just said he was no longer part of it."

And yet, when I revisited the matter with Smith a few years later, he said, "I don't know if Al went to Spahn Ranch." When I reminded him that he'd said otherwise, he made a grudging concession: "He was with them four weeks, *max!*"

So I tracked down Rose himself, who told me in a phone call that he was at the ranch for "probably three or four months." Rose was shocked that I wanted to talk to him—only one other journalist had been in touch—and I found him nonchalant about his time with the Family. More than either of the Smiths, he came across as mild, somewhat naive, and unassuming. His memories of the late sixties had their edges smoothed like stones in the sea. Of course he remembered the girls: "They had a level of self-confidence and dynamism that was pretty amazing," he said. "They could walk into stores and get checks cashed without ID, okay?" And he remembered the power that Manson exuded, recalling a man whose raw charisma was by then tainted with egotism and racism. Still, he obeyed Manson, sincerely feeling that his "destiny was going with Charlie and the girls." He added, "We were all pretty impressionable, very idealistic...Charlie convinced me I didn't need glasses. I stopped wearing them. He'd have me drive the bus up and down the L.A. freeway. I really had to strain."

What had finally made him leave the Spahn Ranch was an

incident in which Manson picked up a prostitute from the freeway and "paraded" her in front of his followers, saying that he "wouldn't have sex with her because she wouldn't give him head. And I just saw that as such an abuse of the power that he had."

It was late autumn 1968 when Rose returned to the Haight. He moved in with Roger and his wife, Carol, in Tiburon, and assisted in writing up two studies. The first was Roger's ARP dissertation. The second was called "The Group Marriage Commune: A Case Study," coauthored with David Smith: the first-ever scholarly study of the Manson Family.

David and Rose believed they had a major research paper on their hands, bolstered by Rose's firsthand observations of the Family. The first published remarks about their "study" appeared six weeks after the Family was charged with the murders, in a January 1970 interview Smith gave to the *Berkeley Barb,* an alt-weekly. The front-page story was headlined, "M.D. on Manson's Sex Life: Psychologist Who Lived with Manson Family Tells About Commune."

Smith discussed Rose's "four months" on the ranch, but he never indicated that his coresearcher had been a follower of Manson. Intentionally or not, Smith gave the impression that Rose's time with the Family was part of a planned study; in fact, they'd decided to write about the Family only *after* Rose left the commune, a point they'd finesse later. And even though Rose was the "psychologist" referred to in the headline, he wasn't, of course, a real psychologist. Smith didn't let him do any of the talking. Instead, the reporter quoted portions of their "scholarly paper," noting that Smith had pulled that article from the presses as soon as he learned that its subjects had been accused of mass murder.

Their paper was eventually published in the *Journal of Psychedelic Drugs* in September 1970. It distanced the HAFMC from Rose's involvement with the Family, and it never identified Manson by his last name, leaving the reader to make the connection. "Partici-pation in the commune at the time of [Rose's] involvement," read the introduction, "was not associated with academic observation and only after leaving the communal setting was thought given to description." Perhaps to exculpate the authors of any responsibility for the murders, it fudged the facts about "Charlie," claiming that during "our observation" he "expressed a philosophy of nonvio-lence…LSD-induced psychedelic philosophy was not a major motivational force."

Smith further downplayed the Family's connection to the HAFMC by claiming that they only spent "three months" living in the Haight, during which their "primary" residence was a bus. In fact, the Family lived in the Haight for more than a year, two blocks from the HAFMC, and after Manson took some followers to Los Angeles, the others moved into Rose's home.

The paper asked why "these young girls" were "so attracted and captivated by a disturbed mystic such as Charlie." That was a great question. Past a certain point, it seemed Rose and Smith had no intention of answering it. Their paper detailed Manson's abusive, controlling methods, especially his sexual tactics, but it steered clear of their true area of expertise: LSD. Most egregiously, the paper was never updated to mention the Tate–LaBianca murders, even though it was published a full year later. The defining event of the "com-mune" that Rose had infiltrated was nowhere to be found.

"Extricated"

Vincent Bugliosi didn't have much use for David and Roger Smith, and he had no use at all for Alan Rose. He didn't interview any of them for *Helter Skelter.* The book's one quote from Roger — "There are a lot of Charlies running around, believe me" — was lifted from his short piece in *Life* magazine and framed to make it look as if Bugliosi had actually spoken to him. The same was true of David.

Bugliosi used him to shrug off the implication that drugs enabled the Family, quoting his assertion that "sex, not drugs, was the common denominator." That quote is also pulled misleadingly from *Life*—David had written about Manson in the same issue. (Given the realm of David Smith's research, I can't see how he really believed it.) Other than that, the Smiths are absent from a story that might never have unfolded without them.

A book is one thing—Bugliosi had dramatic license. Maybe he just didn't think he could do justice to Manson's messy year in Haight-Ashbury. The trial was different. There, Bugliosi had to convince the jury beyond a reasonable doubt that Manson had enough control over his followers to get them to kill for him. He got former Family members to testify in exchange for lighter sentences or dropped charges; they provided vivid illustrations of Manson's domination. But he never called Roger or David Smith, two authorities who'd had almost daily exposure to Manson as he formed the group.

Bugliosi's obsession with convicting Manson of conspiracy is the drama that drives *Helter Skelter* forward. To get Manson's guilty verdict, he had to demonstrate that Manson had ordered the murders and had enough control over the killers that they would do his bidding without question. And he was desperate to do this. He wanted witnesses who could say that "Manson ordered or instructed *anyone* to do *anything*," he told his subordinates. He had to prove *"domination."*

Roger Smith's and David Smith's *Life* essays, the same ones Bugliosi quoted in *Helter Skelter,* came out a month before Bugliosi issued those marching orders to LAPD detectives. Within weeks, the *Berkeley Barb* and *Los Angeles Free Press* ran their front-page stories featuring David Smith's discussion of Manson's "indoctrination" techniques, his "process of reorienting" new recruits, and his "methods of disciplining family members."

Bugliosi told the jury he'd prove that Manson was "the dictatorial leader of the Family." He was still calling witnesses to the stand when David Smith and Alan Rose's research paper came out, featuring such lines as "[Manson] served as absolute ruler."

Yet the Smiths and Alan Rose told me that Bugliosi never got in touch with them. Nor did anyone else from the Los Angeles DA's office or the LAPD. Despite their extensive knowledge of the Family, the researchers never felt it was their duty to tell the authorities what they knew. If anything, David Smith feared testifying. "I remember not wanting to be involved in that trial," he said. "I felt that it would compromise our clinic."

Dr. Dernburg, the psychiatric director of the HAFMC when the Family went there, followed the trial with mounting gloom as he realized that the whole San Francisco chapter of Manson's life was never going to come out. He told me it was "as if Manson's stay up here had been extricated from the whole mass of data."

I couldn't wrap my head around this. Why did Bugliosi ignore the most powerful prosecution evidence available: eyewitness testimony of Manson's control from his parole officer, a laureled medical researcher, and his assistant, who'd lived with the group? Each could've taken the witness stand independently, untainted by the suggestion of a plea arrangement or some type of deal.

I knew I'd have to ask Bugliosi about this eventually, but by that point I didn't trust him, and I wanted to box him in as much as I could. So I called on Stephen Kay, his coprosecutor, to show him all the evidence of the Smiths' relationships with the Family. I was on good terms with Kay, and I felt I could rely on him to be straight with me. At his office, I laid out the two *Life* essays, which I knew Bugliosi had seen, plus press accounts of the Smiths and the HAFMC research papers.

Kay read through them diligently. "I have never seen these before," he said, his mouth open. I asked him if there was any way that Bugliosi had missed this stuff. Absolutely not, Kay said. "Vince

Susan Atkins, right, leaving the grand jury proceedings for the Tate–LaBianca murders with her defense attorney, Richard Caballero. Atkins's testimony was critical to securing indictments against Manson and others in the Family, including herself. But Caballero came to represent her only through an arrangement by prosecutors. (Ralph Crane / The *Life* Picture Collection)

Caballero also sold his client's story to the press and arranged to have it published as a quickie paperback, released the same month as her grand jury appearance—a move that only bolstered the state's case against Atkins and her coconspirators. (Author collection)

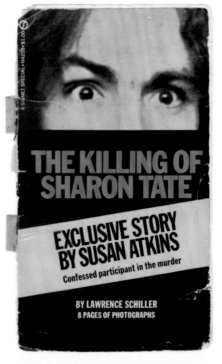

Mary Brunner, one of Manson's earliest followers, with their child, Michael "Pooh Bear" Valentine. (*Life* magazine)

Roger Smith, Manson's parole officer, with his assistant, Gail Sadalla. Manson formed the Family during his time under Smith's supervision in San Francisco. (Elaine Mayes)

ALBERT WAHL
CHIEF PROBATION OFFICER
ROBERT E. SCOTT
DEPUTY CHIEF
PROBATION OFFICER

U. S. COURT HO
BOX NUMBER 3606/
SAN FRANCISCO 94102
CODE 415
TEL. 556-0201

UNITED STATES DISTRICT COURT
NORTHERN DISTRICT OF CALIFORNIA
OFFICE OF THE PROBATION OFFICER

June 3, 1968

REPLY TO: CHIEF PROBATION OFFICER
REFER TO: d

Mr. Charles M. Manson
255 Staples Street
San Francisco, California
    and
14400 Sunset Boulevard
Pacific Palisades, California

Dear Mr. Manson:

Immediately after receipt of this letter, you will
report either to the U. S. Probation Office, U. S.
Courthouse, Los Angeles, California, in person or
to the undersigned in San Francisco. Failure to
follow this direction on or before Monday, June 10,
will result in my recommending that a warrant for
mandatory release violation be issued.

From this point on, you are not to leave your current
residence without written permission from a United
States Probation Officer. Any permission given you
by Mr. Smith who is no longer connected with this
Service is hereby cancelled.

Give this matter your immediate attention. You have
nothing more important to do.

                    Very truly yours,

                    ALBERT WAHL
            Chief U. S. Probation Officer

cc: Mr. Joseph N. Shore
    Parole Executive, Washington, D. C.

A stern letter to Manson from the Federal Probation Office. Manson often
ignored his responsibilities as a federal parolee, but he never faced any
consequences. (Public archive)

Dr. David E. Smith (facing the camera), the cofounder of the Haight-Ashbury Free Medical Clinic, during the summer of love in 1967. Manson and the Family frequented the clinic. (Wayne F. Miller / Magnum Photos)

In clinical experiments, David Smith injected drugs into groups of rodents in confinement. His research echoed the work of John B. Calhoun, a scientist who used rats to study the effects of overpopulation. Illustrations in his landmark 1962 paper, "Population Density and Social Pathology," showed the rodents growing violent in increasingly crowded environments. (*Scientific American*)

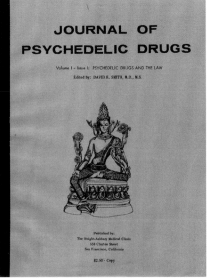

Through his clinic, Smith launched the *Journal of Psychedelic Drugs*, a research periodical that later included a study of the Manson Family's "group-marriage commune." (Haight-Ashbury Medical Clinic)

Dr. Louis Jolyon West, circa 1955. The Central Intelligence Agency subcontracted West for its top-secret MKULTRA program, although he denied it for the rest of his life. (Louis Jolyon West files, UCLA)

Shot of Drug Kills Tusko

By Claire Cawley
A 7,000 - pound research-er gave up his life for sci-ence Friday.
Tusko, the 10-year-old male elephant being board-ed at the Oklahoma City zoo, died shortly after in-jection with an exper-imental drug which has been administered to hu-mans to induce mental ill-ness for study purposes.
The drug is LSD, ly-sergic acid diethylamide. Tusko's reaction was a complete shock to scien-tists who attempted to save his life.
Dr. L. J. West, profes-sor of psychiatry at the University of Oklahoma medical school, who has been directing a series of experiments for which the animal was brought here from Phoenix, said the dos-age was .3 grams.
This is much larger than the proportionate human dose, but 50 percent small-er than the dose ratio for members of the cat family, whose reaction to LSD has been extensively studied, he said.
Dr. West said he and Dr. Chester Pierce, chief of

Dr. L. J. West bends over Tusko as Dr. Warren Thomas looks on.

West found notoriety in 1962 when one of his experiments led him to inject an elephant with enough LSD to kill it in an accidental overdose. While the fact never came out, funding for this debacle came from the CIA. (*The Oklahoman* digital archive)

SAN ANTONIO NEWS HOME EDITION

★ *The Dependable Home Newspaper* ★

36—NO. 258   SAN ANTONIO, TEXAS, MONDAY, JULY 5, 1954   44 Pages   PRICE 5 CENTS

AIRMAN CHARGED IN BRUTAL SEX SLAYING OF S.A. CHILD

★ ★ ★   ★ ★ ★

Thrice-Wed Man Held in Death of Tiny Girl Sunday

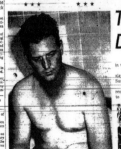

A 31-year-old Lackland A.F.B. drill instructor was in Bexar County jail Monday charged with murder in what veteran peace officers described as Bexar County's most shocking crime of recent years.
Airman 3/C Jimmy N. Shaver, thrice married and the father of two sons, was charged in the rape-slaying of 3-year-old Chere Jo Horton whose battered body was found in a gravel pit off Frio City Road early Sunday. Her disappearance had set in motion a 200-man midnight search.
Constable Ed Schaeffer, who filed the charge, said the airman had signed a statement assuming "full responsibility" for the crime and clearing a 20-year-old Lackland basic trainee who had been with him prior to the attack.

Police Investigator Dean Jones said Shaver "blamed it on drink-ing."
Chere Jo, who apparently had struggled bravely against the man who abducted and ravished her, was the daughter of Mr. and Mrs. J. C. Horton of Trumbo Road.
The child's father was taken to Robert B. Green Hospital about 10:30 p.m. Sunday suffering from shock. After being given a seda-tive, he was returned to his home.

In the 1950s, around the time he researched mind-control techniques for the CIA, West inserted himself into the case of Jimmy Shaver, a Texas airman convicted of raping and murdering a three-year-old girl. Shaver claimed to have no memory of the crime. (*San Antonio News*)

Chemrophyl Associates

P. O. Box 8176
Southwest Station
Washington 24, D. C.

Sherman C. Grifford

2 July 1953

Major Louis J. West
210 Fairchild Lackland Village
San Antonio, Texas

My Good Friend:

I returned from a brief vacation in Maine to find your letter of 11 June
on my desk. I had been awaiting your next communication with considerable
anticipation and curiosity. Frankly, I had been wondering whether your apparent rapid and comprehensive grasp of our problems could possibly be real.
A considerable portion of your letter indicated that you have indeed developed an admirably accurate picture of exactly what we are after. For this I
am deeply grateful.

I am proceeding to take action on developing a practical <u>modus operandi</u>
in the following way:

(1) I am today dispatching a letter to Dr. Hastings enclosing a copy
of your communication and suggesting to him an early conference here in order
to make our initial assault on the top brass in your outfit.
(2) In regard to the remarks you make about the advisability of your
having some leeway in this purchase let me advise that it will be possible
to setup a separate sum of money to be given to you personally for such
matters.
(3) It seems to me that it would be useful for me to obtain Top Secret
clearance from our organization for Steele, Brua and Cowles. We may not favor
to bring them in on the whole story but it would be wise to be in a position
to do so when and if this becomes necessary. For this purpose I would appreciate receiving by return mail the following information on each of these
personalities.

(a) Their full name and title
(b) Their date of birth
(c) Their title of their present job
(d) Their serial number

I gather from your letter that you do not look with favor on attempts
to have you maneuvered out of the Air Force very soon. This would be difficult
to do in any case but I want to know from you whether or not Hastings and I
should pose this as an alternative to the top brass here in the eventuality
that they think it impossible to develop this project within the Air Force
structure.

Sidney Gottlieb, West's handler at the CIA, wrote to him under the pseudonym
Sherman Grifford, using letterhead from "Chemrophyl Associates," a front company. Their correspondence, which confirms West's participation in MKULTRA,
has never before been published. (Author collection)

In 1969, at age twenty-three, Filippo Tenerelli was found dead in a Bishop, California, motel room. Although his death was ruled a suicide, police covered up an abundance of evidence suggesting he was another victim of the Manson Family. (Courtesy Caterina Tenerelli)

After his death, Tenerelli's Volkswagen Beetle was found overturned near the Family's hideout in Death Valley. Manson and his followers routinely stole Beetles to convert them into dune buggies for use in the rough desert terrain. (Courtesy Dallas Sumpter)

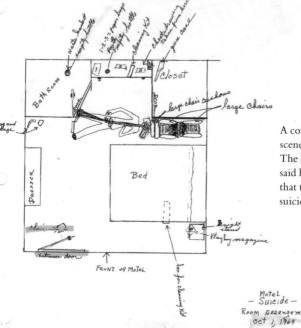

A coroner's drawing of the scene of Tenerelli's death. The autopsy physician later said he was never confident that the incident was a suicide. (Author collection)

The Family in Death Valley, November 1968, in a never-before-published photograph. Manson appears in the back row, fourth from the left. (Special Collections department, University of Nevada)

read all the newspapers, every paper that came out. He subscribed to *every* paper.

"I know everything we had in the files," Kay went on, "because we had a big file cabinet. I'd been through all that." He was positive they didn't have the Smiths' papers and articles there. If Bugliosi knew about them, "he wasn't keeping them in the regular file."

As far as Kay could recall, Bugliosi had never discussed the Smiths and Alan Rose, never entertained the idea of putting them on the stand. But Kay couldn't understand why. "If we had an independent person like that," he told me, "that's much better than calling a member of the Manson Family . . . They would have been *dynamite* witnesses for us."

Although the Smiths never appeared in the courtroom, there's a link between their research and Bugliosi's reasoning that continues to perplex me. In the first phase of the trial, the prosecutor persuaded the jury that Manson had controlled his followers' every thought and action, full stop. In the trial's death-penalty phase, he had to refine that argument somewhat. Because the defendants could be sentenced to death only if they were acting under their own free will, Bugliosi claimed that, regardless of their brainwashing, each of them had the independent capacity to murder. As Bugliosi explained it to me in our first meeting in 1999, Manson had somehow learned that a select few of his followers were willing and able to kill. "Something in the deepest resources of their soul enabled them to do something that you and I cannot do," he said to me that day. "There was something independent of Charles Manson that was coursing through them . . . These people not only killed for him, but they did it with gusto, with *relish*. One hundred and sixty-nine stab wounds! Some of them postmortem! What does that show? I think it's circumstantial evidence that some people have much more homicidal tendencies than others."

It's those "tendencies" that recall David Smith's research. In a

1969 issue of the *Journal of Psychedelic Drugs,* Smith wrote that the main purpose of his experiments with mice was to "isolate" the "behavioral" traits of the rodents that would kill after they'd been aggregated and injected with amphetamines—and then to "modify" their behavior using other drugs. Two years later, writing of the study and its parallels to hippies in the Haight in *Love Needs Care,* Smith admitted that "it has yet to be determined whether amphetamines modify the personality primarily by biochemically altering the central nervous system or by reinforcing or precipitating long-term psychological tendencies." Strikingly, as Bugliosi had it, those "psychological tendencies" were exactly what Manson had learned to exploit.

In the two years before the Manson murders, several papers in the *Journal of Psychedelic Drugs* and other periodicals looked at the increase of psychotic violence in the Haight and its link to amphetamines, LSD, and population density. Some made reference to a forthcoming paper by David Smith, Roger Smith, and Alan Rose on the role that personality factors played in users' reactions to drugs. Why was it that, after just one experience with amphetamines or LSD, certain people experienced hallucinations that lasted for days or even weeks? Were the drugs to blame, or some aspect of the users' psychology? Their paper promised to look into the phenomenon.

But when the article, "Acute Amphetamine Toxicity," finally appeared in the spring 1969 *Journal of Psychedelic Drugs,* both Roger Smith and Alan Rose had been removed as authors. Contradicting his later claim in *Love Needs Care,* David Smith wrote that he "disagreed" with the consensus that "personality was the prime factor in differentiating between psychotic and nonpsychotic reactions," arguing instead that "in the drug subculture of the Haight–Ashbury, the prime determinates of psychotic vs. nonpsychotic reactions were immediate drug environment and experience of the user."

More significant than the contradiction, I felt, was the article's obscurity: when the HAFMC republished bound editions of all the *Journals* five years later, "Acute Amphetamine Toxicity" wasn't included in the collection. All the annotations referring to it in other *Journal* articles had been removed, too. Just as Manson's time in the Haight was "extricated" from the record at trial, the study by the two Smiths and Alan Rose—a study into the origins of the same psychological tendencies found in members of the Manson Family—had disappeared.

Coda: Six Hours with Roger Smith

Even now, more than a decade later, I get excited when I look at the host of documents I showed Kay that day. Flipping through them, I remember how I felt when I was first reporting on Manson's lost year in San Francisco. I thought I'd found the angle that would set my story apart from the reams of others—the beginnings of a working theory about what really motivated the Tate–LaBianca murders. True, it had come too late to work for *Premiere*, but it could be the linchpin for my book.

I pinned a lot of my hopes on one last interview: a sit-down with Roger Smith. It was set for late December 2001. My deal with *Premiere* had been off for a year and I was living off savings, but they were dwindling. If I wanted to earn more money, I'd have to finish my book proposal and sell it to a publisher.

When I spoke to Smith, I knew I had to come away with something so solid that I could finish my reporting. And I sincerely believed that I could. To me, it was obvious that Smith had covered something up, and the evidence was so abundant on this point that I'd have no trouble confronting him about it, even if our exchange got contentious. I would show him documents he hadn't seen in more than three decades. I would press him on his connections to the HAFMC, to Manson, to David Smith, and more; I would ask him why he'd never sent Manson back to prison and why he'd gone along with the bizarre plot to send him to Mexico.

Needless to say, it didn't work out like that.

After the Manson murders, Smith had spent his career behind the well-fortified walls of numerous federal penitentiaries, where he ran specialized units studying or treating sex offenders and drug addicts. It was a path that afforded him plenty of privacy. Over the years, he'd lived on a yacht off the coast of Hawaii; in rural Bend, Oregon; and in a farmhouse more than a century old, surrounded by cornfields, in Ypsilanti, Michigan, outside Ann Arbor.

Smith had agreed to the interview without a moment's hesitation, though I'd called him out of the blue. He was preparing to retire after a decade as director of the Bureau of Mental Forensics for the Michigan State Penitentiary System, and he claimed that none of the many people from his circle I'd interviewed by then had said anything to him about me. On the phone, he told me that he'd been reticent about Manson over the years for fear that the affiliation would tarnish his career. "I'm close to retirement now," he said, "so maybe it's okay to talk."

Our interview began in his office at the prison. It ended at his beautifully restored farmhouse, nearly six hours, a pizza, and several bottles of wine later. It was late December, and snow was falling—outside, the fields were blanketed in white and the houses, his included, twinkled with Christmas lights. Smith lived with his second wife, Carmen, who sat with us in the living room for almost the entirety of the interview. A fire roared in the hearth. Soft rock emanated from a station he'd found on satellite TV. The couple was unfailingly courteous, and I found Smith a patient listener; only a few times did he betray any frustration with my lines of questioning, even as I forced him to examine papers he hadn't seen in thirty-five years.

But the fact was this: he gave me nothing. On the most important questions about his relationship to Manson, he pleaded ignorance, or claimed he had no memory at all.

"I've never been able to understand how he ended up under [your] supervision in San Francisco if he was paroled in L.A.," I said.

"I really don't know, either," Smith said. He posited that parole protocols were more relaxed back in the sixties, and that officials just didn't care if Manson took himself to another city. "Different time, then, I think."

Smith had a memory of interviewing Manson as part of his "prerelease" from prison—a routine process that couldn't have involved him, at least not officially, if Manson was released in Los Angeles.

"Well, I guess I didn't," he replied when I told him that. "I don't even remember that he was released out of L.A."

But I thought I'd have him dead to rights on the question of Manson's arrests during his parole supervision. I had him look over the letter he'd sent to Washington, D.C., asking for permission for Manson to travel to Mexico.

"He was actually in jail then, in Ukiah," I told Smith.

"Really!...I was never notified. This is a mystery to me...I should've been notified."

"By Manson or by the people who arrested him?" I asked.

"By the people who arrested him," Smith said. "There would be some federal record of his arrests, convictions, incarcerations, his criminal justice status."

"Would his parole have been violated for that arrest?"

"Oh, absolutely."

I didn't know it at the time, but Smith was right, in a way. There were two federal documents—Manson's FBI rap sheet and his Bureau of Criminal Identification and Investigation Record— listing his July 31, 1967, conviction, proving that the government *had* been notified. The first of those documents dated to the time of

Smith's supervision, so he would've been notified, too—the probation office receives such papers as a matter of course—but he was saying he wasn't. For good measure, I checked with another federal parole officer who'd worked in the Bay Area in that era. He confirmed that the Justice Department would've automatically notified Smith of Manson's conviction. "Even back then," he said, "the federal guys didn't mess up."

Whenever I reread my interview transcripts, I wince at moments like this. I prepared diligently for these conversations, especially in cases where I thought the right questions could bring major new revelations. Reliving marathon interviews like this, I sometimes kick myself even for having had to stop the conversation to go to the bathroom—maybe if I hadn't taken a break, things would've gone differently.

Even now, I wonder what could've happened if I'd held off on confronting Smith until I'd marshaled every possible resource. In 2001, for example, I hadn't yet found the glowing recommendation he'd provided for Susan Atkins, effectively winning her probation a year before the murders. If I'd had that, I could've challenged a bunch of the assertions he made about Atkins that night—he called her a "hard, hard lady," and he hoped that she never got out of prison. "She was scary. She was aggressive. I thought she was sort of Charlie's operative." Quite an about-face from the man who'd claimed in 1968 that Atkins would "comply willingly with any probationary conditions aimed at her rehabilitation."

I pointed out that Manson had apparently continued to invoke Smith's name after their parole relationship dissolved. Manson and the girls continued visiting him at his office at the HAFMC, and even at his home. I told Smith, "I think he was still trying to pass you off as his PO."

But all he had to say on the subject was: "Oh, really!"

When Smith said he'd never been asked to testify at the trial, despite having served as "an expert witness in lots and lots of trials," I told him and his wife how much that baffled me. They seemed perplexed, too. I asked, "Was there something going on behind the scenes that your testifying would have exposed, a Big Picture, that they didn't want exposed? Maybe like in L.A., where they kept releasing him for offenses without charging him when they had evidence against him?"

For the first time, Smith lost his temper. "Okay, you're operating from the theory that he was tied in — something else was going on. Tom, I can't help you. I don't know." His face reddened, and he shouted, *"I really don't know!"*

"Because you were part of his gestating phase in San Francisco, I thought maybe you might have an indication."

"Yeah, I saw his talent. I saw his bullshit. He was very glib," Smith said. "I had known for a long time how powerful his effect was on people...his particular brand of psychobabble was as persuasive as anybody on the street."

He reminded me that San Francisco in the late sixties may as well have been another country, so different were its customs and mores. I was sympathetic, to a point. By then I'd spoken to so many people about this period that it felt at once totally near and completely alien. So many of my sources, even the most reliable, had trouble explaining their feelings and motivations, not just because so much time had passed but because some schism stood between them and the past. It was irreparable — wherever the sixties had come from, they were gone, even in memory.

As we refilled our wineglasses, Smith conjured the scene: "It was a time when birth control pills first became widely available... You will find this absolutely stupid — women used to walk around and pull up their sweaters to show that they didn't have bras and they would actually seek you out to have sex. Unheard-of." He continued, "Then comes the whole drug thing. Then comes the Haight-Ashbury. The whole Bay Area was one of the most electric places you could possibly be...It was like a magnet."

Manson, he said, had arrived at the tail end of this innocence. When Smith traded his parole job for the ARP, he remembered the Haight already yielding to speed, "the beginning of one of the most incredibly destructive patterns of drug use I'd ever seen... The first six months I was there, there were thirty murders within, like, a six-block radius of the office we had. It was middle-class, totally naive kids...it was the worst maudlin, stupid theater that you've ever seen."

In a scene like that, the Charlie Mansons of the world were a dime a dozen. The Haight was so flooded with weirdos, seekers, addicts, and guru figures that no one batted an eye at him. If anything, Smith said, Manson was a little more respectable than many of them, insofar as he eschewed speed and asked his followers to do the same.

"He was very odd. He was a hippie, it was clear. He was very manipulative—but was he highly dangerous? Didn't see it...I did let him travel, and there were some checks and balances. Basically, when he was in the Bay Area, he was in my office every week. I saw him a lot. Not only in the office...he came in with his girls after a while and I think that became kind of an annoyance to the office."

I made a mental note of that comment. It seemed to confirm that Manson was visiting Smith for official parole meetings at the HAFMC. Later, he backed away from it.

"My association with the clinic really was pretty intermittent," he said. "It wasn't until after I left federal probation that I came down there."

"The chronology confuses me," I said. "The people at the clinic all thought he was coming in for probation."

"No, no, no, I had left probation."

"So he was just coming in to say hello?"

"First of all, he didn't come in that often," Smith said. "I never saw him in any official way and I also never invited him." There could be nothing untoward about Manson's appearances at the HAFMC, he implied, because a conspiracy takes careful planning, and no one there had the capacity to plan anything. "Nothing happened according to schedule in the Haight-Ashbury. You had people walking around jacked up on two grams of speed tempered out with heroin and people carrying guns and tweaking on acid and it was absolutely crazy. Actually, Charlie and his girls were the sanest people around in some ways."

That claim shouldn't have surprised me. Manson had endeared himself to Smith; they were close enough that Smith felt comfortable taking care of Manson's baby. He'd looked after the child for "a couple of months, I think. I know it was long enough to have the baby circumcised, which I think really pissed him off."

When we'd finished our pizza and made our way through most of the final bottle of wine, I steered Smith back toward the subject of Manson's psychology. I still felt that he was trying to have it both ways: to acknowledge Manson's anger and instability and, sometimes in the same breath, to downplay the eccentricities of a man who'd started a cult as Smith watched on.

"There was this unquestioned loyalty to Charlie while they were in San Francisco, [but] there was almost a good-natured quality to it," Smith told me. "There was still the ability to joke with him, and push him." In his mind, the move to the Spahn Ranch was fatal, in that it took the Family out of society. "They were isolated. They were doing acid every day and they were essentially without any reality checks at all... There's a time when everything flips. And I don't know when that was, but it sure as hell wasn't when he was in San Francisco."

Explaining why he refused to talk about Manson for more than twenty-five years, he said, "There were a lot of people who became overnight experts on Manson... particularly back then. Even now. I'm prepared to tell you to get the fuck out of here at some point. You understand what I'm doing here and what's important, which is me. The thing is, Tom, as I look back on that time I don't know what else I could have done...I felt real sadness about it—I don't feel any culpability."

That about summed it up. Soon I thanked Smith and his wife for their generosity and got to my feet. We'd all had some wine, and there was a warmth, if not a trust, in their rustic old farmhouse. I remembered suddenly that it was almost Christmas. They led me to the back door, both of them waving as they saw me out, flakes of snow still falling from the night sky. In my rental car, I took the old highway back past the prison that Smith worked at; apparently he'd personally planned their new, ten-million-dollar mental health care facility. The thought of it made me feel small.

He'd been more than accommodating, hadn't he? And he'd taken a serious look at the papers I'd found, had given serious consideration to my questions...On the face of it, I had no reason to be dissatisfied, having just gotten hours of tape from one of the most reclusive officials connected to Charles Manson.

And yet, as I dwelled on it, the interview felt strange and inconclusive. The closer I got to my motel, the sadder I got. I wasn't finished with the story, or even close to finished. I'd gone to Michigan expecting to shock Roger Smith with incontrovertible evidence of everything he'd overlooked. He had reacted, basically, with six hours of shrugging and some free wine and pizza.

Soon enough, I'd transcribe the interview and start to work away at the little inconsistencies and contradictions in Smith's account, but at the moment I was crestfallen. Even supposing I could find something to push back on, was I right about any of it? Or had Smith entertained six hours of questioning from someone peddling conspiracy theories? His denials felt wrong to me, but I'd had hours to prove my case to him, to get him to break, and I hadn't.

I headed back home to Philadelphia for the holidays. No one knows me better than my family, and over the Christmas break, they noticed right away that something was off. I was aloof, skipping meals to work on the book proposal and figure out my next moves. Stuck in my own head, going through the paces of my story, I tried to construct a coherent narrative out of interview transcripts and dozens of discarded drafts of my dead *Premiere* piece. With no new revelations from Roger Smith, the ending was a big blank.

I'd also told my father, sheepishly, that I was running out of money. He generously offered me a loan, as much as I needed to keep me afloat—and I accepted. I meant it when I promised I'd pay him back.

My father was a tax attorney and law professor, and I realized that I'd never given him a full debriefing on my reporting, even as it became increasingly legalistic. That Christmas I filled him in on everything I'd learned, walking him through my collection of three-ring binders, their pages now dog-eared and marked with a rainbow of neon highlights and plastic reference tabs.

To my relief, I watched as my sober-minded father transitioned to my thinking. He'd told me that he never trusted Bugliosi—too arrogant, too flamboyant—and now he was ready to roll up his sleeves, take out his red pen, and help me in the best way he knew how, by arguing with the U.S. government for records. With his legal knowledge, he helped me fill out new FOIA requests and file appeals to old ones. In the coming months, and for several years, he accomplished what I'd been unable to, forcing unwilling bureaucrats to fill in redacted documents and release information in dribs and drabs. It wasn't enough, of course, to fill in all the gaps, but it got me closer to the truth—and it would never have been possible if I hadn't won over my old buttoned-up dad. He believed in what I'd found. He had the same questions that I did, especially about the parole board's reluctance to release Manson's file. Why were they hiding all this? Everything about the case should be publicly available, he thought. His skepticism kept me going.

After the new year, he drove me to the airport so I could fly back to L.A. I'll never forget the father-son pep talk he gave me. It doesn't matter to us, he said, if you're never able to prove all of this. The fact that you tried so hard is all that matters to us. I headed back to the West Coast feeling reinvigorated, aware of how lucky I was to have my family behind me. At least, I thought, I could have my book out in time for the fortieth anniversary of the murders, in 2009.

11

Mind Control

Off the Deep End

I can still remember the email I sent to my agent. I'd made peace with the fact that I'd never reach a firm conclusion on Manson's involvement with the Smiths. I'd accepted that I had to break off my reporting and move ahead on my book proposal. I'd even taken a full week off—for the first time since I'd started in '99—to clear my head. And then Jolly West happened.

"You're not gonna like this," I wrote to my agent, pausing before I typed the next line: "but I think the JFK assassination is involved." I paused again. "And the CIA's mind-control experiments."

I rewrote it a bunch of different ways, trying to make myself sound less insane, but when I hit send, I still wished right away that I hadn't. I might lose the one publishing professional I had in my corner. And at this point I'd understand if he cut and ran. He always seemed to hold his breath when I mentioned a new "finding," but now I knew I was pressing my luck.

What I'd written was true, though, and I was confident he'd

understand. Through my research on the HAFMC, I'd learned that yet another shadowy researcher kept an office there—and that his LSD research had clearer, more nefarious ties to the CIA than any of the others. At least his name wasn't Smith this time: he was Dr. Louis Jolyon West. His friends called him "Jolly," for his middle name, his impressive girth, and his oversized personality. Pursuing West felt like the logical thing to do, but it also meant swimming deeper into the waters of conspiracy, where, as near as I could tell, only the real nut jobs had wandered before me. I thought of Bill Nelson, the creepy Manson memorabilia dealer I'd once met at a Denny's. Was there something about the isolation and intensity of this work that appealed to me when it pushed most people away?

I'd dared to tell my agent about any of this only because I'd found firm documentation for a long whispered rumor about West. He'd used drugs and hypnosis to conduct behavior-control experiments on Americans without their knowledge or consent. That allegation had landed on the front page of the *New York Times* in 1977, but West had denied it until the day he died, and no one had ever proven the charge. I could, and I thought it was my biggest scoop yet. West's résumé was so chockablock with intrigue and mad-scientist larks that even someone like Reeve Whitson, who behaved like a spy out of a *GQ* spread, paled in comparison.

Born in Brooklyn in 1924, West had enlisted in the army air force during World War II, eventually rising to the rank of colonel. He came to my interest when I learned that he'd accepted an office at the Haight-Ashbury clinic from David Smith himself to recruit subjects for LSD research.

Earlier in his career, West researched methods of controlling human behavior at Cornell University. During the Korean War, he helped to "deprogram" returning prisoners of war who'd allegedly been brainwashed. His success earned him national attention. Around the same time, he achieved still more fame when he joined civil rights activists like his friend the actor Charlton Heston, as well as Dr. Martin Luther King Jr., in marches demanding equal rights for African Americans. Ironically, while he was fighting for the rights of some, he was suspected of infringing on those of others. His detractors alleged that through the fifties and early sixties, at air force bases in Texas and Oklahoma, he performed experiments on unwitting subjects using LSD and hypnosis.

After John F. Kennedy was assassinated in November 1963, West psychiatrically examined Jack Ruby, who'd murdered Kennedy's assassin, Lee Harvey Oswald. Not long before Ruby was due to testify for the Warren Commission, West examined him alone in his jail cell. He emerged to report that Ruby had suffered an "acute psychotic break." Sure enough, Ruby's testimony before the commission succeeded only in making him sound unhinged. He could never fully explain why he'd decided to kill Oswald.

Through the seventies, journalists linked West to the CIA's mind-control research program, MKULTRA. He denied all involvement, vigorously attacking anyone who suggested otherwise. He kept up those attacks until his death in 1999. Then seventy-four, he'd been diagnosed with metastatic cancer, and he prevailed on his son to help him commit suicide with a cocktail of pills.

I had only a fraction of that information at my disposal when I first heard about West, but you can see why I felt I had to expand the frame of my reporting—yet again—just when I'd promised myself to narrow it. Nearly every psychiatrist and researcher I spoke to from Haight-Ashbury had invoked his name, often unfavorably. When I saw that he'd been accused of conducting mind-control experiments, I second-guessed myself; this was not an excursion to be taken lightly.

West had spent the last decades of his career at UCLA, where he'd become something of an institution, heading the psychiatry department's renowned neuroscience center; the university had named an auditorium in his honor. When I called the school, I learned that he'd donated his papers to them, but since no one had asked to see them, they'd never been processed. No one had so much as opened the first box. I would be the first reporter to look at them.

For weeks I convinced myself to leave well enough alone. There was more than enough to fill out my book proposal. I didn't need to involve something as vast and intractable as secret government-sponsored mind-control experiments. But I had a gut feeling that something important was in those files. It gnawed at me.

One day I ran out of willpower. I hopped in my car and drove to the library. Soon I was showing up every day when the building opened, staying for hours to read in the basement, and leaving only when they kicked me out at closing time.

Faking a "Hippie Crash Pad"

Late in the fall of 1966, Jolly West arrived in San Francisco to study hippies and LSD. The Bay Area had seen an unprecedented migration of middle-class youth and an explosion of recreational drug use. West felt he had to witness it firsthand. He secured a government grant and took a yearlong sabbatical from his professorship at the University of Oklahoma, nominally to pursue a fellowship at Stanford, although that school had no record of his participation in a program there.

West was a square—tall, broad, and crew cut, with an all-American look in keeping with his military past. If he wanted a good glimpse of the hippies, he'd have to blend in. He started cobbling together a new wardrobe and skipping haircuts.

At least he had a solid knowledge base. The summer of love had yet to come, and the Tate–LaBianca murders were still years away, but West would effectively predict them both. In a 1967 psychiatry textbook, he'd contributed a chapter called "Hallucinogens," warning students of a "remarkable substance" percolating through college campuses and into cities across the United States. It was LSD, known to leave users "unusually susceptible and emotionally labile" as it caused a "loosening of ego structure." That language was reminiscent of the "reprogramming" spiel that Charles Manson would soon develop, urging his acid-tripping followers to "negate their egos."

When West cautioned against the "LSD cults" springing up in America's "bohemian" quarters, he described exactly the kind of disenchanted wanderers who'd flock to a personality like Manson's in the years to come. West had a hunch that alienated kids "with a pathological desire to withdraw from reality" would crave "shared forbidden activity in a group setting to provide a sense of belonging."

Another paper by West, 1965's "Dangers of Hypnosis," foresaw the rise of dangerous groups led by "crackpots" who hypnotized their followers into violent criminality. Contrary to the prevailing science at the time, West asserted that hypnosis could make people so pliable that they'd violate their moral codes. Scarier still, they'd have no memory of it afterward. Just because such outcomes were rare, he argued, didn't mean they were impossible.

West cited two cases to back up his argument: a double murder in Copenhagen committed by a hypno-programmed man, and a "military offense" induced experimentally at an undisclosed U.S. Army base. He "personally knew" of two other instances, and he'd "heard on excellent authority" of three more, but he didn't elaborate. Later, I'd get a sense of what, or who, he might have had in mind.

When he arrived in Haight-Ashbury, then, West was the only

scientist in the world who'd predicted the emergence of potentially violent "LSD cults." How had he learned so much about acid? You'd never know from his published writing that he'd conducted innumerable experiments with it. In San Francisco, he hoped to conduct more still.

In the Haight, West found a group of kindred spirits at David Smith's new clinic, where plenty of shrinks from the "straight world" were basking in hippiedom. Getting his bearings at the HAFMC, he arranged for the use of a crumbling Victorian house on nearby Frederick Street, where he opened what he described as a "laboratory" disguised as a "hippie crash pad." This would serve as a "semi-permanent observation post," granting him an up-close-and-personal look at the youth. He installed six graduate students in the "pad," telling them to "dress like hippies" and "lure" itinerant kids into the apartment. Passersby were welcome to do as they pleased and stay as long as they liked, as long as they didn't mind grad students taking copious notes on their behavior.

The "pad" opened in June 1967, at the dawn of the summer of love. West took pains to ensure that it felt realistic, decorating it "with posters, flowers and paint." Thus was born the Haight-Ashbury Project, as he called it, or "HAP," for short. For the next six months, he undertook "an ongoing program of intensive inter-disciplinary study into the life and times of the hippies."

To drum up hippie business, West stopped by the HAFMC, where David Smith could furnish willing subjects. Smith even gave him an office. Having a nationally recognized researcher like West working out of the HAFMC would attract sorely needed government funding.

"We helped him with research," Smith told me. He was sympathetic to West's project, even though he admitted that he never bothered to find out what it was, or what its objectives were. He assumed that West, like himself, was diagnosing "psychedelic patterns in the counterculture," trends that others had dismissed as boorish fads.

"They came over and interviewed kids that came into our clinic," Smith said of West and his students. "He wanted to know, 'What is a hippie?'" Smith reminded me that "this was a very new population...the fact that large numbers of white middle-class kids would use illicit drugs was a total mindblower."

Who was paying for all this? According to records in West's files, his "crash pad" was funded by the Foundations Fund for Research in Psychiatry, Inc., which had bankrolled a number of his other projects, too, across decades and institutions. For reasons soon to be clear, I concluded that the Foundations Fund was a front for the CIA.

This wouldn't have been the agency's first "disguised laboratory" in San Francisco. A few years earlier, the evocatively titled Operation Midnight Climax had seen CIA operatives open at least three Bay Area safe houses disguised as upscale bordellos, kitted out with one-way mirrors and kinky photographs. A spy named George Hunter White and his colleagues hired prostitutes to entice prospective johns to the homes, where the men were served cocktails laced with acid. White scrupulously observed the ensuing activities, whatever they were. The goal was to see if LSD, paired with sex, could be used to coax sensitive information from the men—something of a psychedelic honeypot experiment. White so enjoyed the proceedings that he had a portable toilet and a mini-fridge installed on his side of the mirror, so he could watch the action and swill martinis without taking a bathroom break. He later wrote to his CIA handler, "I was a very minor missionary, actually a heretic, but I toiled wholeheartedly in the vineyards because it was fun, fun, fun. Where else could a red-blooded American boy lie, kill and cheat, steal, deceive, rape and pillage with the sanction and blessing of the All-Highest? Pretty Good Stuff, Brudder!"

West knew better than to commit such sentiments to paper, but by 1967 he'd "toiled wholeheartedly in the vineyards," too. Before he moved to the Haight, he'd supervised a similar study in Oklahoma City, hiring informants to infiltrate teenage gangs and engender "a fundamental change" in "basic moral, religious or political matters." The title of the project was Mass Conversion. As I was soon to see, its funds came from Sidney J. Gottlieb, the head of the CIA's MKULTRA program.

In other words, as I said to David Smith, it was all but certain that Jolly West came to the Haight to answer a more ignoble question than "What is a hippie?"

"That would be a cover project," I told Smith.

"Oh, shit," he said.

"Is This an Asphalt Sherwood Forest?"

What was Jolly West really up to in San Francisco? Hanging out at his "crash pad" and roaming the streets of the Haight, he tried to pass as an apostle of free love, but few were fooled. Bob Conrich, a cofounder of the HAFMC, saw through the ruse right away. West "walked into the clinic one day and my first reaction was that he'd read too many Tim Leary interviews," Conrich wrote to me. West was a careerist in hippies' clothing. "What I remember is his enthusiasm for the whole 'summer of love' thing, which seemed exaggerated and insincere."

Conrich was right. West's excitement was a sham, his feelings for hippies dripping with condescension. He soon concluded that the constellation of sex, drugs, and communalism shining over the Haight that summer was "doomed to fail": "The very chemicals they use will inevitably enervate them as individuals and bleed the energies of the hippie movement to its death." He called this an "ineffable tragedy," but it's hard to imagine he saw it that way. For West, the failure of sixties idealism was the most desirable outcome—one that he was quite possibly working toward. A copy of his résumé from this period hints at the thrust of his research. He was at work on a book called *Experimental Psychopathology: The Induction of Abnormal States*. But he never published it. Nor, on the surface, would "the induction of abnormal states" dovetail with the stated goals of his HAP. By the early seventies he removed the title from his résumé and never mentioned it again.

Stephen Pittel, the forensic psychologist, worked briefly with West in 1968 and referred to him as "the only benevolent psychopath I ever met." The man could "charm the pants off of anyone, and manipulate people into doing all sorts of things they didn't want to do."

At the HAP, though, West's motives were so vague that even his charm didn't suffice. No one had a firm grasp of the project's purpose—even those involved in it. The grad students hired to man West's "crash pad" laboratory were assigned to keep diaries of their work. In unguarded moments, nearly all these students admitted that something didn't add up. They weren't sure what they were supposed to be doing, or why West was there. And often he *wasn't* there. Unlike the grad students, he didn't live at the pad. But he wasn't putting in long hours at the HAFMC, either. Those who knew him at both places—and elsewhere in his long career—recalled his chronic absenteeism.

One of the diaries in West's files belonged to Kathy Collins, a Stanford psychology grad student who lived at the HAP pad that summer. The experience was a huge letdown for her, aimless to the point of worthlessness. She was getting paid to do nothing. When "crashers" showed up, "no one made much of a point of finding out about [them]," she put down in neat handwriting. More often, hippies failed to show up at all, since many of them apparently looked on the pad with suspicion. "What the hell have I gotten myself into and what the hell is Jolly doing, it is like a zoo. Is he studying us or them?"

When West made one of his rare appearances, he was "dressed funny," like a hippie; sometimes he would have friends in tow, costumed just as poorly. Collins wrote, "The rest of us tended to look to them in trying to understand what we were supposed to do or what Jolly wanted. Their general reply was that this was a good opportunity to have fun. I gather that they did. They spent a good deal of the time stoned."

Ennui set in. Hoping to feel useful, Collins and the others made inquiries about helping out at the HAFMC. They were swiftly rebuffed. Pressed for specific guidelines, West exuded "phoniness and dishonesty," suggesting that the students answer sweeping, high-flown questions about the Haight, such as "Is this an asphalt Sherwood Forest?" She "got the impression that this question had already been answered."

At the height of her frustration, Collins wrote like someone trapped in an existentialist drama. "I really don't know whether to laugh at Jolly or take him seriously," she fumed. "I feel like no one is being honest and straight and the whole thing is a gigantic put on...What is he trying to prove? He is interested in drugs, that is clear. What else?"

Brainwashing with the Love Drug

Collins was right. West was interested in drugs. His professional fascination with LSD was practically as old as the substance itself, and he was one of an elite cadre of scientists using it in top-secret research. Lysergic acid diethylamide was synthesized in 1938 by chemists at Switzerland's Sandoz Industries, but it was not introduced as a pharmaceutical until 1947. In the fifties, when the CIA began to experiment on humans with it, it was a very new substance. Be that as it may, the agency was not inclined to exercise caution.

Almost right away, government scientists saw LSD as a potential Cold War miracle drug, the key to eradicating communism and seeding global democracy. Its effects on individual minds were extrapolated onto groups, voting blocs, and entire populations. Among psychiatrists, artists, and curious recreational users, LSD augured a different sort of liberty, but they, too, regarded it with awe. Albert Hofmann, the Swiss scientist who'd discovered its hallucinogenic qualities in 1943, described it as a "sacred drug" that gestured toward "the mystical experience of a deeper, comprehensive reality." The actor Cary Grant, on the advice of his shrink, took some one hundred LSD trips during their weekly meetings in the late fifties, experiencing a "rebirth" and picturing himself "as a giant penis launching off from Earth like a spaceship."

Charles Fischer, a drug researcher who worked with David Smith, described to me the early perceptions of acid, when "trips" were planned like literal journeys. "Very few people took LSD without having somebody being a 'trip leader,'" Fischer said. The suggestibility from LSD was akin to hypnosis—and Jolly West, of course, had known well enough to study the two in tandem. "You can tell somebody to hurt somebody, but you call it something else," Fischer explained. "Hammer the nail into the wood, and the wood, perhaps, is a human being...[It] could result in some violent activity, even though LSD was considered a love drug."

The global superpowers considered it anything but. Full-fledged U.S. research into LSD began soon after the end of World War II, when American intelligence learned that the USSR was developing a program to influence human behavior through drugs and hypnosis. The United States believed that the Soviets could extract information from people without their knowledge, program them to make false confessions, and perhaps persuade them to kill on command.

The CIA, then in its infancy, saw mind control as a natural extension of communism, spreading like fire where the forces of unreason prevailed. In 1949 it launched Operation Bluebird, a mind-control program whose chipper name belied its brutal ambitions and its propensity for trampling on human rights. In its yen to best the Soviets, the CIA tested drugs on American citizens—most in federal penitentiaries or on military bases—who didn't even know about, let alone consent to, the battery of procedures they underwent.

Their abuse found further justification in 1952, when, in Korea, captured American pilots admitted on national radio that they'd sprayed the Korean countryside with illegal biological weapons. It was a confession so beyond the pale that the CIA blamed Communists: the POWs must have been "brainwashed." The word, a literal translation of the Chinese *xi nao,* didn't appear in English before 1950. It articulated a set of fears that had coalesced in postwar America. Soviets were using guile to force an evil philosophy on the world. Technology had destabilized every atom of human nature, and a new class of chemicals with unpronounceable names could reduce people to machines. The human mind, like any other appliance, could be rewired and automated.

Once the Korean War was over and the American POWs returned, the army brought in a team of scientists to "deprogram" them. Among those scientists was a young psychiatrist from Cornell, Dr. Louis J. West. He would later claim to have studied eighty-three prisoners of war, fifty-six of whom had been forced to make false confessions. West interviewed them at length, undoing the treacheries of the "thought reform" they'd undergone in enemy hands. He and his colleagues were credited with reintegrating the POWs into Western society and, maybe more important, getting them to renounce their claims about having used biological weapons.

West's success with the POWs gained him entrée to the upper echelons of the intelligence community. As the Cold War bred paranoia, the CIA accelerated its mind-control efforts, and West, I learned, carved out a niche he'd occupy for decades to come. Initially, the agency wanted only to prevent further brainwashing by the Soviets. But the extraordinary power of psychotropic drugs, particularly LSD, was hard to ignore. Thus a defensive program became an offensive one. Operation Bluebird morphed into Operation Artichoke, a search for an all-purpose truth serum.

Dr. Sidney Gottlieb, a poisons expert who headed the chemical division of the CIA's Technical Services Staff, had convinced the agency's director, Allen Dulles, that mind-control ops were the future. Gottlieb, whose aptitude and amorality had earned him the nickname the "Black Sorcerer," developed gadgetry straight out of schlocky sci-fi: high-potency stink bombs, swizzle sticks laced with drugs, exploding seashells, poisoned toothpaste, poisoned handkerchiefs, poisoned cigars, poisoned anything. Mind control became Gottlieb's pet project. Dulles, convinced that the American dream was at stake, ensured that Gottlieb was well funded. In a speech at Princeton University, Dulles warned that Communist spies could turn the American mind into "a phonograph playing a disc put on its spindle by an outside genius over which it has no control." Just days after those remarks, on April 13, 1953, he officially set Project MKULTRA into motion.

The project's broadest goal was "to influence human behavior." Under its umbrella were 149 subprojects, many involving research that used unwitting participants. Having persuaded an Indianapolis pharmaceutical company to replicate the Swiss formula for LSD, the CIA had a limitless domestic supply of its favorite new drug. The agency hoped to produce couriers who could embed hidden messages in their brains, to implant false memories and remove true ones in people without their awareness, to convert groups to opposing ideologies, and more. The loftiest objective was the creation of hypno-programmed assassins.

In their defense, CIA spooks weren't above experimenting on themselves. The same substance that held the promise of controlling minds and quashing communism was used in churlish office pranks, with agents quietly slipping LSD into their colleagues' drinks to achieve much needed "firsthand knowledge." A plan to spike the punch bowl at the CIA Christmas party was quashed when higher-ups reminded the office that it could cause insanity.

The most sensitive work was conducted far from Langley— farmed out to scientists at colleges, hospitals, prisons, and military bases all over the United States and Canada. The CIA gave these scientists aliases, funneled money to them, and instructed them on how to conceal their research from prying eyes, including those of their unknowing subjects. Feeling that it was their patriotic duty, the scientists accepted their secret missions in defiance of the Hippocratic oath: "First, do no harm."

In 1949, at the Nuremberg trials that adjudicated the crimes of World War II, the United States adopted the International Code for Human Experimentation: "A person must give full and informed consent before being used as a subject." MKULTRA scientists flouted this code constantly, remorselessly—and in ways that stupefy the imagination. Their work encompassed everything from electronic brain stimulation to sensory deprivation to "induced pain" and "psychosis." They sought ways to cause heart attacks, severe twitching, and intense cluster headaches. If drugs didn't do the trick, they'd try to master ESP, ultrasonic vibrations, and radiation poisoning. One project tried to harness the power of magnetic fields.

Operated on a strict need-to-know basis, MKULTRA was so highly classified that when John McCone succeeded Dulles as CIA director late in 1961 he was not informed of its existence. Fewer than half a dozen agency brass were aware of MKULTRA at any period during its twenty-year history. When Gottlieb retired, in 1972 or '73, the project retired with him. By then it had been pared down to almost nothing, as the agency focused on other ways to halt communism and sway policy making abroad and at home.

Still, when the Watergate scandal, and the CIA's involvement in it, consumed the nation in the early seventies, it occurred to agency leadership that it would be prudent to cover their tracks. Director Richard Helms ordered Gottlieb to destroy all MKUL-TRA files. In January 1973, the Technical Services Staff shredded countless documents describing the use of hallucinogens, including every known copy of a manual called "LSD: Some Un-Psychedelic Implications." MKULTRA evaporated.

Grandiose and Sinister

In their haste to purge their misdeeds, the agents forgot about a cache of some sixteen thousand additional papers in an off-site warehouse. Even internally, those files would remain undiscovered for several years, but it was only a matter of time until the story broke; MKULTRA had become fodder for rumors around Washington.

In December 1974, the project finally came to light in a terrific flash of headlines and intrigue. Seymour Hersh reported it on the front page of the *New York Times:* "Huge C.I.A. Operation Reported in U.S. Against Antiwar Forces." Three government investigations followed, all hobbled by the CIA's destruction of its files. When records were available, they were redacted; when witnesses were summoned, they were forgetful.

First came the Church Committee and the Rockefeller Commission, each mentioned earlier regarding CHAOS and COIN-TELPRO. The Church Committee's final report unveiled a 1957 internal evaluation of MKULTRA by the CIA's inspector general. "Precautions must be taken," the document warned, "to conceal these activities from the American public in general. The knowledge that the agency is engaging in unethical and illicit activities would have serious repercussions." A 1963 review from the inspector general put it even more gravely: "A final phase of the testing of MKULTRA products places the rights and interests of U.S. citizens in jeopardy."

In fact, as the Church Committee's report went on, MKULTRA had caused the deaths of at least two American citizens. One was a psychiatric patient who'd been injected with a synthetic mescaline derivative. The other was Frank Olson, a CIA-contracted scientist who'd been unwittingly dosed with LSD at a small agency gathering in the backwoods of Maryland presided over by Gottlieb himself. Olson fell into an irreparable depression afterward, which led him to hurl himself out the window of a New York City hotel where agents had brought him for "treatment." (Continued investigation by Olson's son, Eric, strongly suggests that the CIA arranged for the agents to fake his suicide; they threw him out of the window themselves out of fear that he would blow the whistle on MKULTRA and the military's use of biological weapons in the Korean War.)

The news of Olson's death shocked a nation already reeling from Watergate, and now less inclined than ever to trust its institutions. The government tried to quell the controversy by passing new regulations on human experimentation. But scrutiny and internal pressure on the CIA continued to mount until the agency was forced to make an admission: It hadn't destroyed everything. It had come to their attention that thousands of pages about MKULTRA were collecting dust in the off-site warehouse.

So came another congressional investigation, more robust than the last, with sixteen thousand additional pages of documentation at its disposal. Senators Ted Kennedy and Daniel Inouye subpoenaed a number of CIA spooks. Among them was Gottlieb, rousted from his retirement in California and forced to defend his actions before the Senate. Or rather, before some of the Senate. Gottlieb claimed that his heart condition precluded the possibility of his addressing the whole chamber; instead, he was installed in an anteroom, where he answered questions from a select group while the masses listened over a public address system.

As the *New York Times* pointed out, Gottlieb "managed to elude the lights and microphones and the crush of reporters waiting for him in the Senate hearing room." He was spared the sight of the incredulity that spread over their faces as he admitted that he had destroyed MKULTRA's files not to cover up "illegal activity," but "because this material was sensitive and capable of being misunderstood." He resented the harm done to his reputation, and he was loath to provide specifics about MKULTRA experiments, saying that he'd never witnessed any himself.

Gottlieb's destruction of the MKULTRA files was a federal crime. It was investigated by the Justice Department in 1976, but, according to the *Times,* "quietly dropped." His brutal courses of experimentation broke any number of laws, and his perjury that day did, too. But he was never prosecuted. He'd testified before the Senate only under the condition that he receive total criminal immunity.

As for those sixteen thousand new pages, they were mainly financial records, but a few more tantalizing documents found the CIA explicating its ambitions. "Can we obtain control of the future activities (physical and mental) of any individual, willing or unwilling… with a guarantee of amnesia?" they asked. "Can we force an individual to act against his own moral concepts?" And: "Can an individual…be made to perform an act of attempted assassination?"

Senate investigators condemned MKULTRA unanimously. Kennedy branded it "perverse" and "corrupt," an erosion of the "freedom of individuals and institutions in the name of national security." Inouye called it "grandiose and sinister." The CIA's new director, Stansfield Turner, swore that he'd sent all existing MKULTRA files to the Justice Department, which would mount a thorough investigation.

Still, between the destruction of records and the subpoenaed agents' sudden memory lapses, everyone knew that "the full facts," as the *New York Times* editorialized, "may never come out." The Senate demanded the formation of a federal program to locate the victims of MKULTRA experiments, and to pursue criminal charges against the perpetrators. That program never coalesced. Surviving records named eighty institutions, including forty-four universities and colleges, and 185 researchers, among them Louis J. West. The *New York Times* identified him, in a front-page lead story, no less, as one of seven suspected scientists who'd secretly participated in MKULTRA under academic cover. And yet not one researcher was ever federally investigated, and only two victims were ever notified. The *Times* had called MKULTRA "a secret twenty-five year, twenty-five million dollar effort by the CIA to learn how to control the human mind." It looked like no one would suffer any consequences for it.

Griffin Bell, the Attorney General at the time of the revelations, told me the files never arrived at the Justice Department, despite Stansfield Turner's sworn claim to the contrary. Bell said they must've just "fall[en] through the cracks." As for Turner himself, he told me he could no longer remember having testified that the CIA sent the files. "I'm just drawing a total blank here," he said. I read his remarks back to him. "I guess I did testify about this," he said. "Somebody fed me the stuff and I played it back."

The *New York Times* ran twenty-seven stories on MKULTRA, eight on the front page. But no one in the press corps, and none of the senators involved, followed up to see that the promised investigations took place. Since then, the program's bewildering significance has been engulfed many times over by other controversies. Receding in the rearview mirror, it looks like just another example of the CIA's megalomania at the zenith of the Cold War.

Jolly West, CIA Asset

When I started visiting the UCLA library, I had no idea that Jolly West had created a "laboratory disguised as a hippie crash pad" in the Haight. I'd found early research papers of his, but not much else. And for a long while, my days in the library were fruitless. West's archive comprised two hundred boxes, most of them full of ephemera. There were tons of press clippings. West had tracked the media's coverage of assassinations, the CIA, aggression in cats, psychosurgery, capital punishment, alcoholism among Native Americans, behavior modification, and the civil rights movement, among other subjects. I was intrigued to see many clippings on the Manson murders, and papers by Roger Smith, David Smith, and Alan Rose.

Part of the reason that West became my white whale was that, improbably enough, I'd already interviewed him once in 1995, a few years before his death, when I was still reporting celebrity features for *Us* and *Premiere*. I was doing a piece on the uptick in celebrity stalkers, and West was one of the scientific "experts" I consulted. When I'd spoken with psychiatrists before, I was the one who did all the talking—this time it was all West, who droned on for so long that I cut the interview short.

Now that felt like a lifetime ago. As I settled in for the long haul at the library, my early certainty began to falter. My first visit had been on June 12, 2001. I'd leave the campus every evening wondering if I was wasting my time, having found nothing and gotten no closer to wrapping up my reporting. The basement of the library came to feel like my underground bunker. More than two months went by. I kept sifting and taking notes. On August 25, among a batch of research papers on hypnosis, I found them: letters between West and his CIA handler, "Sherman Grifford."

I didn't recognize the name, so as soon as I got home, I began tearing through every book I had that mentioned MKULTRA, hoping that it would jump out at me. In the first and most definitive of the bunch, John Marks's *The Search for the Manchurian Candidate*, there it was, buried in a footnote: "CIA operators and agents all had cover names," it said, "even in classified documents. Gottlieb was 'Sherman R. Grifford.' "

So West really had lied all those years. Not only was he a part of MKULTRA, he'd corresponded with the "Black Sorcerer" of MKULTRA himself. Preserved in his files, the letters picked up midstream, with no prologue or preliminaries. The first one was dated June 11, 1953, a mere two months after MKULTRA started. West was then chief of psychiatric service at the airbase at Lackland, Texas.

Addressing Gottlieb as "S.G.," he outlined the experiments he proposed to perform using a combination of psychotropic drugs and hypnosis. Enumerating short- and long-term goals, he offered a nine-point list, beginning with a plan to discover "the degree to which information can be extracted from presumably unwilling subjects (through hypnosis alone or in combination with certain drugs), possibly with subsequent amnesia for the interrogation and/or alteration of the subject's recollection of the information he formerly knew." Another item proposed honing "techniques for implanting false information into particular subjects . . . or for inducing in them specific mental disorders." West wanted to reverse someone's belief system without his knowledge, and make it stick. He hoped to create "couriers" who would carry "a long and complex message" embedded secretly in their minds, and to study "the induction of trance-states by drugs." All of these were the goals of

MKULTRA, and they bore a striking resemblance to Manson's accomplishments with his followers more than a decade later.

"Needless to say," West added, the experiments "must eventually be put to test in practical trials in the field."

West's colleagues wouldn't approve of his activities. He yearned to "cut down considerably the number of people who can properly call me to account." Because he'd be using drugs that were "not on the Air Force list of standard preparations," he wanted to secure "some sort of *carte blanche*." (He would go on to suggest a number of security measures in his letters, including disguised funding, double envelopes, and false names.)

Next West addressed a sensitive matter: who would the guinea pigs be? He listed four groups—basic airmen, volunteers, patients, and "others, possibly including prisoners in the local stockade." Only the volunteers would be paid. The others could be unwilling, and, though it wasn't spelled out, unwitting. It'd be easier to preserve his secrecy if he was "inducing specific mental disorders" in people who already exhibited them. "Certain patients requiring hypnosis in therapy, or suffering from dissociative disorders (trances, fugues, amnesias, etc.) might lend themselves to our experiments."

As if to prove his thoroughness, he affixed two addenda to his four-page letter, begging Gottlieb to get one of his superiors, a Major Robert Williams, "transferred to another base." Williams was "an uncomfortably close scrutinizer of all my activities" who believed that hypnosis was "tampering with the soul," West complained.

Gottlieb's reply came on letterhead from "Chemrophyl Associates," a front company he used to correspond with MKULTRA subcontractors. "My Good Friend," he wrote, "I had been wondering whether your apparent rapid and comprehensive grasp of our problems could possibly be real...you have indeed developed an admirably accurate picture of exactly what we are after. For this I am deeply grateful." He would arrange top-secret clearances for anyone who might become ensnared in their work, giving West "a separate sum" for the purchase of materials.

Gottlieb saluted his new recruit: "We have developed quite an asset in the relationship we are developing with you."

West returned the camaraderie. "It makes me very happy to realize that you consider me 'an asset,'" he replied. "Surely there is no more vital undertaking conceivable in these times."

With that, the record of their correspondence ceased for nearly nine months. When it resumed, in April 1954, West had begun arrangements to relocate to the University of Oklahoma School of Medicine, which wanted him to head its psychiatry department. He would be a civilian again. Gottlieb commended his "new look," noting, "it appears at the moment to be a move which would in the long run be beneficial for us." He signed off intimately, "Give my regards to your family."

West had lied to his prospective employer, writing, "My present job is purely clinical and I have been doing no research, classified or otherwise." The university took him at his word. Now performing his duties for Gottlieb at both the university and the air force base, West asked the judge advocate at Lackland for permission to accept money from the Geschickter Fund for Medical Research, which he called "a non-profit private research foundation." In fact, as the CIA later acknowledged, Geschickter was another of Gottlieb's fictions, enabling him to keep West and other researchers properly paid.

By April 1955, West had moved permanently to Oklahoma City. But the air force insisted he return to Lackland weekly to serve out the remainder of his contract. Gottlieb, who'd evidently attempted to pull some strings, wrote in September 1954 to relay some frustrating news: "The Air Force will not release you... Although this rather adequately stops our present effort, it does not erase the need for research in the field. I'm suggesting therefore that you give some thought to the period some 20 months hence and the plans which might be made in the interim."

Twenty months would've put them in April 1956. That year, West reported back to the CIA that the experiments he'd begun in 1953 had at last come to fruition. He was ensconced in a civilian institution, and evidently he found it a less oppressive setting than Lackland had been. In a paper titled "The Psychophysiological Studies of Hypnosis and Suggestibility," he claimed to have achieved the impossible: he knew how to replace "true memories" with "false ones" in human beings without their knowledge. In case the CIA didn't grasp the significance of this, he put it in layman's terms: "It has been found to be feasible to take the memory of a definite event in the life of an individual and, through hypnotic suggestion, bring about the subsequent conscious recall to the effect that this event never actually took place, but that a different (fictional) event actually did occur."

The document, marked "classified," was right there in West's files; I had to assume that the CIA had destroyed any copies. They've never publicly acknowledged West's groundbreaking deed. He'd done it, he claimed, by administering "new drugs" effective in "speeding the induction of the hypnotic state and in deepening the trance that can be produced in given subjects."

As in his initial experiments, West performed most of these psychiatric feats on mental health patients. "The necessity to obtain most of the subject material from a population of psychiatry patients made standardized observations very difficult," he groused. In the report, which doubled as a request for continued funding—a successful request; West received government backing through 1965 at the least—he enthusiastically described a high-tech laboratory he planned to construct at Oklahoma. It would include "a special chamber [where] various hypnotic, pharmacologic, and sensory-environmental variables will be manipulated."

West had hypnotized mental patients and "normal subjects" and exposed them to a host of drugs, including chlorpromazine, reserpine, amphetamines, and LSD—the same ones that David Smith would inject in his confined rodents about a decade later. Of course, at least two of these, LSD especially, would prove instrumental in the Manson Family's group psychology.

But when it came to elaborating on his findings about implanting memories and controlling thoughts, West skimped on the details. He seemed to have been in a rudimentary phase of his research. Acid, he wrote, made people more difficult to hypnotize; it was better to pair hypnosis with long bouts of isolation and sleep deprivation. Using hypnotic suggestion, he claimed, "a person can be told that it is now a year later and during the course of this year many changes have taken place...so that it is now acceptable for him to discuss matters that he previously felt he should not discuss...An individual who insists he desires to do one thing will reveal that secretly he wishes just the opposite."

Since West's paper was light on specifics, it's hard to know if it was only a ploy for more funding. Whatever it was, the CIA felt it had to keep it under wraps. When the agency was forced to disclose MKULTRA to the public, they submitted an expurgated version of West's paper to Congress, an act of deception that's never been exposed. At the National Security Archives in D.C., I found the version of "The Psychophysiological Studies of Hypnosis and Suggestibility" that the CIA had turned over to the Senate. West's name and affiliation were redacted, as expected. But what shocked me was that the Senate's version didn't include West's nine-page attachment, but rather an unsigned summary. There was no mention of West's triumphant accomplishment, the replacement of "the memory of a definite event in the life of an individual" with a "fictional event."

In sworn testimony, the CIA said that everything it shared with Congress was intact except for the redactions of researchers' and institutions' names. Now it turned out they hadn't just censored West's report; they'd completely misrepresented its contents. The one-page summary of West's accomplishments in the lab doesn't exist in West's original. The new page was only a theoretical discussion of LSD—of its *possible* effects on "dissociative states." It concluded, "The effects of these agents [LSD and other drugs] upon the production, maintenance, and manifestations of disassociated states *has never been studied*."

West, of course, had studied those effects for years and years. I could only conclude that the CIA misrepresented the original document to mislead the Senate committee, thus striking West's research from the official record. As was my habit whenever I found hard evidence of a cover-up, I started dwelling on one question after another. Didn't this counterfeit paper cast doubt on the entire cache of documents released to the Senate in 1977? If West's authentic paper had been so fuzzy about the effects of drugs, including LSD, on dissociative states, why had the CIA felt the need to generate a fake version?

Maybe because West had achieved one of MKULTRA's most coveted goals. Despite testimony to the contrary, the CIA had, in fact, learned how to manipulate people's memories without their knowledge. Agency officials claimed the program had been a colossal failure, leading newspapers to run mocking headlines like "The Gang That Couldn't Spray Straight." It could've been exactly what the agency wanted—for the world to assume MKULTRA was a bust, and forget the whole thing. One thing was indisputable: The CIA's falsified documents invalidated the Senate investigation's findings. The agency lied, obstructed justice, and tampered with evidence, and the West documents prove it.

Given the furtive nature of his research, West could be surprisingly garrulous. Among the press clippings in his file were two items from Portland, Oregon, newspapers, both dated October 1963—the murky period between his Oklahoma hypnosis studies and the Haight-Ashbury Project. West had given an address to the Mental Health Association of Oregon, letting it slip that he was inducing insanity in the lab. He framed these studies as positive developments: they might someday cure mental illness.

"We are at the dawning of a new era," West told the crowd, "learning for the first time to produce temporary mental derangement in the laboratory." The *Oregon Journal* noted that West "listed the new hallucination drug LSD, along with other drugs, hypnosis, and sleep deprivation as some of the things that [he was] using to produce temporary mental illness effects in normal people." Reporting that West had done "extensive work" with LSD, the *Journal* continued: "The most important contribution of the drug so far is in producing model mental illnesses."

Almost fifteen years later, besieged by reporters after the *New York Times* alleged that he'd taken part in MKULTRA's secret LSD experimentation program, West insisted that all of his LSD work "had been confined to animals," denying any CIA affiliation. When reporters pointed out that he'd received an awful lot of money from the agency, he retorted that he'd had no idea that the Geschickter Fund and other sources were CIA fronts. Legally, the CIA was obligated to tell the University of Oklahoma that one of its faculty had been on the agency payroll. Oklahoma revealed a heavily redacted memo saying that an unnamed professor—West, I confirmed through financial records—had been investigating "a number of dissociative phenomena" on humans "in the lab," including an exceptionally rare clinical disorder known as "latah," "a neurotic condition marked by automatic obedience."

None of the allegations harmed West's reputation. By then he'd left Oklahoma for UCLA, where he offered a steady stream of denials and continued to thrive through his retirement in 1988. Irascible and arrogant, he was quick to threaten lawsuits when anyone brought up the charges. Sometimes he threw in diversionary tactics: in a 1991 rebuttal, he claimed, "My secret connection to Washington, D.C. is not as a spook, but rather as a confidential advisor to Presidents...From Eisenhower to Bush, Democrat and Republican Presidents alike have freely sought and received my counsel." In a 1993 letter to the editor of the UCLA *Bruin,* he had the temerity to compare his accusers to Nazi propagandists "in Goebbels' tradition of the Big Lie." West added, "I have never taken part in 'mind-control' experiments funded by the CIA or anybody else": a statement belied by his own files.

The Misadventures of Jolly West

Even before his CIA connections came out, West's experiments got him in plenty of trouble. In 1972, he announced plans to build a lab in an abandoned Nike Missile base in the Santa Monica Mountains. He would call it "The Center for the Study and Reduction of Violence," or the Violence Center, for short. There, in perfect isolation, he could study the origins and control of human violence by experimenting on prisoners. Governor Ronald Reagan gave the Violence Center a full-throated endorsement.

But West's proposal for grant money landed him in hot water. He planned to test radical forms of behavior modification, implanting electrodes and "remote monitoring devices" in prisoners' brains. A federal investigation concluded that the program involved "coercive methods" that threatened "privacy and self-determination."

The committee's disclosures stymied the Violence Center before it got past the planning stages. The California legislature vetoed the project; UCLA's student body rose up in protest of West. And this, to reiterate, was *before* anyone had a clue about his CIA work.

Now I could tie West to the highest, most clandestine echelons of the Central Intelligence Agency. I could tie him to both of the

Smiths, the authority figures from Manson's lost year in San Francisco. And through his efforts to open the Violence Center, I could tie him to bigwigs in the LAPD and the DA's office who'd helped to prosecute Manson. But I could never prove that he'd examined Manson himself—or even that they'd ever met. Nor had West taken part in Manson's trial. His absence was conspicuous. One of the world's leading experts on brainwashing and cults, he was hardly averse to publicity. He'd appeared as a witness many times before. Manson was tried in his own backyard; the proceedings were international news. Yet West went nowhere near them.

I told David Smith about the CIA's research and its parallels with Manson: the agency had wanted to accomplish exactly what Manson succeeded in doing with the girls. I was wondering whether someone in the CIA influenced Manson while he was in San Francisco.

"I don't know," he said, "but the military experiments are added proof that my hypothesis is correct—that it can be done."

"That you can brainwash with LSD?"

He nodded.

"The CIA maintained that they never were able to accomplish it," I said.

"In part because they were basically taking normal subjects," he said, "not susceptible girls in a reinforcing environment." When he'd evaluated Susan Atkins for a parole hearing ten years after she'd separated from Manson, she was still under his control. "I can't get him out of my head!" she told him. "He's still in my brain!"

But was brainwashing really even possible? I'd always believed that Cold War–era paranoia had overstated the potential for "Manchurian Candidates" taught to kill by dastardly commies. On the other hand, I accepted that Charles Manson had altered his followers' minds, and that LSD did a lot of the heavy lifting. He'd seemed to have an endless supply of the drug, though no one said how he got it. Plus, he was so often described as "hypnotic." Ed Sanders had written in *The Family* of a hypnotist, William Deanyer, who managed a Sunset Strip club and alleged that he'd taught Manson how to hypnotize. It seemed dubious. But I confirmed that Deanyer had learned hypnosis in the navy. And his daughter told me she'd seen her father teaching Manson at the club.

With Alan Scheflin, a forensic psychologist and law professor who'd written a book on MKULTRA, I laid out a circumstantial case linking West to Manson. Was it possible, I asked, that the Manson murders were an MKULTRA experiment gone wrong? "No," he said, "an MKULTRA experiment gone right."

In the back of my mind was the most confounding passage in *Helter Skelter*—one that I'd underlined, highlighted, and finally torn out and taped above my computer. "The most puzzling question of all," Bugliosi wrote, was how Manson had turned his docile followers into remorseless killers. Even with the LSD, the sex, the isolation, the sleep deprivation, the social abandonment, there had to be "some intangible quality... It may be something that he learned from others." *Something that he learned from others.* Those had become the six most pivotal words in the book for me.

I was more compelled than ever to peel back every layer of West's past, hoping that some tie to Manson would come out, or that I'd get the name of someone who knew the name of someone who could confirm that the two had met. On the way, I discovered some fearsome episodes from West's past. As a self-styled brainwashing expert, he'd been present whenever mind control reared its ugly head in American culture. Murders, assassinations, kidnappings, cults, prisoners of war—his fingerprints were on all of them.

The Curious Case of Jimmy Shaver

After midnight on July 4, 1954, a three-year-old girl named Chere Jo Horton disappeared outside the Lackland Air Force Base, where Jolly West was stationed. Horton's parents had left her in the parking lot outside a bar; she played with her brother while they had a drink inside. When they noticed her missing, they formed a search party.

Within an hour of Horton's disappearance, the party came upon a car with her underwear hanging from the door. They heard shouting nearby. Two construction workers had been napping in a nearby gravel pit when a Lackland airman wandered out of the darkness. He was shirtless, covered in blood and scratches. Making no attempt to escape, he let the search party walk him to the edge of the highway. Bystanders described him as "dazed" and "trance-like."

"What's going on here?" he asked. He didn't seem drunk, but he couldn't say where he was, how he'd gotten there, or whose blood was all over him. Meanwhile, the search party found Horton's body in the gravel pit. Her neck was broken, her legs had been torn open, and she'd been raped. Deputies arrested the man.

His name was Jimmy Shaver. At twenty-nine, he was recently remarried, with two children, no criminal record, no history of violence. He'd been at the same bar Horton had been abducted from, but he'd left with a friend, who told police that neither of them was drunk, though Shaver seemed high on something. Before deputies could take Shaver to the county jail, a constable from another precinct arrived with orders from military police to assume custody of him.

Around four that morning, an air force marshal questioned Shaver and two doctors examined him, agreeing he wasn't drunk. One later testified that he "was not normal...he was very composed outside, which I did not expect him to be under these circumstances." He was released to the county jail and booked for rape and murder.

Investigators interrogated Shaver through the morning. When his wife came to visit, he didn't recognize her. He gave his first statement at 10:30 a.m., adamant that another man was responsible: he could summon an image of a stranger with blond hair and tattoos. After the air force marshal returned to the jailhouse, however, Shaver signed a second statement taking full responsibility. Though he still didn't remember anything, he reasoned that he must have done it.

Two months later, in September, Shaver's memories still hadn't returned. The base hospital commander told Jolly West to perform an evaluation: was he legally sane at the time of the murder? Shaver spent the next two weeks under West's supervision, subject to copious psychological tests. They returned to the scene of the crime, trying to jog his memory. Later, West hypnotized Shaver and gave him an injection of sodium pentothal, "truth serum," to see if he could clear his amnesia.

While Shaver was under—with West injecting more truth serum to "deepen the trance"—Shaver recalled the events of that night. He confessed to killing Horton. She'd brought out repressed memories of his cousin, "Beth Rainboat," who'd sexually abused him as a child. Shaver had started drinking at home that night when he "had visions of God, who whispered into his ear to seek out and kill the evil girl Beth." (This "Beth" was never sought for questioning.) At the trial, West argued that Shaver's truth-serum confession was more valid than any other. And West was testifying for the *defense*—they'd hoped he could get an acquittal on temporary insanity.

Instead, West's testimony helped the prosecution. Here was a psychiatric expert who believed wholeheartedly that Shaver had committed the crime, and who'd gotten him to admit it in colorful detail. While West maintained that the airman had suffered a bout of temporary insanity, he also said that Shaver was "quite sane now." In the courtroom, he didn't look that way. One newspaper account said he "sat through the strenuous sessions like a man in a trance," saying nothing, never rising to stretch or smoke, though he was a known chain-smoker. "Some believe it's an act," the paper said, "others believe his demeanor is real."

West often treated Lackland airmen for neurological disorders. During the trial, it came out that Shaver had suffered from migraines so debilitating that he'd dunk his head in a bucket of ice water when he felt one coming on. He sought regular treatment, and the air force had recommended him for a two-year experimental program. The doctor who'd attempted to recruit him was never named.

Shaver's medical history was scrutinized at trial, but little mention was made of the base hospital, where West had conducted his MKULTRA experiments on unwitting patients. On the stand, West said he'd never gotten around to seeing whether Shaver had been treated there. I checked—Lackland officials told me there was no record of him in their master index of patients. But, curiously, all the records for patients in 1954 had been maintained, with one exception: the file for last names beginning with "Sa" through "St" had vanished.

Articles and court testimony described Shaver's mental state just as West had described his experiments the previous summer: amnesias and trance states, a man violating his moral code with no memory of doing so. And West had written that he planned to experiment on Lackland airmen for projects that "must eventually be put to test in practical trials in the field."

This was all the more difficult to ignore after I got the transcript of Shaver's truth-serum interview. West had used leading questions to walk the entranced Shaver through the crime. "Tell me about when you took your clothes off, Jimmy," he said. And trying to prove that Shaver had repressed memories: "Jimmy, do you remember when something like this happened before?" Or: "After you took her clothes off what did you do?"

"I never did take her clothes off," Shaver said.

The interview was divided into thirds. The middle third, for some reason, wasn't recorded. When the record picked up, the transcript said, "Shaver is crying. He has been confronted with all the facts repeatedly."

West asked, "Now you remember it all, don't you, Jimmy?"

"Yes, sir," Shaver replied.

For West, this seems to have been business as usual, but it left an indelible mark on the psychiatrists who worked with him. One of them, Gilbert Rose, was so baffled by the Shaver case that he went on to write a play about it. When I reached Rose by phone in 2002, he said Shaver still haunted him.

"In my fifty years in the profession," he said of the truth-serum interview, "that was the most dramatic moment ever—when he clapped his hands to his face and remembered killing the girl." But Rose was shocked when I told him that West had hypnotized Shaver in addition to giving him sodium pentothal. After I read Rose citations from articles, reports, and the transcript, he seemed to accept it, but he was adamant that West had never said any-thing—hypnotism was not part of the protocol.

He'd also never known how West had found out about the case right away.

"We were involved from the first day," Rose recalled. "Jolly phoned me the morning of the murder," Rose said, giving me flashbacks to Shahrokh Hatami's memory of Reeve Whitson. "He initiated it."

West may have shielded himself from scrutiny, but he made only a minimal effort to exonerate Shaver. The airman was found guilty. Though an appeals court ruled that he'd had an unfair trial, he was convicted again in the retrial. In 1958, on his thirty-third birthday, he was executed by the electric chair. He maintained his innocence the whole time.

West claimed he was in the courtroom the day Shaver was sentenced to death. Around this time, he became vehemently against capital punishment. I couldn't help but wonder if it was because he knew his experiments might've led to the execution of an innocent man and the death of a child. What if his correspondence with Gottlieb, predating the crime by just a year, had been presented at trial? Would the outcome have been the same?

Tusko Goes Down

If the Shaver incident was the most harrowing chapter of West's career, the most surreal belonged to Tusko: an elephant. Of all West's experiments, this one netted the most press, much of it scathing. But the public didn't know that the CIA's Sidney Gottlieb had funded it.

On August 2, 1962, West headed to Oklahoma City's Lincoln Park Zoo, where he'd invited a crowd of eager onlookers to watch his latest test. To their delight, he'd secured an Asian elephant named Tusko, an exotic specimen in Oklahoma. West would attempt, he explained, to induce musth, "a form of madness" that occurred in male elephants during the rutting season. Musth caused violent behavioral changes. "Normally cooperative and tamable, the elephant now runs berserk for a period of about two weeks, during which time he may attack or destroy anything in his path," West explained, claiming that whole villages had been wiped out by a single musthing animal. In his rage, the elephant secreted "a mysterious fluid," brown and sticky, from his temporal gland. Could it prove medically useful? He intended to find out. His method was simple: he would simulate musth by injecting the elephant with a lot of LSD.

But West had miscalculated the dosage. Tusko weighed a whopping 7000 pounds. West shot him with 2800 milligrams of acid, about 1400 times the quantity given to a human to produce "a marked mental disturbance," by West's measurement. "Five minutes after the injection," West later wrote, "Tusko trumpeted, collapsed, fell heavily onto his right side, defecated and went into status epilepticus," a respiratory seizure resulting in death.

The next morning's paper featured a front-page photo of the portly psychiatrist bent over the deceased pachyderm. There were no animal-rights groups then—Tusko's death was received more as comedy than tragedy. For a time, West became the laughing-stock of the scientific community, and he was soon making fun of the mishap himself; he liked to inform his lecture audiences that he was the doctor famous for killing an elephant with LSD. When I asked Roger Smith about West, he exclaimed, "He's the guy that killed the elephant. Great story. Wonderful story. He always told it!"

The mystery behind the joke was why LSD had been used on an elephant in the first place. What good did it do to simulate musth? West, true to form, never gave the same explanation twice. Speaking to an interviewer from the *Medical Tribune,* and to another from the *Daily Oklahoman,* West said his objective was to find an "animal model" for "recurring psychoses in humans." Elephant brains were useful analogs for the human mind: they had excellent memories, "creative judgment," sophisticated problem-solving abilities, and even an "individual personality." Looking at elephant violence offered an opportunity "to learn what changes are correlated with this gross behavior," and to see if those changes happened in people, too.

And yet in a December 1962 article for the journal *Science,* West

and his coresearcher acted as if their ambitions were purely zoo-
logical. If they surgically removed an elephant's glands before
puberty, "he might grow up to be a sexually capable but behaviorly
tractable animal."

Their recommendations were so preposterous that they occa-
sioned an avalanche of letters to *Science*. Outraged scientists questioned West's true objectives, labeling him "capricious" and
"irresponsible." "I fail to see any scientific merit," one wrote, "or
purpose."

West left his position at the University of Oklahoma in January
1969. His successor, Dr. Gordon Deckert, found records in the
department's files about the Tusko debacle. "When [the elephant]
died, the department was worried: How in the world are we going
to pay for that?" Deckert recalled. "All Jolly would say to anybody
was that he would find a way to pay for it. I learned then, when I
became chair, that the source was payment from the CIA." Having
known about West's involvement in "the so-called brainwashing
issue in the Korean War," Deckert conceded that he "wasn't terribly surprised." The financial cover was the Foundations Fund for
Research in Psychiatry, Inc.: the same group that paid for West's
Haight–Ashbury Project.

Jack Ruby's Psychotic Break

At UCLA, I kept requesting boxes of West's papers, and they kept
leading me over trapdoors. Next they dropped me into a quagmire
I wanted no part of: the assassination of John F. Kennedy, an event
that plausibly qualified as the most discussed crime of all time.
Certainly it had bred more conspiracy theories, skepticism, and
enmity than any other incident in U.S. history, altering the way
Americans digested their news, and breaking the nation's belief in
its institutions. I flipped through West's pages cautiously, hoping

that his involvement was peripheral. It wasn't. Down through the trapdoor I went.

Kennedy was shot as his motorcade passed through Dallas's Dealey Plaza on November 22, 1963. Two days later, at the Dallas police headquarters, officers escorted Kennedy's assassin, Lee Harvey Oswald, to an armored car that would drive him to the county jail. A man stepped out from the crowd and aimed a revolver at Oswald's chest. It was Jack Ruby, a nightclub proprietor with connections to Cuban political groups and organized crime. He fired once at point-blank range, sending a fatal bullet into Oswald's stomach.

According to a first-person account that Ruby produced with a ghostwriter—published in newspapers in a scenario close to Susan Atkins's, and again involving Lawrence Schiller—Ruby "lost [his] senses" when he pulled out his gun. Next thing he knew, the cops had him pinned to the floor, and he had no memory of what he'd just done. "What am I doing here?" he asked. "What are you guys jumping on me for?" A psychiatric analysis solicited by Ruby's defense attorneys said he'd suffered "a 'fugue state' with subsequent amnesia."

On the advice of his attorney at the time, Ruby said he'd murdered Oswald to spare the widowed First Lady, Jackie Kennedy, the ordeal of testifying against Oswald at trial. Another of Ruby's attorneys, Melvin Belli, later wrote that Ruby had "a blank spot in his memory," and that any explanation he provided was simply "confabulating." Potential justifications "had been poured like water into the vacuum in his pathologically receptive memory and, once there, had solidified like cement."

Seemingly as soon as the story of Oswald's murder hit the presses, Jolly West tried to insinuate himself into the case. He hoped to assemble a panel of "experts in behavior problems" to weigh in on Ruby's mental state. He took the extraordinary measure of approaching Judge Joe B. Brown, who'd impaneled the grand jury that indicted Ruby. West wanted the judge to appoint him to the case. At that time, police hadn't revealed any substantial information about Ruby, his psychological condition, or his possible motive. And West was vague about *his* motive, too. Three documents among his papers said he'd been "asked" by someone, though he never said who, to seek the appointment from Brown "a few days after the assassination," a fact never before made public.

The judge turned him down. For the moment, it seemed, West would be getting nowhere near Ruby, who was soon convicted of first-degree murder and sentenced to death. Ruby was reportedly unmoored by the news. He'd killed the president's assassin, and the citizens of Dallas had rewarded him with a trip to the gallows. He fired his attorney and hired Hubert Winston Smith, a psychiatrist with a law degree who'd assisted in the trial, to represent him on appeal.

Meanwhile, at Langley, the CIA's Richard Helms was making the case that MKULTRA's human guinea pigs had to be entirely unaware of the experiments performed on them. This was "the only realistic method," he wrote, "to influence human behavior as the operational targets will certainly be unwitting."

Once Dr. Smith was driving Ruby's legal team, one of his first acts was to request a new psychiatric examination of Ruby. He had one candidate in mind: Dr. Louis Jolyon West, whom he noted in a court brief had enjoyed acclaim for his studies of brainwashed American POWs. Perhaps, Smith wrote, West could use his "highly qualified" skills as a hypnotist and an administrator of the "truth serum, sodium pentothal" to help Ruby regain his memory of the shooting. (West may have rewarded Smith for the plum assignment by helping him land a teaching position at Oklahoma.)

And so, on April 26, 1964, West boarded a plane bound for Dallas. He was scheduled to examine Jack Ruby in the county jail that afternoon.

The Dallas papers reported it in their final editions that evening: West emerged from Ruby's cell to announce that the previously sane inmate had undergone "an acute psychotic break" sometime during the preceding "forty-eight hours." Whatever transpired between West and Ruby in that cell, only the two of them could say; there were no witnesses. West asserted that Ruby "was now positively insane." The condition appeared to be "unshakable" and "fixed."

In a sworn affidavit accompanying his diagnosis, West described a completely unhinged man who hallucinated, heard voices, and had suddenly acquired the unshakeable belief that a new holocaust was under way in America. "Last night," West wrote, "the patient became convinced that all Jews in America were being slaughtered. This was in retaliation for him, Jack Ruby, the Jew who was responsible for 'all the trouble.'" The delusions were so real that Ruby had crawled under the table to hide from the killers. He said he'd "seen his own brother tortured, horribly mutilated, castrated, and burned in the street outside the jail. He could still hear the screams...The orders for this terrible 'pogrom' must have come from Washington."

West said the trouble had started sometime in the evening before the exam, when Ruby ran headfirst into his cell wall in an apparent suicide attempt. But Ruby's jailer, Sheriff Bill Decker, shrugged it off as a cry for attention. "He rubbed his head on the wall enough that we had to put a little Merthiolate [antiseptic] on it," Decker told a reporter. "That's all."

From that day forward, every doctor who examined Ruby made similar diagnoses: he was delusional. West, however, was hardly the first to have evaluated him. By then nearly half a dozen psychiatrists, many equally renowned, had taken stock of Ruby's condition, finding him essentially compos mentis. West had been briefed on these opinions, but in his hubris, he wrote that he'd hardly bothered with them, having been "unable to read them until earlier today on the airplane. Tonight, my own findings make it clear that there has been an acute change in the patient's condition since these earlier studies were carried out."

The change was too "acute" for Judge Brown's liking. In the preceding five months, he'd spent many hours in the courtroom with Ruby, and he'd never witnessed anything resembling the behavior West described. Presumably it wasn't lost on him that this was the same doctor who'd clamored to see Ruby months earlier. After the judge heard West's report, he ordered a second opinion, saying, "I would like some real disinterested doctors to examine Ruby for my own benefit. I want to get the truth out of it."

That opinion came from Dr. William Beavers, who examined Ruby two days after West. Beavers's report to the judge, never before made public, confirmed West's findings. Ruby "became agitated," Beavers wrote, and "asked if I did not hear the sounds of torture that were going on." Like Judge Brown, he was alarmed by the abruptness of Ruby's disintegration. He considered the possibility that Ruby was malingering—but quickly ruled it out, explaining that it was "highly unlikely that this individual could have convincingly faked hallucinations." Beavers wondered if Ruby had been tampered with or drugged by an outsider. "The possibility of a toxic psychosis could be entertained," he wrote, "but is considered unlikely because of the protected situation."

The truth, by that point, was sealed up behind West. Beavers couldn't have known that one of his fellow caregivers was capable of anything so diabolical as inducing mental illness in a patient. His report would have turned out differently, no doubt, if he'd been apprised of West's unorthodox fortes, and his long relationship with the Central Intelligence Agency.

Dozens of West's colleagues offered me assessments of his character. There was praise, especially from those who'd worked with him at UCLA, but there was also condemnation, most of it from his former colleagues at Oklahoma, where he'd done the bulk of his MKULTRA research. He was a "devious man," "egotistical," an inveterate "narcissist" and "womanizer." The few who hadn't already suspected his involvement with the CIA accepted it readily. But the most relevant insight came from Dr. Jay Shurley, his good friend of forty-five years, who'd worked with West at Lackland Air Force Base and the University of Oklahoma. Shurley was one of the few colleagues who admitted that West was an employee of the CIA. I asked him if he thought West would've accepted an assignment from the CIA to scramble Jack Ruby's mind.

"I feel sort of disloyal to Jolly's memory," Shurley said, "but I have to be honest with you, my gut feeling would be yes. He would be capable of that." Calling West "a very complex character," he explained, "he had a little problem with grandiosity. He would not be averse at all to having influenced American history in some way or other, whether he got the credit for it or not...Jolly had a real streak of—I guess you'd call it patriotism. If the president asked him to do something, or somebody in a higher office...he would break his back to do that without asking too many questions."

"Even if it meant distorting American history?"

"I suppose so," Shurley said. "He was a pretty fearless kind of guy."

"A Deliberate Gangland Killing"

West's "fearless" intervention set the stage for decades of confusion and conspiracy in Washington. A week after Kennedy's assassination, the newly installed president, Lyndon Johnson, hand-selected a group of thirteen men to investigate the crime. The President's Commission on the Assassination of President Kennedy—better known as the Warren Commission, after its chairman, Chief Justice of the United States Earl Warren—had some dubious members in its ranks. One was Allen Dulles, the former CIA director. Kennedy had fired him two years earlier, after he'd bungled the

Bay of Pigs invasion. Another was the official CIA liaison to the group, Richard Helms, soon to become the agency's director. A protégé of Dulles, Helms was the longtime secret employer of Jolly West, and one of the few agency officials aware of MKULTRA. But no one else on the commission—except, presumably, Dulles, who started the program—was aware that a CIA "asset" trained in mind control had assumed responsibility for the psychiatric care of Jack Ruby, whom the commission regarded as their "most important witness."

In June 1964, Earl Warren and others from the group flew to Dallas to give Ruby a hearing in the interrogation room of the county jail. The bulk of his testimony was a morass of paranoid rambling. He begged Warren to get him out of Dallas. "The Jewish people are being exterminated at this moment," he warned. "I know I won't live to see you another time...Do I sound sort of screwy?" He demanded to speak with a Jew, whispering frantically, "You have to get me to Washington! They're cutting off the arms and legs of Jewish children in Albuquerque and El Paso!"

The commission, unable to extract a cogent account from their main witness, concluded that Lee Harvey Oswald acted alone in assassinating Kennedy, and that Ruby did not act in a conspiracy to silence Oswald. Although they saw no evidence of a secret plot, they couldn't definitively rule out such a thing. But their integrity was compromised the minute West set foot in Ruby's jail cell. The group was required to investigate the CIA as a routine suspect in the assassination of a sitting president. Neither Dulles nor Helms ever reported their knowledge of West's employment by the CIA. And soon Jack Ruby was no longer around to tell his own story. He died in 1967 of complications from lung cancer.

In the seventies, when Congress looked into abuses by intelligence agencies, it found evidence that the CIA and FBI had obstructed the Kennedy investigation. Dulles and Helms had deliberately concealed failed CIA plots to assassinate Cuba's dictator, Fidel Castro. Allegedly, the CIA had aligned with organized crime figures, many sworn enemies of President Kennedy and his brother, Attorney General Robert Kennedy; they teamed up with anti-Castro Cubans in Miami and New Orleans to assassinate the dictator. Helms had personally overseen those schemes.

The evidence, wrote House officials, "impeaches the process by which the intelligence agencies arrived at their own conclusions about the assassination." Feeling it had no choice but to start over again, the House voted overwhelmingly to impanel the House Select Committee on Assassinations (HSCA) and reinvestigate.

The HSCA openly aspired to make the Warren *Report* "persuasive." Its final five-volume report—arriving in 1979, after two and a half years and $5.4 million in taxpayer money—did just the opposite. Based on new ballistic evidence of a second gunman in Dallas, the HSCA rejected the Warren Commission's finding that Oswald had acted alone. There was a "probable conspiracy," it announced, to assassinate the president.

The committee had to be measured; it didn't identify any potential coconspirators in the president's murder. A few years later, freed of their congressional restraints, the committee's G. Robert Blakey and Richard Billings published *The Plot to Kill the President,* an unmuzzled account of the investigation. "The murder of Oswald by Jack Ruby had all the earmarks of an organized crime hit, an action to silence the assassin, so he could never reveal the conspiracy," they wrote. "Jack Ruby, working for the mob, after stalking Oswald for two days, silenced him forever. This was a deliberate gangland killing."

The coauthors saw no evidence implicating the CIA, but they remained suspicious. Their suspicions were borne out in the hulking twenty-seven-volume appendix of the HSCA witnesses' published testimony, which described behind-the-scenes maneuvering by Dulles and Helms to obstruct the Warren Commission. Along with the FBI's J. Edgar Hoover, Dulles and Helms were determined to present Oswald as a crazed lone assassin and Ruby as a distraught citizen. Hoover released the FBI's initial findings just two weeks after the killing, concluding that Oswald acted alone.

"Hoover lied his eyes out," the Warren Commission's Hale Boggs later testified in HSCA hearings, "on Oswald, on Ruby, on their friends, the bullets, the gun, you name it."

Dulles was no less complicit. He'd urged the Warren Commission to limit itself to reviewing the FBI's investigation, rather than mounting its own. In secret, he met with Helms and other CIA officials to coach them on what questions the commission planned to ask.

Faced with these revelations, the HSCA could only conclude that intelligence groups were hiding their links to Oswald and Ruby, if not a CIA effort to assassinate Castro. Some believed that the plot on Castro may have been turned on Kennedy, after his Bay of Pigs invasion failed and he embraced other policy changes that curtailed the agency's influence, like reducing the U.S. presence in Vietnam, warming diplomatic relations with the Soviet Union, and decreasing military spending. Even President Johnson had his doubts. "The President felt that [the] CIA had had something to do with the plot," said an Oval Office memo from '67.

If the CIA wanted to shut Ruby up, what was it that he had on it? Burt Griffin, an attorney for the Warren Commission, appeared before the HSCA to say that he and his partner had nearly confirmed Ruby's ties to gunrunning schemes by anti-Castro Cubans, who were shipping arms from the United States to Cuba in hopes of deposing the dictator.

At the time, Griffin had no idea that the CIA sponsored these gunrunning schemes. In March 1964—when Ruby was weeks away from his "examination" by Jolly West—Griffin and his partner approached Richard Helms, requesting all the information the CIA had on Ruby. They believed it was possible "that Ruby was involved in illegal dealings with Cuban elements who might have had contact with Oswald."

Helms offered only a curt reply: "The CIA would be very limited in its possibility of assisting." Griffin was baffled—this was someone who was supposed to be helping him. He appealed again. By the time Helms mustered a response, months had passed, and West had long since paid his fateful visit to Ruby. "An examination of Agency files," Helms wrote, "has produced no information on Jack Ruby or his activities."

As for Jolly West, he also did his part to keep Ruby untainted from any whiff of conspiracy. As the Warren Commission tried to divine Ruby's motive, West sent a confidential letter to Earl Warren himself, a copy of which I discovered in the HSCA's files. Dated June 23, 1964, and addressed to "My Dear Mr. Chief Justice," West's note contends that his "examinations" of Ruby gave him unique insight into the man's "motivations for the murder." (This despite the fact that West had said Ruby was "positively insane.") He was confident that Ruby had acted in an "irrational and unpremeditated" manner when he shot Oswald, "wanting to prove that the Jews—through himself—loved their President and were not cowards." Moreover, West asserted that Ruby "had never seen [Oswald] in his life" before his involvement in the Kennedy assassination broke. Without consent from his patient or his patient's lawyers, West was offering confidential medical assessments tailored to political ends. "Please let me know if there is anything else that I can do to be of assistance," he added. Warren didn't. In an internal note, he dismissed the psychiatrist as an "interloper," writing, "I see no need to do anything with this material." Had he known of West's CIA connections, he may have reacted differently.

If West couldn't foist his version of events onto the Warren

Commission, he could at least make sure that no compromising information about Ruby emerged. At his urging, a psychiatrist named Dr. Werner Tuteur examined Ruby in July 1965 to prepare for an upcoming hearing on his sanity. Tuteur submitted a twelve-page report to West—it was there in his files, bundled with an edited version that West had submitted to the court. He struck just one passage, the most vital: "There is considerable guilt about the fact that he sent guns to Cuba," Tuteur had written. "He feels he 'helped the enemy' and incriminated himself. 'They got what they wanted on me.'" Erasing those lines, West expunged the very evidence Griffin had been looking for.

West kept meticulous notes on the Ruby case, all dutifully filed. As investigators, scholars, and journalists struggled to piece together the puzzle, he watched from afar, compiling records for his own book about Ruby. He never ended up writing it, but he paid close attention to an exhaustive 1965 volume, *The Trial of Jack Ruby,* by John Kaplan and Jon R. Waltz. They wrote, "The fact is that nobody knows why Jack Ruby shot Lee Harvey Oswald—and this includes Jack Ruby."

Jolly West had jotted down that line with a note to himself: "good quote." It was, until now, the closest he ever came to receiving public credit for his work.

Coda: "The Data-Spew"

Libra, Don DeLillo's 1988 novel about Lee Harvey Oswald, features a character named Nicholas Branch—a retired CIA analyst tasked with internally reviewing the agency's conduct in the JFK assassination, once and for all. The assignment swallows him for fifteen years. The agency pays for the construction of a lavish, fireproof home office, which becomes, to Branch, "the book-filled room, the room of documents, the room of theories and dreams." He reposes in "a glove-leather armchair," surrounded by shelves and filing cabinets bursting with folders, cassettes, legal pads, and books. Branch "sits in the data-spew of hundreds of lives." He comes to feel that "the past is changing as he writes." And his ultimate subject, he knows, isn't crime or politics. It's "men in small rooms."

Although I had a sagging sofa instead of a glove-leather armchair, and while nothing in my apartment was fire-insured, let alone fireproof, I identified a lot with Nicholas Branch. I was immersed in records, voices from the past, competing narratives, complexity that sometimes seemed to multiply for its own sake. No matter which way I moved, the stories shifted beneath my feet. I was a man in a small room reading about men in small rooms. But where Nicholas Branch had the full backing of the CIA, I had only myself.

As I worked to fill out my book proposal and, I hoped, draw my reporting to a close, I had dreams of sharing my findings with the members of the Warren Commission, brandishing evidence they'd never been able to prize out of the CIA. But most of the commission's members were long dead. Gerald Ford wasn't, but he wanted nothing to do with me. Burt Griffin, who'd been responsible for handling the Ruby aspect of the investigation, said in a phone interview that my findings were "very scary stuff," and that West's relationship with the CIA "should be investigated." But he was long retired—if anyone was going to launch an investigation, it wouldn't be him.

I had better luck with Arlen Specter, then the senior senator from my home state of Pennsylvania. Late in 2002, visiting my parents in Philadelphia, I decided to see if he was interested in the papers I'd uncovered.

Specter had joined the Warren Commission as a young investigative attorney. He'd participated in Ruby's appearances before the commission. When Ruby dilated on his anti-Semitic conspiracy theories, he thought he had an ally in Specter, one of the commission's only Jewish staff members. Specter was also responsible for the Warren Commission's controversial "single bullet theory," which argued that one bullet had taken a circuitous route through the bodies of John F. Kennedy and Governor John Connally, who had been sitting in front of Kennedy when he was shot. This theory ruled out the possibility of a second gunman, and Specter regarded it as gospel truth; he referred to it as the Single Bullet *Conclusion*. Since his role in the commission had launched his career, Specter had been unusually forthcoming about it over the years, eager to defend his position and to remind voters of his role in a seminal chapter of American history.

Getting Specter's attention took months. Through his aides, I wrangled what was supposed to be a two-minute phone interview. He called me from the Senate floor. I laid out my case as quickly as possible, with background on West, his involvement with the CIA's MKULTRA experiments, and his examination of Ruby.

Specter was intrigued. Our call ended up running to twenty minutes. Though he had no knowledge of the agency's mind-control program or the congressional investigation into it, he seemed open to the possibility that West could have tampered with Ruby and, thus, with the Warren Commission's findings.

"Can you fax me these documents?" he asked, offering to approach the CIA about them.

I wanted him to see them in person. Once they were out of my hands, there was no telling where they might end up, and alerting the CIA to them right away might not be in the best interest of my reporting. Specter sighed.

Knowing that congressmen usually went home for weekends, I took a chance: "If you're going to be in Philadelphia..."

He had a squash match that Saturday at the Wyndham Plaza Hotel. He suggested I meet him there. His aide would call to set it up.

I was thrilled—a sitting senator, a key investigator for the Warren Commission, was willing to hear me out in person. I followed up with a fax sharing some of the *New York Times*'s reporting on MKULTRA and more information on West.

And then I got paranoid.

I hadn't gone through every box of West's files yet. What if divulging my findings to Specter jeopardized my access to those? Someone could get there first and remove anything incriminating.

But that was outlandish, I thought. I was flying back to L.A. at the end of the weekend. If I went to the UCLA files right away, I'd be fine—even the CIA couldn't act so quickly.

And yet the more I thought about it, the more distrustful I got. Why was Specter so eager to see the documents? He didn't seem to care a whit about my credentials, or lack thereof. And could it really be true that a longtime senator had never heard of MKULTRA? Specter was the chairman of the Senate Select Committee on Intelligence, the same group that had investigated MKULTRA back in the day. He had the power to open doors for me, but if he was bent on upholding the Warren Commission's findings, wouldn't he just as soon close those doors?

I was overthinking everything, and then overthinking my overthinking. At the end of the day, I decided to err on the side of caution and postpone our meeting. Maybe in the future I could have an attorney accompany me, or some impartial observer.

The next morning, I left messages at Specter's hotel and with his press office: I was profoundly sorry, but an emergency had come up, and I really had to leave for L.A. that afternoon. I went to run a few errands, trying to convince myself I hadn't made a huge mistake. To this day, I wonder about that.

While I was out, the phone rang and my mom picked up. It was Arlen Specter, sounding confused. Having been briefed on my plan, my mom told Specter I was on my way to the airport. (Her feelings were mixed, she told me later—her son was important enough to merit a call from a senator on a weekend, but her son had also made her lie to that senator.)

Specter was gobsmacked. "So he's *not* going to meet with me?"

"I'm afraid not," my mom said.

I tried to reschedule our meeting for years. When I finally got him on the phone again, I was so shocked to have gotten through that I realized I'd long since stopped preparing for our talk. It had been months since I'd rehearsed the particulars of West and Ruby. I was much less convincing. He wasn't interested in seeing any of my papers.

"I just don't see where this all leads," Specter said. That was a phrase I'd be hearing a lot in the coming years.

12

Where Does It All Go?

Writing the Music

Jolly West's MKULTRA letters were my biggest discovery, I thought. If there were an answer to that question of questions—how Manson got his followers to kill—I felt it had to be there. I marshaled my energy in the hopes of discovering that they'd crossed paths, or that Manson's enormous success in creating the Family had some debt to the CIA's mind-control techniques. Even if I turned up nothing, I thought considering Manson and West in parallel was a worthy effort. Theirs was one of the great non sequiturs of the sixties. Manson, the ex-con, the Hollywood striver, the oversexed, unwashed guru who'd been discarded from society, had used LSD to collect and reprogram his followers. In the summer of love, he walked the same streets and frequented the same clinic as Jolly West, the upright air force officer, the world-renowned psychiatrist, the eloquent hypnotist who wrote to his CIA handler that there was "no more vital undertaking conceivable" than to dose unwitting research subjects with LSD and replace their memories.

Both men were moralizers, hypocrites, and narcissists. And both were determined to make their presence felt in an America they felt had gone rotten. On the stand at his own trial, Manson said, "Is it a conspiracy that the music is telling the youth to rise up against the establishment?...It is not my conspiracy. It is not my music. I hear what it relates. It says rise, it says kill. Why blame it on me? I didn't write the music." On some level, he was right.

I resumed work on my proposal feeling that I had enough to make even hardened skeptics doubt themselves a little bit. Though it took me years to get all my words in fighting condition, I finally finished in 2005. It came in at a whopping eighty thousand words, as long as many actual books. On the merits of the proposal, Penguin Press agreed to publish the book. I was elated, and more than a little relieved. I hadn't known whether any respectable publisher would vouch for a project that mentioned Manson, Jack Ruby, and CIA mind control in the same breath. Penguin's support was vindicating, and the advance payment it offered was more than enough to let me tie up my reporting.

The complete manuscript was due in early 2008, a little less than three years away. Now all I had to do was finish my reporting and write the thing. The following year would be the fortieth anniversary of the murders—I'd only missed my *Premiere* deadline by a decade. But that had been a magazine story. This would be a book.

I had big plans for the money from my advance, which was more lucrative than I'd allowed myself to imagine it could be. I upgraded my computer, junked my old Acura, and bought...a used '85 Volvo, for four hundred bucks. Everything else would go back into the book. Although my friends advised me to buy property and take an exotic vacation, I didn't even consider it. I had at least three years of rigorous reporting and writing ahead of me. The money could help me accomplish what had been too costly or labor-intensive before. I hired two research assistants to help me get organized. They transcribed the endless hours of taped interviews I'd amassed—more than two hundred cassettes by then, most of their ninety minutes completely filled. They helped type out the handwritten notes on my sixty legal pads and thirty notebooks, and some of the passages I'd highlighted in some three hundred books. Most of my papers were in one of the 190 binders I had, and yet I'd allowed a half dozen stacks of unfiled documents to grow to about four feet high apiece. (At least they were separated by subject.) Reviewing the massive material record of my work was unsettling. I was rediscovering the fragments, micro-obsessions, and niggling questions that had tugged me onward when I began my reporting. Many I'd simply forgotten about; others were unresolved and probably always would be. But a few started to tempt me again. Now that I was finalizing everything, I had to be sure I hadn't missed a lead. If a doubt sat in the back of my mind long enough, I added it to my to-do list. Soon it was dangerously long for someone with a book to write.

One of the most basic problems I'd had over the years was tracking people down. Many former members of the Family had gone to great lengths to make themselves unreachable: they'd changed their names and severed ties with anyone who might've known about their pasts. At least the celebrities who'd said no to me once upon a time could be reached through publicists. Now I was looking for people who'd gone off the grid. I didn't necessarily want to force anyone to speak to me. But what if someone in the Family remembered Jolly West, or Reeve Whitson, or any of the shadowy figures I'd investigated? What if, like the detective Charlie Guenther, they had something they'd wanted to get off their chest for thirty years? Some of my hostile interviewees had thawed when they saw that I didn't have the sensational, tabloid-style agenda that fueled most reporting on Manson.

So I also hired a private detective, a retired LASO deputy

nicknamed Moon, who worked out of an office in Arizona. To this day, I've never met him, though we've shared thousands of emails and calls. Moon found people and police records I never could've turned up on my own. He'd participated in the LASO raid of the Spahn Ranch, and he reached out to other retired cops, urging them to speak to me. He also schooled me in skip tracing, the art of finding people who don't want to be found. Before long I was paying to access digitized cross-directories and databases, including one called Merlin that required a PI license to use, which I managed to obtain. Between the two of us, Moon and I located just about everyone who'd hung around with Manson, most of them scattered up and down the West Coast. I added them to my interview list, along with the usual mix of cops, lawyers, drug dealers, researchers, Hollywood has-beens, and congressmen.

The extra help freed me up to do what I did best: dive into the archives. I had about a dozen places I needed to visit to fill in holes in my paper trail. There were old LAPD and LASO homicide detectives; district attorneys who'd offered to show me their stuff; files on the Family from courts, police departments, parks departments, and highway patrols that I'd persuaded the state of California to let me see for the first time; and personal files from reporters who'd long ago tried to investigate the same stuff I was after, most of them hitting the same dead ends.

My to-do list was now as long as it'd been in the heaviest days of my reporting. And sometimes, behind my excitement and anxiety, I could feel a lower, deeper dread. Even if I could strengthen the bridge between Manson and West, I didn't have a smoking gun—some fabled needle at the Spahn Ranch with Jolly West's fingerprints on it, or a classified memo from the Los Angeles DA's office to the FBI. I worried I never would. The evidence I'd amassed against the official version of the Manson murders was so voluminous, from so many angles, that it was overdetermined. I could poke a thousand holes in the story, but I couldn't say what really happened. In fact, the major arms of my research were often in contradiction with one another. It couldn't be the case that the truth involved a drug burn gone wrong, orgies with Hollywood elite, a counterinsurgency-trained CIA infiltrator in the Family, a series of unusually lax sheriff's deputies and district attorneys and judges and parole officers, an FBI plot to smear leftists and Black Panthers, an effort to see if research on drugged mice applied to hippies, and LSD mind-control experiments tested in the field... could it? There was no way. To imagine state, local, and federal law enforcement cooperating in perfect harmony, with the courts backing them up—it made no sense. What I'd uncovered was something closer to an improvised, shambolic effort to contain the fallout from the murders. I couldn't walk myself through the sequence of events without tripping on something. I was a lousy conspiracy theorist, at the end of the day, because I wanted nothing left to the realm of the theoretical.

I was sure that at least one person had a better idea of the truth than I did. Before I went delving into any more archives or darting up the coast to confront former Family members, I had to return a phone call I'd been putting off for years. I had to talk to Bugliosi.

My Adversary

Back in 1999, Bugliosi had told me, "If there's something about my handling of the case—anything at all—that you had a question about, I would appreciate if you would call me to get my view on it." I'd promised to hear him out, imagining I'd circle back in another few months. Now seven years had passed, and I had so many questions that it took me weeks of preparation just to remember all of them.

If I was reluctant to pick up the phone, it was because I was about to engage with a man who went to criminal lengths to protect his reputation. I've already mentioned Mary Neiswender, the reporter who told me that Bugliosi was "terribly dangerous": he'd sent an emissary warning that he knew where her kids went to school and implied that "it would be very easy to plant narcotics in their lockers." And I knew that Bugliosi had been indicted for perjury as a result of his prosecuting the murders—as mentioned earlier, he'd leaked information about Manson's "hit list" to a reporter and had threatened professional consequences for his coprosecutors if they told anyone.

Those turned out to be two of the milder incidents in his quest for self-preservation. In 1968, Bugliosi fell into a scandal kept under wraps by the DA's office until '72, when he was running for district attorney of Los Angeles. (He lost the election.) He'd stalked and terrorized someone he was convinced had carried on an affair with his wife and fathered his first-born child, Vincent Jr. As clichéd as it sounds, Bugliosi suspected his milkman, Herbert Weisel, who was married with two children.

Weisel had left his job in 1965, eight months before Vincent Jr. was born. Bugliosi was sure that Weisel had quit because of his transgression—the evidence must've been in Weisel's personnel file at the dairy. He made anonymous phone calls to Weisel's wife and then to Weisel himself, demanding him to release his files. The couple began to notice "strange cars" circling their block after dark. They changed their phone number, which was already unlisted. Two days later, they got a typed letter postmarked from L.A. "You shouldn't have changed your phone number," it said. "That wasn't nice."

Eventually, Bugliosi's wife, Gail, approached the Weisels, revealing her identity in the hopes that she could arrange a détente. The Weisels told her that her husband should be getting psychiatric help. "She told us that she'd tried many times, but that he wouldn't do it," they later testified in a civil deposition. She'd apparently taken paternity and lie-detector tests to prove the child was his, but he still harbored doubts. "I know he's sick," the Weisels reported her to have said. "He's got a mental problem."

The couple became so frightened that they stopped allowing their children to take the bus to school. They hired a lawyer and, after a mediation, Bugliosi agreed to stop harassing them and to pay them $100 for their silence. They refused the money. In '72, with Bugliosi on the ballot, they decided it was their civic duty to go public—their tormentor aspired to the most powerful law enforcement job in the city. They told the papers of his yearlong harassment and intimidation campaign.

Enlisting his well-documented talent for fabrication, Bugliosi retaliated, telling the press that Weisel had stolen money from his kitchen table seven years earlier. Weisel sued him for slander and defamation. It wasn't a tough case to win. In depositions, Bugliosi and his wife swore they'd only been worried about the alleged robbery of their home. The Weisels argued otherwise, bringing in witnesses who, they claimed, exposed the Bugliosis as perjurers. Soon it came out that Bugliosi had twice used an investigator in the DA's office—*his* office—to get confidential information about Weisel, claiming he was a material witness in a murder case. Fearing the disclosure would cost him his job, Bugliosi settled out of court, paying the Weisels $12,500. He paid in cash, on the condition that they sign a confidentiality agreement and turn over the deposition tapes.

No sooner was the milkman imbroglio resolved than Bugliosi fell into another fiasco, again abusing his connection to the criminal justice system to straighten it out. His mistress, Virginia Cardwell, the single mother of a five-year-old, told him she was pregnant. It was his. With visions of public office still dancing in his mind, and *Helter Skelter* on the eve of publication, he ordered Cardwell, a Catholic, to get an abortion. She refused, but after Bugliosi threatened her and gave her money for the procedure, she lied and said she'd done it. He wasn't about to take her word for it. He got her doctor's name, called him, and learned that she'd never been to see him, after which he headed to her apartment and beat her so savagely that she suffered a miscarriage. He choked her, struck her in the face several times with his fists, threw her onto the floor, pulled her up by her hair, and threatened to kill her if she had the baby, saying she wouldn't leave the apartment alive if she lied to him: "I will break every bone in your body—this will ruin my career." Bruised and battered, Cardwell gathered herself and went to the Santa Monica Police Department, where she filed a criminal complaint. The cops photographed her bruises and then, evidently, did nothing.

That evening, an eagle-eyed reporter spotted the incident on the police blotter and wrote about it in the next day's paper. Bugliosi returned to Cardwell's apartment that morning, this time with his secretary. The pair held her hostage for four hours until she agreed to tell the police she'd filed a false complaint the previous day. Bugliosi assured her he'd use his contacts in the DA's office to make sure she was never brought to trial for the false report. He and his secretary used Cardwell's typewriter to forge a backdated bill for legal services, telling her to show it to the police. He listened in on an extension as she called to turn herself in. The dispatcher said they'd send a patrol car to get her. He vigorously shook his head, and Cardwell told the dispatcher she'd be fine getting in on her own.

The dispatcher sent a car anyway. One of the detectives who'd seen Cardwell that day, Michael Landis, told me Bugliosi and "a couple of his associates" answered the door "and tried to discourage us from talking to her. We were persistent and we did see her—and she was pretty well banged up." Cardwell claimed that the bruises were from an accident: her son had hit her in the face with a baseball bat. She'd only blamed Bugliosi because she was angry that he'd overcharged her for legal advice concerning her divorce. "This outrageous charge, even though false, can be extremely harmful," Bugliosi told police.

Cardwell's brother persuaded her to file a lawsuit against Bugliosi. Bugliosi's story fell apart before the suit was even filed, and he settled with Cardwell in exchange for her confidentiality—ensuring, he hoped, that his lies to the police, fabrication of evidence, and obstruction of justice would never see the light of day. He was wrong. The Virginia Cardwell story hit the papers in 1974, when his primary opponent in the California state attorney general's race, William Norris, caught wind of it. (Bugliosi lost that election, too.) Because of his clout in the DA's office, he was never prosecuted for assaulting Cardwell. Landis, the detective, called him "a whiney, sniveley little bastard," saying, "I wanted to prosecute the son of a bitch."

All of which is to say that I approached Bugliosi with extreme caution.

And at first, he refused to grant me another interview. In the intervening years, he explained, he'd heard from two unnamed "sources" that I'd done "terrible things" in my "private life." He refused to say what these things were. I knew I'd done nothing wrong. I told him to go ahead and expose whatever it was he had on me—it would never hold up to scrutiny. I added that I'd amassed a lot of documents, including some in his own hand, that raised questions about the integrity of the prosecution. But he was adamant: no interview. Furthermore, if my book defamed or libeled him, he would hold me liable to the greatest degree of the law. "You don't want to be working for me the rest of your life," he said. "I think you know what I mean." He hung up.

And then, ten minutes later, he called back. He wanted to repeat the same conversation we'd just had, to pretend like we were having it for the first time. His wife, Gail, would be listening in on another extension as a "witness," so I wouldn't misrepresent what he'd said.

"You want us to repeat the conversation word for word, like it hadn't already happened?" I asked.

"Yes," he said. "Or, you know, the essence of the conversation."

It was a ridiculous exercise. I agreed anyway; I wanted to keep our lines of communication open, and I had a morbid desire to see how it played out. I told him I'd only do it if I could tape the call, so I'd have a "witness," too. He agreed.

Listening back to it now, I'm amazed: we really did it. We had the same talk again, with occasional corrections. ("No, Vince, you said you'd sue me for 100 million dollars, not millions of dollars.") Every few minutes, Bugliosi would make sure that Gail was still listening. "Yes," she'd sigh. "I'm here." As for the papers I had, he told me, "Documents may be accurate…but it doesn't make the document itself truthful." And even if he wanted to sit down with me—which he didn't, because of the "terrible things" I'd done—he couldn't, because he was "absolutely swamped." He didn't even have time to go to a Super Bowl party that "some prominent people" had invited him to.

"I kind of doubt that under any circumstances I'd be willing to give you an interview," he said. "But if you send me a letter specifying everything you want to talk about, or the essence of what you want to talk about, there's an outside possibility that I may find the time, or make the time."

I never sent that letter. Experience had taught me that the longer I stayed silent, the more agitated Bugliosi would become. Despite his protestations, he really wanted to know what I'd write about him. A week later, he called and said that his wife had persuaded him to sit down with me. The interview was on.

Bugliosi Redux

And so we return to that sunny day in February 2006, when Bugliosi gave me a stern dressing-down at his home in Pasadena, his wife looking on phlegmatically. That was the day he announced himself as my "adversary" and issued a forty-five-minute "opening statement," his kitchen now his courtroom as he mounted the case that he was a "decent guy" who'd "never hurt anyone in the first instance." He would retaliate "in the second instance," in self-defense or "to get even, or to get justice."

As if to prove that point, he kept threatening to sue me, making it clear that he wouldn't tolerate any allegation of misconduct. He spoke so quickly, and with such a flurry of hyperbole and legalism, that I could hardly rebut one of his points without three more rising up to take its place. Just as my encounter with Roger Smith had, my interview with Bugliosi lasted for some six hours, and I came out of it with little more than a list of denials and evasions. But at least Smith had given me wine and pizza. Bugliosi gave me only vitriol.

Before we met, I rehearsed my questions with an actor friend who stepped into Bugliosi's shoes. We developed a plan on how best to deploy my findings and parry his denials. I brought binders full of documents and carefully highlighted passages from *Helter Skelter* so that I could refresh his memory if he claimed not to recall certain particulars from the case.

But right away, Bugliosi threw me off. "Ask me your hardest question," he said at the outset. And so I started with everything I had on Terry Melcher, suggesting that Bugliosi had covered up for him and that he'd been much friendlier with Manson than had been revealed. It was the wrong move—I'd intended to build to this moment, and now I was leading with it, giving him every reason to take a contentious tone. Pulling out a passage from *Helter Skelter,* I showed Bugliosi what he'd written about Dean Moorehouse, the member of the Family who, according to the prosecutor, stayed at the house on Cielo Drive "for a brief period" after Melcher moved out.

"That's not true," I said. "He never lived there after Melcher moved out. He lived there the summer before, off and on *with*

Melcher." I showed him that Dean Moorehouse was actually in prison when Bugliosi had said he lived at the Cielo house.

"I forget what you're telling me," Bugliosi said. "The matter of where and how, I forget that kind of stuff. Thirty-five years ago, I've gone after a million things since then... There's a lot of errors in the book." He'd authored it with a cowriter, and he'd been too busy running for district attorney to fact-check every last word.

"This may have gotten past me," he said. "I'm [more] interested in anything you would have that would indicate that I may have misled the jury, because I don't believe that happened intentionally."

I took out the pages in Bugliosi's own handwriting: notes from his interview with Danny DeCarlo, one of his main witnesses, who'd said that Terry Melcher had visited Manson three times *after* the murders, contravening what Melcher had said on the stand.

"This was *after* the murders?" Bugliosi clarified, reading through his own notes. "Are you sure about that?"

"You wrote it," I said. He confirmed they were his notes and read them again.

"You have to know, Tom, that when people are talking to you they garble things up... My god. They tell a story—"

"But this is not ambiguous. You write, 'Definitely saw Melcher out at Spahn Ranch. Heard girls say, Terry's coming! Terry's coming!' And you make a point of writing down that it was after the August 16th bust. There's nothing ambiguous about when it was."

"I'm being a hundred percent candid with you," Bugliosi said, "this is new to me. I'm not saying I didn't know it at the time, don't get me wrong, but I absolutely have no impression, no recollection of this at all." He sighed. "What's the point?... How does it help me with the jury?"

I thought it impeached Melcher's testimony, which had been essential to the case. It made him a dirtier witness, I said, because he had a relationship with the murderers after the murders. I showed him the sheriff's interview with the Family's Paul Watkins, who remembered seeing Melcher on his knees, on acid, begging for Manson's forgiveness at the Spahn Ranch—again, after the murders. Didn't it suggest some kind of complicity?

Bugliosi leveled an intense stare at me. "I was not trying to protect Terry Melcher," he said. "Why would I try to deceive the jury on something that the opposition had? I turned over everything to them."

But Paul Fitzgerald, the defense attorney, "said he never saw any of that. He said he was shocked," I explained.

"He may have forgotten about them himself!" Bugliosi shouted. "Look, if I'm going to try to hide them, I throw them away! Why wouldn't I throw them away? Everything that I had was turned over to the defense. *Everything.*"

"He didn't say he didn't *remember,* he said he never *saw* it."

Bugliosi scoffed. "Terry would never have associated with these people if he thought they committed these murders," he said. "If he did go out there afterward, it wasn't because he was complicit... I'm investigating this case, I'm handling all the witnesses, things could have gotten past me. But you've got to ask yourself this question, what could I possibly gain?"

I told him how Stephen Kay, his own coprosecutor, had reacted to these documents: "If Vince was covering this stuff up... what else did he change?"

Bugliosi gave a brittle laugh. "Oh, Jesus, that is so laughable it's just unbelievable. Just absolutely unbelievable. That I'd cover up that Terry Melcher had gone out to Spahn Ranch after the murders. It's just so extremely insignificant, it wouldn't help me at all." But it wasn't insignificant, and from his reaction I could tell he knew it. These pages rewrote the narrative of the case. That's why Melcher had threatened to throw them from his rooftop; that's why Bugliosi would sue me if I printed them.

Around and around we went. Bugliosi said, "When Terry was on the witness stand, did he testify that he never saw Manson after May?"

"Yeah," I said. "So, that's perjury."

"So you're saying that Terry lied on the witness stand." Still, he didn't see the point, or pretended not to. Until I read him his own closing argument, he refused to recognize that he'd even used Melcher as part of the motive for the murders. He'd said in his summation, "indirectly [Manson] was striking back at Terry Melcher personally. By ordering a mass murder at Melcher's former residence, Manson obviously knew that Melcher's realization that these murders took place at a residence in which he lived just a couple of months earlier would literally paralyze Melcher with fear." If that were so, why did Melcher go out to visit Manson at least three times afterward? All Bugliosi could say about the matter was that it "must have slipped past me." To accuse him of conspiring with Melcher was "mind-boggling craziness."

What about Reeve Whitson, the mysterious figure who'd helped gain the testimony of Sharon Tate's photographer friend, Shahrokh Hatami? Did Bugliosi remember Whitson?

"Oh, possibly," he said.

The hours ticked by, and whatever I threw at him, he deflected. The replacement of Susan Atkins's attorney? I showed him the memos. "I don't remember any of this stuff."

Manson's mysterious move to San Francisco, which violated his parole even though Bugliosi had wrongly written that he "requested and received permission" for it? "I can't even remember that."

How about the warrant for the massive August 16 raid at the Spahn Ranch? Bugliosi had asserted, incorrectly, that it was "misdated." "I don't know where I got that," he said.

"I wanted to ask you about Roger and David Smith," I said. (I wasn't about to get into the matter of Jolly West; I knew it'd be met with a blank stare.)

"Who are they?" I gave him my spiel on the paramount significance of Manson's year in San Francisco. "That's good stuff that you've come up with," he said. "Are they mentioned in my book?" Barely, I said. He was unfazed. "Must've gotten past me."

To present our back-and-forth in granular detail would be excruciating—reading through the transcript never fails to give me a headache. Suffice it to say that the subject of Terry Melcher always riled him up. Anything and everything else, he hardly cared about; if it didn't involve him directly, he had no use for it. He reiterated that he was "the fairest prosecutor in the land," and that a hefty hundred-million-dollar lawsuit awaited me if I suggested otherwise. This is when he fell into his refrain about "the Man in the Mirror." Because he was ethical "to an unprecedented degree," he could live with the sight of his own reflection. He didn't understand how I could live with mine. Manson himself had a fondness for the same phrase: "I am the man in the mirror," he said. "Anything you see in me is in you, I am you, and when you can admit that you will be free."

When Bugliosi and I finished, at last, he confessed that he was sometimes obsessive and overreactive—Gail had told him he might have a psychiatric disorder. But he'd done nothing wrong, and he didn't want his admittedly frenetic behavior to color my impressions of his conduct as a prosecutor.

It was a rare moment of self-awareness, probably the last I ever saw in him. The aftermath of our meeting was a series of alternately coaxing and acrimonious phone calls at all hours of the day and night, conveying a thinly veiled ultimatum: I could drop anything negative about him from my book or fear his wrath. If I published such "outrageous," "preposterous," and "unbelievable" lies, the lawsuit was a foregone conclusion.

Before the litigation, though, would come *the letter*: a cri de coeur to my editor at Penguin, with the publisher and president of the company in cc. It would be "very, very, very long," Bugliosi warned. He'd take "six, seven, eight hours" to write the first of "many drafts." He didn't want to do it—he'd gladly tear it up if I called to apologize.

"There is nothing to decide, here, Tom," he continued, sounding like a used-car salesman. "It's so damn easy."

When I declined for the last time, he said, "We should view ourselves as adversaries," and told me to expect *the letter.*

Now that Bugliosi was my sworn adversary, his next move hardly came as a surprise: the smear campaign. First thing next morning, I got a panicked message from Rudi Altobelli, the flamboyant talent manager who'd owned the house on Cielo Drive. We hadn't spoken in four years.

"Please give me a call so I can understand what I'm talking about," the elderly Altobelli said. "I still love you."

Altobelli had gotten a disturbing call from Bugliosi. "The first thing he wanted to know about was your relationships with young boys," he told me when I called back. As Bugliosi remembered it, Altobelli had told him years ago that I "dated ten, twelve, and fourteen-year-olds," Altobelli said, adding that he knew it was a lie. I'm gay, and when Altobelli and I became friends, I was dating someone younger—but he was twenty-nine, not twelve. At that time, Bugliosi was in regular communication with Altobelli, who felt he must've told him I was dating a younger guy. But then and now, Bugliosi knew he meant a young *man,* not a kid. "You're creating something that isn't so," Altobelli told him.

"I'm not going to talk to him anymore," Altobelli said. *"Ever."* Bugliosi kept calling for weeks; in just one morning, he left seven messages on Altobelli's machine. He wanted Altobelli to sign a letter saying I'd lied about Melcher. Altobelli refused.

At least now I knew the "terrible things" about me that Bugliosi had referred to; they were as transparently false as I'd suspected.

I could see why he'd twice been sued for defamation. In his long career, Bugliosi had lied under oath; he'd lied to newspapers; he'd lied to police and investigators from his own office. Now that I'd called him a liar, he was plenty willing to lie about me, too.

His letter arrived at Penguin on July 3, 2006. It had taken five months to write. It was thirty-four pages, single-spaced. And, as it turned out, it was the first of many such letters. As Bugliosi had promised, copies were delivered to my editor and my publisher, so we could take in its distortions, ad hominem attacks, and vigorous self-aggrandizement as a team. Often referring to me as "super-sleuth O'Neal"—the misspelling was intentional, I believe; he'd done the same to his nemesis Stephen Kay in *Helter Skelter*—Bugliosi claimed that I'd first approached him for the sole purpose of discovering titillating factoids about Sharon Tate and Roman Polanski's "private sex and drug lives." (Easy to disprove—I'd taped the whole interview.) He hinted at his allegations of pedophilia and claimed that I'd accused him of framing Manson. Most of all, he attacked the significance—or lack thereof—of my findings on Terry Melcher.

"Can you see why there is a part of me that actually wants O'Neal's dream to come true," he wrote, "so that I can have the opportunity to get even with him and destroy his life more than he's trying to destroy mine?" If Penguin moved forward with my book, the publisher "would almost assuredly be perceived by the national media as taking a position in defense of Charles Manson, one of history's most notorious murderers." He followed up with letters to all of the Family's imprisoned murderers except Manson himself, asking if they'd refute my claims about Melcher's involvement with the group. No one replied.

When it became clear that Penguin would stand behind me, Bugliosi sent another letter in 2007. And another in 2008, inveighing against my project and the irreparable harm it would do to his children, especially if, as I'd told him I would, I detailed the law-suits he'd faced over the years.

I'd promised my editor that I'd finish my reporting by August 1, 2006. Though I may never have hit that deadline anyway, Bugliosi's letter derailed me. Everyone I knew urged me not to respond on a point-by-point basis. But how could I not? I had no intention of reply-ing to him directly, but he'd gotten the best of my inner obsessive, and I spent a while collating all the evidence that refuted his claims. If he did plan on suing me, I'd be ready. In light of his threats, I told him I was now treating everything he'd said to me as on the record. Back in 1999, he'd given me my first shred of new information on the case, claiming off the record that there was a videotape found at Cielo Drive which showed Sharon Tate being forced to have sex with two men. Since Bugliosi had detailed this allegation in one of his letters to Penguin, I saw no need to keep it off the record.

My fastidiousness distracted me from that looming dread, per-haps best articulated by Bugliosi himself: "Where does it all go, Tom? *Where does it all go?*" I thought his apoplexy confirmed that I was on the right track, but I'd have to find the answers without any help from him. And now there was another unanswerable ques-tion: Was it all worth it? All the lonely hours in my car, the endless days poring over transcripts at archives from the edge of Death Valley to small towns in Washington and Nevada; begging and battling for police records; studying obscure medical journals and academic papers; filing hundreds of FOIA requests; fielding death threats and promises of litigation . . . could I really say it was worth it? Honestly, I didn't know anymore. And this was before I fell into a debt of more than half a million dollars.

Digging for Bodies in the Desert

Bugliosi had rattled me, but I tried to shake him off. I had a book to finish—or, more realistically, a book to start. Whenever I sat down, opened up Microsoft Word, and confronted a blinking cursor over a snowy expanse of white, I found it easy to make other plans. Sometimes I'd eke out ten or fifteen pages only to recoil at the holes in my story. My theory that Manson and West were linked was tenuous, circumstantial, lying solely in the fact that they'd walked the corridors of the same clinic. Wouldn't it be more effective to argue that the entire prosecution of Manson was a sham, with *Helter Skelter* as a cover-up? Bugliosi had said he "must have missed" Manson's San Francisco chapter—but everyone who knew him said he'd never miss it. I had to show that he concealed more, that witnesses besides Melcher lied, that there was an elaborate scheme to misrepresent the facts. Sure, I told myself: that would be better. I'd go back to the trial transcripts—maybe a few weeks here, a spare weekend there, while I wrote. Maybe Jolly West didn't even belong in the book. Maybe Reeve Whitson was just padding. Maybe, maybe…

I put more effort into begging for deadline extensions than I did into writing the book. And the world kept concocting reasons for me to keep reporting. Toward the end of 2007, a homicide cop named Paul Dostie claimed to have found forensic evidence of at least five bodies buried at the Barker Ranch in Death Valley, where Manson was captured in 1969. Dostie's trained cadaver dog had sniffed out unidentified remains in the area. As part of a big PR push, Dostie asked me for information supporting the possibility that these could be Manson's long rumored additional victims. His comrade-in-arms was Debra Tate, Sharon's sister, who had become a good friend of mine. Their effort garnered national media coverage. Soon the Inyo County Sheriff's Office authorized a dig in the desert.

Skeptics liked to ask: What did it matter if the police had taken so many months to bring the Family to justice after the murders? Even if they fudged the investigation, they still found him eventually. My answer was always that the Family may have used those extra months to continue their murder spree. At the trial, a ranch hand told police that Manson had bragged about killing thirty-five people; Bugliosi thought the number "may even exceed Manson's estimate." The bodies had been buried or staged to look like suicides. Just because the Family had never been prosecuted for these killings didn't mean they hadn't happened. If I could put a human face on the death toll, I could say with certainty that we were right to question the official narrative—that the failures of the police, deliberate or not, had a steep cost.

Dostie's dig could help me with that, but I already had a lead on a promising unsolved murder from the Family's time in Death Valley. In January 2008—motivated by the surge of support for Dostie's work, petitions from Debra Tate, and my own preliminary reporting—police announced that they were reopening an investigation into this death. This was great news, except when it came to my book. I worried that the renewed attention would compromise my final reporting. Former Family members might go back underground after I'd taken months to find out where they lived. The police might flush out information about the unsolved murder that I'd been on the brink of finding myself. I had to hit the road right away. The writing was on hold yet again.

A good part of my trip was a bust. I spent six months living out of cheap motels and crashing on friends' couches, racing across the Pacific Northwest to confront Family members at their doorsteps, along with a slew of other boldfaced names from *Helter Skelter,* most of whom had never been found. They were not happy to see me. Very few of them agreed to speak to me at all. Several chased me off their property—two with gardening shears.

Just when I was starting to think that the trip was a total wash, I made my last big break. I had proof—beyond a reasonable doubt, I thought—that the Manson Family had killed a young man in the desert, and that investigators had covered it up.

What Happened to Filippo Tenerelli?

On September 29, 1969, a twenty-three-year-old named Filippo Tenerelli left his parents' home in a brand-new Volkswagen Beetle. Tenerelli, a native Italian, had immigrated to Los Angeles with his family in 1959. He had no history of mental illness and no arrests.

Tenerelli made the long drive from Culver City to Father Crowley Point, an overlook at Death Valley National Park offering majestic desert vistas. He was there to drive his car over the cliff.

But at the precipice, the Beetle got caught on boulders, thwarting his suicide. Frustrated, Tenerelli took a pickax and a shovel from his trunk and dislodged the car. Then, his fury overpowering his suicidal impulses, he pushed it over the edge. The car fell some four hundred feet, coming to rest wheels up at the bottom of the canyon. He clambered down the steep, rocky terrain, reached into the car to retrieve his belongings, and cut his hands on something inside, leaving blood splatters on the ceiling.

No one knew how Tenerelli spent the rest of the day, or the day following. On the evening of the thirtieth, he wound up in Bishop, California, one hundred miles away. He checked into unit 3 of the Sportsman's Lodge motel, where he again tried and failed to kill himself, slashing his right wrist. The cut was superficial, and he covered it with a bandage.

The next day, October 1, Tenerelli went to the town's sporting-goods store and bought a twenty-gauge shotgun, some ammo, a case, and a cleaning kit. Elsewhere, he picked up two fifths of whiskey, two pairs of underwear, a safety razor, and an issue of *Playboy*.

That night Tenerelli emerged from his motel room when he heard fire engines. The fire department was doing a controlled demolition of a building across the street. The motel owner, Bee Greer, was watching, and she told Tenerelli what was going on. He observed the fire for a while and returned to his room. No one saw him alive again.

A maid tried to get into Tenerelli's room the next morning. The door was barricaded from the inside. Around noon, Greer's husband and son pushed it in. There was Tenerelli, dead of a gunshot to the face.

Police reports concluded that Tenerelli had blocked the door with a chair, put the loaded shotgun into his mouth, and pulled the trigger with his toe. He was lying on his back on the floor, dressed only in jeans, with "two Turkish bath towels under his head, possibly to soak up blood," and "a bed pillow over his head, apparently to muffle the sound." He'd shaved all of his pubic hair—some of it was between the pages of the *Playboy* he'd bought. But when he'd checked in to the motel, he'd given someone else's name. With no ID to be found, he was listed as a John Doe.

Tenerelli's family filed a missing persons report on October 3. The next day, two hunters spotted his overturned Beetle at the bottom of Father Crowley Point and notified the California Highway Patrol. An officer went to look and, noticing the blood on the ceiling, suspected foul play. The Tenerelli family learned that their son's abandoned car had been discovered in Death Valley.

For three weeks, the Bishop Police Department tried to ID their John Doe while the county sheriff's office looked for the missing Tenerelli. They never connected their parallel investigations, though they had stations next door to each other in Bishop, and the same coroner's office served them both.

On October 30, the Inyo *Register* reported that the "suicide victim" had been positively identified as Filippo Tenerelli of Culver City. Tenerelli had been IDed by X-rays that matched his patient records at an L.A. hospital. But the case was soon pushed from the local papers by an even wilder story: in a remote area of

Death Valley, a band of nomadic hippies had been arrested for destroying government property and operating an auto-theft ring. In the coming weeks, they'd be charged with the grisly murders of Sharon Tate and seven others in Los Angeles.

Although it wasn't reported at the time, the Inyo County Sheriff's Office and the California Highway Patrol did briefly consider the possibility that the Family was responsible for Tenerelli's death. According to documents I found, investigators doubted that Tenerelli had died by his own hand; they had evidence linking Family members to his death. Their suspicions were obliquely referenced in a *Los Angeles Times* story two weeks after the Family was charged in the Tate–LaBianca murders. The paper reported that law enforcement was looking into other potential Family murders, including a "motorcyclist killed in Bishop." Six months later, a *Rolling Stone* story quoted an "insider" in the Los Angeles DA's office — later identified as Aaron Stovitz — who suggested that the death of "a Philip Tenerelli" might've been the Family's doing. But no one had reported what, if anything, led investigators to their suspicions. In 2007, when I began looking into Tenerelli's death, no one outside of law enforcement had seen documents linking Tenerelli to the Family.

I started with three people: the mayor of Bishop, Frank Crom, who'd been on the police force in 1969; Lieutenant Chris Carter, currently of the Bishop Police Department; and Leon Brune, the chief deputy coroner in '69, and still coroner of Inyo County.

Carter said the records of Tenerelli's suicide had been "purged." Only unsolved homicide records were kept indefinitely. (Another cop who'd worked the case said he'd seen the records as recently as 1993.) Brune, meanwhile, faxed me the autopsy report and his investigation of the death. His record gave me a much clearer picture of Tenerelli's death, but I found some glaring inconsistencies. The story got even murkier when I tracked down the original

Bishop Police Department investigative report, which suggested a far more sinister ending to Tenerelli's life—and, perhaps more disturbing, a possible cover-up of that ending by investigators that appeared to continue into the present. Something was wrong.

I met Brune at his mortuary in Bishop, where I was ushered into a somber reception area and asked to wait: he was with someone at the moment. That someone turned out to be Mayor Frank Crom, who didn't offer me his hand when he emerged from Brune's office. Instead, he followed me back into the room—he intended to sit in on our interview, whether I minded or not. As we took our seats, I got out my tape recorder. Crom said he wouldn't allow our conversation to be recorded. Things didn't get much better from there. Crom answered or amended my questions to Brune, constantly interrupting us.

I tried to ask Brune about the sketch of the murder scene I'd found among the pages he'd faxed. Why weren't the motel room windows included in the sketch? No mention was made of them in the report. How big were they? When the body was discovered, were they open or closed, locked or unlocked?

Crom answered for him: "No one could've gotten in or out of those windows. They were too small."

Barely ten minutes after we started, Brune shot a nervous glance at Crom and ended the meeting. He had business to attend to. I'd asked him only half of my questions. Crom got me out of the building and followed me to my car, repeating that there was no way the death was anything but a suicide. He suggested I was wasting my time. Everything in his behavior said the opposite.

The Sportsman's Lodge, where Tenerelli died, was long gone. But Bee Greer, the owner, wasn't. A spry eighty-one-year-old widow with a razor-sharp memory, she flatly contradicted the mayor's statement that her motel windows were too small to climb in or out of. Maybe even two people at a time could fit through

them, she said. Her son, Kermit, who'd helped push in the barricaded door of Tenerelli's room, was with us that day. He added that
his parents had often punished him by locking him in the same
unit. He'd always climb out the windows, he said, and he wasn't
much smaller then than he was now. (And he was a big guy.)

If I didn't believe him, why not go see for myself? The motel
hadn't been demolished, he reported. It'd been sold to an alfalfa
ranch just outside of town: they picked up the whole structure and
moved it out there a few years before.

I drove out to Zack's Ranch to have a look. Just as the Greers
had said, the windows were big enough for two people to climb
through at the same time. Andi Zack, whose late father had bought
the motel units, told me that all the windows were original. She
showed me unit 3 and let me photograph it.

Bee Greer remembered when Tenerelli showed up to the motel.
He arrived without a car, she said, which was why he had to show
her a driver's license — something the police and the newspapers
had explicitly said he didn't do.

"I never would've checked anyone in who came without a car
and a license," she said — without those, she'd have no collateral if
there were damages to the property or the customer tried to bolt
without paying. She copied the license information into her register, which she later gave to the police. But the cops, Crom among
them, refused to believe that the victim had showed her ID, or
even that he had a wallet. "They kept coming back and trying to
talk me out of it," she said, still angry all these years later. "It was a
wallet with a driver's license — but they didn't want me to say that."

Later, I found a registration form from the Sportsman's Lodge. It
had Tenerelli's name on it — misspelled — and it showed that he paid
for a thirty-three-day stay beginning on October 1, 1969. The total
was $156, paid in full. Bee Greer told me it was "exactly" the same
registration form she would've used in 1969, but a couple of things

didn't seem right. The customer always filled out the form. Why would Tenerelli have spelled his own name wrong? There should've been a home address and a driver's license number, but neither was there. Tenerelli's sister later confirmed that this wasn't his handwriting. Plus, Tenerelli had a noticeable Italian accent. The man Greer spoke with had no accent at all. Maybe someone had checked in under Tenerelli's name, paying for a month in advance to ensure that the body wouldn't be discovered right away.

The police reports contained no photographs of the crime scene. They made no mention of any forensics tests — no ballistics, blood splatters, fingerprints, rigor mortis. Officials I spoke to said these would have been routine in an unattended shooting death, even in 1969. There was a lab report showing that Tenerelli's blood-alcohol level at the time of his death was .03%, which doesn't even qualify as under the influence. But he'd bought those two fifths of whiskey the night before he died. When his body was found, one bottle was sitting empty in the wastebasket; the other was on a shelf, only a third full. If Tenerelli didn't drink all that whiskey, who did?

The documents made me wonder when exactly Bishop police and the coroner's office had figured out the identity of the John Doe in their morgue. On October 17, a radiologist at Washington Hospital in Culver City examined X-rays of the John Doe sent to her by the Inyo County coroner. They were "similar or identical," she wrote, to those of a patient who'd been operated on at the hospital after a motorcycle accident in '64: Tenerelli. The Inyo coroner had been notified of the match "within twenty-four hours," so they'd identified their John Doe as Tenerelli no later than October 18. And yet the chief of police had told the Inyo *Register* that the identification came ten days later, on October 28.

The Inyo County Sheriff's Office was investigating the case from the other side: they'd found Tenerelli's totaled Beetle in the desert, and they wanted to know where he'd gone. Documents from their investigation suggested that the coroner's office withheld information from them. When an Inyo detective asked about Bishop's John Doe on October 28, Brune didn't tell him they'd identified the victim nearly two weeks earlier.

Had Brune deliberately kept this from the sheriff? Why wasn't Tenerelli's identification shared with the other agencies—or his own family—sooner? I could never ask Brune. Neither he nor Crom spoke to me again.

Robert Denton, the surgeon who'd conducted Tenerelli's autopsy, told me he'd never believed the case was a suicide; he only called it that under pressure from the coroner's office. Looking over his own report, Denton said, "See where I wrote, 'This man *seems* to be a suicide'? I wasn't happy with this. That's why I wrote *seems.*" He shook his head. "There were bum things going on here." It appeared to him now, as it probably did then, that Tenerelli had been "in a fight or dragged" before he was shot. In those days, he said, a lot of "questionable deaths" were "signed off as suicides": "It was too expensive to investigate . . . People didn't want to be involved."

On the other side, the sheriffs and the California Highway Patrol were looking into the abandoned Volkswagen with blood on its interior.

A report filed by one of the sheriff's deputies on October 5 said, "From indications at the scene . . . the vehicle has not been at the location for more than two days." If that was true, Tenerelli couldn't have dumped the car. His body had been found three days earlier, on October 2, and the estimated time of death was between 9:30 and 10:30 p.m., October 1.

And yet all the newspapers, working on information from the police, reported that Tenerelli had ditched his car there after a failed suicide attempt. Why did police put out this story when it didn't fit the timeline?

There were clues among the evidence recovered from the scene near the car. Cops found a pickax and a shovel with a broken handle, as well as beer and soda bottles—all covered in what was thought to be Tenerelli's blood. Then there was a cache of unused shotgun shells, a loaf of French bread and a package of lunch meat, maps, "miscellaneous papers," and several documents indicating that Tenerelli might not have been alone in the car: a "meal" and "laundry" sheet from Brentwood Hospital, where he had neither worked nor been a patient; and a Santa Monica bus schedule, which he wouldn't have needed because he owned a car and a motorcycle.

The two hunters who'd chanced upon Tenerelli's car had observed someone "coming up from the wreck" as they climbed down to it, sheriffs' reports said. There was far more blood in and around the vehicle than the papers had reported: blood on the fender and bumper, inside the driver's-side door and under the dash, palm prints in dried blood, scratch marks going through the dried blood…a lot of blood from just one man who had no noticeable wounds when he arrived in Bishop. Bee Greer had told police that when she talked to Tenerelli he "seemed quite natural and told her that he was here to look the area over and possibly find a job." If the coroner's time of death was correct, Tenerelli had shaved his pubes, downed a bottle and a half of whiskey, and shot himself within two hours of that conversation.

Meanwhile, memos from the California Highway Patrol suggested suspects for the murder: the group of hippie car thieves they'd recently taken into custody. In Bishop, "around the 1st of October," a highway patrolman had stopped a "late model" blue Volkswagen; Tenerelli drove a '69 blue Volkswagen, and October 1 was the day before his body was found. The patrolman questioned the driver, who, like his two male passengers, was a "hippie" type. Later, investigators showed the patrolman a photograph of the Family, including Manson, Steven Grogan, and Danny DeCarlo. He "was sure" that DeCarlo was the driver of the car.

The report continued: "Even though Tenerelli was supposed to be a definite suicide, perhaps Bishop PD would be interested, especially if we can place DiCarlo [*sic*] in Bishop after 9-29-69 and prior to or on 10-1-69." I checked, and DeCarlo was in Death Valley on exactly the dates in question. But there was no indication that the Highway Patrol had shared their findings with the Bishop Police Department.

Records from the Inyo District Attorney contained a morgue photograph of Tenerelli's face, with a note attached. DAs wanted to find another photo of Tenerelli to show to "Kitty": the Family's Kitty Lutesinger, who'd run away from Death Valley before her friends were caught, and who'd briefly cooperated with investigators. If she told detectives anything about Tenerelli, we'll probably never know—there were no other documents linking the two, and she refused to speak to me when I knocked on her door in 2008.

Neither of the officers who investigated Tenerelli's abandoned Volkswagen believed he committed suicide. One of them, the California Highway Patrol's Doug Manning, called the official story "a bunch of malarkey." The other, Inyo sheriff's deputy Dennis Cox, called it "bullshit."

Cox was sure the car was "dumped" in Death Valley after Tenerelli's death in Bishop. He'd been to Father Crowley Point the day before the hunters discovered the Beetle, and "it wasn't there." After the Manson Family was arrested for their auto-theft ring, one of the girls told investigators that she was "involved" with Tenerelli, and that he'd been with the Family in Death Valley before his death. But Cox couldn't remember who'd said that.

When police in Death Valley finally captured the Family, they'd been tracking the group's car thefts and burglaries since September 29 at the latest. They might not have known yet that their suspects were killers, but they *did* know that they'd been stealing vehicles all over Inyo County, with a special predilection for Volkswagen Beetles, which they liked to convert into dune buggies for use in the rugged desert terrain.

One last thing bothered me: the pubic hair. If, as police reports stated, Tenerelli had shaved his pubes just before killing himself, and a "few strands" had been found "between the pages" of a *Playboy* magazine—what happened to the rest? The Family's Bill Vance had a "magic vest" he liked to wear that was "made of pubic hair," per a report from the Los Angeles County Sheriff's Office. The LASO report never said where the pubic hair came from—and how could it, really?—but I found it relevant that Vance, an associate of Manson from prison, was arrested for stealing a gun from a car in Death Valley on October 5, 1969, the day Tenerelli's car was pulled from the nearby ravine.

Coda: "Out of the Loop"

In January 2008, Bishop's new chief of police, Kathleen Sheehan, called to say she'd heard about my investigation from Debra Tate. In light of my findings she was reopening the investigation into Tenerelli's death. She assigned a homicide detective, David Jepson, to the case, asking me to share my findings with him. "Murder doesn't happen every day around here," she said.

I was happy to help. For once, I thought my reporting might yield positive results, rather than dead ends and obfuscation. Jepson and I spoke on the phone more than a dozen times before he decided to visit me in L.A. That July, he and his superior, Chris Carter, drove 275 miles to meet with me in the dining room of the Embassy Suites Hotel in El Segundo.

During our four-hour meeting, which Jepson recorded, I showed them everything. Both officers agreed that the death was a "probable" murder and vowed to continue their investigation in Bishop. Carter said he didn't "believe in coincidences," and there were "too many" here. But toward the end of the meeting they turned off the recorder and made an odd request.

Carter asked me to copy the documents I'd shared that day and mail the file to a "personal" P.O. box in Bishop. The detectives were concerned that their chief, Sheehan, would use this case to get publicity. They wanted to keep her "out of the loop on this one" until the investigation was over.

I didn't like the sound of that, and I told them so. Sheehan had been the one who reopened the case. We wouldn't be meeting if not for her.

Making sure the recorder was still off, Carter said he believed Sheehan would "kill the investigation" if she found out that "it involved a cover-up or even incompetence." And the mayor, Frank Crom—who'd already tried to persuade me to leave well enough alone—would "pull the plug if [we] discover cover-up aspects." The detectives assured me they'd prevent any derailment of the investigation, and they promised to share anything new they uncovered. Against my better instincts, I agreed to continue cooperating with them.

That was a big mistake. I never heard from either officer again. Through intermediaries, I learned they were telling people in Bishop that their investigation had turned up no pursuable evidence and the case had been closed.

The three of us had discussed people they'd want to interview when they returned to Bishop. I called a lot of those people—they'd never heard from the detectives. In fact, in the six months between the reopening of the case and their visit to me in L.A., they had interviewed only three people. That number never went up.

According to the scant record Jepson finally shared with me in 2011, he never conducted another interview after our meeting.

When I finally got Jepson on the phone, I reminded him that he'd promised to share his findings with me. He said his files were in a storage shed in his backyard. It took him weeks to dig through this shed. Because I kept leaving him messages, he eventually called me back and, sounding triumphant, told me that he'd found one of his notebooks. He faxed me the pages from it: they covered the same period I already knew about, during which he'd spoken to all of three people. Jepson was sure there were later interviews, but he kept searching in his shed, and nothing turned up.

I had to ask if the investigation had been quashed, as he and Carter had warned it would be if it disclosed a "cover-up" or "incompetence" in the old department.

After a lot of prodding, Jepson recalled "conversations" at the police department before their meeting with me—something to the effect that they weren't going to have "people come up here and smear a retired lieutenant's [Frank Crom's] name and smear the department."

I knew I had to go to Jepson's superiors, beginning with Sheehan. By then she'd left Bishop to become chief of police in Port Hueneme, another small town in California. Although she sounded happy to hear from me again on the phone, by the time I drove out to see her the next day, her mood had darkened. Like Jepson, she said the investigation was over, and that was all there was to it. When I explained that Carter and Jepson had said that she craved publicity and should be kept "out of the loop," she didn't believe it. I showed her my notes from that meeting, and she accused me of fabricating them. I'd seen these reversals many times before, almost exclusively from law enforcement officials. But Sheehan's was so abrupt, so hard, that I left her office shaken—whatever had happened in Bishop, I was certain she knew more than she was admitting.

Chris Carter, who'd succeeded Sheehan as chief of the Bishop

Police Department, was clearly prepared for my call. He denied everything he'd said to me in L.A. while his recorder was off. I asked for a copy of the tape—he'd be happy to provide it. I knew he'd made his incriminating remarks when the recorder wasn't running, I said, but I still expected to hear the click of the machine going off and on again. I should've kept that to myself. Two weeks later, when I called again, he claimed the tape had been lost or destroyed.

Nevertheless, I filed an Open Records Act Request with the Bishop Police Department for all files on their reinvestigation of the Tenerelli death. I received a response saying no records had been found.

Through all this, I never stopped thinking of Tenerelli's mother, Caterina, whom I'd met in 2008, when she was ninety-four. With one of her daughters translating her Italian, she told me she never accepted that her son killed himself. She believed God had kept her alive to learn the truth about him. But she'd died at ninety-nine, never knowing the answers.

Paul Dostie, the detective with the cadaver dog, had no better luck than I did. The sheriff halted his dig in Death Valley after less than two feet of earth had been removed.

And now my book was even more overdue than my article to *Premiere* had ever been. Penguin had granted me extension after extension, approving another advance payment to me to keep me afloat. In the meantime, my editor had left the house, and the 2008 recession had editorial departments tightening their belts. Author contracts had once come with implicit latitude. Now, with lots of money on the line, editors wanted something to show for their investments, especially when an untested writer had received a significant advance.

The fortieth anniversary of the Tate–LaBianca murders came and went. It had now been ten years since my report for *Premiere* was supposed to appear. The magazine didn't even exist anymore. On cable news, my fellow reporters and dozens of my interview subjects showed up as talking heads, discussing the continuing significance of the murders. There was Bugliosi, still hawking *Helter Skelter,* calling the crimes "revolutionary, political."

I fumbled and fiddled, trying to find a workable structure for the book. Should it begin with MKULTRA? The night of the Tate murders? No matter where I dropped in, I tripped myself up with parentheticals and long digressions; there was no starting point that didn't entail a herculean amount of exposition. I sent in outlines, synopses, addenda, half-starts, revised proposals. None of them hit the mark, and I knew that. I'd come to feel like a prisoner of my own story. Everyone agreed that it would make for an outstanding book; no one, least of all me, could describe what that book might look like, or how it would accommodate a plot that had no end. By 2011, I'd taken so long to deliver that my original editor had come back to Penguin. He proposed bringing on a collaborator, someone who could metabolize my reporting into a cogent narrative.

I was all for it. Penguin helped me find an ideal candidate: a journalist with decades of political reporting and many books under his belt, someone with experience and sangfroid. When he signed on, I felt like I could see a lifeboat on the horizon. He wrote yet another synopsis, one that yielded the first unabashedly positive note from Penguin I'd gotten in years. "We find this very encouraging: full speed ahead."

That was in October 2011. By December, he'd quit. Our deadline—the last one—was only six months away, and now I was flying solo.

After he walked, Penguin offered to buy me out. If I let someone else write the book—completely—I'd receive no more money, no credit, no input, nothing. All I'd get was the portion of the advance I'd already received—and spent, years before, on nothing but reporting the book. I told my agent to tell them to go to hell.

I decided to use those remaining six months to write the book myself. Before he'd even seen my manuscript, my editor warned that there was only a one in a million chance they wouldn't reject it. I typed out pages in furious haste. I tried to be thorough, to be linear. I wrote in the first person, hoping to give readers a sense of what I'd been thinking. And in June 2012, I turned in what I had: 129 pages, single-spaced, amounting to 117,228 words. It covered barely the first three months of my reporting.

If you've inspected the spine of this book, you've already noticed that the Penguin Press colophon isn't on it. They canceled the book. I like to believe my editor was sorry it came to this, and that he believed in the project. I don't believe Penguin's lawyers shared his sorrow—they wanted their money back. If I didn't pay up by the start of 2013, they would have no choice but to sue me.

I didn't have that money, of course. I'd been living on it, as the publisher had intended me to, for years. A few months earlier, I'd been hoping to repay my parents for their loan. Now I was in the hole with them and one of the biggest publishers in the world. In 2012, I became one of a dozen authors Penguin sued for failing to deliver manuscripts. Most were far more established than I was. The lawsuits sent waves of panic through the industry. Even though mine was for the most money, it came half a year later than the others, and so, mercifully, it didn't make the papers. That was one humiliation I was spared.

But I was still devastated. I felt like I'd failed everyone. I had one job to do, and I hadn't done it. Paul Krassner, the journalist who'd warned me that the story would "take over my life," was more than right: it had chewed me up and spit me out. I didn't know how I could ever report on anything else now. My agent shopped the book around to other publishers, and while a few were interested in buying the rights, the offers never materialized. Some documentary filmmakers had courted me, too, and one, an Oscar winner, went so far as to make some test footage, which he sold as a series to a premium cable station. But there, too, things fell apart. In all honesty, though, I was the one who backed out of these projects. Inevitably, the conversations ran aground on questions of ownership—some legal, others more figurative. Whose story was this? How far did you have to step back before you could fit a frame around it? And, of course: Where did it all go?

I remember a day soon after the deal fell apart. My neighbor, a good friend, was walking his dogs and saw me sitting outside, looking miserable. He invited me to join him. After trying to distract me with pleasantries for a while, he turned the conversation to the lawsuit.

"Do you regret all this?" he asked.

"Not at all," I said. I shocked myself with my answer, but I really believed it. "This has been the most exciting thirteen years of my life. There's nothing like the adrenaline rush of catching these people in lies, and documenting it—knowing that you've found something no one else has found."

I kept little pieces of cardboard around my office. Sometimes I folded them up and carried them in my pocket. Whenever I started doubting myself, which was a lot, I had a list of bullet points I'd write down on them and read to myself for encouragement—a reminder of what I'd discovered that no one else had, what I knew I had to share with the world. Like: Stephen Kay telling me that my findings were important enough to overturn the verdicts. Lewis Watnick, the retired DA, saying that Manson had to be an informant. Jolly West writing to his CIA handlers to announce that he'd implanted a false memory in someone; the CIA removing that information from the report they shared with Congress. The DA's office conspiring with a judge to replace a defense attorney. Charlie Guenther, fighting back tears to tell me about the wiretap he'd heard. People had confided in me. I'd wrested documents from places other reporters had never penetrated. What did it mean, and what would I do with it?

When I got back from the walk with my neighbor that day, I fished out one of the cardboard squares and read the bullet points again. Each one set off a chain of reminders to myself: People I needed to call. FOIA requests I had to follow up on. A new book on the CIA I hadn't read yet. A retired detective whose files were probably, at this very second, quietly turning to dust in his garage...

What else could I do?

I kept reporting.

The Manson murders have an aura of finality. In 2016, *The Guardian* marveled at how they compel us despite "the lack of any meaty mystery": "There are no questions about what happened... We know pretty much exactly who did what to whom, when and why." In a sense, that's true: the material evidence is sickeningly conclusive, and it still shocks today. But it doesn't make sense. The mystery is there.

In my nearly twenty years of reporting on this case, people have asked me all the time: What do I think really happened? I hate that question more than anything. The plain answer is, I don't know. I worry that as soon as I speculate, I undermine the work I've done. In a sense, had I been more willing to fill in the blanks, I might've finished this book a lot sooner.

That's not to say I haven't entertained a lot of pet theories over the years. They've fallen in and out of favor as I learned more or shifted my focus. For a while, I was convinced the victims at the Tate and LaBianca houses knew their killers in the Family, that they'd been targeted—maybe not by the girls, but by Manson and Tex Watson. It may have had something to do with a drug burn, or an unknown middleman with connections to Hollywood. Or there's the possibility that the Family was caught up in a CHAOS or COINTELPRO operation, goaded into violence as sheriff's deputies and the LAPD looked the other way, necessitating a cover-up. And there's the most "far out" theory: that Manson was tied to an MKULTRA effort to create assassins who would kill on command.

It's when someone claims that I've "found the truth" that I get anxious. I haven't found the truth, much as I wish I could say I have. My goal isn't to say what *did* happen—it's to prove that the official story *didn't*. I've learned to accept the ambiguity. I had to, I realized, if I ever wanted to finish this book. For every chapter here, there are a dozen I've left out. There's more, there's always more.

But I haven't stopped trying. If there's hope anywhere, it's in the documents. I remain shocked by the state's lack of transparency. For reasons I can't understand, district attorneys, law enforcement agencies, federal bureaus, and other outposts of officialdom continue to suppress their files, even as they claim they have nothing to hide.

This position assumes a certain amount of complacency in the public. If the truth turns out to exist on a photocopy of a photocopy of a photocopy, on the 3,005th page of a transcript so dry that no one has read it from start to finish, they're counting on our not caring. To get to that kernel of truth, you have to generate a paper trail of your own: of FOIA requests, public hearings, and concerned letters to your congressperson, all eventually housed in their own sleepy archives.

As of this writing, the LAPD and the DA's office are still in legal battles about their unfathomable refusal to release information—a refusal that extends to the victims' families and to the defendants themselves.

The latest front is a battle over the Tex Watson tapes. Less than two weeks before the Family's capture in the desert. Watson absconded to his parents' place in Copeville, Texas. On November 30, 1969, he turned himself in for questioning after learning that two LAPD detectives were on a plane heading his way. He got a lawyer, Bill Boyd, of Dallas, who sat him down to make a taped confession. This is, as far as anyone knows, the first known recorded account of the crimes—before Bugliosi or anyone else could impose narrative order on it. It's all the more valuable because Watson hadn't even been identified as a suspect yet. He was speaking of his own accord to his lawyer, not as a man defending himself to the police.

According to Boyd, Watson described the duration of his time with the Family and, in chilling detail, the killing of Tate and the other victims. He was "very straightforward" and "candid" about his involvement in the crimes, Boyd told me. He also described other murders that the group committed—murders that hadn't been discovered.

In 2009, Boyd agreed to let me listen to the tapes, but only with Watson's permission, which I knew he'd never get. He wouldn't go into granular detail about them, perhaps realizing that he'd already violated Watson's confidentiality. Boyd died a year after we spoke. By 2011, his law firm had gone bankrupt, and its holdings were in receivership—including the cassettes, which he'd kept in a safe in his office.

A Dallas bankruptcy trustee had come into possession of the tapes, and she seemed on the verge of releasing them to me. Instead, she offered them to Patrick Sequeira, the deputy district attorney in L.A. who handled Watson's parole hearings. Sequeira supported my effort to get them, and he assured me he'd let me hear them—"We wouldn't even know they existed if it weren't for you," he said. Watson tried to halt their release, filing an injunction in Texas and setting off a yearlong battle. The DA's office won. But since gaining custody of the recordings, they have been played for no one outside the justice system, not even the victims' families, who asked to hear them. The DA's office and the LAPD have released only minimal and at times contradictory statements about their content.

Sequeira told me there were no unknown homicides mentioned on them—there was nothing new at all. But if the DA's office released them to me, they'd have to release them to everyone, and they didn't want the information to be distorted by the public. Soon after, he cut off communications with me.

Richard Pfeiffer, the attorney for Leslie Van Houten, wanted to hear the tapes, too—what if they contained exculpatory information that could be used at parole hearings? Pfeiffer tried to get them but to no avail. Soon the DA's office trotted out a different reason for not releasing them: "There are unsolved crimes Manson Family members are suspected of committing. The information in the tape(s) are part of the investigation of those crimes and could be used to solve them."

The case reached the California Supreme Court. Pfeiffer suggested that the judge could review the tapes and make his own decision. But the DA's office did not "believe it necessary for the court to arduously labor through the 326 pages of [Watson's] rambling musings." The court decided in the DA's favor. Since then, Leslie Van Houten has been approved for parole for the first time ever. California's governor at the time, Jerry Brown, vetoed her release on the recommendation of the DA's office. Although Pfeiffer made it clear that it was his idea to go after the tapes, the DAs had lambasted Van Houten for trying to get them, saying it was clear evidence that she still hadn't accepted full responsibility for her crimes.

Pfeiffer vowed to go back to court and get the tapes, and he's pursued a number of legal avenues, all unsuccessful, thus far. To this day, the DA's office is guarding them with more fervor than ever. I keep the parole hearings in my calendar, making sure to get transcripts of them as soon as they're available. At these hearings, the state tries to turn the mind-bending events of August 9, 1969, into inert history—and they're one of the only places left to hope for the truth.

Whenever I tell people about my work, they want to know if I interviewed Charles Manson himself. I did, over the phone, in 2000. Our first conversation, disconcertingly enough, was on Valentine's Day.

Our exchanges were mediated through two of Manson's associates, Pin Cushion and Gray Wolf. The former, nicknamed for the frequency with which he'd been stabbed, was born Roger Dale Smith. He was Manson's guy on the inside, his prison gofer. The latter, born Craig Hammond, had been anointed Gray Wolf by Manson himself, and brokered all outside access to Manson. A retiree, he'd moved to Hanford, California, decades earlier just to be near the prison that housed Manson, whom he believed to possess "deep insight into environmental issues." (Many of Manson's latter-day followers claimed to be enchanted by his ecological "ATWA" philosophy—"Air, Trees, Water, Animals," or "All the Way Alive"—through which he endorsed the use of a seed gun called "the Savior" to repopulate California's plant species.) Later, Hammond was arrested for smuggling a cell phone to Manson in prison. A few years after that, when Manson had gotten engaged to a young woman named Star, it was claimed that Hammond had been sleeping with her, and Manson rechristened him "Dead Rat."

In 2000, when Gray Wolf set up my interview, he urged me to "protect myself." "You don't know what powers are pushing against you," he said.

He patched me through to Pin Cushion, who put on Manson himself. We would have five minutes to talk before the prison terminated the call automatically.

"Hello, Tom," Manson said.

"Hi, Charlie, how you doing?"

"Aw, hanging loose, man."

"Happy Valentine's Day," I said.

"Yeah, same to you, man."

I'd only caught Manson's interest because his handlers had told him I had information about potential perjury during the trial—Terry Melcher's. But now that I had him on the line, he wanted to talk about anything but Terry Melcher. I gave him a brief introduction to my angle for *Premiere,* which he dismissed as "hype." He wanted me to speak "to the heart." I rattled off a list of names to see if he knew them.

"I don't know anyone, man," he said. "I barely know myself."

Manson spoke in riddles when he spoke at all. He claimed that there was a lot of money behind the murders, and that the "United States Navy" held the purse strings. "I'm Vincent Bugliosi's godfather," he said. But he wasn't a snitch, so he wasn't going to give me any names. "There's a lot of people playing a lot of games, man," he said. He added: "I pitched horseshoes when I was seventeen."

Whenever he didn't feel like answering, he'd say something like that. "I got five red wheels on that truck." Or: "When Reagan went to Greenland we locked all the weather stations to the heart project."

Our five minutes vanished before I even got my bearings. Hammond dialed again. If I wanted to connect with Charlie, he said, I had to show him my human side, my heart. I took a breath while Manson got back on the line.

"Look it, man," he said. "See, I have no way of knowing what you're biting into."

I tried again to explain. Even in Manson's more lucid moments, the only thing we saw eye to eye on was that the prosecution had played dirty. But he didn't think Melcher was the problem—"He didn't say anything." He seemed to have written Melcher off. "The simplicity of the whole thing is that Terry gave his word for something," he said, "and he didn't do it, and we didn't realize that the Korean War was lost." To him, the real villain was Linda Kasabian, his lapsed follower, who'd flipped for the prosecution.

"She gave the souls of her children up to the devil in a sacrificial trip that came down in an agreement with the universal mind," he explained. "You just tell her that the key to Red Skelton's house is in the ventilator and it's still there. And that crypt is still there with the dogs at attention."

Our time was nearly up again. Manson passed the phone back to Pin Cushion, who offered to write down my remaining questions and send me Manson's answers, verbatim.

But the next night, Gray Wolf called and said that would never happen. Manson—who was apparently much less gnomic with his friends than he'd been with me—was upset with me. He and Pin Cushion wouldn't talk again or send answers. Gray Wolf seemed surprised by all of it. He wasn't used to Manson taking calls from journalists, and he said that he, too, was still processing everything he'd heard last night, as if some of it had been news to him. I wondered if this had more to do with Pin Cushion, who'd made some bold claims as he'd jotted down my questions. He said Manson personally knew Mama Cass Elliot. He'd brought his girls to orgies for the Hollywood elite. He'd left a bunch of "bodies out in that motherfucking desert, man!" And, most mystifying of all, other members of the Family may have gone to the Tate house the night she was killed. I wondered if Manson had been standing next to him while he said all this, and gotten angry afterward.

In 2008, I reached out to Manson again through Gray Wolf. This was after my many run-ins with Manson's former followers, many of whom were not as former as I thought. The people I'd asked about Filippo Tenerelli and other possible victims must have relayed those communications to Manson. Gray Wolf told me never to get in touch again.

"People are upset with you and you're in trouble," he said. "You don't have permission to do what you're doing." He wouldn't say more. I was cut off. *"And I don't know you,"* he added. He hung up.

So concluded my dealings with Charles Manson and his inner circle. When Manson died, in November 2017, the moment aroused little feeling in me. My investigation orbited him, but he mattered hardly at all to me. At some point, as a cottage industry rose up around him and he became a true-crime icon, he'd been made brittle, toothless. His image had become a repository for our fears. Everyone preferred the idea of him to the reality, and in death, he was more ideal than ever: the killer hippie from the sixties, a decade that feels further removed from the present than many that occurred before it.

Always willing to play the madman, he slipped too easily into our understanding of the criminal mastermind. In that rictus of his, those glinting eyes, the X carved into his forehead, we're supposed to recognize what Bugliosi famously called "a metaphor for evil." But the full extent of that evil isn't in what we know about Manson. It's in what we don't know. That's what kept me going all these years, even when I was broke, even when people said I was crazy, even when I had death threats lobbed at me.

As Manson said to me with an air of disgust: "The bottom line is that you want information."

"Exactly," I said.

ACKNOWLEDGMENTS

The twenty-year journey culminating in this book began with a phone call from Leslie Van Buskirk at *Premiere* magazine. For that I am forever grateful and, yeah, sometimes resentful. Jim Meigs bet the bank on this—I wish he could've stuck around to the end, but who wants to live with Manson that long, except for me? Others at *Premiere* who kept me on my toes for nearly two years were Kathy Heintzelmen and Anne Thompson.

Without my agent, Sloan Harris of ICM, this book wouldn't exist. His tenacity and faith—not to mention his extraordinary ability to think outside the box when cancelations, lawsuits, and threats became routine—should be enshrined in the Agentry Hall of Fame. Also life-preserving at ICM were Sloan's assistants over the years: Kristyn Keene, Heather Karpas, and Alexa Brahme. Kudos, too, to the lawyers who kept me out of jail or, at least, bankruptcy court: John DeLaney and Heather Bushong. And to Rich Green, Michael McCormick, and Will Watkins, who wrangled much-needed sustenance from Hollywood.

At Little, Brown, editor-in-chief Judy Clain went where others before her wouldn't (or did, then fled). Reagan Arthur bravely put pen to paper, making it real. Their team—Alex Hoopes, Katharine Myers, Alyssa Persons, Ira Boudah, Ben Allen, Trent Duffy, and Lauren Harms—pulled off the amazing feat of producing and publicizing this book. Thanks also to Eric Rayman and Carol Ross, whose close reading safeguarded (hopefully) my future mobility.

When you work on a book for twenty years—examining crimes that occurred decades prior—you lose many of your sources along the way. Among the many who are no longer with us, but who must be acknowledged for excavating memories of a dark, horrifying time, are: Rudi Altobelli, Bill Garretson, Elaine Young, Dominick Dunne, Bill

Tennant, Shahrokh Hatami, Richard and Paul Sylbert, Polly Platt, Charles Eastman, Julia Phillips, Denny Doherty, Christopher Jones, Gene Gutowski, and Victor Lownes.

From the law enforcement and legal worlds, and also gone: Charlie Guenther, Paul Whiteley, Bill Gleason, Preston Guillory, Mike and Elsa McGann, Danny Bowser, Paul Caruso, Gerald and Milton Condon, Paul Fitzgerald, Lewis Watnick, Buck Compton, and George Denny.

To thank everyone I interviewed would require dozens of pages—and many of my sources never appear in this book. I'll limit this list to the ones who endured my inquiries for years, if not decades, and who deserve accolades for their patience.

From the world of Cielo Drive and slightly beyond: Allan Warnick, Gregg Jakobson, Sharmagne Leland-St. John, Jim Mitchum, Elke Sommer, Peter Bart, Tanya and Michael Sarne, Corrine Sydney, Joe Torrenueva, Witold Kaczanowski, Sheilah Welles, Joanna Pettet, Bob Lipton, and Mark Lindsay.

From the Beach Boys' arena, including authors, researchers, and associates of the band: Alan Boyd, Brad Elliot, Karen Lamm, Nick Grillo, Steve Despar, John Parks, David Anderle, Stanley Shapiro, Ryan Oskenberg, and especially Eddie Roach and Jon Stebbins. Richard Barton Campbell, the webmaster of CassElliot.com, was a tremendous help.

Witnesses who testified at the trial or provided information that helped break the case: Virginia Graham, Jerrold Friedman, Harold True, Joe Dorgan, Father Robert Byrne, and Christine and Michael Heger.

The Hinman case: Cookie Marsman, Marie Janisse, Jay Hofstadter, Eric Carlson, John Nicks, Glen David Giardenelli, Glenn Krell, Michael Erwin, Mark Salerno, Jim and Julie Otterstrom.

Los Angeles Sheriff's Office: Bill "Moon" Mullin, Louie Danhof, John C. Graham, Jim White, Harold White, John Kolman, Lee Koury, Tony Palmer, Frank Merriman, Bill McComas, Michael Devereaux, Garland Austin, Gil Parra, Jerome Stern, Frank Salerno, Bob Lindbloom, Beto Kienast, George Grap, Samuel Olmstead, Bob Wachsmuth, Bob Payne, George Smith, Paul Piet, Robert Osborne, Don Dunlop, Paul George, Carlos DeLaFuente, John Sheehan, D. C. Richards, Fred Stemrich, and Donald Neureither. Los Angeles Police Department: Carl Dein, James Vuchsas, Charles Collins, Mike Nielsen, Bob Calkins, Jerry Joe DeRosa, Robert Burbridge, Dudley Varney, Wayne Clayton, Walt Burke, Freddy McKnight, Sidney Nuckles, Danny Galindo, William Lee, Cliff Shepard, Ed Lutes, Ed Meckel, and Edward Davis.

Federal law enforcement and the U.S. Attorney's Office: Roger "Frenchie" LaJeunesse, Werner Michel, John Marcello, Rich Gorman, Samuel Barrett, Richard Wood, Bob Lund, Bob Hinerfeld, Timothy Thornton, Gerald O'Neill, and Ray Sherrard. Los Angeles District Attorney's office: Stephen Kay, Burton Katz, Jeff Jonas, Robert Schirn, Ronald Ross, Anthony Manzella, and John Van de Kamp. Defense attorneys for Manson Family: Irving Kanarek, Gary Fields, Leon Salter, Jeffrey Engler, Deb Fraser, and Rich Pfeiffer.

Los Angeles media: Sandi Gibbons, Mary Neiswender, Pete Noyes, Dick Carlson, and Brent Zackie.

Las Vegas Police Department: Loren Stevens.

San Francisco: David Smith, Roger Smith, Al Rose, Gail Sadalla, Ernest Dernburg, Eugene Schoenfeld, Steve Pittel, Lyle Grosjean, Charles Fischer, John Frykman, Bob Conrich, John Luce, and Joel Fort. Mendocino County: Margo Tomkins, David Mandel, Thomas Martin, and Duncan James.

Inyo County Sheriff's Department: Jim Bilyeu, Wayne Wolcott, Harry Homsher, Joe Redmond, Alan George, Dave Walizer, Dennis Cox, Ben Anderson, Jerry Hildreth, and Randy Geiger. Inyo County District Attorneys: Art Maillett and Tom Hardy. California Highway Patrol: officers Jim Pursell, Doug Manning, and George Edgerton. Regarding the investigation and capture of the Family in Death Valley, thanks also to former Death Valley National Park superintendent (and author of the indispensable *Desert Shadows*) Bob Murphy, and Parks Department rangers Homer Leach, Al Schneider, Paul Fodor, Don Carney, and Richard Powell. And thanks to Darlene Ward, the daughter of late Inyo deputy sheriff Don Ward.

The Tenerelli case would've remained in the shadows were it not for the invaluable assistance of Bee and Kermit Greer, Robert Denton, and Billy Kriens, the original investigating officer at the Sportsman's Lodge. A special thank you to Sue Norris, a medical doctor with experience in forensic pathology who provided a detailed analysis of the Tenerelli coroner's findings. Finally, while I wasn't able to comfort Filippo's mother, Caterina, with a final answer about what happened to her son, I hope I have provided some solace to his sisters, Angela, Lucia, Maria, and Chiara, and his nieces and nephews, especially Cosimo Giovane, who has worked so tirelessly to have the cause of death on his uncle's death certificate changed from "suicide" to "unknown."

Lastly, in Inyo, a heartfelt expression of gratitude to Paul Dostie, who has committed the last twelve years of his life to searching for the remains of possible unidentified victims of the Manson Family.

My detour into the murky world of government intelligence and covert operations would have been impossible without the pioneering work of previous CHAOS, COINTELPRO, and MKULTRA authors and researchers, many of whom provided guidance, moral support, and files. Among those who offered generous help are Eric Olson, John Marks, Alan Scheflin, Doug Valentine, Dick Russell, Sid Bender, William Turner, Peter Dale Scott, John Judge, Rex Bradford, Larry Hancock, John Kelly, Phil Melanson, Robert Blair Keiser, Shane O'Sullivan, Brad Johnson, Jim DiEugenio, and Rose Lynn Mangan.

Especially helpful in my investigation of Reeve Whitson was his daughter, Liza, and his former wife, Ellen. Likewise, thanks to Cindy Hancock and Margot Silverman for welcoming me into their homes and opening their fathers' (William Herrmann and Charles Tacot, respectively) files. A big thanks also to Paul LePage Jr. for allowing access to his late father's files, and to Joseph Boskin, who served on the Riots and Disorders Task Force with William Herrmann and gave me his entire archive on the committee.

I interviewed dozens of Jolly West's colleagues and associates. I must express gratitude to the few who helped me understand him the most: Elizabeth "Libby" Price, Gilbert Rose, James R. Allen, and Margaret T. Singer, West's partner in studying the returned prisoners of the Korean War who beseeched me not to publish the West-Gottlieb letters because they'd destroy "all the good research" they'd done "showing how brainwashing and thought reform works."

I talked to relatives of the doomed airman Jimmy Shaver and his victim, Chere Jo Horton. His sister, Brenda Hoff, shared family secrets with me as well as the absolute conviction that her brother did not wittingly kill Horton.

Thanks to the archivists across the country who endured my unending requests: at the Los Angeles Court of Appeals, Oscar Gonzalez; Los Angeles Superior Court, Mark Hoffman and Don Camera; Federal Bureau of Prisons, Dana Hansen, Ben Kingsley, Traci Billingsly, and Ann Diestel; Federal Parole Office, Pamela Posch and Debbie Terrell; Inyo County District Attorney's office, Janet and C.J.; University of Nevada Reno, Jacque Sundstrand; National Archives, Greg Badsher, Richard Boylan, Will Mahoney, John Taylor, Fred Romanski, Marjorie Ciralante, Martha Murphy, Marty McGann, Carl Wisenbach, Sam Bouchart, Ken

Schlesinger, Rod Ross, Steve Tilley, Ramona Oliver, and Janis Wiggins; National Security Archive, Kevin Symonds; California State Archives, Linda Johnson; and the Special Collections Department of the Charles E. Young Library at UCLA, Charlotte Brown.

Authors who shared information on the Manson case include Ivor Davis, Simon Wells, Greg King, Marlin Maryneck, Barney Hoskyns, and Paul Krassner.

Independent researchers who helped me include Jedidiah Laub-Klein, Tommy Schwab, Jason Majik, Jon Aes-Nihil, John Michael Jones, and Mark Turner. Also Bo Edlund and Glenna Schultz, the proprietors of the best websites on the crimes, CieloDrive.com and TruthOnTateLaBianca.com, respectively. These two case "scholars" often found information I'd long given up on. Their knowledge on the crimes surpasses anyone I've encountered in my twenty years researching them.

Helpful members and associates of the Family include Dean Moorehouse, Sherry Cooper, Catherine "Cappie" Gillies, Dianne Lake, Brooks Poston, Paul Crockett, Vern Plumlee, and Barbara Hoyt. There were also those who intersected with the group, including Bob Berry, Bob April, Charlie Melton, Corrine Broskette, Rosina Kroner, and Lee Saunooke.

A host of my friends provided unwavering moral support—not to mention beds, couches, and floors when I turned up in their towns with a car full of files and addresses of local criminals I planned to confront. Among them (the friends, not the criminals) are Jenny Jedeikin, Patricia Harty, Holly Millea, Gail Gilchrist, Greg and Erin Fitzsimmons, Jay Russell, Lee Cunningham, Paul Lyons, Nick Smith, Jaceene Margolin, Jane Campbell, Daisy Foote, Mary Fitzgerald, Bryan Northam, Eileen O'Conner, Elaine DeBuhr, Daina Mileris, Beena Kamlani, Anne McDermott, Sean Jamison, Val Reitman, Kim Stevens, Karla Stevens, Fernando Arreola, Brad Verter, and Liz Heskin. Thanks also to Mike Gibbons (who gave me a car), Jesse Despard (who held forty boxes of my files in her basement for two years), Tim and Kyle Dilworth (basement storage for even more boxes), and Tim Guinee (an actor who roleplayed an antagonist with me in preparation for an interview).

I've had the best researchers and tape transcribers, including Jim and Desi Jedeikin, Tanya McClure, Chris Kinker, Tucker Capps, Phil Brier, and Julie Tate. The one who hung in the longest and found out the most is Bob Perkins, a true investigator and an excellent writer.

A few lawyers who provided invaluable support are Joe Weiner, David Feige, Richard Marks, Jessica Friedman, Paul McGuire, and Tim

O'Conner. And some filmmakers who briefly journeyed with me as we pursued possible collaborations: Errol Morris, John Marks, and Ken Druckerman.

In 2016, my collaborator, Dan Piepenbring, became the final component to finishing this odyssey, breathing life into my moribund pages, making sense of nonsense, and allowing me to see my findings again, with fresh eyes. For that, I will be forever indebted to the best collaborator an overwhelmed author could have. (Also thanks to Dan's equally talented agent, Dan Kirschen of ICM.)

But my deepest gratitude is reserved for two people without whose support I never would've survived these past twenty years: my father, William, who believed in the project from day one, even when others stopped believing; and my mother, Jean, who outlived him, making our joy at the conclusion bittersweet. My siblings, Bill, Tim, and Ellen, and their spouses and kids, were an enormous source of spiritual, sometimes financial, and (with Tim, particularly) legal sustenance. (Thank God there are three lawyers in my family, and thank God they were determined enough to keep me from moving into their basements to make sure all my contracts were ironclad and my lawsuits settled.)

These acknowledgments would mean nothing without a word of thanks to the people who sacrificed, and continue to sacrifice, the most in this story. The survivors of the victims of the crimes described in these pages have to be reminded, yet again, of pain and trauma that needs no reminding. Their generosity and bravery never fail to humble me. Their grace in the face of such tragedy is a far greater testament to the lives of the loved ones they lost than any book could be.

Thank you to the sister of John Philip Haught, Paula Scott Lowe, and to the mother of Marina Habe, Eloise Hardt, who died in 2017 at age ninety-nine, never knowing who killed her only child, and to Marina's stepbrother and best friend, Mark McNamara.

And my sincerest gratitude to the survivors of the known victims of the Manson group, who shared their stories with me: Frank Struthers, Suzanne LaBerge, Eva Morel, Janet Parent, and, especially, Anthony DiMaria and Debra Tate.

NOTES

Prologue

4 Vince's own handwriting: Vincent Bugliosi interview with Terry Melcher, Los Angeles District Attorney's office.

6 I believed he'd framed Manson: Author interview with Rudolph Altobelli.

1. The Crime of the Century

Helter Skelter was published in 1974. An updated edition was published in 1994 to commemorate the twenty-fifth anniversary of the murders. All citations are from that 1994 edition. The accounts of the crimes and investigation in this chapter are taken from the trial transcripts and *Helter Skelter*. Where information is used from the trial transcript that was either not used or abridged by Bugliosi in *Helter Skelter*, that information will be cited.

14 "a metaphor for evil": Vincent Bugliosi with Curt Gentry, *Helter Skelter* (New York: Norton, 1994), 640.

14 "the dark and malignant side of humanity": Bugliosi quoted in Richard C. Paddock, "The Long, Chilling Shadow of Charles Manson," *Los Angeles Times*, Aug. 8, 1994.

15 "We're going to get some fucking pigs!": Bugliosi and Gentry, *Helter Skelter*, 442.

16 would often molest her: Susan Atkins testimony, Subsequent Parole Consideration Hearing, State of California Board of Prison Terms, in the Matter of the Life Term Parole Consideration Hearing of Susan Atkins, CDC Inmate W-08340, Dec. 16, 1988.

16 "'You're going downhill'": This and all quotations from the Manson trial in this chapter are from the court transcripts, *California v. Charles Manson, Susan Atkins, Leslie Van Houten and Patricia Krenwinkel,* case 22239.

18 At the top of the driveway they found Steven Parent: I uncovered ample evidence suggesting that Parent's relationship with William Garretson was significantly different than the one depicted at trial and in *Helter Skelter*, including the purpose of his visit to the guesthouse on August 8, 1969.

19 put on "a crooked orbit.": Steven V. Roberts, "Polanskis Were at Center of a Rootless Way of Life," *New York Times*, Aug. 31, 1969.

20 she'd apparently stopped traffic: Author interview with Martin Ransohoff.

20 the home she called the "Love House": Author interview with Rudolph Altobelli,
    who added that Tate got the name from the house's prior occupant, Candice Bergen.

20 her child would strengthen her marriage: Author interview with Elaine Young.

22 "It was like I was dead": Susan Atkins testimony, *California v. Manson et al.*

22 called the murders a "blood orgy": Bugliosi and Gentry, *Helter Skelter,* 45.

22 others reported "ritualistic slayings": Dial Torgerson, "Ritualistic Slayings," *Los
    Angeles Times*, Aug. 10, 1969.

22 "overtones of a weird religious rite": Kay Gardella, "Actress and 4 Slain in
    Ritual," New York *Daily News,* Aug. 10, 1969.

22 "It's like a battlefield": Bugliosi and Gentry, *Helter Skelter,* 37.

23 "Eeny meeny miney mo": Associated Press, "Two More Killings Spur Coast
    Manhunt," Aug. 11, 1969.

23 breaking in and moving their furniture: LAPD Second Homicide Investigation
    Progress Report, DR 69-586-381, 4.

26 "breaking off a minute piece": Tex Watson and Chaplain Ray, *Will You Die for
    Me?* (Old Tappan, N.J.: Fleming H. Revell, 1978), 79.

27 as many as thirty-three people: Bugliosi reported in *Helter Skelter* (615–16) that
    ranch hand Juan Flynn told him that Manson bragged that he had killed thirty-
    five people; Bugliosi believed the actual number might've been higher. (Flynn,
    a strapping, authentic cowboy from Panama, spent considerable time with the
    Family at both the Spahn and Barker Ranches, and later provided key prosecution
    testimony for Bugliosi).

27 "invitation to freedom": "Hippies and Violence," *Time*, Dec. 12, 1969.

29 "I am a mechanical boy": Watson and Ray, *Will You Die for Me?,* 80.

29 antisocial behavior and psychic trauma: Bugliosi and Gentry, *Helter Skelter*, 193.

30 "If there ever was a man": Ibid., 200.

30 "an evil Pied Piper": United Press International, "Leader Played Part of Evil Pied
    Piper," Dec. 8, 1969.

31 "a nomadic band of hippies": Associated Press, untitled article, Dec. 2, 1969.

31 "pseudo-religious cult": United Press International, "Pseudo-Religious Cult
    Members Suspects in Bloody Slayings," Dec. 2, 1969.

31 "power to control their minds and bodies": Steven V. Roberts, "3 Suspects in
    Tate Case Tied to Guru and 'Family,'" *New York Times*, Dec. 3, 1969.

31 "man of the year" and "Offing those rich pigs": Bugliosi and Gentry, *Helter
    Skelter,* 297.

32 "hippie drug-and-murder cult": "The Demon of Death Valley," *Time,* Dec. 12, 1969.

32 "bushy-haired, wild-bearded": Associated Press, "Charles Manson, Hippie
    Leader Key Figure in Tate Murder Case," Dec. 4, 1969.

32 "a psyche torn asunder": "The Demon of Death Valley."

33 "even-toned arguments": Associated Press, "Beatles Song Inspired Tate Murders,
    Says D.A.," July 24, 1970.

34 That house was no longer occupied: I was able to document that the house was, in
    fact, occupied at the time, by the owner's son, Leonard Posella. (His mother, the
    owner, lived in the guesthouse in the back.)

35 a .38 revolver under his robes: Bugliosi and Gentry, *Helter Skelter,* 487.

36 "Over and over": Watson and Ray, *Will You Die for Me?*, 180.

36 "It's better than a climax": Bugliosi and Gentry, *Helter Skelter,* 139.

39 "agreements from his followers" and "got right up": Bugliosi and Gentry, *Helter Skelter,* 318.

39 "locating deep-seated hang-ups" through "melt-twisted": Paul Watkins with Guillermo Soledad, *My Life with Charles Manson* (New York: Bantam, 1979), 80–81.

39 "were like computers": Brooks Poston testimony in *California v. Charles Manson, Susan Atkins, Leslie Van Houten and Patricia Krenwinkel,* case 22239.

40 "to a purity and nothingness": Watson and Ray, *Will You Die for Me?*, 78–79.

42 "coursing through their veins": Steve Oney, "Manson: An Oral History," *Los Angeles Magazine*, Jul. 1, 2009.

43 "Death? That's what you're *all* going to get": Bugliosi and Gentry, *Helter Skelter,* 594.

2. An Aura of Danger

45 "unreality and hedonism": Stephen V. Roberts, "Polanskis Were at Center of Rootless Way of Life," *New York Times*, Aug. 31, 1969.

49 "Los Angeles sewer system is stoned": Thomas Thompson, "A Tragic Trip to the House on the Hill," *Life*, Aug. 29, 1969.

53 sound tests that supported Garretson: The police, nonetheless, were hardly convinced, as noted in the LAPD First Homicide Investigation Progress Report, DR 69-059-593 (p. 29): "It is highly unlikely that Garretson was not aware of the screams, gunshots and other turmoil that would result from a multiple homicide such as took place in his near proximity." Stephen Kay told me he believed Garretson had fled the guesthouse during the murders and hid in the hills above the house. In interviews with me and other reporters before his death in 2017, Garretson claimed that he'd recovered memories of the night of the murders after seeing a reenactment on television in the 1990s. He believed he'd been picked up by associates of the killers who were casing the house earlier that evening. He added that Barry Tarlow, the attorney who represented him at the time of his arrest, had said he'd been sent "by a friend," refusing to identify who that "friend" was. (Tarlow's office confirmed that he had been sent by a "friend," but insisted he wasn't paid and never learned the friend's identity.)

53 that a drug dealer had once been tied up: Among the books reporting this story are Steven Gaines, *Heroes and Villains: The True Story of the Beach Boys* (Boston: Da Capo, 1995), Barney Hoskyns, *Waiting for the Sun: Strange Days, Weird Scenes, and the Sound of Los Angeles* (New York: St. Martin's, 1996), and Ed Sanders, *The Family*, 3rd ed. (New York: Thunder's Mouth, 2002).

54 a tape of Roman and Sharon: Vincent Bugliosi with Curt Gentry, *Helter Skelter* (New York: Norton, 1994), 47.

54 "climbed the ladder to the loft": Ibid., 88.

55 assigned the Tate murder case until November: Ibid., 166–67.

56 Kaczanowski finally consented to be interviewed: The account of Kaczanowski's interactions with the police, victims, Polanski, and original suspects comes from my interviews with Kaczanowski and the LAPD files on the case (provided by retired LAPD Sgt. Mike McGann).

57 Billy Doyle, Tom Harrigan, and Pic Dawson: First Homicide Investigation Progress Report; individual subject interviews by LAPD; author interviews with William Tennant, Kaczanowski, Billy Doyle, Thomas Harrigan, and Charles Tacot.

57   Gene Gutowski and two friends: Author interviews with Gutowski, Victor
     Lownes, and Richard Sylbert.

57   Denny's parking lot: Author interviews with Kaczanowski, Gutowski, and Lownes.

58   barred from entering Polanski's suite: Robert Helder and Paul Tate, *Five Down
     on Cielo Drive* (unpublished manuscript; Talmy Enterprises, Inc., 1993), 27.

58   "Polanski was taken to an apartment": Bugliosi and Gentry, *Helter Skelter,* 79.

58   denied knowing Kaczanowski: Roman Polanski, LAPD Polygraph Examination,
     Aug. 11, 1969.

58   a turbulent time at the Cielo house: The information in this chapter about the
     activities at Cielo Drive in the months leading up to the murders—including the
     details about the drug dealing by Doyle, Harrigan, Dawson, and Tacot—is from
     First Homicide Investigation Progress Report; LAPD Second Homicide
     Investigation Progress Report, DR 69-059-593; witness interviews by LAPD (from
     McGann files); numerous author interviews; and Helder and Tate, *Five Down.*

64   Tennant's fall from grace: Peter Bart, "Exec Comes Full Circle After Descent into
     Despair," *Variety,* Feb. 8, 1993.

67   subject of Interpol surveillance: Eddi Fiegel, *Dream a Little Dream of Me: The Life
     of "Mama" Cass Elliot* (London: Sidgwick and Jackson, 2005), 244–45; Author
     FOIPA Request, 1122260-000, Dawson, Harris Pickens, III, Nov. 24, 2008.

67   The young son of a diplomat: "Evelyn Parks Dawson" (obituary), *Washington Post,*
     Aug. 20, 1987; LAPD First Homicide Investigation Progress Report, DR 69-059-
     593, 9–10.

67   1966 London arrest: Fiegel, *Dream a Little Dream,* 244–45.

67   Polanski's circle through Mama Cass: LAPD First Homicide Investigation
     Progress Report.

67   According to police reports: Ibid.

67   selling drugs in Los Angeles: Author interview with Margot Tacot Silverman.

67   conviction was later overturned: LAPD First Homicide Investigation Progress
     Report, 30.

68   anally raped him: Accounts of this incident come from individual LAPD
     interview subject reports; the LAPD Homicide Progress Reports; author
     interviews with Doyle and Tacot; Gaines, *Heroes and Villains;* Hoskyns, *Waiting for
     the Sun;* and Sanders, *The Family.*

68   Candice Bergen, in an interview with the LAPD: LAPD Interview with Bergen,
     #145, by Warren and Gilmore, Aug. 21, 1969.

68   Dennis Hopper told the *Los Angeles Free Press*: Sanders, *The Family,* 195. Sanders
     says Hopper also told the *Press* that Doyle's rape was filmed, quoting Hopper:
     "They had fallen into sadism and masochism and bestiality—and they recorded it
     all on videotape too. The L.A. police told me this. I know that three days before
     they were killed, twenty-five people were invited to that house to a mass
     whipping of a dealer from Sunset Strip who'd given them bad dope."

69   In short, he told: All quotations and summaries in this section are from Billy
     Doyle, LAPD Interrogation (transcript), by Earl Deemer, Aug. 28, 1969.

71   "if they'd fucked me or not!": Helder and Tate, *Five Down,* 63.

71   Dawson had died: Fiegel, *Dream a Little Dream,* 143; "Harris Pickens Dawson, III"
     (obituary), *Washington Post,* Aug. 20, 1986.

71 Harrigan was nowhere to be found: I did find and interview Harrigan, but not until 2014.

72 "chained a sign to the tree": Doyle, LAPD Interrogation transcript.

72 No footage from this film has ever surfaced: Doyle admitted to me that the movie was a ruse, but gave differing reasons for the trip's true purpose. Reed B. Mitchell, a Los Angeles disc jockey, told the LAPD that he'd been approached by Tacot before the murders "regarding a boat to bring back some drugs possibly [from] Jamaica" (Mitchell, LAPD Interview, #106, by Celmer, Burke, and Stanley, Aug. 19, 1969).

72 "I took a lie-detector test," Tacot told me: I have never been able to find this lie detector test, or any reference to a polygraph being administered to Tacot in the LAPD files.

72 "You can't kill somebody long-distance": The LAPD was never able to corroborate that the two men were in Jamaica when the murders occurred. Several interview subjects told police they saw Doyle in Los Angeles around the time of the murders. According to the Homicide Investigation Report, Harrigan visited the Tate house the day before the murders (Aug. 7) to discuss "a delivery of MDA in the near future" with Frykowski (First Homicide Investigation Progress Report, 11); Harrigan's attorney, when he was a suspect in the Tate murders and questioned by police, was Paul Caruso, who would later represent Susan Atkins with his law partner, Richard Caballero. Caruso told me that Harrigan sold drugs to Frykowski but was never paid for them.

73 pallbearer at the gangster Mickey Cohen's funeral: Author interview with Jim Dickson.

73 Though many confuse him with a fictional character from *The Godfather*, Johnny Fontaine really was born with that name. After his affiliation with mobster Micky Cohen became public in the 1950s, Fontaine was forced to adopt the stage name "Jeffrey Stone" by his studio (which put out the false story that the change was made because his name sounded too much like the actress, Joan Fontaine).

73 "controlling" him with voodoo: United Press International, "Corrine Calvet Denies Threatening with Hex," Dec. 12, 1967.

73 "The only thing that I can tell you": Author interview with Corrine Calvet. As for Calvet's assertion that the FBI told her she was in danger, even though the FBI wasn't supposed to have been involved in the investigation, several dozen people told me they were certain they were interviewed by investigators who identified themselves as FBI agents. Roger "Frenchie" LaJeunesse, an FBI field agent in Los Angeles, confirmed to me that he participated in the investigation in an "unofficial" capacity.

75 sued the *Los Angeles Times*: Case 963676, Los Angeles Superior Court, Oct. 23, 1969. The case was dismissed after Tacot missed several hearings.

75 acknowledged by the federal government: Carina A. Del Rosario, *A Different Battle: Stories of Asian Pacific American Veterans* (Seattle: University of Washington Press, 2000), 95.

75 Hersh Matias Warzechahe: Los Angeles Superior Court Archives, Case C36566, *Henry Martin Fine v. Bloch, Robert D.,* Aug. 15, 1972.

76 an assassin for the CIA: Author interview with Peter Knecht. Knecht, a Hollywood defense attorney, had been Jay Sebring's lawyer and accompanied Roman Polanski

and the psychic Peter Hurkos to the Cielo house after the murders. He represented Tacot on a charge of carrying an army-issued firearm. Knecht said one of Tacot's assignments from the CIA included a failed assassination attempt against Fidel Castro. In a unpublished memoir shared by his widow, Knecht wrote, Tacot "was scary . . . [he] was dangerous, and I was glad that I managed to beat that [firearm] case because I was a little concerned about him, although I didn't really fear for my own safety. I was just being cautious. As a defense attorney, you can't do your job if you get caught up worrying about your clients and what they might or might not do, even the Charles Mansons and Charlie Tacots of the world."

76 "soldier of fortune": David Crosby and Carl Gottlieb, *Since Then: How I Survived Everything and Lived to Tell About It* (New York: Putnam, 2006), 209.

76 ex-marine who'd served in Korea: Author interview with Mitchum; William Rinehart, LAPD Polygraph and Interview transcript, by Earl Deemer, Sept. 30, 1969.

76 grew pot in Arizona: Author interview with Mitchum; author interview with Silverman.

76 a child molester: Author interview with a person who wishes to remain anonymous.

76 coke smuggler: Author interview with Silverman; author interview with David Berk.

76 "Hey, man, aren't you?": Author interview with Mitchum.

77 a movie PR man from the 1940s: Margot Tacot Silverman shared Fine's personal papers, which her father inherited, with me. They included countless press clippings and promotional photographs of Fine with stars like John Wayne and Kim Novak.

77 Office of Strategic Services: Author interviews with colleagues and friends of Fine, including Eddie Kafafian, Vernon Scott, Bob Thomas, Joe Hyams, and Eddie Albert; author interview with Shalya Provost Spencer, Fine's daughter (she has changed her first name from the one she was given at birth, Sheila).

77 German landing sites: Author interview with Albert; author interview with Spencer.

77 espionage operations through the sixties: Author interviews with Kafafian, Scott, Thomas, Hyams, Albert, and Spencer.

78 vast amounts of cocaine: Doyle, LAPD Interrogation transcript.

80 Cass Elliot knew Manson: Sanders, *The Family*, 147. I have never been able to corroborate Manson and Elliot meeting, but it has also been reported by Hoskyns, *Waiting for the Sun*, 183; and Fiegel, *Dream a Little Dream*, 305. Michael Caine, in his memoir, *What's It All About?* (New York: Random House, 1992), 318, claimed to have met Manson at a party at Elliot's house that was also attended by Sharon Tate and Jay Sebring.

80 Elliot had been friends with Frykowski and Folger: There are multiple references to this in both the First and Second Homicide Investigation Progress Reports.

80 Elliot's bandmates were close: LAPD Homicide Investigation Progress Report I, 10; John and Michelle Phillips, LAPD Interview, #22, by Celmer, Stanley, and Burke, Aug. 12, 1969 (1–2).

81 renamed himself after a racetrack: Author interview with Larry Geller.

81 Frank Sinatra and several casino owners: Author interview with Joe Torrenueva.

82 "shot two guys who were going": United Press, "Pistols Roar as Fans Scrap: Quarrel on Griffith Fight Ends with Gun Duel," Dec. 1, 1929; Ovid DeMaris,

Captive City (Secaucus, N.J.: Lyle Stuart, 1969), 230; William F. Roemer Jr., *Roemer: Man Against the Mob: The Inside Story About How the FBI Cracked the Chicago Mob by the Agent Who Led the Attack* (New York: Ivy Books, 1989), 100.

82   He later went to Havana: Baron FOIPA, 0926058-00, released Oct. 3, 2001; DeMaris, *Captive City,* 230; Roemer, *Roemer,* 100.

82   Lansky's eyes and ears: Roemer, *Roemer,* 100. Baron was "the closest associate" of Johnny Rosselli at the time that Rosselli was part of the top-secret CIA effort to assassinate Fidel Castro known as "Mongoose" (Peter Dale Scott, *Deep Politics and the Death of JFK* [Berkeley: University of California Press, 1993], 199, 178).

82   some type of security-intelligence clearance: Baron FBI FOIPA 92-251 LV (sec. 1, pt. 1); DeMaris, *Captive City,* 225; untitled article, *Chicago Tribune,* Jan. 14, 1961.

82   a cabal of right-wing military intelligence: The others named by Torrenueva were Virgil Crabtree, the head of intelligence for the IRS in Los Angeles in the fifties and an undercover investigator for the L.A. District Attorney's office in the sixties; Jack Entratter, who ran the Sands Casino until his death in the early seventies; Sy Bartlett, a retired army intelligence officer who moved to Hollywood and had a successful career as a screenwriter; and Tony Owen, the ex-husband of wholesome actress Donna Reed.

83   General Curtis E. LeMay: See Curtis LeMay with MacKinlay Kantor, *Mission with LeMay* (Garden City, N.Y.: Doubleday, 1965); Warren Kozak, *LeMay: The Life and Wars of General Curtis LeMay* (Washington, D.C.: Regnery, 2009); and I. F. Stone, "LeMay: Cave Man in a Jet Bomber," in *In a Time of Torment, 1961–1967* (Boston: Little, Brown, 1989), 92–104.

83   "He was a bad businessman": Sebring's nephew, Anthony DiMaria, who is making a documentary film about his uncle, adamantly refutes the notion that his uncle was anything but flush at the time of his death, but I found ample evidence in police interviews and elsewhere suggesting the opposite was true. A few samples: In *Restless Souls: The Sharon Tate Family's Account of Stardom, the Manson Murders, and a Crusade for Justice* (New York: It Books/HarperCollins, 2012), Alisa Statman and Brie Tate say that Sebring was "over a quarter million dollars in debt" (p. 85). Art Blum, a business partner, told me that Sebring "always had financial problems, spent it as fast as he could… [and] was losing his shirt at the salon."

83   a group of his stylists had defected: Author interview with Felice Ingrassia.

83   "roughed up" several employees: Ibid.; author interview with Phillips.

3. The Golden Penetrators

87   Bugliosi had to give him a tranquilizer: Author interview with Vincent Bugliosi.

88   "shaved a couple of visits to the ranch": Karina Longworth, "Charles Manson's Hollywood, Part 5: Doris Day and Terry Melcher," *You Must Remember This* (podcast), June 23, 2015.

89   divorced for the second time: According to State of California Marriage Records, Carole married Dennis Wilson on July 29, 1965, divorced him in December 1966, remarried him at an unrecorded date (and location), and divorced him again in June 1967.

89   during his "rampages": Case 711515, Superior Court of Los Angeles, Los Angeles.

89   two young children: Scott, born in 1962, to Carole and her first husband (Scott Vanerstrom), was adopted by Dennis; the couple's daughter, Jennifer, was born in 1967.

89   Ella Jo Bailey and Patricia Krenwinkel: The story of Wilson's introduction to the Manson Family is from the Tate-LaBianca trial transcripts and *Helter Skelter*, unless otherwise indicated.

90   "just because we were men": Tex Watson and Chaplain Ray, *Will You Die for Me?* (Old Tappan, N.J.: Fleming H. Revell, 1978), 57.

90   "I Live with 17 Girls": David Griffiths, "Dennis Wilson: I Live with 17 Girls," *Record Mirror*, Dec. 21, 1968.

90   "another artist for Brother Records": Keith Altman, "Dennis Wilson: This Is Where It's At," *Rave*, May 1969.

90   "Cease to Exist": Ed Sanders, *The Family*, 3rd ed. (New York: Thunder's Mouth, 2002), 64. The key word "exist" was changed to "resist" and the song title was changed to "Never Learn Not to Love." It was released as the B side of the first single from the Beach Boys album *20/20* on December 8, 1968. The band performed the song, with Dennis singing the lead vocal, on *The Mike Douglas Show* on August 22, 1969, less than two weeks after the Tate–LaBianca murders (see IMDB.com, *The Mike Douglas Show,* episode 8.240). Bugliosi didn't report that Wilson had stolen a song from Manson until the twenty-fifth anniversary edition of *Helter Skelter*—and then, only in a footnote (Vincent Bugliosi with Curt Gentry, *Helter Skelter* [New York: Norton, 1994], 667).

90   "though they'd probably deny it now": Nick Kent, *The Dark Stuff: Selected Writings on Rock Music* (Boston: DaCapo Press, 2002), 310.

90   the "Golden Penetrators": Steven Gaines, *Heroes and Villains: The True Story of the Beach Boys* (Boston: Da Capo, 1995), 190; Barney Hoskyns, *Waiting for the Sun: Strange Days, Weird Scenes, and the Sound of Los Angeles* (New York: St. Martin's, 1996), 156.

90   "roving cocksmen": Gaines, *Heroes and Villains*, 190.

91   he crossed paths with Manson: Melcher testimony, *California v. Charles Manson, Susan Atkins, Leslie Van Houten and Patricia Krenwinkel,* case 22239, 15083.

91   Manson came along in the back seat: Ibid., 15097–98.

91   upward of $100,000: Bugliosi and Gentry, *Helter Skelter*, 335–36.

91   Wilson gave three interviews: Griffiths, "I Live with 17 Girls"; Altman, "Dennis Wilson"; Lon Goddard, "The Continuing Story of Beach Boy Dennis and His House of Seventeen Women," *Record Mirror*, July 5, 1969. Bugliosi omitted from *Helter Skelter* the fact that these three interviews were published before the murders.

91   a Malibu beach house: Author interview with Gregg Jakobson.

91   Melcher stood him up: Bugliosi and Gentry, *Helter Skelter*, 323.

92   ask the owner of the property: Ibid., 308, 306.

92   visiting twice over four days: There are multiple references to this in Melcher testimony, *California v. Manson et al.*

92   his friend Mike Deasy: Ibid.

92   "Don't draw on me, motherfucker!": David Felton and David Dalton, "Charles Manson: The Incredible Story of the Most Dangerous Man Alive," *Rolling Stone*, June 25, 1970, 39.

93   the Family repeated their audition: Melcher testimony, *California v. Manson et al.*, 15124.

93   a frightening LSD trip: Bugliosi and Gentry, *Helter Skelter,* 250.

93   Melcher conveyed his rejection through Jakobson: Melcher testimony, Grand Jury, A253156, *The People of the State of California vs. Charles Manson, Charles*

Watson, aka Charles Montgomery; Susan Atkins, aka Sadie Mae Glutz; Linda Kasabian, Patricia Krenwinkel, and Leslie Sankston, Dec. 5, 1969, 127.

93 Wilson and Jakobson knew that Manson had shot: I located more than a half dozen documents in the Los Angeles District Attorney files and the Los Angeles County Sheriff's Office files indicating that Manson had discussed the Bernard Crowe shooting with Wilson within a week of the Tate murders, although it's unclear if the name Crowe was ever mentioned.

93 "upward of a hundred times": Jakobson testimony, *California v. Charles Watson,* 2 Crim 22241, 2851.

94 "scatter [their] limbs": Ibid., 2836.

94 Tate was hanged from the ceiling: Coroner Thomas Noguchi testified, "Based on the wound findings on the left side of her cheek and the way the rope was tied at the scene . . . I would form the opinion that Miss Tate had been suspended"—see *California v. Manson et al.,* 8907.

94 Jakobson apparently didn't make the connection: Jakobson testimony, ibid., 14235.

94 "Tell Dennis there are more," "The electricity," and "Don't be surprised": Bugliosi and Gentry, *Helter Skelter,* 336–7.

94 "I know why Charles Manson": David Leaf, *The Beach Boys and the California Myth* (New York: Grosset and Dunlap, 1978), 136.

94 "Me and Charlie": Joel Selvin, untitled article, *San Francisco Chronicle,* Jan. 8, 1984.

95 including Henry Fonda: Bugliosi and Gentry, *Helter Skelter,* 305.

95 filing a lawsuit: *Rudolph Altobelli v. Polanski et al.,* Superior Court of the State of California, Nov. 16, 1969.

97 "about the musician that Manson": Stephen Kay has said at various parole hearings (and in interviews with me) that Hinman met Manson through Wilson, Jakobson, and Melcher, something else left out of *Helter Skelter.*

98 Altobelli moved back into the house: Melcher eventually admitted to me that he'd lived in the house with Altobelli after the murders. He'd said the opposite in his mother's biography: "I hadn't been in the house since the day I moved out," Melcher wrote of the day in late November 1969 when he learned of Manson's involvement in the murders (Melcher, quoted in A. E. Hotchner, *Doris Day* [New York: Bantam, 1976], 242).

99 both privileged children of Hollywood royalty: Bergen's father was the famous ventriloquist Edgar Bergen.

99 "snuck out in the middle of the night": Author interview with Allen Warnick.

100 "'we'll kill you'": Author interview with Genevieve Waite.

100 "these people who have been harassing me there": Ibid.

100 Carole had had photos taken: Author interview with Dean Moorehouse.

100 she pursued a romance with Jay Sebring: Carole Wilson, LAPD Interview, #66, by Gilmore, Aug. 15, 1969, which includes: "Miss Wilson states she slept with Sebring at his home off and on for the past two years."

101 longest and costliest in California history: "The Manson Murders at 40: 'Helter Skelter' Author Vincent Bugliosi Looks Back," *Newsweek,* Aug. 1, 2009.

102 stating in an official letter: Lorenzo Quezada, LAPD Discovery Unit, to author, June 4, 1999.

102 stalked former members of the Family: Author interviews with multiple former Family members, including Dianne Lake, Sherry Cooper, and Catherine Gillies;

author interviews with the children of Rosemary LaBianca, Suzan LaBerge, and Frank Struthers.

102 falling-out before her death in 1992: Author interview with Bill Nelson; author interview with Debra Tate.

103 Like Ed Sanders: Author interview with Ed Sanders.

105 Carole Wilson, and Carole Jakobson: The wives of Dennis Wilson and Gregg Jakobson were both close to Sebring, Tate, and Altobelli, and they were frequent visitors to the Tate house. Both women also had harrowing encounters with Manson before and after the murders.

105 "August 10": I later learned that Carole Jakobson was the third person interviewed by the LAPD (Carole Jakobson, LAPD Interview, #63, by Varney, Aug. 10, 1969). According to Gregg Jakobson's testimony at the Tate–LaBianca trial, he was also present for the interview, although his name doesn't appear in the LAPD summary. Jakobson told the jury the detectives "really did not come to speak to me. They spoke to my wife more than me. I was there so they spoke to me, too" (Jakobson testimony, *California v. Manson et al.*). During his closing argument to the jury, Irving Kanarek noted the impossible "coincidence" that the man who knew most about Manson, outside of the Family, was among the first to be interviewed by police, and somehow never mentioned his friend as a possible suspect in the murders (Kanarek, final statement, ibid., 20274).

105 spoken to police within a week: Carole Wilson's interview was on August 15, 1969.

107 "his way of living and how groovy it was": Altobelli testimony, *California v. Manson et al.*, 14769.

107 "I think I have seen him at Dennis Wilson's house": Melcher testimony, Los Angeles Grand Jury, 128.

107 he'd met Manson no more than three times: Multiple references in Melcher testimony, *California v. Manson et al.*

108 "Manson and Watson attended a party": Author interview with Stephen Kay.

108 never once saw Watson inside his house: Melcher's recollections about Watson changed dramatically according to the needs of the prosecution. Before the grand jury, when shown a photo of Watson, Melcher testified that he didn't "know him" (Melcher testimony, Los Angeles Grand Jury, 128). When pressed, he said he may have seen him at Dennis Wilson's house, but wasn't certain (ibid.). He was never asked about Watson at the Tate–LaBianca trial (Watson wasn't a defendant), but when Watson was tried by Bugliosi after the Tate–LaBianca verdicts and the prosecution needed to place the Texan inside the Cielo Drive house prior to the Polanskis' residency, Melcher delivered. Asked by Bugliosi if he'd ever seen Watson in his house, Melcher replied that he had "approximately six times" (Melcher testimony, *California v. Watson,* 2207). These discrepancies were never reported in *Helter Skelter.*

109 Gentry was working on the book: Gentry, Stephen Kay, and more than six other people who were present during the trial confirmed this in interviews with me.

109 "obstructionist tactics": Bugliosi and Gentry, *Helter Skelter,* 371.

109 opprobrium from every corner: Kanarek first gained fame as the attorney for one of two defendants who killed a LAPD officer in a case that would later be immortalized as a book and movie called *The Onion Field.*

109 Manson wanted the worst: Author interview with Burton Katz; Burton Katz, *Justice Overruled: Unmasking the Criminal Justice System* (New York: Grand Central, 1997), 163; author interview with Peter Knecht; author interview with Gary Fields.

109 He objected nine times: Bugliosi and Gentry, *Helter Skelter*, 417, 424.

109 The judge jailed him twice for contempt: Ibid., 466.

110 "the Toscanini of Tedium": Ibid., 530.

110 confidentiality prevented him: Several sources told me they believed Kanarek was paid by Melcher, accounting for, they said, Kanarek's highly uncharacteristic decision to forgo cross-examining Melcher on the stand.

111 living out of his car: Author interview with Fields; author interview with Kay.

111 Over the ten years previous to our meeting: Unless otherwise indicated, all the information about Kanarek came from interviews with him and with George Denny, an attorney and longtime friend. Kanarek also shared the story of his nervous breakdown and the loss of his law license with a *Los Angeles Times* reporter; see Dana Parsons, "Barred from World He Loved, Just Getting by Is a Trial," *Los Angeles Times,* Oct. 25, 1998.

112 they colluded, that is, to protect the convictions: After the judge ruled that Farr had immunity as a newsman and didn't have to testify about who gave him the sealed documents, the state withdrew its charges.

4. *The Holes in* Helter Skelter

116 "After Terry Melcher": At that time, I was relying on the first edition of *Helter Skelter*, published by W.W. Norton in 1974. The relevant passage ("Gregg Jakobson had arranged for a Dean Moorehouse to stay there . . .") appears on p. 377, and is presented identically in later editions (1994 Norton paperback, p. 275; 1995 Bantam paperback, p. 511). However, I later discovered that some editions of the book (i.e., the 2001 Norton paperback) did identify Dean Moorehouse as the father of Ruth Moorehouse ("Jakobson had arranged for Dean Moorehouse, Ruth Ann Moorehouse's father, to stay there for a brief period," p. 496). As Bugliosi and his coauthor, Curt Gentry, were both deceased at the time of my discovery, I couldn't ask them about the discrepancy.

117 the ex-con was fresh out of federal prison: The information in this chapter about Dennis Moorehouse is from my interviews with him and from his parole file, which I received from the State of California after obtaining his consent. Details about the arrest of Manson in Leggett in July 1967 are from police reports and news articles.

117 prompting her mother to report her: G. Campbell, Bureau of Criminal Identification and Investigation, Crime Report, Mendocino County Sheriff's Office, File 25544, Suspect: Charles Willis [sic] Manson, July 28, 1967; "Deputies End Leggett Tryst," *Ukiah* [Calif.] *Daily Journal*, July 31, 1967, 8.

117 The legend is that Manson persuaded: Author interview with Dean Moorehouse.

118 "They convicted me in December of '68": Moorehouse's first trial had ended in a hung jury the previous August (see ibid. and "LSD Trial Ends in Hung Jury; New Trial Date Set," *Ukiah Daily Journal,* Aug. 28, 1968).

118 for the long drive to Ukiah: Melcher testimony, *California v. Charles Watson,* 2 Crim 22241, 2208; Ed Sanders, *The Family,* 3rd ed. (New York: Thunder's Mouth, 2002), 83; Tex Watson and Chaplain Ray, *Will You Die for Me?* (Old Tappan, N.J.: Fleming H. Revell, 1978), 62; author interview with Moorehouse.

118 "he gave me his credit card": Author interview with Moorehouse. See also Sanders, *The Family,* 83; Watson and Ray, *Will You Die for Me?,* 62. In August 1968, Watson was ticketed for speeding while driving Melcher's car in San Luis Obispo County with Moorehouse. When Watson failed to pay the fine or appear for the court date, a warrant was issued for his arrest, identifying Melcher as the registered owner of the vehicle (case T-3504, citation F221471, *California v. Charles Denton Watson,* Order to Appear, County of San Luis Obispo Justice Court, Sept. 5, 1968—from the files of Los Angeles Sheriff's Office).

118 entered the prison system on January 2, 1969: Moorehouse, Dean Allen, Cumulative Case History, State of California, Department of Corrections, case 4482-C, Jan. 3, 1969.

119 left her deeply skeptical of Bugliosi...for Terry Melcher: Author interview with Sandi Gibbons.

120 my visits weren't exactly authorized: Since my last visit to the files in 2006, to the best of my knowledge all other requests from researchers wanting similar access have been denied.

120 the Straight Satans: DeCarlo helped found the bike club in 1966, according to testimony from his trial for drug smuggling. See *United States v. DeCarlo et al.,* no. 37502-SD-Criminal, U.S. District Court, Southern District, March 28–June 30, 1967.

120 in the spring of '69: Bugliosi and Gentry, *Helter Skelter,* 146.

121 DeCarlo's father was in the firearms business: Ibid., 144.

121 got access to drugs: Ibid., 132; Bill Nelson, audio interview with Vincent Bugliosi, 1999, Mansonmurders.com.

121 His testimony did a lot of heavy lifting for Bugliosi: The prosecutor wrote in *Helter Skelter* that he "succeed[ed] in getting a tremendous amount of evidence in through DeCarlo" (468).

121 he identified the weapons used in the murders: Ibid., 464–69.

121 In the crossed-out sections of Bugliosi's notes: Vincent Bugliosi interview with Danny DeCarlo, Feb. 11, 1970, 2.

122 Melcher replied under oath: Grand Jury, A253156, *The People of the State of California vs. Charles Manson, Charles Watson, aka Charles Montgomery; Susan Atkins, aka Sadie Mae Glutz; Linda Kasabian, Patricia Krenwinkel, and Leslie Sankston,* Dec. 5, 1969, 128.

122 "After this second occasion": Melcher testimony, *California v. Charles Manson, Susan Atkins, Leslie Van Houten and Patricia Krenwinkel,* case 22239, 15127.

122 "Yeah, just a few days after May 18": Ibid., 15144–45.

123 might never have gotten his convictions: Bugliosi interview, "Charlie's Friends," *The Fifth Estate* (Canadian TV series), 1975.

123 to "instill fear" in Melcher: Richard Caballero and Paul Caruso interview with Susan Atkins, transcript, Dec. 1, 1969, 3.

123 Bugliosi had crossed out: Bugliosi interview with DeCarlo.

123 legendary in L.A. legal circles: Fitzgerald was the model for the title character of John Gregory Dunne's crime novel *Dutch Shea, Jr.,* about a scrappy, hard-drinking Los Angeles defense attorney.

124 a girlfriend of his: Author interview with Cupertina Vega.

125 Melcher had expressly denied: Melcher testimony, *California v. Manson et al.*, 15124.

125 "He did not record Manson": Bugliosi, closing argument, ibid., 21370. When Bugliosi executive-produced a remake of the TV movie of *Helter Skelter* in 2004, he included a scene depicting Melcher and Wilson recording Manson in a studio (John Gray, *Helter Skelter* script, page 9).

125 Donald "Shorty" Shea: Bugliosi and Gentry, *Helter Skelter,* 661.

125 "After one of the girls told me that they killed the caretaker": Parks probably believed, erroneously, that Shea was the "caretaker" of the ranch.

127 "Melcher was on acid": Unsigned handwritten notes, Paul Watkins interview, LASO, Dec. 19, 1969, 7.

131 "Dennis and Greg had been there": In police interviews and interviews with me, Jakobson described several visits he made with Wilson to the Family's outpost in Death Valley. This suggested that Wilson wasn't done with the Family after he allegedly threw them out of his home in August 1968. The Family didn't start going to the desert until mid-November 1968, according to police reports, trial testimony, and *Helter Skelter.*

133 "And they said, probably not": Melcher was less kind in his mother's biography, writing: "The cops said that five or six of the Manson girls claimed that Manson had set me up with them and that I was the father of their babies. I finally got so fed up with the cops over these sex inquiries that I got out the pictures of the most recent ladies in my life, real beauties, all of them, and I said, 'Listen, when I've got beauties like these to get in bed with, why would I want to screw any of Manson's clap-ridden, unwashed dogs?'" (A. E. Hotchner, *Doris Day* [New York: Bantam, 1976], 247).

136 soon rubbing elbows with the sons: All the Jakobson information comes from my interviews with him, unless otherwise noted.

136 racking up a few arrests along the way: According to testimony at Tex Watson's trial, Jakobson had been arrested on a drug charge in November 1968; Watson said that Manson sent him to Melcher's house to get money to bail Jakobson out of jail. Melcher refused, and had his chauffeur drive Watson down to Sunset Boulevard so he could hitchhike back to the Spahn Ranch (Watson testimony, *California v. Watson,* 3251, 3310). The second arrest, according to Melcher's first police interview (LAPD Interview, #231, by Patchett, Nov. 31 [*sic*], 1969), occurred on his and Jakobson's third visit to the Spahn Ranch. LAPD detective Frank Patchett wrote, "It was on that visit that the three were stopped by LA County sheriffs and Jakobson was arrested for a ticket. Melcher bailed him out." It seemed curious to me that there was actually a sheriff's officer at the Spahn Ranch who arrested Jakobson during his and Melcher's "final" visit to Manson in May 1969.

137 "He doesn't anymore": Jakobson testimony, *California v. Manson et al.,* 14182.

137 "how much of that is legend and how much of it is true": Though both Melcher and Jakobson's testimony about the spyglass was brought out by Bugliosi—and the prosecutor also included it in his summation—for some reason Bugliosi never mentions this vital bit of information in *Helter Skelter.* Melcher wrote about it in his mother's biography: Manson had "stolen a telescope from the deck of the

Malibu house, presumably to let me know he knew my whereabouts" (Hotchner, *Doris Day,* 249).

137 "Jakobson frequently smiled at Manson": Associated Press, "Defendant in Tate Trial Well Liked," Nov. 16, 1970.

137 "thank Mr. Melcher for his presence": *California v. Manson et al.*, 15152. Although Bugliosi omitted the cordial remarks from Kanarek to Melcher in *Helter Skelter,* he did note (without editorial comment) that Kanarek chose not to examine Melcher, "probably at Manson's request" (495).

138 all sourced to Jakobson: Jeff Guinn, *Manson: The Life and Times of Charles Manson* (New York: Simon and Schuster, 2013), 157, 182, 198.

138 "all and any references": I counted five changes between the original hardcover edition (1996) and the paperback reissue (1999). References to Melcher's involvement with the Manson women were removed and the number of times he visited the Spahn Ranch was changed from "several" to "twice." Any suggestions that he was aware of Manson's propensity for murder were excised entirely. All the changes to *Waiting for the Sun* can be seen by comparing the following pages (the 1996 hardcover versus the 1999 paperback): 176/181, 176/181 (a second set of changes here), 179/183, 179/184, 179/184 (a second set of changes here), and 181/186.

5. Amnesia at the L.A. County Sheriff's Office

143 A soft-spoken Buddhist: All the information about Hinman in this chapter comes from the Hinman murder trial transcripts (A-057452, *The People of the State of California v. Robert Kenneth Beausoleil*) or *Helter Skelter,* unless otherwise noted.

143 Atkins and Brunner took turns: Atkins and Brunner both admitted smothering Hinman with a pillow. But at Atkins's 1978 parole hearing, she said it was Beausoleil who smothered Hinman (Atkins testimony, Subsequent Parole Consideration Hearing, State of California Board of Prison Terms, in the Matter of the Life Term Parole Consideration Hearing of Susan Atkins, CDC Inmate W-08340, July 20, 1978, 24–25).

144 They spent five days: Paul Whiteley testimony, *California v. Robert Beausoleil (I),* A-057452, 9; Ed Sanders, *The Family,* 3rd ed. (New York: Thunder's Mouth, 2002), 188.

144 a woman had been in his house: Bill Gleason (retired LASO), timeline of Hinman murder (provided by Gleason to author); author interview with Jay Hofstadter; Hofstadter testimony, *California v. Charles Manson* (for Hinman and Shea murders), A-267861, 4124; Richard Siegel testimony, ibid., 4345. Gleason's timeline contains these entries:
7-26-69 and 7-27-69: Jay Hofstadter calls Hinman home, phone answered by Atkins; second call by Mary Brunner.
7-26-69 and 7-27-69: Richard Siegal calls Hinman, Atkins answers, speaks with English accent.

145 he had at least one accomplice: Gleason timeline; the applicable entry reads:
7-26-69: Dave Ewing knocks on front door of Gary Hinman's home, Susan Atkins answers door carrying candle, said Hinman in Colorado. (He was being tortured at the time.)
 In addition, according to documents in the LASO files, Ewing was a biker known as "preacher" who lived with Hinman in 1968 and knew the Family well.

Ewing could have provided a physical identification of Atkins at the Hinman house during the period he was being tortured and murdered, but for reasons unknown he never testified in any of the Hinman murder trials. He refused to be interviewed for this book.

145   that led them to overlook Manson: Vincent Bugliosi with Curt Gentry, *Helter Skelter* (New York: Norton, 1994), 113.

145   the two detectives did the right thing: Ibid., 62.

146   kept the Manson Family at large: Ibid.

146   arrest was for stolen vehicles: They were also charged with possession of stolen property, possession of illegal firearms (a sawed-off shotgun), and arson (they'd set fire to a federally owned earth-moving vehicle, a "Michigan Loader"). See "28 'Hips' Nabbed in Death Valley, Goler Wash Raids," *Inyo* [Calif.] *Independent,* Oct. 16, 1969, 1.

146   On August 16, 1969: Unless otherwise noted, all the information on the Spahn Ranch Raid is from the reports I obtained from the LASO files and from interviews with officers who participated in the raid, some of whom shared additional records from the raid, including its "operational plan."

147   "It was the most flawlessly": Author interview with John Kolman.

147   perhaps even sending undercover agents to investigate: Frank Salerno, a retired LASO narcotics detective, told me that LASO intelligence sent undercover agents wired with recording devices into the Spahn Ranch to purchase narcotics from Family members but were unsuccessful. Another retired detective, Gil Parra, who worked LASO intelligence and homicide, told me that when he started working intelligence in May 1969, the sheriffs already had "informants" planted at the ranch.

147   "on a misdated warrant": Bugliosi and Gentry, *Helter Skelter,* 90.

148   Ellroy still hailed him: James Ellroy, *My Dark Places* (New York: Knopf, 1996), 217; the author also praised Guenther as the cop "who *really* broke the Charles Manson case" (ibid.).

149   "Same knife. Same wound": In a phone conversation, Noguchi told me he "thinks" he remembers telling Guenther this but isn't certain. He also said he was "surprised" when the LAPD announced two days after the LaBianca killings that the couple's murders were committed by different perpetrators than the ones who killed the Tate victims.

149   Bugliosi had discredited it: Bugliosi, in his words, "demolished" the false scenario by exposing its many holes. Among those he listed: If Tate and LaBianca were to be a "carbon copy" of Hinman, why weren't the words "Political Piggy" written at the Tate house, rather than just "Pig," and why were there no paw prints like the ones left at Hinman's? How did the words "Helter Skelter" on the LaBiancas' refrigerator mimic the Tate or Hinman murder scene? (Bugliosi and Gentry, *Helter Skelter,* 586–87; author interview with Vincent Bugliosi).

150   No one in law enforcement: More than two dozen investigators, from both LASO and the LAPD, didn't believe the Helter Skelter motive. Many of Bugliosi's own colleagues at the DA's office didn't, either. Among those who said this on the record were: Aaron Stovitz, Bugliosi's original coprosecutor, who told me he never believed the murders were committed for any other reason than to free Bobby Beausoleil; Burton Katz, who prosecuted two Family members (Beausoleil in his retrial for Hinman, and Grogan for the Shea murder), was certain it was a

copycat, too, saying Bugliosi used Helter Skelter because he wanted "something sexy"; and Jeff Jonas, who appeared for the state against Beausoleil and Bruce Davis at parole hearings.

150 allegedly Linda Kasabian: In my interview with him, Beausoleil denied making any such phone call; Kasabian, through her family, turned down repeated requests for an interview.

150 "Pig" in blood: Atkins Testimony, Grand Jury, A253156, *The People of the State of California v. Charles Manson, Charles Watson, aka Charles Montgomery; Susan Atkins, aka Sadie Mae Glutz; Linda Kasabian, Patricia Krenwinkel, and Leslie Sankston,* Dec. 5, 1969.

150 on the wall at Hinman's: Both Atkins and Beausoleil have taken credit for writing "Political Piggy" in Hinman's blood at his house. It's difficult to know which one actually did it (author interview with Bobby Beausoleil; Atkins testimony, Grand Jury, 69).

151 other journalists had sniffed around: Both Guenther and his partner Whiteley worked closely with Ed Sanders on his book *The Family* (their names appear in the acknowledgments). However, when I asked Sanders whether they'd ever told him about the tape and, if so, why he hadn't written about it, Sanders said he'd heard only about the phone call, not that there had been a recording of it.

151 made sure that someone else did: It's difficult to determine whether it was illegal in 1969 to tape an inmate's call in the Los Angeles County jail without his or her knowledge. Some experts told me it was legal as long as the inmates were informed of the possibility, either verbally or by posted notice. Others told me calls could be recorded only by court order.

151 magazine in June 1970: David Felton and David Dalton, "Charles Manson: The Incredible Story of the Most Dangerous Man Alive," *Rolling Stone,* June 25, 1970, 28.

152 Tate–LaBianca murders were copycat crimes: Author interview with Aaron Stovitz.

153 "I heard it, yes,": Author interview with Paul Whiteley.

153 they never even drove out there: Author interview with Guenther.

154 Reading through the transcript: Mae Brussell interview with Preston Guillory, "Assassination Dialogue," KLRB News, tape 21, side 2, Nov. 17, 1971.

154 cache of firearms: Preston Guillory testimony, *California v. Manson* (Hinman/Shea), 9557; author interview with Guillory.

154 Manson's lawlessness: Guillory testimony, *California v. Manson* (Hinman/Shea), 9585–86, 9598–99; author interview with Guillory.

154 Family toting machine guns: Paul Krassner, *Confessions of a Raving, Unconfined Nut: Misadventures in the Counter-Culture* (New York: Simon and Schuster, 1993), 203; author interview with Guillory.

154 "Make no arrests": Brussell interview with Guillory, side 1.

154 statutory rape: George Smith, County of Los Angeles Sheriff's Department, Complaint 469-0084-1071-724, S: Charles Milles Manson, April 2, 1969; William C. Gleason, Affidavit in Support of and Petition for Search Warrant, State of California, County of Los Angeles, no. 2029, Aug. 13, 1969, 4.

155 running surveillance on the Spahn Ranch: Guillory testimony, *California v. Manson* (Hinman/Shea), 9584; Brussell interview with Guillory; author interview with Guillory.

155   cover sheets to protect: Ibid. (all).

155   "was just a local thing": Brussell interview with Guillory.

155   cover its tracks after the murders: Ibid.

155   thinking the press: Ibid.; author interview with Guillory.

155   sent him packing: Given the option to "quit or be fired," Guillory chose to resign (Guillory testimony, *California v. Manson* (Hinman/Shea), 9570; author interview with Guillory).

155   discuss his previous employment there: Brussell interview with Guillory.

157   it would've cost Pitchess the next election: Pitchess, a former FBI agent, was sheriff of Los Angeles County for twenty-three years (1953–1982).

158   "the raid was more or less staged": Krassner, *Confessions*, 203.

159   "kind of an off-the-wall guy": Author interview with Gleason.

159   "a gigantic chip on his shoulder": Author interview with Robert Wachsmuth.

159   "a motel room in Malibu": Author interview with Bill McComas.

160   "Not that I know of": Author interview with John Graham.

161   Running to sixteen pages: William C. Gleason, Affidavit in Support of and Petition for Search Warrant, State of California, County of Los Angeles, no. 2029, Aug. 13, 1969.

161   "automatic pistols, and revolvers": Ibid., 1.

161   the only suspect identified by name: Manson is named nineteen times in the document, beginning on the first page.

163   "from a tree, upside down, dead.": Richard W. Pearson, Captain/Commander, Malibu Station, to John P. Knox, Chief, Patrol Division West, LASO, "Spahn Ranch Summary," Aug. 11, 1969, 5.

163   "a large amount of narcotics": Gleason, Sergeant, Motorcycle File, to James C. White, Captain, Records and Data Bureau, LASO, "Additional Information Regarding Narcotics Activity at Spahn Movie Ranch in Chatsworth," Aug. 7, 1969, 1.

163   one-page arrest report: P. R. George, Supplementary Report, File 469-02614-1071-029, S: Charles Milles Manson, Aug. 16, 1969.

164   a warrant is good for ten days: Section 1534(a) of the California Penal Code reads: "A search warrant shall be executed and returned within 10 days after date of issuance."

164   because of insufficient evidence: Sanders, *The Family,* 268.

165   never caught attempting to use the cards: According to Manson's arrest report (P. R. George, Supplementary Report), the four cards—each for a different gasoline company—belonged to Irvin H. Weiland, M.D., of Encino, whom I located and spoke to. Dr. Weiland told me the cards had been in his wallet, which was stolen from the glove compartment of his car. He didn't remember whether they had ever been used, but, as several retired LASO officials told me, the possession of stolen goods itself is a crime.

166   On a bedside table were several joints: Unless otherwise noted, the information about this arrest is from the Manson and Schram arrest reports (R. Wachsmuth, Complaint Report, Charles Milles Manson, Carol Matthews [Schram], File 469-02723-1071-181, Aug. 24, 1969); a transcript of a sheriff's interview with Schram and her parents ("Statement of Stephanie Schram," and parents, File 069-02378-1076-036, by Dep. George A. Palmer and Sgt. William Gleason, LASO, Dec. 4,

1969); and an interview with Robert Wachsmuth, the sheriff's deputy who made the arrests.

166 no pot in the cigarettes: Sanders, *The Family,* 269.

166 on August 26: Charles Milles Manson, Supplementary Report, LASO, File 469-07223-1071-181, by V. W. Jones, Aug. 27, 1969.

166 No reason was given for the decision: Statement of Stephanie Schram, 29. In the statement, Schram's mother rebukes Gleason and Palmer, saying that her daughter is now on probation for "possession of marijuana...and it's on her record, but *he* [Manson] was just set free!" Mrs. Schram adds, "He was violating federal parole [and] they let him loose!"

166 found with drugs and a juvenile: Manson, Supplementary Report.

167 never even bothered going to arrest him: This is my assumption based on the fact that I was unable to find any documentary evidence indicating that it had been done.

167 he moved to Death Valley: The September 10 date is an estimate based on police interviews of Family members, trial testimonies, and witness reports.

167 The DA's order rejecting the pot charges: Manson, Supplementary Report.

167 The LASO deputies who'd arrested Manson: Author interview with Paul George.

167 "ample reason for a parole revocation": Bugliosi and Gentry, *Helter Skelter,* 546.

168 Gleason's duty to have told the parole office: Author interview with Guenther.

168 Kitty Lutesinger, sixteen, was pregnant: Kathern [*sic*] Rene Lutesinger, AKA Kitty, LASO "Wanted for Questioning—Murder," by Guenther and Whiteley, Aug. 17, 1969.

168 to be with Beausoleil: Lutesinger testimony, *California v. Beausoleil (I),* 26.

168 leave the group and raise their child: Bugliosi and Gentry, *Helter Skelter,* 115.

168 heaping abuse on anyone: Lutesinger, Arrest Report, LASO, DR-156-774, by Officer Peterson, Sgt. Bell, July 30, 1969, 2.

169 ran away from the ranch: Ibid.

169 LASO sheriffs found her on July 30: Ibid., 2–3; "Additional Information Regarding Spahn Movie Ranch, and the Stolen Vehicle Activity at That Location," LASO Correspondence, Gleason to James C. White, Capt., Aug. 11, 1969, 3–5.

169 interview her again eleven days later: Ibid., 3.

169 "I had been programmed to believe": Sanders, *The Family,* 259.

170 On August 15: [Unsigned] Lutesinger, "Sheriff's interview at San Dimas Station on 10/12/69," 1–2.

170 they never checked the Spahn Ranch: Author interview with Guenther.

170 all-points bulletin: [Unsigned memo], "Hinman, Tate, et. al [sic], LaBianca Murder Cases," 2. The teletype that went out after the radio broadcast was dated August 17 (Lutesinger "Wanted for Questioning").

170 Whiteley's interview notes in the LASO files: Paul Whiteley, Case 069-02378-1076-06, July 31, 1969.

170 though they didn't know where: Whiteley notebook in ibid.

170 She'd been picked up: Katherine Lynn Drake, LASO Booking and Property Report, File 469-02614-1071-029, Booking 892 975, Aug. 19, 1969.

170 posted the bulletin for Lutesinger's arrest: Lutesinger "Wanted for Questioning."

170 living at the Spahn Ranch: Whiteley notebook. The "Wanted for Questioning" bulletin lists "Spawn [sic] Ranch, Malibu," as one of Lutesinger's "possible addresses."

170 They did nothing: Author interview with Guenther.

170 at the Malibu station: They were released without charges on Monday, August 18, 1969.

171 a few stray LAPD squad cars: I confirmed this in other reports in the LASO file as well as in interviews with LASO deputies who participated in the raid, but I was never able to identify the LAPD officers.

171 beside a story about the still unsolved Tate murders: Bugliosi and Gentry, *Helter Skelter*, 89–90.

171 "Whitely [*sic*] & Guenther tell Gleason": Gleason timeline, Oct. 29, 1969.

171 Lutesinger herself had told him: "Additional Information Regarding Spahn Movie Ranch," 4.

171 true identities of each suspect: Teletype to Malibu Station, SBI and IRC, "Make Following Corrections as to AKA's", refer: Gleason, Aug. 18, 1969.

172 when they all moved to Death Valley: Vincent Bugliosi interview with Kitty Lutesinger, undated, Los Angeles District Attorney files, 1.

173 "had his finger in a bigger pie": Author interview with Gil Parra.

173 "ratting out other people": Ibid.

174 Manson's fear of the Black Panthers: Gleason, Search Warrant, 6.

174 "carloads" of "negroes": Pearson to Knox, "Spahn Ranch Summary," 13.

174 A fire patrolman reported: Ibid., 2.

176 "offer the sheriff department's cooperation": Author interview with James C. White.

176 I arrived to find not one but three deputies: Author interview with Captain Raymond Peavy, Lt. Joe Hartshorne, and Det. Paul Delhauer.

180 "Your actions embarrass": Matt Stevens, "Ex–Los Angeles Sheriff Lee Baca Is Sentenced to 3 Years in Prison," *New York Times,* May 12, 2017.

6. Who Was Reeve Whitson?

185 before the Polanskis' maid had arrived: Police estimated she arrived at the front gate at approximately 8:30 a.m. (LAPD First Homicide Investigation Progress Report, DR 69-059-593, 15).

185 It appeared four times: Hatami testimony, *California v. Charles Manson, Susan Atkins, Leslie Van Houten and Patricia Krenwinkel,* case #22239, 14483, 14508, 14542, 14554.

187 "Just Reeve Whitson, myself, and Mr. Hatami": *California v. Manson et al.*, 14554.

187 The judge decided that Hatami: Judge Older refused to allow Hatami to make a physical identification of Manson in court because of his uncertainty over who he saw that day. He permitted him only to testify that the person *resembled* the defendant (ibid., 14566–67).

188 "about eight lives simultaneously": Author interview with William Whitson (who is unrelated to Reeve Whitson).

191 The coroner described blood smears: First Homicide Investigation Progress Report (4–5) reads: "There was dried blood smeared over the entire body. It appeared to investigating officers that someone had handled the victim, as in moving her from one location to another and the blood from the wounds had been smeared over the body in the process."

191 heard gunshots and arguing: First Homicide Investigation Progress Report, 19–21. Bugliosi described two incidents of sounds heard after the killers were supposed to have left the property in his book but omitted two more reports of

shouting and gunfire that occurred hours after the murders—one from a second private security officer on patrol in the vicinity; see Vincent Bugliosi with Curt Gentry, *Helter Skelter* (New York: Norton, 1994), 20–21.

191 "see what my children did": Ed Sanders, *The Family*, 3rd ed. (New York: Thunder's Mouth, 2002), 220.

191 another researcher had raised the possibility: Bill Nelson videotaped interview with Vincent Bugliosi, in author's possession.

192 a traveling family act: Author interview with Hope Hirschman.

192 "His great strength": Author interview with William Whitson.

192 According to a few people I spoke with: Author interview with the Edlunds; author interview with Rosenfelt; author interview with Julie Newmar.

195 how many powerful friends he had: Among other Whitson friends I spoke to were Leon Uris (author of *Exodus*), John Raitt (actor-singer), and Art Linkletter (the television entertainer, who told me Whitson was "a spook").

197 "He always wanted to go": Author interview with Baron Oswald von Richthofen.

197 "neither confirm nor deny": Whitson, CIA FOIA response, no. 2000-01269, June 23, 2000.

197 unpublished book: Robert Helder and Paul Tate, *Five Down on Cielo Drive* (unpublished manuscript; Talmy Enterprises, Inc., 1993).

198 They secured a contract: Author interview with Roger LaJeunesse; author interview with Shel Talmy.

198 a ghostwriter came on board: Author interview with LaJeunesse; author interview with Stanley Ralph Ross.

198 "appeared to be running the LAPD": Author interview with Charles Guenther.

198 growing a beard and long hair: Helder and Tate, *Five Down*, 72.

198 "a somewhat shady character": Ibid., 22.

199 "He sure did get around": Ibid., 27.

199 especially those in Mama Cass's circle: Ibid., 28.

199 "an amateur sleuth on the case": Ibid., 138.

199 "Mr. Anonymous": Ibid., 60.

200 was eligible for parole: Associated Press, "Doris Tate, Victims' Rights Activist, 68," *New York Times*, July 1, 1992.

200 something deeper than Helter Skelter: Author interview with Ed Sanders; Sanders, *The Family*, 512; author interview with Judy Hanson.

200 Cielo house was under surveillance: Author interview with Sanders; author interview with Hanson.

201 her daughter wasn't supposed: Ibid. Hanson, a private investigator and close friend of Doris and Paul Tate, also told me that Doris "confirmed" to her that a call had been made from the Spahn Ranch to Cielo Drive a few hours before the murders. In *Helter Skelter*, however, Bugliosi maintained that records for the Spahn Ranch pay phone from April to October 1969 didn't show any calls to the Tate house (the months of April and July were "lost or destroyed," he added). See Bugliosi and Gentry, *Helter Skelter*, 333.

201 Sharon's red Ferrari: Author interview with Sanders; Sanders, *The Family*, 512; author interview with Hanson.

201 book about her theories: Author interview with Debra Tate; author interview with Greg King.

201 separate parts of their house: Author interviews with sources who requested anonymity.

202 "knew just about everyone": Helder and Tate, *Five Down,* 23.

203 who surveilled Baron for decades: Peter Dale Scott, *Deep Politics and the Death of JFK* (Berkeley: University of California Press, 1993), 199.

203 "could be more dangerous": I. F. Stone, "LeMay: Cave Man in a Jet Bomber," in *In a Time of Torment, 1961–1967* (Boston: Little, Brown, 1989), 104.

203 vice president of a missile-parts manufacturer: LeMay was hired by Networks Electronic in 1965. The high-security facility, which had a contract with the Defense Department, was located in Chatsworth, California, less than five miles from the Spahn Ranch. The company's founder and president, Mihai Patrichi, was a former Romanian army general who was a member of the Iron Guard, a far-right political group in Romania ("General Radescu's Relations with the Iron Guardists in Argentina," Nov. 24, 1948, declassified document in National Archives, College Park, Md.; Alan Goldstein, "Patrichi Is the Main Power at Explosives-Maker Networks Electronic," *Los Angeles Times,* May 29, 1986).

204 United Nations listed Otto Skorzeny: Glenn B. Infield, *Skorzeny: Hitler's Commando* (New York: St. Martin's, 1981), 160.

204 one of Hitler's most trusted operatives: Charles Higham, *American Swastika: The Shocking Story of Nazi Collaborators in Our Midst from 1933 to the Present Day* (New York: Doubleday, 1985), 244; Martin A. Lee, *The Beast Reawakens* (Boston: Little, Brown, 1997), 4–18.

204 new lives around the world: Infield, *Skorzeny,* 235.

204 "the most dangerous man in Europe": Ibid. See also Lee, *The Beast Awakens,* 6.

204 once a member of the Hitler Youth: Skorzeny, Intelligence Report, Museum of Intolerance, Los Angeles, Calif., 1951.

204 contracts for German engineering companies: Skorzeny, Defense Intelligence Agency Report, Sept. 12, 1962. Ilse was the niece of Hjalmar Schacht, Hitler's finance minister (he was tried at Nuremberg, and acquitted); see Infield, *Skorzeny,* 171.

204 "American system from within": Author interview with von Richthofen.

204 "we should kill the drug lords": Ibid.

205 "The entire Manson situation": Author interview with Andreas Gross.

205 His résumé…racing enthusiast: The projects described in this paragraph come from author interviews with the Edlunds; Neil Cummings; Gross; von Richthofen; McGann; Clyde Whitson; Art Linkletter; William Whitson; Robert Whitson; James Paul; Shelly Wile; Alastair Buchan; Louise Batchelor; Gloria Krachmalnick; Hope Hirschman; Will Layman; Carroll Shelby; Dan Gurney; and Maurice Phillips.

205 he stowed it in his freezer: Author interview with William Whitson; author interview with Clyde Whitson; author interview with the Edlunds.

205 "on a cot in his parents' kitchen": Author interview with Simone Zorn Hunt.

205 drove an economical Ford Pinto: Author interview with von Richthofen.

205 destitute and disgruntled: Author interview with the Edlunds; author interview with Robert Whitson.

205 "You really are a pawn": Author interview with Robert Whitson.

205 "You didn't even exist to us": Ibid.

206 a rat dropped in the tube: Ibid.

206 half a million dollars: Author interview with Rosenfelt.

206 may have been foul play: Author interview with Clyde Whitson; author interview with the Edlunds.

206 "an extraterrestrial": Author interview with William Whitson.

207 "no open or officially acknowledged relationship": Whitson, CIA FOIA 2000-01269, reply, May 21, 2003.

7. Neutralizing the Left

In June 2002, the *San Francisco Chronicle* published an award-winning series of investigative articles about the rise of the Free Speech movement at Berkeley and the attendant crackdown by Governor Ronald Reagan, the CIA, and the FBI. Using information from files won in three Freedom of Information lawsuits against the FBI, the reporter Seth Rosenfeld's six-story series exposed the previously unreported lengths that Reagan, the FBI Director J. Edgar Hoover, and the CIA Director John McCone went to in order to dismantle and smear the leaders of the left-wing movement in California. Much of the information in this chapter is from Rosenfeld's series, later expanded into a book, *The FBI's War on Student Radicals, and Reagan's Rise to Power* (New York: Farrar Straus Giroux, 2012). I also relied heavily on the published reports of the Rockefeller Commission and Church Committee (*The President's Commission on CIA Activities Within the United States* [Washington, D.C.: GPO, 1975]; hereinafter, the Rockefeller Commission); and *The United States Senate Select Committee to Study Governmental Operations with Respect to Intelligence Activities* [Washington, D.C.: GPO, 1976]; hereinafter, the Church Committee), as well as the reporting of Seymour Hersh in the *New York Times* and Ward Churchill and Jim Vander Wall's indispensable *The COINTELPRO Papers: Documents from the FBI's Secret Wars Against Domestic Dissent* (Boston: South End Press, 1990).

209 three congressional committees: These were the aforementioned Rockefeller Commission and Church Committee, as well as *The United States House Permanent Select Committee on Intelligence* (referred to as the Pike Committee, and active in 1975–1976).

210 "No more appeasement": Todd Gitlin, *The Sixties: Years of Hope, Days of Rage* (New York: Random House, 1987), 415.

211 respective operations in San Francisco: Seymour Hersh, "Hunt Tells of Early Work for a C.I.A. Domestic Unit," *New York Times,* Dec. 31, 1974, A-1, 4.

212 "in the heart of every longhair": Gitlin, *The Sixties,* 404.

212 First launched in 1956 to "increase factionalism": Carl J. Jensen III, David H. McElreath, and Melissa Graves, *Introduction to Intelligence Studies* (Boca Raton, Fla.: CRC Press, 2012), 34.

212 "to expose, disrupt, misdirect": Quoted in Churchill and Vander Wall, *COINTELPRO Papers,* 92–93.

213 "their potential for violence": Quoted in Alexander Cockburn and Jeffrey St. Clair, *Whiteout: The CIA, Drugs and the Press* (London: Verso, 1999), 69.

213 tripped on acid: Martin A. Lee and Bruce Shlain, *Acid Dreams: The CIA, LSD, and the Sixties Rebellion* (New York: Grove Weidenfeld, 1985), 223.

213　arrange for the bloodshed themselves: Jack Olson, *Last Man Standing: The Tragedy and Triumph of Geronimo Pratt* (New York: Doubleday, 2000), 45.

213　"power to determine the destiny": Stephen Shames and Bobby Seale, *Power to the People: The World of the Black Panthers* (New York: Abrams, 2016), 12.

214　Newton shot and killed: Newton was convicted of voluntary manslaughter in 1968 and sentenced to two to fifteen years in prison. An appellate court decision later reversed the conviction.

214　a seventeen-year-old Panther was killed: While awaiting trial on attempted murder charges, Cleaver fled to Cuba. He returned from foreign exile in 1978 and pleaded guilty to a lesser charge in exchange for a sentence of 1,200 hours of community service.

214　gunfights led to four Panther deaths: Three were killed by the LAPD on August 5, 1968, and one on October 5, 1968. See Edward Jay Epstein, "The Black Panthers and the Police: A Pattern of Genocide?," *The New Yorker*, Feb. 13, 1971.

214　suspected of being a snitch: Paul Bass and Douglas W. Rae, *Murder in the Model City: The Black Panthers, Yale, and the Redemption of a Killer* (New York: Basic Books, 2009), 20–34.

214　a "hate-type organization": James E. McKeown and Frederick Inglebrit Tietze, *The Changing Metropolis* (Boston: Houghton Mifflin, 1971), 86.

214　the personal bodyguard for Fred Hampton: Much has been written about the murder of Fred Hampton, but nothing as thorough as Jeffrey Haas's *The Assassination of Fred Hampton: How the FBI and the Chicago Police Murdered a Black Panther* (Chicago: Chicago Review Press, 2011), from which most of the information about Hampton has been taken.

215　a small FBI field office in Media: Betty Medsger, *The Burglary: The Discovery of J. Edgar Hoover's Secret F.B.I.* (New York: Knopf, 2014).

215　only in 2014 did they reveal themselves: Ibid.

215　"hastened the growth of a vine": James Bovard, *Terrorism and Tyranny: Trampling Freedom, Justice, and Peace to Rid the World of Evil* (New York: St. Martin's, 2015), 187.

216　"injury or death to targets": Associated Press, "Black Panthers Affected," *New York Times*, May 6, 1976.

216　"a staggering range of targets": Church Committee, book 3, *COINTELPRO: The FBI's Covert Action Programs Against American Citizens,* April 23, 1976, 19, 11, 15.

216　exploits in Los Angeles: Ibid., 35, 58, 64, 67.

217　Black Student Union meeting: Olson, *Last Man Standing,* 223–24.

217　"The Los Angeles Division": Church Committee, 3:189.

218　"the bloodshed that occurred": Ibid.

218　"carnage as a positive development": Ibid., 3:192.

218　flirting with other women: Ibid., 3:158; Richard Gid Powers, *Broken: The Troubled Past and Uncertain Future of the FBI* (New York: Simon and Schuster, 2004), 246.

218　"a fraud, demagogue, and scoundrel": William C. Sullivan to Alan H. Belmont, Jan. 8, 1964, FOIA no. 77-56944-19; Church Committee, 3:136.

218　"Will it get us what we want?": Church Committee, 3:135.

219 "responsibilities to the American people": Statement of Clarence M. Kelley, Director, Federal Bureau of Investigation, *Cong. Rec.,* House of Representatives, Feb. 4, 1975, 2247.

219 "simply because they are Negroes": Joshua Bloom, Waldo E. Martin Jr., and Waldo E. Martin, *Black Against Empire: The History and Politics of the Black Panther Party* (Berkeley: University of California Press, 2015), 202.

219 Hollywood's liberal whites: [Redacted name], Field Agent, SAC, Los Angeles, to, Director, FBI, Nov. 29, 1968, quoted in Churchill and Vander Wall, *COINTELPRO Papers,* 132.

219 reportedly under FBI surveillance: For Jane Fonda, see ibid., 159, 212, 214; Church Committee, 3:209. For Cass Elliot, see FBI File 62-5-38112, cited in Jon Johnson, *Make Your Own Kind of Music: A Career Retrospective of Cass Elliot* (Detroit: Music Archives Press, 1987), 99–124. For Warren Beatty, see Paul Young, *L.A. Exposed: Strange Myths and Curious Legends in the City of Angels* (New York: St. Martin's Griffin, 2002), 34.

219 outspoken civil rights activist: LAPD First Homicide Investigation Progress Report, DR 69-059-593, 27. It reads, "In the past year, Abigail had been an active participant in Negro social work. She sponsored and attended rallies in the Watts area and is reported to have been an active participant in civil rights activities in the San Francisco bay area. This contention is borne out by several civil rights placards found at the Cielo address."

220 "The Peace and Freedom Party": Churchill and Vander Wall, *COINTELPRO Papers,* 132.

220 the framing of Gerard "Geronimo" Pratt: The information in this section is from Jack Olson's *Last Man Standing,* unless otherwise noted.

221 "the arrest of the militants": Ibid., 231.

221 "to serve the white man": Vincent Bugliosi with Curt Gentry, *Helter Skelter* (New York: Norton, 1994), 303.

221 "go pick the cotton": Ibid., 330.

221 planning an attack on him: William C. Gleason, Affidavit in Support of and Petition for Search Warrant, State of California, County of Los Angeles, no. 2029, Aug. 13, 1969, 6.

222 with powerful telescopes: Ibid.; Bugliosi and Gentry, *Helter Skelter,* 344.

222 Bernard "Lotsapoppa" Crowe: Bugliosi and Gentry, *Helter Skelter,* 372–73 (all Crowe information is taken from *Helter Skelter,* unless otherwise indicated).

222 "speed along the race war": Author interview with Vincent Bugliosi.

222 Manson was already frightened: Bugliosi maintained that Manson began warning of an impending race war in February 1969 (*Helter Skelter,* 329).

223 three more Panthers, one of them fatal: Olson, *Last Man Standing,* 225.

223 infiltrate "subversive" groups and then "neutralize" them: Seymour Hersh, "Huge C.I.A. Operation Reported in U.S. Against Antiwar Forces, Other Dissidents in Nixon Years, *New York Times,* Dec. 22, 1974, 1, 26; Charles J. V. Murphy, "Assassination Plot That Failed," *Time,* v. 105, Jun. 30, 1975, 28.

223 born of Lyndon Johnson's neurosis: Unless otherwise indicated, all the information in this section is taken from the Seth Rosenfeld 2002 investigative series, mentioned in the headnote to this chapter's notes, or directly from the Rockefeller Commission.

224 "bigger than My Lai": William Egan Colby and Peter Forbath, *Honorable Men: My Life in the CIA* (New York: Simon and Schuster, 1978), 15.

224 Angleton resigned from the agency: Tim Weiner, *Legacy of Ashes: The History of the CIA* (New York: Anchor, 2007), 389.

224 he ordered the destruction: Ibid., 375.

224 Rockefeller, had worked with the CIA: Tad Szulc, "Why Rockefeller Tried to Cover Up the CIA Probe," *New York*, Sept. 5, 1977. Szulc called the commission's investigation "the most blatant cover-up since Watergate," reporting that Vice President Rockefeller argued that "for national security reasons, it was not necessary for his commission to be told 'everything.'"

225 Gerald Ford fired him: Seymour Hersh, "Colby Says His Dismissal as CIA Chief Arose from His Cooperation in Domestic Spying Activities," *New York Times*, Mar. 14, 1978, 12.

225 "very much on its periphery": Colby and Forbath, *Honorable Men*, 317.

225 the *New York Times* revealed: Seymour Hersh, "CIA Reportedly Recruited Blacks for Surveillance of Panther Party," *New York Times*, Mar. 17, 1978, A-1, 16.

226 A longtime lieutenant with the LAPD: Herrmann retired on August 29, 1968, with the rank of lieutenant, according to my interview with a Public Information Officer in the LAPD Pensions and Retirement Office.

226 he specialized in quelling insurgencies: William Drummond, "State Intelligence System: Stigma of a 'Big Brother,'" *Los Angeles Times*, Mar. 18, 1970.

226 predict violent outbreaks in cities: Charles Foley, "Reagan's Plan to 'Beat Revolution,'" *The Observer* (London), May 17, 1970, 2.

226 "genius," praising his technical aptitude: Daryl F. Gates with Diane K. Shah, *Chief: My Life in the LAPD* (New York: Bantam, 1992), 163.

226 yielded a collection of redacted documents: Eighty-three pages were released by the Washington, D.C., office of the FBI (FOIPA no. 0966502); a second request to the Los Angeles Field Office produced an additional thirty-eight pages (FOIPA no. 190-231795). Many of the redactions are preceded or followed by phrases like "project which was very sensitive in nature" or "Top Secret (The D.O.D. [Department of Defense] Clearances are still active)." One report revealed that Herrmann's work for the White House Office of Science and Technology (at unspecified dates in the 1960s) was "so sensitive in nature" that the White House "was unable to provide any further information"—and the information that *was* provided to the FBI was then redacted by the agency. Other records revealed that Herrmann received his first "secret clearance" from the federal government on February 7, 1957. That was elevated to a "top secret security clearance" on April 16, 1965, by the Office of Security, Treasury Department (FOIPA no. 0966502).

227 the company claimed that Herrmann never: FOIPA no. 0966502, July 21, 1972, 10.

227 "neither confirm or deny": CIA F-2002, 02097, March 7, 2003. I also received the same response from the CIA for records of the Systems Development Corporation (Systems Development Corporation, CIA FOIA F-2002-01413, Feb. 10, 2003: "Neither confirm nor deny any confidential or covert relationship . . ."), where, according to an article in the *Honolulu Advertiser* ("University Post Seen for Herrmann," Mar. 26, 1971), Herrmann was "responsible for research, development and related activities connected with public order, counterinsurgency and security systems" between 1967 and 1971.

227 training Thai police: FBI FOIPA no. 0966502; "University Post Seen for Herrmann"; CORDS Historical Working Group Files, NARA (National Archives), 1967–73, box 25, Folder—Pacification Task Force/General Correspondence, ARPA, DAHC04-69-C-0010.

227 a scientific "advisor" to the army: CORDS Historical Working Group Files.

227 CIA project called Phoenix: Unless otherwise indicated, the information in this section is from Douglas Valentine, *The Phoenix Program* (New York: William Morrow, 1990).

227 "a set of programs": Colonel Andrew R. Finlayson, USMC (Ret.), "A Retrospective on Counterinsurgency Operations: The Tay Ninh Provincial Reconnaissance Unit and Its Role in the Phoenix Program, 1969–70," Central Intelligence Agency, Library (accessed via CIA website).

228 a 1971 congressional investigation: Cong. Rec., Proceedings and Debates; Congress, vol. 117, pt. 4 (Washington, D.C.: GPO, 1971), 4240–49.

228 the atrocities were the work of the Viet Cong: Ibid.

228 "They wanted me to take charge": Anthony B. Herbert, *Herbert: The Making of a Soldier* (New York: Hippocrene, 1982).

228 "The good guys": John Pilger, *Heroes* (Boston: South End Press, 2001), 258.

228 prisoners were shot and their bodies burned: Cockburn and St. Clair, *Whiteout,* 210.

228 later revealed as a CIA front: Seymour Hersh, *Cover-up: The Army's Secret Investigation of the Massacre at My Lai 4* (New York: Random House, 1972). Wrote Hersh, "By 1968, Phoenix Committees were set up in each of South Vietnam's 44 provinces and directed by an agent from the CIA, who sometimes operated under cover as an employee of the Agency for International Development (AID)."

229 he was a part of AID: CORDS Historical Working Group Files. In addition, Herrmann told two interviewers that he went to Thailand for AID in 1967: see James Wrightson, "Computer Replaces Spy-in-Street for Antiriot Sleuthing," *Sacramento Bee*, Aug. 2, 1970, and "University Post Seen for Herrmann."

229 nicknamed "Blowtorch Bob": Tim Weiner, "Robert Komer, 78, Figure in Vietnam, Dies," *New York Times*, April 12, 2000.

229 behind the program's notorious kill quotas: Valentine, *Phoenix Program,* 98.

230 series of "research" gigs: FOIPA no. 0966502; FOIPA no. 190-231795.

230 to prevent future outbreaks of violence: Ibid. (both); "University Post Seen for Herrmann."

230 the task force was hardly: Foley, "Reagan's Plan to 'Beat Revolution.'" (All the information in this section is taken from this article, unless otherwise indicated.)

231 depicting him as a pig: "Big Pig on Campus" (SDS document), collection of Cindy Hancock.

231 more circumspect interview: "Computer Replaces Spy-in-Street for Antiriot Sleuthing."

232 the CIA had "operatives": Gaeton Fonzi, *The Last Investigation* (New York: Thunder's Mouth, 1993), 239. Fonzi, an investigator for the House Select Committee on Assassinations (which in 1978 examined the assassinations of John F. Kennedy, Martin Luther King Jr., and Robert F. Kennedy), reported that the committee discovered a CIA operative had also infiltrated New Orleans DA Jim Garrison's 1966 investigation and prosecution of Clay Shaw, an alleged CIA operative, for the John F. Kennedy assassination. In her *Farewell to Justice: Jim Garrison, JFK's Assassination, and the Case That Should Have Changed History*

(Dulles, Va.: Potomac Books, 2007), Joan Mellen alleges that two Garrison investigators, William Martin and William C. Wood, were secretly contracted by the CIA to "sabotage" his prosecution.

232 "one of the top agents": R. Harris Smith, *OSS: The Secret History of America's First Central Intelligence Agency* (Berkeley: University of California Press, 1972), 18.

232 the Office of Strategic Services: Ibid., 18; Office of Strategic Services, Declassified Files, Record Group no. 226, National Archives, College Park, Md.

232 Trained in espionage and counterintelligence techniques: Office of Strategic Services, Declassified Files (multiple files); Steven Edington interview with Evelle Younger, "Evelle J. Younger: A Lifetime in Law Enforcement," Oral History Program, Powell Library, University of California, Los Angeles, 1982, 6–7.

232 becoming Los Angeles district attorney in 1964: John Balzar, "FBI: Ex-Atty. Gen. Evelle Younger Is Dead at 70," *Los Angeles Times*, May 5, 1989.

232 a friend of Governor Reagan: Ibid.; "Evelle J. Younger: A Lifetime," 7–10.

232 internal threats to the nation's security: "Evelle J. Younger: A Lifetime," 15–16, 17.

232 "better training and equipment": Steve Weissman, ed., *Big Brother and the Holding Company: The World Behind Watergate* (Palo Alto, Calif.: Ramparts, 1974), 29.

232 "the General": Balzar, "FBI: Ex-Atty. Gen."

233 absence of a black studies program: Ron Einstoss, "20 Found Guilty in Disturbances at Valley State," *Los Angeles Times*, Nov. 19, 1969.

233 deputy DA who tried the case: Ibid.

233 Nor did his second in command: All the Compton information is from Lynn "Buck" Compton with Marcus Brotherton, *Call of Duty: My Life Before During, and After the Band of Brothers* (New York: Berkley Caliber, 2008) or from author interview with Lynn Compton. Compton also was an advisor to Herrmann's Riots and Disorders Task Force, according to "California Council on Criminal Justice Records, 1968–74," F3869, California State Archives, Sacramento, Feb. 7, 1969.

233 role was "nonoperational": "Computer Replaces Spy-in-Street for Antiriot Sleuthing."

234 next to a piece on the LAPD's theory: Ron Einstoss, "Panther Killings Result of Power Play, Jury Told," *Los Angeles Times*, Aug. 12, 1969; Lee Dye, "Police See 'Copycat Killer' in Slaying of Los Feliz Couple," *Los Angeles Times*, Aug. 12, 1969.

8. The Lawyer Swap

237 ordered all three sets of slaughters: Stephen Kay, who joined the prosecution after the trial began, said as far as he knew there was never any thought to try the cases together, but he would've done it. "When you're trying a conspiracy, you want as many cases as possible," he explained. Hinman's murder was also further "proof" of the Helter Skelter motive, Kay added; Manson wanted Hinman's money to get the Family to the desert during "the race war."

238 a closed meeting with the judge: Bugliosi omits this episode from his book, mentioning only that the first Beausoleil trial ended in a hung jury because DeCarlo, "brought in at the last minute...hadn't been a convincing witness" (Vincent Bugliosi with Curt Gentry, *Helter Skelter* [New York: Norton, 1994], 206–7). My account of the Beausoleil prosecution relies on interviews with Leon Salter and Ron Ross, the opposing attorneys, the trial transcript, and Jerry LeBlanc and Ivor Davis's *5 to Die*, which has the best rendering of the first Beausoleil trial (Los Angeles: Holloway House, 1970).

239 already a convicted felon: *United States v. DeCarlo et al.,* no. 37502-SD-Criminal, U.S. District Court, Southern District, March 28–June 30, 1967.

239 facing new charges: DeCarlo, Case A058069, Los Angeles Superior Court Archives.

240 "a long sword": DeCarlo testimony, *California v. Robert Beausoleil* (I), A-057452.

243 their daughter was in custody...Atkins agreed to speak: Guenther and Whiteley, LASO Supplementary Report, File 069-02378-1076-016, Arrested: Lutesinger, Atkins, Oct. 13, 1969.

243 her role in the Tate–LaBianca murders: Bugliosi and Gentry, *Helter Skelter,* 117–30.

243 "warm and sticky and nice": Ibid., 126.

244 On the evening of November 19: The information in this passage comes from ibid., 172–73.

245 Atkins's attorney was Gerald Condon: The account that follows is based on documents discovered in the files of the Los Angeles Sheriff's Office; the Los Angeles Superior Court Archives; the Los Angeles District Attorney's office; the personal files of Paul LePage, the LAPD detective who supervised the LaBianca murder investigation (shared by his son, Paul LePage Jr.); the files of Mike McGann, the LAPD detective who worked the Tate investigation; as well as from interviews with Gerald Condon, F. Milton Condon (his brother, who assisted Gerald), and others, as noted.

245 Beausoleil...was already represented: This public defender was Leon Salter.

245 Condon was appointed on November 12: Susan Atkins, County of Los Angeles Sheriff's Department, Supplementary Report, Nov. 12, 1969.

245 seven-page memo: "Hinman, Tate, et. [sic] al., LaBianca murder cases," LASO Files. This document is undated and unsigned.

245 entry for November 20: Ibid., 4.

246 a three-page summary: Paul LePage, "Chronology of Information on the LaBianca/Tate Murder Investigation," Oct. 15–Nov. 31, 1969.

246 minutes of Atkins's November 26 arraignment: *California v. Atkins,* Case no. A058031, Los Angeles Superior Court Archives, Nov. 26, 1969.

247 produced no results: Mary Hearn, Director of Public Information, Los Angeles Superior Court, told me this.

247 worked there himself for eight years: Dial Torgerson and Ron Einstoss, "Jury Hears Tate Case Girl Today, *Los Angeles Times,* Dec. 5, 1969.

247 close with his former colleagues: *California v. Charles Manson, Susan Atkins, Leslie Van Houten and Patricia Krenwinkel,* case 22239, 25063. Caballero acknowledged that—like his law partner who assisted him in the case, Paul Caruso—he was a member of the "EJY Club," a steering committee of citizens dedicated to electing DA Evelle J. Younger as attorney general of California in 1970. The club was disbanded after Younger's opponent charged that its members received favors from Younger in exchange for donations.

248 Police Chief Edward Davis: "3 from Bay Commune Named in Tate Slaying," Santa Monica [Calif.] *Evening Outlook,* Dec. 1, 1969, 1.

248 well-known mob lawyer: Jeanie Kasindorf, "The Case Against Evelle Younger," *New West Magazine,* Oct. 23, 1978. This eight-page cover story alleged that DA Younger protected organized crime figures through the help of friends like

Caruso. The story focused on a notorious 1967 case involving Caruso's representation of Maurice Friedman, a mobster, who, with Johnny Rosselli—Charles Baron's associate—was tried for fixing card games at the Hollywood Friars Club.

248 she'd been "at the scene": All the quotes in this paragraph from an unbylined front-page story, "8 Women, 2 Men Held in Tate Killings," Santa Monica *Evening Outlook*, Dec. 2, 1969, 1.

248 Atkins had accepted their deal: Bugliosi and Gentry, *Helter Skelter,* 223.

249 Manson's dictatorial methods: Charles Hillinger and Dial Torgerson, "Revenge Claimed: Grudge Against Doris Day Son Linked to Slaying in Tate Case; Deaths Were Ordered, Suspect Says," *Los Angeles Times,* Dec. 3, 1969, 1.

249 "to a snack from the icebox": "Attorney for Girl Member of Cult Tells Her Version," Santa Monica *Evening Outlook*, Dec. 3, 1969, 1.

249 a four-day fusillade of specificity: Associated Press, "Attorneys Accuse Hippies in Sharon Tate's Murder," Dec. 4, 1969.

249 the president of the Los Angeles County Bar: Marilyn Elias, "Bar Chief Scores Atkins Attorney over Tate Comments," Santa Monica *Evening Outlook,* Dec. 5, 1969, 1.

249 "might save her from the gas chamber": Torgerson and Einstoss, "Jury Hears Tate Case Girl Today."

249 Bugliosi described it as "excellent": Bugliosi and Gentry, *Helter Skelter,* 232.

249 nothing was ever formalized or signed: When pressed by Kanarek about not having a signed agreement, Caballero said, the "common practice is such that these agreements aren't written down. It is just normally not done. These people are lawyers, professional people. You make an agreement and you keep it" (Caballero testimony, *California v. Manson et al.,* 25803). Kanarek made sure to point out that Linda Kasabian's attorneys had received a fully executed contract for her deal with the prosecution.

250 "Do the French drink wine?": Lawrence Schiller, *The Killing of Sharon Tate* (New York: Signet, 1969), 63.

250 unstable witness and a murderer: Bugliosi and Gentry, *Helter Skelter,* 234.

250 "unusual" but "not unprecedented": Ibid., 221.

250 Atkins spoke on tape: Ibid., 229–30.

250 that she didn't kill Sharon Tate: Atkins testimony, Los Angeles Grand Jury, Dec. 5, 1969, 66.

251 *consider* not asking for the death penalty: Bugliosi and Gentry, *Helter Skelter,* 218.

251 But after the grand jury, the deal changed: In *Helter Skelter,* Bugliosi wrote that once he learned Atkins wouldn't testify against the others the deal was all but over, despite their promise to Atkins about not having to testify at trial (ibid., 338).

251 "we still didn't have a case": Ibid., 285, 295.

251 who came bearing messages from Manson: Ibid., 295, 338.

251 in negotiations with the attorney of Linda Kasabian: In *Helter Skelter,* Bugliosi made it appear that they didn't begin negotiations with Kasabian's attorney until after they'd been notified on February 26, 1970, that Atkins wouldn't testify at trial (which, again, she didn't have to do anyway). But according to documents I found, they'd already started discussing a Kasabian deal on or before January 22.

471

One such document from the LePage files, dated January 22, 1970 and titled "Minutes of Meeting at Robbery Homicide, LAPD," contained the following: "Present [at meeting], LePage [eight other LAPD detectives], Stovitz and Bugliosi...On Kasabian, for us to agree to a plea of manslaughter she would have to give full testimony in each trial. Her attorneys strike me (Stovitz) as being sincere..."

252 "joyous"..."both burst into laughter": Associated Press, "Happy Jail Reunion: Miss Atkins, Manson Rejoined," Mar. 6, 1970.

252 "Charlie doesn't give orders": William Farr, "Manson, Atkins in 'Joyful' Meeting," Los Angeles Herald Examiner, Mar. 5, 1970.

252 Atkins fired Caballero and Caruso: Bugliosi and Gentry, Helter Skelter, 353.

252 declined to testify for the state: William Farr and Charles Sterling, "Susan Atkins to Deny Her Story," Los Angeles Herald Examiner, Mar. 10, 1970.

252 "outlandish" and "nonsensical" motions: Bugliosi and Gentry, Helter Skelter, 353.

252 "to testify before the grand jury": "2 New Tate Suspects?," Hollywood Citizen News, Mar. 24, 1970.

253 "instrumental in getting Dick Caballero": Author interview with Gary Fleischman (now Gary Fields).

253 "Hollywood journalist and communicator" named Lawrence Schiller: Bugliosi and Gentry, Helter Skelter, 261; Schiller testimony, California v. Manson et al., 24875.

253 far from the eyes of any potential jurors in Los Angeles: Bugliosi and Gentry, Helter Skelter, 262.

254 Atkins's byline landed: "Susan Atkins' Story of 2 Nights of Murder," Los Angeles Times, Dec. 14, 1969, A1.

254 "world's great real estate sections": David Felton and David Dalton, "Charles Manson: The Incredible Story of the Most Dangerous Man Alive," Rolling Stone, June 25, 1970, 25.

254 "a fair trial in Los Angeles": "Checkbook Journalism," Newsweek, Dec. 29, 1969, 46.

254 Claiming to be "shocked and surprised": City News Service, "Atkins Lawyer Raps Story, Threatens Suit," Santa Monica Evening Outlook, Dec. 17, 1969.

255 "could not have been produced": Schiller, Killing of Sharon Tate, 5.

255 landed on his doorstep: Bugliosi and Gentry, Helter Skelter, 260–62.

255 Helter Skelter left all of this out: All the information—including direct quotes—in this section is taken from the transcripts of the death-penalty phase testimony of Susan Atkins, Richard Caballero, Paul Caruso, Carmella Ambrosini, Lawrence Schiller, Vincent Bugliosi, and Aaron Stovitz, unless otherwise indicated. Ed Sanders also wrote a series of articles in the Los Angeles Free Press in 1970 (under his own name and various pseudonyms) detailing his suspicion that Caballero and Caruso had been planted by the prosecution and sabotaged the Family's defense: "Manson Can Go Free: Distinguished Attorney Maps Out Manson's Defense," Jan. 16, 1970, 1, 6, 7; Dunbar J. Van Ness, "Changing Focus on Manson," Jan. 23, 1970, 2, 12, 13; A. J. Stapleton, "Manson Case: A Fair Trial?," Feb. 13, 1970, 21, 22; Ed Sanders, "Talk to Charles Manson—$1000 a Crack," June 5, 1970, 3; and Ed Sanders, "The Case of the Susan Atkins Rip-Off," July 24, 1970, 3, 20, 24.

255 the comedian Lenny Bruce: Grace Lichtenstein, "Gilmore's Agent an Entrepreneur Who Specializes in the Sensational," *New York Times,* Jan. 20, 1977; author interview with Richard Shackleton.

257 "until her fate is decided": Schiller, *The Killing of Sharon Tate,* 66.

257 $40,000 for exclusive English rights: Bugliosi and Gentry, *Helter Skelter,* 262. The *New York Times* reported Schiller's gross at $175,000—see Lichtenstein, "Gilmore's Agent an Entrepreneur."

257 collaborating with Cohen on a book of his own: Author interview with Vincent Bugliosi.

258 said reporter worked for the same newspaper: Schiller testified that Cohen had taken a three-day leave of absence from the *Times* to write the story (Schiller testimony, *California v. Manson et al.,* 24911).

258 afterward he claimed in interviews: See David Margolick, "Letter from Los Angeles: O.J.'s Ghost," *Vanity Fair,* Nov. 1996, 116; David Scheff, "Playboy Interview: Lawrence Schiller," *Playboy,* Feb. 1997, 23; Lichtenstein, "Gilmore's Agent an Entrepreneur"; Norman Mailer, *The Executioner's Song* (New York: Warner, 1980), 599.

258 if not for Pete Miller: All the information in this section is taken from the transcripts of the death-penalty phase testimony of Pete Miller, Caballero, and Bugliosi, unless otherwise indicated.

260 "the prosecution didn't put up any obstacles": "Checkbook Journalism."

260 wanted the publicity from the case: Ed Sanders, "'Gas Chamber' Prosecution Girds Its Loins for Battle," *Los Angeles Free Press,* June 12, 1970, 12.

261 Lawrence Schiller wouldn't talk: His assistant in 2005, Kathleen, told me the Manson case was "the one subject he doesn't discuss" (of course, from his interviews with *Playboy, Vanity Fair,* and more, that hardly appears to be true).

261 supporting the official explanation: Richard Warren Lewis, *The Scavengers and Critics of the Warren Report: Based on an Investigation by Lawrence Schiller* (New York: Delacorte Press, 1967).

261 Ruby's confessing to the murder: Released by Capitol Records in 1967 as an LP, it's titled *The Controversy.*

261 *hadn't* killed Oswald: According to documents I found at the National Archives, Schiller sent a prerelease transcript of the Ruby interview to, among others, J. Edgar Hoover, offering it as proof that Ruby shot Oswald "on an impulse and there was no conspiracy" (House Select Committee on Assassinations, Rec. 180-10019-10176, File 62-109060-4429, Jan. 20, 1967, 2). In an effort to refute Warren Commission critic Mark Lane, who claimed that a famous photograph of Kennedy's alleged assassin Oswald holding the rifle used in the crime was doctored, Schiller appeared in a 1967 TV documentary to present the findings of his "independent study" of the picture, showing it was authentic (*The Warren Report,* CBS, June 25, 1967). A decade later, in Carl Bernstein's groundbreaking exposé, "The CIA and the Media" (*Rolling Stone,* Oct. 20, 1977), Bernstein reported that "CBS was unquestionably the CIA's most valuable asset," adding, "over the years the network provided cover for CIA employees, including at least one well-known foreign correspondent and several stringers" (61).

261 Their identities were never revealed: Bernstein, "The CIA and the Media," 55–67.

261 believed Schiller was one of those assets: Author interview with Mark Lane. Lane told me he couldn't prove Schiller was working for intelligence, but if he wasn't, he said, "He should have been." Lane added, "Every time [Schiller] said or wrote anything, it was exactly what the intelligence organizations wanted."

261 "smear" him in the press: HSCA, Rec. 180-10019-100034, File 008976, June 6, 1978.

261 Schiller had been acting as an informant: Most of the information in this section is taken from the records of the National Archive's Kennedy Assassination Collection. However, I also relied heavily on a book by Joan Mellen, a Temple University professor, about New Orleans District Attorney Jim Garrison's unsuccessful prosecution of alleged CIA "asset" Clay Shaw, for the murder of President Kennedy. *A Farewell to Justice: Jim Garrison, JFK's Assassination, and The Case That Should Have Changed History* (Dulles, Va.: Potomac Books, 2005) used many of the same documents I found to make a compelling case that Schiller and Cohen were among many CIA and FBI media assets tasked to obstruct and derail the controversial DA's investigation.

262 publications that provided CIA employees with cover: Bernstein, "The CIA and the Media," 63. Bernstein reported that Henry Luce, the founding publisher of *Time* and *Life* magazines, "readily allowed certain members of his staff—at *Time* and *Life*—to work for the Agency and agreed to provide jobs and credentials to other CIA operatives who lacked journalistic experience" (ibid.).

262 and then sharing his findings with the FBI: HSCA, Rec. 180-10046-10153, File 105-82555-unrecorded, Mar. 16, 1967, 1–6; FBI, Rec. 124-100048-10455, File 62-109060-4876, Mar. 15. 1967, 1; FBI, Rec. 124-10050-10025, File 62-109060-4907, Mar. 22, 1967, 1–4; FBI, Rec. 124-10050-10018, File 62-109060-4903, Mar. 29, 1967, 1–4.

262 "in possession of the names": FBI, Rec. 124-100048-10455, File 62-109060-4876, Mar. 15. 1967, 1. A week later, according to two follow-up memos, Schiller met with agent A. Rosen of the FBI's Los Angeles Field Office and provided the name, aliases, and likely addresses of Lane's informant—see FBI, Rec. 124-10050-10025, File 62-109060-4907, Mar. 22, 1967, 1–4; FBI, Rec. 124-10050-10018, File 62-109060-4903, Mar. 29, 1967, 1–4.

262 According to memos, the FBI eagerly awaited: FBI, Rec. 124-10050-10006, File 62-109060-4897, Mar. 28, 1967, 1. In addition, Schiller informed the FBI of articles "under consideration" at *Life* that "attacked the conclusions of the Warren Commission" (FBI, Rec. 124-10043-10283, File 62-109060-4846, Mar. 21, 1967) and of articles in preparation at other publications—in this case *The New Yorker*—with information about Garrison's investigation that hadn't been made public yet (FBI, Rec. 124-10050-10006, File 62-109060-4897, Mar. 28, 1967, 3).

262 President Kennedy and his brother Robert: Noyes's book, *Legacy of Doubt* (New York: Pinnacle, 1973), blamed right-wing intelligence operatives and organized crime for the assassinations of both Kennedys.

262 pressured him to abandon the project: Author interview with Pete Noyes.

262 Noyes was fairly certain that Cohen: The CIA never responded to my 2002 FOIA for information on Cohen. His widow, Dorothy, a former journalist and two-term mayor of South Pasadena, declined my request for an interview. His daughter, Cassy, also a journalist, spoke to me briefly but said she couldn't continue without consulting an attorney.

262 It bears mentioning that Bugliosi spent twenty years of his life working on what he called his "magnum opus," a 1630-page book (with 1000-plus additional pages of footnotes on a CD-ROM) that attacked every major conspiracy theory ever introduced in the Kennedy assassination. Published in 2007 by W.W. Norton, *Reclaiming History: The Assassination of John F Kennedy,* "proved," he told an interviewer, "literally beyond all doubt that there was no conspiracy in the Kennedy Assassination." Many esteemed assignation researchers criticized the book, saying it presented a one-sided, cherry-picked argument that omitted critical evidence implicating, among others, the Central Intelligence Agency.

263 interview with Howard: "Interview of Rena Howard—Sybil Brand Institute," Nov. 18, 1969, 1–4, LePage personal files.

263 drugs on the nights of the murders: Kasabian testified more than a dozen times that she didn't take drugs anytime around the murders. "I just know," she said under cross-examination by Kanarek (*California v. Manson et al.,* 6302). "Do I have to give a further explanation? I just know."

263 all the killers had taken speed: Kasabian voice-over, *Manson,* Cineplex Productions, 2009: "Before we left the ranch, I remember that we all took some speed. A white capsule was handed to me and I took it."

264 repeated incessantly in Atkins's later accounts: In the Dec. 14, 1969, *Los Angeles Times* story, Schiller quoted Atkins saying Manson "instructed" her to do things five times in just the opening column of the multipage article.

264 They may not even have known: Keith Ditman testimony, *California v. Manson et al.,* 25347.

265 he had no explanation for why: By the end of Manson's life, this had evolved to his saying he might've had an idea what they were going to do, but he had nothing to do with it. "I didn't direct anyone to do a motherfucking thing," Manson told *Rolling Stone* in 2013 (Erik Hedegaard, "Charles Manson Today: The Final Confessions of a Psychopath," *Rolling Stone,* Nov. 21, 2013).

265 eyeglasses recovered from Tate's living room: LAPD First Homicide Investigation Progress Report, DR 69-059-593, 16.

266 "a misleading clue for the police": Nuel Emmons, *Manson in His Own Words* (New York: Grove Press, 1986), 207.

266 Manson himself vaguely disavowed: Author interview with Craig Hammond.

266 several televised interviews to promote it: Manson, with Emmons, was interviewed in prison by Tom Snyder for Snyder's eponymous show on June 12, 1981, and again, for *Today* on Jan. 27, 1987.

266 "So what if I did make you": Charles Manson to Linda Kasabian, Mar. 21, 1970, LASO files.

266 she told Atkins to stop cooperating: Bugliosi and Gentry, *Helter Skelter,* 294.

267 never given an interview about Manson: Author interview with Danny Bowser.

267 covert surveillance on known criminals: All the information about SIS in this section is from a series of investigative pieces the *Los Angeles Times* ran about the secretive unit, beginning with David Freed, "Special Investigations Section: Watching Crime Happen—LAPD's Secret SIS Unit, Citizens Terrorized as Police Look On," Sept. 25, 1988; and including Matt Lait, "SIS: Stormy Past, Shaky Future; LAPD's Special Investigation Section," *Los Angeles Times,* Nov. 29, 1998.

267 "We weren't even connected": Ibid.

267 SIS was called the "Death Squad": Lait, "SIS: Stormy Past."

267 "documented numerous instances": Freed, "Special Investigations Section."

268 "Even within the LAPD": Lait, "SIS: Stormy Past."

268 The later piece in the *Times* reported: Ibid.

268 "One of his responsibilities": Roman Polanski, *Roman by Polanski* (New York: William Morrow, 1984), 310.

268 his real eye had been shot out: Ibid.

269 taken into custody on August 9, 1969: First Homicide Investigation Progress Report, 16.

9. Manson's Get-Out-of-Jail-Free Card

274 The events of June 4, 1969: All information about the June 4, 1969, arrest is from the two-page police report (Officer G. M. Heidrich, LAPD, Arrest Report, DR 69-469997).

275 The police had discovered a warrant: The information about the arrests and prosecution of Atkins, Brunner, and other female Family members in Mendocino, as well as the probation violations of Atkins after her sentence, and Mendocino County's effort to revoke her probation, comes from arrest reports, court minutes, probation reports, news clippings, and interviews with principal subjects. Sources are cited below whenever a document, news report, or interview is quoted. If information is presented without quotation marks, it comes from the more than two dozen documents, clips, and interviews compiled for this section. The same goes for the almost identical events in Oregon a year earlier.

275 "no intentions of abiding by it": "Probation Officer's Report and Recommendation for Revocation in Absentia," Sadie Mae Glutz, Case no. 4503-C, Dept. 2, Filed in the Superior Court of the State of California, Mendocino County, Statement of Fact, Margo S. Tompkins, May 29, 1969, 3.

276 "the defendant has not violated": "Minute Order on Probation Hearing," Glutz, Case no. 4503-C, Dept. 2, Filed in the Superior Court of the State of California, Mendocino County, June 18, 1969, 1.

276 murders of at least eight people: Atkins was convicted in the seven Tate–LaBianca killings and pleaded guilty to the murder of Gary Hinman.

277 a "traveling minister": Mary Yates, Senior Probation Officer, City and County of San Francisco, letter to C. H. McFarlan, Deputy Administrator, Interstate Probation and Parole, Sacramento, Re: Susan Denise Atkins, Case CJ 4771-Oregon, Nov. 10, 1967, 1–2.

278 "is in love with all of them": Ibid., 1.

278 "certain she will do as she pleases": Ibid., 2.

278 "Her speech was quite disorganized": M. E. Madison, Memo to File, Re: Atkins, CJ Prob. 4771, Nov. 14, 1967.

278 they wrote to the original sentencing judge: M. E. Madison, Supervisor, Interstate Unit, letter to Honorable Judge George A. Jones, Marion County Court House, Re: Atkins, CJ Prob. 4771, Dec. 12, 1967, 1–2.

278 *terminating* Susan Atkins's probation: George A. Jones, Circuit Judge, State of Oregon, County of Marion, no. 61487, *Oregon v. Atkins,* "Order Terminating Probation," Jan. 4, 1968.

279 Manson sent his girls there: The information in this section is from the same records, clippings, and interviews, with additional arrest, court, and probation files of the others arrested in Mendocino on May 22, 1968: Mary Brunner, Ella Jo Bailey, Patricia Krenwinkel, and Stephanie Rowe. Additional information comes from such books as David E. Smith and John Luce, *Love Needs Care* (Boston: Little, Brown, 1971), Ed Sanders, *The Family,* 3rd ed. (New York: Thunder's Mouth, 2002), and Vincent Bugliosi with Curt Gentry, *Helter Skelter* (New York: Norton, 1994).

280 "saw flashes when he closed his eyes": David Mandel, "Probation Officer's Report and Recommendation, Sadie Mae Glutz aka Susan Denise Atkins," Superior Court of the State of California, in and for the County of Mendocino, Case no. 4503-C, Dept. 2, Aug. 30, 1968, 3.

280 Brunner's had just begun: Brunner was arrested in April 1968 with Manson and about a dozen other Family members while sleeping beside their parked bus on the Pacific Coast Highway in Ventura County. The officers found her week-old baby, Michael Valentine, sleeping alone in the bus and charged her with endangering the welfare of a child. She pleaded guilty to a reduced charge of contributing to the delinquency of a minor and was sentenced to two years' probation, though there's no record she ever met with a probation officer ("'Hippie' Mom on Probation, Returned Baby," *Oxnard* [Calif.] *Press Courier,* May 14, 1968, 9).

280 Smith and his wife decided: This was first reported by Sanders in *The Family.* It was also confirmed by Roger Smith, and his ex-wife, Carol, in interviews with me.

281 Pooh Bear's temporary foster parents: Ibid.

281 Alan Rose repaired to Mendocino County: Alan Rose's involvement with the Family was first reported in "M.D. on Manson's Sex Life: Psychologist Who Lived with Manson Family Tells About Commune," *The Berkeley Barb,* Jan. 16–22, 1970, 1, 13, and later by Sanders in *The Family* and Smith and Luce in *Love Needs Care.* It was also confirmed by Rose, David Smith, Roger Smith, and others in interviews with me.

282 "former federal parole officer": Mandel, "Probation Officer's Report and Recommendation, Sadie Mae Glutz," 4.

282 Manson and his "guru"-like hold: David Mandel, "Probation Officer's Report and Recommendation, Mary Theresa Brunner," Superior Court of the State of California, in and for the County of Mendocino, Case no. 4503-C, Dept. No. 2, Sept. 6, 1968, 6.

282 used her name without her knowledge: Author interview with Carol Smith (who asked to be identified by her former last name).

282 "hostile and possibly vengeful": Mandel, "Probation Officer's Report and Recommendation, Sadie Mae Glutz," 10.

282 "comply willingly": Ibid., 4. According to the report, Smith said he knew Atkins for "approximately three years." If true, that meant he'd known Atkins since about August 1965, two years before she even met Manson.

282 "manipulated by her present group": Mandel, "Probation Officer's Report and Recommendation, Mary Theresa Brunner," 8.

283 his leniency with the Manson girls: Author interview with Duncan James (one of the deputy district attorneys who prosecuted Atkins, Brunner, and the others).

283 Winslow resurfaced in Los Angeles: The judge's last day on the bench was January 6, 1969, according to the Mendocino County Office of Human Resources.

283 the attorney for Doris Day and her son, Terry Melcher: Winslow represented the pair in their lawsuit against the business partner of Day's late husband for breach of contract and fraud.

283 Winslow who accompanied him: Author interview with Tom Johnson; also confirmed by Winslow's widow, Betty, via Johnson (Mrs. Winslow declined to speak to me).

284 began to use LSD: Smith and Luce, *Love Needs Care,* 257–58.

284 Manson had been released from Terminal Island: The information in this section comes from a variety of sources, most prominently, Manson's federal parole file, which I petitioned the U.S. Parole Commission for in a nearly two-year-long FOIA process. Other sources were police reports and case files I was able to obtain from various county, state, and federal offices, newspaper clippings, books (including *Love Needs Care* and *The Family*), and interviews, chief among them, Roger Smith, David Smith, and Alan Rose.

284 "sustained history of violence": Bugliosi and Gentry, *Helter Skelter,* 203.

285 "criminally sophisticated": Ibid.

285 Years earlier, Manson had had his parole revoked: Angus D. McEachen, Chief U.S. Probation Officer, U.S. District Court for the Southern District of California, "Petition for Action...Praying that court will order issuance of bench warrant...," *United States v. Charles Milles Manson,* Central Division, Docket no. C-27806-CD ("Probationer has failed to submit written monthly report since Feb. 5, 1960 [and] to keep the Probation Office notified as to his whereabouts and current address"), filed May 25, 1960. Manson's probation was also revoked in 1956 by the federal probation office in Los Angeles for missing a hearing (Bugliosi and Gentry, *Helter Skelter,* 196). I was unable to determine if McEachen was in the office at that time.

285 "requested and received permission": Bugliosi and Gentry, *Helter Skelter,* 203.

285 The prosecutor had a copy of Manson's parole file: Ibid., 190–203.

285 "now within the city of Berkeley, California": John A. Sprague, Supervising U.S. Probation Officer, Northern District of California, letter to Angus D. McEachen, Chief U.S. Probation Officer, U.S. Court House, Los Angeles, Apr. 11, 1967.

286 Robert Heinlein's: Robert Gillette, "Manson's Blueprint?: Claim Tate Suspect Used Space-Fiction Plot," *Los Angeles Herald Examiner,* Jan. 8, 1970, A1–2; "A Martian Model?," *Time,* Jan. 19, 1970, 44–45; Smith and Luce, *Love Needs Care,* 258.

286 Roger Smith got a nickname: Gillette, "Manson's Blueprint?," A2.; Smith and Luce, *Love Needs Care,* 260.

287 "no powers of invention": "A Martian Model?," 44.

287 But Roger Smith approved: Smith and Luce, *Love Needs Care,* 258.

287 hazy on the details of how he became: I interviewed Smith on the phone several times and in person twice, first at his home in Michigan in 2001, and then at his home in Oregon in 2008.

287 funded by the National Institute of Mental Health: James Robison, Leslie T. Wilkins, Robert M. Carter, and Albert Wahl, "Final Report," *The San Francisco Project: A Study of Federal Probation and Parole,* April 1969, 1 ("This study was

supported by a $275,000 Mental Health Project Grant from the National Institute of Mental Health").

287 The project studied the relationship between: I reviewed the study's papers at the Special Collections Department of the University of California Bancroft Library, Berkeley. This archive—catalogued officially as The San Francisco Project, University of California, School of Criminology, 1965–1969, Call no. NRLF (UCB) HV9303. C2 no. 14—consists mostly of academic papers, with no individual case files or specifics about clients ("No substantive estimate of the number and *characteristics* of these cases appears to be available"—William P. Adams, Paul M. Chandler, and M. G. Neithercutt, "The San Francisco Project: A Critique," *Federal Probation*, Dec. 1971, 46). Neither Smith's nor Manson's names appear in the collection. The information in this section comes from these UC Berkeley files, as well as news articles and interviews with Smith and several other parole and probation officers who worked on the four-year-long study.

287 The six participating parole officers: Ibid.; author interviews with William P. Adams, M. G. Neithercutt, and Roger Smith.

288 winnowed his set of parolees: Roger Smith was vague about when and if Manson ever became his only client, but Gail Sadalla and Alan Rose, both of whom assisted Smith at the Amphetamine Research Project, said Manson was the only parolee they were aware of who came to the HAFMC for meetings with Smith (author interview with Gail Sadalla; author interviews with Rose).

288 a few days in 1956: According to Manson's FBI "rap" sheet, he was held in the Chicago County Jail from March 9 through 12, 1956, while awaiting transfer to Los Angeles on a federal probation violation ("Charles Milles Manson," U.S. Department of Justice, FBI Rec, no. 643 369 A, April 15, 1959).

288 violent behavior in Oakland gang members: Wallace Turner, "Addiction Linked to Violent Youth: 'Rowdies' Likely to Become Heroin Users, Study Finds," *New York Times,* April 30, 1967.

289 through his own "immersion": Author interview with R. Smith.

289 He and the other researchers created "outposts": Ibid. One of the "projects" initiated by Blumer and Smith in 1965—with Smith serving as director—was the Juvenile Add-Center Project, an "action research program" for at-risk youth in the flatland district. In an academic paper, Smith described the center as a way "to penetrate the drug world…its primary goal is to obtain a clear view of the ways into and the ways out of the drug world" (Roger Smith, "Status Politics and the Image of the Addict," *Issues in Criminology*, Fall 1966, 157, 307–8).

289 They embraced a "participant-observer" approach: As Smith explained to me, the best way to "understand how young people got involved with gangs, how they rationalized what they did, how they were able to justify it to recruit other people" was to "suspend judgment" and observe them. This included, he acknowledged, not reporting criminal activity he or his researchers might witness.

289 expert on gangs, collective behavior: "Seminar to Explore Use, Abuse of Drugs," *Oakland Tribune,* Apr. 18, 1967.

289 to send Manson to live in the Haight: Author interview with R. Smith; Smith and Luce, *Love Needs Care,* 257 (Smith and Luce maintain that Roger originally turned down Manson's request to relocate to the Haight, but later changed his mind and approved it).

290 "The summer of love was just": George Varga, "The Summer of Love, an Epic Tipping Point for Music and Youth Culture, Turns 50," *San Diego Union-Tribune*, May 27, 2017.

290 "A new nation has grown": Peter Conners, *White Hand Society: The Psychedelic Partnership of Timothy Leary and Allen Ginsberg* (San Francisco: City Lights, 2010), 199.

290 dropped acid on a daily basis: Smith and Luce, *Love Needs Care*, 258.

290 "seemed to accept the world": Ibid., 257.

291 "He appears to be in better shape": Roger Smith to Joseph Shore, Parole Executive, U.S. Board of Parole, July 31, 1967.

291 At the time, Manson was sitting in a jail cell: All the information about Manson's arrest and conviction in July 1967 is from police reports, news clippings, and interviews with the officers involved in the arrest, as well as with Dean Moorehouse (the father of Ruth Ann Moorehouse), who witnessed it.

291 merited only a footnote: Bugliosi did mention that Manson received a three-year probation sentence (Bugliosi and Gentry, *Helter Skelter,* 315), but he never said what happened to Manson's probation supervision for his 1967 conviction. And I've never found any evidence that it was enforced, let alone enacted.

291 permitted into evidence during the trial: The information in this section is from the testimony of Samuel Barrett (Manson's final parole officer), who was called during the death-penalty phase of the trial by Kanarek, in an effort to gain access to Manson's parole records (*California v. Charles Manson, Susan Atkins, Leslie Van Houten and Patricia Krenwinkel,* case 22239, 22132–203).

291 he dispatched David Anderson: Ibid., 22161–74.

291 "incriminate the Attorney General": Ibid., 22193.

292 "four inches thick": Ibid., 22177.

292 occurred under his watch: Author interview with R. Smith.

292 to travel to Mexico: Smith to Shore, July 31, 1967.

292 Manson had been arrested in Mexico: *Manson v. United States,* "Forma Pauperis Affidavit," no. 64-585-WM, filed Apr. 8, 1964 (Manson filed a motion arguing that his 1959 arrest in Mexico and reparation to the United States were unfair because he was unable to understand the proceedings in the Mexican court).

292 "Manson is not to leave": There were two overlapping notes, one typed and one handwritten; the first, cited here, is Joseph Shore to Albert Wahl, Chief U.S. Probation Officer, San Francisco, Aug. 25, 1967.

292 record was "lengthy and serious": Handwritten note with illegible signature to illegible recipient, on "U.S. Board of Parole" letterhead, Sept. 5, 1967.

293 "additives and mineral food supplements": Roger Smith to Joseph Shore, Aug. 15, 1967.

293 The parole board rejected: Shore to Wahl, Aug. 25, 1967.

293 study of Mexican drug trafficking: Author interview with R. Smith.

293 Mazatlán, which was the main port city: Elijah Wald, *Narcocorrido: A Journey into the Music of Drugs, Guns, and Guerrillas* (New York: Rayo, 2001), 39.

293 "Was I a career, committed parole officer? *No!*": Author interview with R. Smith.

293 to meet with "recording agents": Roger Smith [to Manson], "Permission to Travel" ("Ft. Lauderdale, Fla., via Los Angeles...leaving Nov. 10, 1967 and returning within 20 days...to contact recording agents in Los Angeles and

Florida regarding sale and recording of your music"), Nov. 16, 1967; Roger Smith [to Manson], "Permission to Travel" ("Miami, Fla...leaving 11-30-67 and returning within 20 days...to further the possibility of obtaining a record contract"), Dec. 4, 1967.

294 If they went anywhere: Mandel, "Probation Officer's Report and Recommendation, Mary Theresa Brunner," 5 ("They have also visited Southern California and Mexico lately").

294 Susan Atkins's probation officers: Yates to McFarlan, Nov. 10, 1967, 1–2. Yates wrote: "Today they leave for Los Angeles and then on to Florida. I told her she was not to leave without the permission of the Oregon Probation Department, but I am just as certain she will do as she pleases." See also Madison, Memo to File, Nov. 14, 1967. Madison wrote: "At 3:15 pm Atkins called and advised she was going on trip with or without permission."

294 quite a bit of time in Mexico: Mandel, "Probation Officer's Report and Recommendation, Mary Theresa Brunner."

295 "your status leaves much to be desired": Samuel Barrett to Charles Manson, June 12, 1968, in Manson's federal parole file.

295 Barrett was the parole officer: Bugliosi and Gentry, *Helter Skelter,* 546–47.

295 three hundred parole cases between 1967 and 1969: Author interview with Samuel Barrett.

295 only twenty-one words for Roger Smith: Bugliosi and Gentry, *Helter Skelter,* 225.

295 "apparently did not retain": Pamela A. Posch, General Counsel, United States Parole Commission, letter to author, June 4, 2001, 1. Posch conceded that this was unusual in a follow-up phone conversation.

295 the files of "notorious felons": Author interview with Ann Diestel, Archivist, Federal Bureau of Prisons; Posch to O'Neill, June 4, 2001, 1.

296 that file was missing, too: Author interview with Victoria Hardin, Director, Office of History, National Institute of Health. Using the information I gave her, Hardin was unable to find any record of the San Francisco Project in her archive, which inherited the NIMH files after several reorganizations of the program.

296 The headline: Charles Hillinger, "Wayward Bus Stuck in Ditch: Deputy Finds Nude Hippies Asleep in Weeds," *Los Angeles Times,* Apr. 23, 1968, 3, 23. See also: "Nine Nude Hippies Arrested; Found Huddled Around a Bonfire," *Oxnard Press Courier,* Apr. 23, 1968, 9; Associated Press, "No Disaster: Just Hippies Sleeping Nude," *Ontario Daily Report,* Apr. 23, 1968, A-4; United Press International, "14 Nude Hippies Found Beside a Wayward Bus," *Oakland Tribune,* Apr. 23, 1969, 14.

296 "Wait, my baby's on the bus": Hillinger, "Wayward Bus Stuck in Ditch," 3.

297 She was later convicted: "'Hippie' Mom on Probation," 9.

297 traveling "freely between San Francisco": Albert Wahl, Chief Probation Officer, U.S. District Court, Northern District of California, letter to Angus D. McEachen, Apr. 26, 1968, 1.

297 "Be sure to read the clipping": Ibid., 2.

297 legal owner of the bus: Angus D. McEachen, letter to Albert Wahl, May 7, 1968, 1–2.

298 sending Manson back to federal prison: McEachen, "Petition for Action."

298 "his adventuresome nature": McEachen to Wahl, May 7, 1968, 2.

298 sitting in the Los Angeles County jail: Ibid.

298 DA had declined to file: Angus D. McEachen, letter to Albert Wahl, May 29, 1968.

299 "Failure to follow": Albert Wahl, letter to Charles Manson, June 3, 1968.

299 "It would appear that Mr. Manson": Albert Wahl, letter to Angus D. McEachen, June 11, 1968.

299 "succumbed to Manson's obsequious manner": Angus D. McEachen, letter to Albert Wahl, June 12, 1968.

299 The record label "would have to be idiotic": Ibid.

300 On June 12, Barrett: Samuel Barrett, letter to Charles Manson, June 12, 1969.

300 The next letters came: Angus D. McEachen, letter to Joseph Shore (Attn.: James Jones), Aug. 7, 1968.

300 hosted Manson at their home: Author interview with C. Smith; author interview with R. Smith.

300 The National Institute of Mental Health funded: Smith and Luce, *Love Needs Care,* 36.

301 used by the CIA as a funding front: Edwin M. Long Jr., Deputy Director, Scientific and Public Information, NIMH, letter to Joseph J. Petrillo and Timothy Sullivan, Sept. 30, 1976, National Security Archives, George Washington University, Washington, D.C.

301 "way in which violence": Roger Smith, "The Marketplace of Speed: Violence and Compulsive Methamphetamine Abuse" (PhD diss., University of California, Berkeley, 1969), 5.

301 "asking me to help them with the law": Smith and Luce, *Love Needs Care,* 36.

301 Hiding in a "deviant group": Smith, "The Marketplace of Speed."

302 anonymity in all reports: Ibid., 136.

302 opened the previous summer: When it finally received funding in May 1968, ARP was moved to the clinic's "annex," one block away (Smith and Luce, *Love Needs Care,* 36).

302 why not just meet: Smith was vague in his interviews with me (as were David Smith and Luce in their book) about when his professional relationship with Manson ended and the personal one began. Smith told Ed Sanders, for instance, that he stopped being a parole officer in January 1968, when he began work at the clinic (Sanders, *The Family,* 460–61), but in a résumé Smith shared with me, he lists the date of his departure from the probation office as May 1968. David Smith and Luce put the start of Roger's work at the HAFMC as January 1968 (36) but other sources told me it was the fall of 1967 (author interviews with Rose, Sadalla, and Ernest Dernburg). Whatever the case, Manson was visiting Roger Smith at the clinic in *some* capacity in the spring of '68, as Smith and Luce report Roger saying in their book: "I ceased being his parole officer in 1968, when I started working at the Medical Section, so [Manson] had no real reason to spend so much time with me. But he came anyway, preaching about love" (257).

302 Soon Manson became a mainstay: Smith and Luce, *Love Needs Care,* 36, 255–62.

10. *The Haight-Ashbury Free Medical Clinic*

305 David Elvin Smith grew up: This section relies primarily on Smith's writing in *Love Needs Care* (cowritten by John Luce; Boston: Little, Brown, 1971) and in his self-published *Journal of Psychedelic Drugs.* A biography of Smith by Clark S.

Sturges, *Dr. Dave: A Profile of David E. Smith, M.D., Founder of the Haight Ashbury Free Clinics* (Walnut Creek, Calif.: Devil Mountain Books, 1993), was also heavily resourced.

306 "high on the same substance": Ariel Zeitlin Cooke, "Volunteer Doctor, The Free Clinic at 33: How a Radical Idea Became a Model Institution," *Diversion*, April 2000.

308 "Charlie's girls," as they were known: Author interview with Robert Conrich.

308 They referred to him as Christ, or "J.C.": Vincent Bugliosi with Curt Gentry, *Helter Skelter* (New York: Norton, 1994), 315.

308 "reprogram" his followers: The information about Manson's methods of "reprogramming" his followers during the Haight period is from Smith and Luce, *Love Needs Care*, 259–63, unless otherwise noted.

308 a phrase David claims to have coined: Author interview with David Smith.

308 But Manson had an aversion: Smith and Luce, *Love Needs Care*, 258–59.

309 "mitigating circumstances": Ibid.

309 a "capsule" of speed: *Manson*, Cineplex Productions, 2009.

309 In books and at parole hearings, Susan Atkins: Susan Atkins with Bob Slosser, *Child of Satan, Child of God* (Plainfield, N.J.: Logos International, 1977), 135; Susan Atkins, Subsequent Parole Consideration Hearing, State of California Board of Prison Terms, in the Matter of the Life Term Parole Consideration Hearing of Susan Atkins, CDC Inmate W-08340, June 1, 2005, multiple references.

309 both nights of the murders: Tex Watson and Chaplain Ray, *Will You Die for Me?* (Old Tappan, N.J.: Fleming H. Revell, 1978), 131, 141.

309 brooding on his delusions: Susan Atkins-Whitehouse, *The Myth of Helter Skelter*, (San Juan Capistrano, Calif.: Menelorelin Dorenay, 2012), 63.

309 a short essay for *Life* magazine: Roger Smith and David Smith, "A Doctor and a Parole Officer Remember Manson," *Life*, Dec. 1, 1969, 26.

310 only the third reporter: Not counting his December 1969 *Life* essay and his interview for 1971's *Love Needs Care*, Roger Smith spoke to Ed Sanders for *The Family* in 1971 (but his quotes weren't attributed to him until Sanders's 2002 update, 460–61) and the cable channel A&E for its documentary *Charles Manson: Journey into Evil* (1995).

310 "If you love everything, you don't": Smith and Luce, *Love Needs Care*, 257–58.

311 "Charlie's ability to draw": Author interview with Alan Rose.

311 "was always kind of fascinated": Author interview with Carol Smith.

311 "he had made an error": Author interview with Ernest Dernburg.

311 "bringing operations to a standstill": Smith and Luce, *Love Needs Care*, 260.

311 One reason the HAFMC was free: Much of *Love Needs Care* recounts David Smith's never-ending battle to keep the clinic open in the first few years. Although he told me in interviews that it never received federal grants, he clearly states in the book (36) that Roger Smith's ARP was funded by a $37,000 grant from the NIMH in May 1968, and several papers published by Smith and his colleagues at the HAFMC acknowledge the NIMH for funding.

311 "I always thought there would be problems": Author interview with Lyle Grosjean.

312 "He was going to soothe the savage beast": Author interview with Dernburg.

312 never actually received his PhD: Author interview with D. Smith.

312 published a brief article: The story is an almost word-for-word copy of the thesis of Charles M. Fischer, one of the four researchers, who received his master's in pharmacology at the University of California, San Francisco, in 1968. I obtained a copy of the thesis from the university. Smith told me that it was originally *his* PhD dissertation; he "gave" it to Fischer when he realized he wasn't going to finish his doctorate. Fischer denied Smith's assertion. Fischer's name—along with those of Smith, Eugene Schoenfeld, and Charles H. Hine—appeared on the paper when it was published the following year in the HAFMC's *Journal of Psychedelic Drugs* under the same title, "Behavioral Mediators in the Polyphasic Mortality Curve of Aggregate Amphetamine Toxicity" (vol. 2 [Spring 1969]: 55–72). A revised version of the article was published in a bound collection of *Journal* articles in 1973.

312 sixteen albino mice: The information in this section comes from interviews with David Smith and Schoenfeld and Fischer, Smith's coresearchers in the mice study. (Hine died in 1991.) The scientific data is taken directly from version of the paper published in 1969 in *Journal of Psychedelic Drugs*, except where specified. The similarities of Smith's animal research to the formation of the Manson Family were first reported by Carol Greene (a pseudonym) in a German book published by the right-wing Lyndon LaRouche Organization, *Der Fall Charles Manson: Mörder aus der Retorte* (n.p.: E.I.R., 1992). I was able to obtain an English translation (*The Test Tube Murders;* no publication data available) and speak to "Greene" in 2003. Some of her findings were substantiated during my independent investigation and expanded on (others were impossible to corroborate). "Greene" told me she'd severed ties with the LaRouche organization and no longer had her research files. She didn't interview anyone for her book and relied mostly on Smith's articles and *Love Needs Care*, from which she drew her theories.

313 "frenzied attacks of unrelenting rage": Smith and Luce, *Love Needs Care,* 16. See also author interview with D. Smith.

313 dismembered body parts: Fischer, a twenty-four-year-old graduate student at the time, had to check on the mice in eight-hour intervals, often in the middle of the night. "It was brutal," he told me of the carnage he'd encounter. "There was no rhyme or reason—it was just helter skelter."

313 "consume the drugs in crowded atmospheres": Smith and Luce, *Love Needs Care,* 16.

314 "lashed out with murderous rage": Ibid., 19.

314 "like rats in a cage": Ibid., 222.

314 Suggestibility was among: According to the *Journal of Psychedelic Drugs* article, the objective of research was twofold: to discover which drugs would "modify" the violence of the animals caused by amphetamine and aggregation and and, more important, what existing "behavioral" factors made some animals violent enough to kill, and to isolate those factors. See Fischer et al., "Behavioral Mediators," 56.

314 they're rats: Smith and Luce, *Love Needs Care,* multiple references; David Smith and Donald R. Wesson, eds., *Uppers and Downers* (Englewood Cliffs, N.J.: Prentice Hall, 1974), 47.

314 Schoenfeld insisted that he'd worked with rats: Author interview with Eugene
     Schoenfeld. Fischer asked me whether David Smith was on "drugs" when he told
     me the research was on rats. "I'm surprised that David wouldn't remember that,"
     he said during our interview, "they were *Balt-C*. I was the one who ordered those
     damn mice and I was the one who shot them up."

315 David Smith's research was funded: D. E. Smith, C. M. Fischer, and C. H. Hine,
     "Effects of Chlorpromazine, Phenobarbital, and Iproniazid on the Polyphasic
     Mortality Curve of Aggregate Amphetamine," from "Abstracts of Papers for the
     Sixth Annual Meeting of the Society of Toxicology, Atlanta, Georgia, March
     23–25, 1967," *Toxicology and Applied Pharmacology* 10 (1967): 378–411. The abstract
     contains this notation on p. 403: "Supported in part by U.S. Public Service
     Toxicology Training Grant No. 5 TO1 GM01304-02."

315 rape, murder, cannibalism, and infanticide: The information in this section is
     from Calhoun's paper, unless otherwise noted: John B. Calhoun, "Population
     Density and Social Pathology," *Scientific American* 206, no. 2 (Feb. 1962): 139–49.

315 "that can be found within [the] group": Ibid., 144.

318 "a lasting impact on the individual's personality": William McGlothlin, Sidney
     Cohen, and Marcella McGlothlin, "Long Lasting Effects of LSD on Normals,"
     Journal of Psychedelic Drugs 3, no. 1 (Sept. 1970): 20–31 (reprinted from *Archives of
     General Psychiatry* 17, no. 5 [Nov. 1967]: 521–32).

318 feelings of "frustrated anger" led people: Kay Blacker, "Chronic Users of LSD:
     The 'Acidheads,'" *Journal of Psychedelic Drugs* 3, no. 1 (Sept. 1970): 32.

319 "the psychedelic syndrome": According to a paper he later wrote, Smith first
     presented this theory in a lecture at the University of California, San Francisco,
     between the fall of 1967 and spring of 1968. See David E. Smith, "Changing
     Patterns of Drug Abuse in Haight-Ashbury," *California Medicine,* Feb. 1969.

319 "the emergence of a dramatic orientation": David E. Smith, "LSD and the
     Psychedelic Syndrome," *Clinical Toxicology* 2, no. 1 (Mar. 1969): 69–73.

319 "Charlie could probably be diagnosed": R. Smith and D. Smith, "A Doctor and a
     Parole Officer Remember Manson," 26.

320 a criminology paper: Roger Smith, "Status Politics and the Image of the Addict,"
     Issues in Criminology, Fall 1966. All of the information in this section is taken
     directly from Smith's article.

321 But as Grogan wrote: Emmett Grogan, *Ringolevio: A Life Played for Keeps* (Boston:
     Little, Brown, 1972), 290.

322 Rose was a friend of Roger: Author interview with Rose.

322 A former rabbinical student: The information about Rose comes primarily
     from Smith and Luce, *Love Needs Care*, and from interviews with Rose, David
     Smith, Roger Smith, Gail Sadalla, and others who worked alongside him at the
     clinic.

322 Rose and David went on to coauthor three studies of the Haight's drug culture in
     the *Journal of Psychedelic Drugs:* "LSD: Its Use, Abuse, and Suggested Treatment,"
     vol. 1, no. 2 (Winter 1967–68): 117–28; "Incidents Involving the Haight-Ashbury
     Population and Some Uncommonly Used Drugs," vol. 1, no. 2 (Winter 1967–
     68), cowritten with Frederick Meyers; and "The Group Marriage Commune: A
     Case Study," vol. 3, no. 1 (Sept. 1970): 115–19.

322 probably on Manson's orders: Smith and Luce, *Love Needs Care,* 263; author interview with Rose; author interview with D. Smith; author interview with Sadalla.

323 until Manson summoned them: Smith and Luce, *Love Needs Care,* 263; author interview with Rose.

323 he was living on money funneled: Author interview with Rose; author interview with D. Smith.

323 he stayed with them: Ibid. (both); Smith and Luce, *Love Needs Care,* 263.

323 "in the strange communal phenomenon": Smith and Luce, *Love Needs Care,* 263.

323 one's subjects broke the law: Roger Smith, "The Marketplace of Speed: Violence and Compulsive Methamphetamine Abuse" (PhD diss., University of California, Berkeley, 1969), 3, 136.

325 The first was Roger's ARP dissertation: author interview with Rose.

325 the first-ever scholarly study: Smith and Rose, "The Group Marriage Commune," 115–19.

325 a January 1970 interview: "M.D. on Manson's Sex Life: Psychologist Who Lived with Manson Family Tells About Commune," *The Berkeley Barb,* Jan. 16–22, 1970.

325 a point they'd finesse later: Smith and Rose, "The Group Marriage Commune," 115–16.

326 the others moved into Rose's home: Smith and Luce, *Love Needs Care,* 256–64.

326 He didn't interview any: author interviews with D. Smith, R. Smith, Rose, and Vincent Bugliosi. Rose isn't mentioned in *Helter Skelter.*

326 as if Bugliosi had actually spoken to him: Bugliosi and Gentry, *Helter Skelter,* 225.

327 "sex, not drugs, was the common denominator": Ibid., 226.

327 to prove "*domination*": Ibid., 287.

327 ran their front-page stories: The *Los Angeles Free Press,* sister publication to the *Barb,* ran the identical story a week later (Jan. 23–29, 1970).

327 "the dictatorial leader of the Family": Bugliosi and Gentry, *Helter Skelter,* 413.

328 "served as absolute ruler": Smith and Rose, "The Group Marriage Commune," 116.

329 if they were acting under their own free will: Bugliosi addressed the quandary in *Helter Skelter,* writing: "I was giving the attorneys for the three girls a ready-made defense. In the penalty phase of the trial they could argue that since Atkins, Krenwinkel and Van Houten were totally under Manson's domination, they were not nearly as culpable as he" (Bugliosi and Gentry, *Helter Skelter,* 415).

330 to "modify" their behavior: Fischer et al., "Behavioral Mediators," 28.

330 "long-term psychological tendencies": Smith and Luce, *Love Needs Care,* 16.

330 Some made reference to a forthcoming paper: In Charles Fischer's own master's thesis, a footnote refers to D. E. Smith, C. M. Fischer, A. J. Rose, and F. M. Meyers, "Patterns of Amphetamine Toxicity in the Haight-Ashbury," which is forthcoming from the *Journal of Psychedelic Drugs*; and a footnote in Smith, "Changing Drug Patterns in the Haight-Ashbury," refers to D. E. Smith, C. M. Fischer, and R. Smith, "Toxicity of High Dose Methamphetamine Abuse," which is then "in press" at the same journal.

330 both Roger Smith and Alan Rose: David E. Smith and Charles M. Fischer, "Acute Amphetamine Toxicity," *Journal of Psychedelic Drugs* 2, no. 2 (Spring 1969).

333 the government *had* been notified: The two documents are: Manson, Charles
Willis [sic], Bureau of Criminal Identification and Investigation, Sacramento,
"Crime Report," Case no. 25544, "Date and Time Reported to Department:
7-28-1967, 01:00 PM"; and Manson, Charles Milles, U.S. Department of Justice,
Federal Bureau of Investigation (Rap Sheet), Record no. 643 369 A, Apr. 30,
1968, 5.

334 "the federal guys didn't mess up": Author interview with Richard Wood.

334 "comply willingly with any probationary conditions": David Mandel, "Probation
Officer's Report and Recommendation, Sadie Mae Glutz aka Susan Denise
Atkins," Superior Court of the State of California, in and for the County of
Mendocino, Case no. 4503-C, Dept. 2, Aug. 30, 1968, 4. I was able to finally
show Roger Smith his probation recommendations for Atkins and Brunner at our
last meeting in 2008. He said he had no recollection of making the statements
attributed to him and added they didn't "sound" like him, anyway. "I would
never say 'unconventional lifestyle,'" he told me.

11. Mind Control

342 Born in Brooklyn in 1924: Two invaluable books I relied on for West's
biographical information are Anthony Kales, Chester M. Pierce, and Milton
Greenblatt, eds. *The Mosaic of Contemporary Psychiatry in Perspective* (New York:
Springer-Verlag, 1992) and John West, *The Last Goodnights: Assisting My Parents
with Their Suicides* (Berkeley, Calif.: Counterpoint, 2009). The latter is a memoir
by one of West's three children, recalling life with his father and the decision he
made to assist both his parents when they chose to end their lives after being
diagnosed with terminal illnesses. No one in West's family would talk to me, but
I interviewed dozens of his colleagues and friends, dating all the way back to his
time as the head of the psychiatric unit at the Lackland Air Force Base. His
archive at the Department of Special Collections at the Charles Young Library at
UCLA—hereinafter cited as West Archive—provided me with the clearest
picture of the true nature of his research.

343 equal rights for African Americans: Robert S. Pynoos, "Violence, Personality,
and Post-Traumatic Stress Disorder: Development and Political Perspectives," in
Mosaic of Contemporary Psychiatry, 71–72.

343 suffered an "acute psychotic break": Hubert Winston Smith, letter to Joe
Tonahill, May 11, 1964, West Archive.

343 making him sound unhinged: "Testimony of Jack Ruby," Warren Commission
volumes, 5H208-211, June 7, 1964, 181–213.

343 he prevailed on his son: West, *The Last Goodnights.*

344 no record of his participation: Douglas McAdam (former director of the Center
for Advanced Study in the Behavioral Science at Stanford, after West's time
there), email to author; Julie Schumaker (Center for Advanced Study,
researcher), email to author. McAdam and Schumaker said that West never
provided a "Statement of Purpose" or "Year End Report," both required of all
participants.

344 and skipping haircuts: West, letter to Fred Pumpian-Mindlin (one of the
researchers), June 20, 1967, West Archive.

345 a "remarkable substance": West and A. Mandell, "Hallucinogens," *Comprehensive Textbook of Psychiatry,* ed. Alfred M. Freedman and Harold I. Kaplan (Baltimore: Williams and Wilkins, 1967), 247–53. According to the book's editors, West's chapter was completed in 1966.

345 "negate their egos": David E. Smith and John Luce, *Love Needs Care* (Boston: Little, Brown, 1971), 259.

345 in America's "bohemian" quarters: West and Mandell, "Hallucinogens," 252.

345 "crackpots" who hypnotized: West and Gordon H. Deckert, "Dangers of Hypnosis," *Journal of the American Medical Association* 192, no. 1 (Apr. 1965): 9–12.

346 You'd never know from his published writing: In the many papers written by West, he never once mentioned his own drug experiments with human subjects, just those conducted by *other* researchers.

346 a crumbling Victorian house: West published several academic papers about the Haight-Ashbury Project, all of which will be cited in this section, but the most relevant information was obtained from his archive at UCLA, which contains the diaries of many of the researchers who participated in the program. I interviewed several of the researchers as well as others who knew of the project through their work with West at the HAFMC that summer.

346 a "laboratory" disguised as a "hippie crash pad": West and James R. Allen, "Flight from Violence: Hippies and the Green Rebellion," *American Journal of Psychiatry* 125, no. 3 (Sept. 1968): 365; West, James R. Allen, and Joshua Kaufman, "Runaways, Hippies and Marijuana," *American Journal of Psychiatry* 126, no. 5 (Nov. 1969): 163.

346 "semi-permanent observation post": West and James R. Allen, "The Green Rebellion," *Sooner,* Nov. 1967, 6.

346 "with posters, flowers and paint": Ibid.

346 could furnish willing subjects: Author interview with David Smith; author interview with James Allen.

347 records in West's files: See, for instance, West, Allen, and Kaufman, "Runaways, Hippies and Marijuana," which contains this acknowledgment: "This study was supported in part by a grant from the Foundations Fund for Research in Psychiatry, by a fellowship award from the Center for Advanced Study in Behavioral Sciences, Stanford, Calif., awarded to Dr. West, and by Public Health Service Grant MH–35063 from National Institute of Mental Health."

347 the agency's first "disguised laboratory": The first and still definitive book on the MKULTRA program is by the former State Department official who compelled the agency to release its financial records: John Marks, *The Search for the Manchurian Candidate: The CIA and Mind Control* (New York: Norton, 1979). I also reviewed Marks's files (CIA Behavior Experiments Collection—John Marks Donation, National Security Archive, Gehlman Library, George Washington University, Washington, D.C.); for records of "Operation Midnight Climax," the "safe house" projects run by George Hunter White in New York City and San Francisco in the 1960s, I reviewed White's papers (George White Papers, 1932–1970, collection no. M1111), at Stanford University, in the library's department of special collections. Other invaluable books on MKULTRA include Martin A. Lee and Bruce Shlain, *Acid Dreams: The CIA, LSD, and the Sixties Rebellion* (New

York: Grove Weidenfeld, 1985); Alexander Cockburn and Jeffrey St. Clair, *Whiteout: The CIA, Drugs and the Press* (London: Verso, 1998); and Alan W. Scheflin and Edward M. Opton, *The Mind Manipulators* (New York: Paddington Press, 1978). An additional resource was the published transcripts of *Project MKULTRA, the CIA's Program of Research in Behavioral Modification,* Joint Hearing Before the Select Committee on Intelligence and the Subcommittee on Human Resources, U.S. Senate, 95th Congress, 1st Sess., Aug. 3, 1977 (Washington, D.C.: GPO, 1977); and *Human Drug Testing by the CIA, 1977,* Hearings before the Subcommittee on Health and Scientific Research of the Committee on Human Resources, U.S. Senate, 95th Congress, 1st Sess., Sept. 20–21, 1977 (Washington, D.C.: GPO, 1977); hereafter referred to as the Kennedy-Inouye Hearings. The information that follows comes primarily from these sources.

347 "I was a very minor missionary": Troy Hooper, "Operation Midnight Climax: How the CIA Dosed S.F. Citizens with LSD," *S.F. Weekly,* Mar. 14, 2012.

348 Mass Conversion: Marks, *Search for the Manchurian Candidate,* 170. A sanitized description of the project was released to the university by the CIA in 1977 (CIA MORI DocID: 17358); see Mick Hinton, "1950s OU Study Funded by CIA," *Oklahoman,* Sept. 21, 1977, 4.

348 funds came from Sidney J. Gottlieb: Marks, *Search for the Manchurian Candidate,* 170; Hinton, "1950s OU Study," 4. As both Marks and Hinton reported—and I documented in West's files—the research was paid for by the Society for the Investigation of Human Ecology (also called the Human Ecology Fund), run by an air force colonel named James Monroe, and by the Geschickter Fund for Medical Research, both exposed during the 1970s congressional investigations as "cut-outs" for the CIA's MKULTRA program.

348 "bleed the energies of the hippie movement": West and Allen, "The Green Rebellion," 32.

349 He was at work on a book: Memorandum of Agreement: Louis Jolyon West and the McGraw-Hill Book Company, for a work entitled *Experimental Psychopathology: The Induction of Abnormal States,* Aug. 27, 1968, West Archive.

349 By the early seventies he removed the title: I found the book listed as "in preparation" in a curriculum vitae dated Apr. 10, 1967 and another dated with just the year 1968, but in no version of West's CVs after that (West Archive).

349 Kathy Collins: All the information regarding Collins's experience is taken directly from her diary, which is in the West Archive. I searched for Collins for years, only to learn in 2012 that she died around 2007.

350 When West made one of his rare appearances: Ibid., entry of July 11, 1969.

350 the CIA began to experiment on humans: Much of the information in this section comes from the books cited above: Marks, *Search for the Manchurian Candidate;* Lee and Shlain, *Acid Dreams;* Scheflin and Opton, *The Mind Manipulators;* and Cockburn and St. Clair, *Whiteout.* Also indispensable were the files of John Marks at the National Security Archive; the Rockefeller Commission report: *The President's Commission on CIA Activities Within the United States* (Washington, D.C.: GPO, 1975); the Church Committee report: *The United States Senate Select Committee to Study Governmental Operations with Respect to Intelligence Activities* (Washington, D.C.: GPO, 1976); and the transcripts of the Kennedy-Inouye Hearings from 1977.

351 "deeper, comprehensive reality": Albert Hofmann, *LSD My Problem Child: Reflections on Sacred Drugs, Mysticism and Science* (MAPS.org., 2009), 209.

351 "from Earth like a spaceship": Xan Brooks, "Cary Grant: How 100 Acid Trips in Tinseltown 'Changed My Life,'" *The Guardian,* May 12, 2017.

352 forced to make false confessions: West, I. E. Farber, and Harry F. Harlow, "Brainwashing, Conditioning and DDD (Debility, Dependency, and Dread)," *Sociometry* 20 (1957): 271–83. The information in this section about West's work with POWs is from this paper.

353 the "Black Sorcerer": Kris Hollington, *Wolves, Jackals, and Foxes: The Assassins Who Changed History* (New York: St. Martin's, 2015), 34.

353 "a phonograph playing a disc": Lee and Shlain, *Acid Dreams,* 27.

353 "to influence human behavior": Kennedy-Inouye Hearings, Aug. 3, 1977, Appendix A, 82.

354 hypno-programmed assassins: Nicholas M. Horrock, "C.I.A. Documents Tell of 1954 Project to Create Involuntary Assassins," *New York Times*, Feb. 9, 1978, A17.

355 In December 1974: Seymour Hersh, "Huge C.I.A. Operation Reported in U.S. Against Antiwar Forces," *New York Times,* Dec. 22, 1974.

355 "Precautions must be taken": Church Committee, Book 1; XVII, 394.

356 "rights and interests of U.S. citizens in jeopardy": Ibid., 390.

356 deaths of at least two American citizens: Ibid., 386.

356 The other was Frank Olson: Ibid. ("The Death of Dr. Frank Olson"), 394–403.

356 strongly suggests that the CIA: Eric Olson, personal communications with author; *Wormwood*, Netflix (Errol Morris, dir.), 2017.

357 "waiting for him in the Senate hearing room": Jo Thomas, "Key Witness Testifies in Private on C.I.A. Drug Tests," *New York Times*, Sept. 22, 1977, 1.

357 "quietly dropped": Anthony Marro, "C.I.A. Head Offers Drug-Test Files If Justice Department Has Inquiry," *New York Times*, Aug. 10, 1977, 1.

357 receive total criminal immunity: Thomas, "Key Witness Testifies," 1.

357 "Can we obtain control": "Objectives and Agencies" (CIA document), May 23, 1951, 1, 7, CIA Behavior Experiments Collection—John Marks Donation, National Security Archive, Gehlman Library, George Washington University, Washington, D.C.

357 "Can we force an individual to act": Untitled CIA document, 1952, ibid.

357 "an act of attempted assassination?": Untitled CIA document, Jan. 1954, ibid.

357 "perverse" and "corrupt": Kennedy-Inouye Hearings, 1st Sess., Aug. 3, 1977, 16.

357 "freedom of individual and institutions": Ibid., Sept. 20, 1977, 1.

358 Inouye called it "grandiose and sinister": Ibid., Aug. 3, 1977, 13.

358 Stansfield Turner, swore: Ibid., Sept. 20, 1977, 145.

358 "may never come out": "Control C.I.A., Not Behavior," editorial, *New York Times,* Aug. 5, 1977, 16.

358 That program never coalesced: The closest thing was an in-house investigation by the CIA, called the Victims Task Force. Unsurprisingly, the three-man team of agents (two from the CIA, one from the DEA) turned up only two victims of MKULTRA, both women. Each had been unwittingly dosed with LSD at a party in Greenwich Village on January 11, 1953 (one of the women received a $15,000 settlement from the federal government, the other was deceased).

358 The *New York Times* identified him: Nicholas M. Horrock, "Private Institutions
Used in C.I.A. Effort to Control Behavior: $25 Million Program," *New York
Times,* Aug. 2, 1977, A-1.

358 not one researcher: Further, I spoke to Robert H. Wiltse and Frank Laubinger,
the two CIA agents on the task force, and they told me they never even contacted
a university or other facility where MKULTRA research had occurred. Their
seven-month investigation consisted of contacting less than half a dozen people
who were named in the diary of George H. White, the CIA agent who conducted
experiments in safe houses in New York and San Francisco between 1953 and
1965. When I asked Wiltse why the academic institutions and federal facilities
where most of the MKULTRA research occurred had been ignored, he replied
that he "didn't know." When pressed, he said it "didn't seem necessary," adding
that he never even left the CIA headquarters in Langley, during the investigation.
Laubinger told me that he was the one who investigated the safe houses operated
by White, and that he believed Wiltse was responsible for investigating the
academic institutions. Laubinger called Gottlieb "an honorable man who was
dealt a blow" by the congressional investigations. He said if the communists had
mind control technology in their arsenal, "Well, maybe we ought to have it too."

358 "a secret twenty-five year": Horrock, "Private Institutions."

358 "I'm just drawing a total blank here": Author interview with Stansfield Turner.

360 "CIA operators and agents": Marks, *Search for the Manchurian Candidate,* 97.

360 The first one was dated June 11, 1953: All the information that follows is taken
directly from this document in the West Archive.

361 "My Good Friend": "Sherman R. Grifford," letter to West, July 2, 1953, West
Archive.

362 "you consider me 'an asset'": West, letter to "Sherman R. Grifford," July 7, 1953,
ibid.

362 his "new look": "Sherman R. Grifford," letter to West, Apr. 21, 1954, ibid.

362 "I have been doing no research": West, letter to Dr. Mark R. Everett, Dean,
University of Oklahoma, School of Medicine, June 8, 1954, ibid.

362 "a non-profit private research foundation": West to Staff Judge Advocate,
Lackland Air Force Base, Dec. 13, 1954, ibid.

362 keep West and other researchers properly paid: Marks, *Search for the Manchurian
Candidate,* 63.

362 "The Air Force will not release you": "Sherman R. Grifford," letter to West,
Sept. 16, 1954, West Archive.

363 he claimed to have achieved: West, "The Psychophysiological Studies of Hypnosis
and Suggestibility," n.d., 1–5, ibid. I found this five-page document in the
West Archive attached to a nine-page paper called "Report on Research in
Hypnosis."

363 "true memories" with "false ones": West, "Report on Research in Hypnosis,"
6–7, ibid.

363 "a different (fictional) event actually did occur": Ibid., 7.

363 "deepening the trance that can be produced": West, "Psychophysiological Studies
of Hypnosis and Suggestibility," 2.

363 "made standardized observations very difficult": West, "Report on Research in
Hypnosis," 8.

363 "sensory-environmental variables will be manipulated": West, "Psychophysiological Studies of Hypnosis and Suggestibility," 5.

364 chlorpromazine, reserpine: West, "Report on Research in Hypnosis," 2–4.

364 "he wishes just the opposite": Ibid., 7.

364 that the CIA had turned over to the Senate: CIA MORI DocID: 17441.

365 "The effects of these agents": CIA Document 43–18.

365 mocking headlines like the "The Gang That Couldn't Spray Straight": Bill Richards, "The Gang That Couldn't Spray Straight," *Washington Post*, Sept. 21, 1977, A-1. Richards described the previous day's testimony as "more a portrayal of a group of bumbling amateurs than of American James Bonds."

366 inducing insanity in the lab: Ross Corduff, "Driving of Patient to Insanity to Perfect Treatment Explained," *Corvallis Gazette-Times*, Oct. 5, 1963.

366 "mental derangement in the laboratory": Marge Davenport, "Sleep Linked to Sanity of Humans," *Oregon Journal*, Oct. 4, 1963, 2.

366 "had been confined to animals": United Press International, "C.I.A. Tells Oklahoma U. of Mind-Research Role," *New York Times*, Sept. 3, 1977; see also John Greiner, "Ex-OU Psychiatrist Reports Contact with CIA Mind Control Research," *Sunday Oklahoman*, Aug. 21, 1977, 1; Mick Hinton, "O.U. Mind Control Experiments Bared: School Told CIA Funded Secret Tests," *Saturday Oklahoman and Times*, Sept. 3, 1977.

366 were CIA fronts: "C.I.A. Tells Oklahoma U."; Hinton, "O.U. Mind Control Experiments Bared"; Andy Rieger, "Sharp Informed of CIA Projects," *Oklahoma Daily*, Sept. 30, 1977, 1.

366 Oklahoma revealed a heavily redacted memo: Rieger, "Sharp Informed of CIA Projects," 1; Steve Walden, "CIA Grants Shown: Report 'Heavily Censored,'" *Oklahoma Daily*, Oct. 1, 1977, 1–2.

366 through his retirement in 1988: West, letter to the editor, *San Francisco Examiner*, Mar. 31, 1988, 1–3, West Archive. "The statement that I was a paid consultant to the CIA and one of its 'top hypnotists' is false," wrote West. A few months later, West wrote to another magazine: "I have never worked for the CIA" (West, letter to Michael Sigman, editor of *LA Weekly*, June 2, 1988, West Archive).

367 "sought and received my counsel": West, letter to Marvin Karno, M.D., Robert O. Pasnau, M.D., and Joel Yager, M.D., Jan. 15, 1991, ibid.

367 "in Goebbels' tradition of the Big Lie": West, letter to the editor, *Summer Bruin*, June 27, 1993, 2, ibid.

367 "The Center for the Story and Reduction of Violence": The information about West's Violence Center is from news articles; congressional and state assembly testimony; interviews with colleagues of West (both involved in the proposed project and opposed to it); and, most prominently, several drafts of the project in West's hand from his files in the West Archive—these documents reveal his efforts to tamp down the project's more radical objectives in response to the growing public outcry.

367 Governor Ronald Reagan: Reagan unveiled West's plan in his State of the State address to the legislature on January 11, 1973. See William Endicott, "$850 Million Surplus in Taxes Told; Reagan Calls for Refunds," *Los Angeles Times*, Jan. 12, 1973, A-1.

367   "remote monitoring devices": West, "Center for Prevention of Violence, Neuropsychiatric Institute, UCLA," Sept. 1, 1972 (first draft of project proposal), 5, West Archive; Staff of the Subcommittee on Constitutional Rights of the Committee of the Judiciary, U.S. Senate, 93rd Congress, 2nd Sess., *Individual Rights and the Federal Role in Behavior Modification* (Washington, D.C.: GPO, November 1974), 13, 35–37.

367   threatened "privacy and self-determination": *Individual Rights and the Federal Role,* 34.

368   helped to prosecute Manson: Among the agencies contacted by West for help in "developing plans" for the Violence Center were the Los Angeles Police Department, Los Angeles District Attorney's office, and the office of California Attorney General Evelle Younger (ibid., 348).

368   He'd appeared as a witness many times: West's highest profile appearance as an expert witness in a brainwashing case came later, however, at the trial of kidnapped heiress Patty Hearst in 1976. Two of West's staff at the UCLA Neuropsychiatric Institute, Keith Ditman and Joel Hochman, testified for the defense during the death-penalty phase of the Tate–LaBianca trial (Vincent Bugliosi with Curt Gentry, *Helter Skelter* [New York: Norton, 1994], 572–79).

368   "that it can be done": Author interview with D. Smith. In the same interview, Smith expressed surprise when I mentioned MKULTRA, saying he'd never heard of it—or that the CIA gave LSD to citizens, even in San Francisco, without their knowledge.

369   so often described as "hypnotic": Bugliosi and Gentry, *Helter Skelter,* 615.

369   taught Manson how to hypnotize: Ed Sanders, *The Family,* 3rd ed. (New York: Thunder's Mouth, 2002), 43.

369   Deanyer had learned hypnosis in the navy: A FOIA to the FBI resulted in the release of forty-seven heavily redacted pages of a forty-nine-page file (FOIPA no. 0961945-000). The file confirmed that Deanyer, born Burnie William Smith Jr., on June 3, 1934, in Wheeling, West Virginia, learned hypnotism while stationed in Pearl Harbor with the U.S. Navy, between 1942 and 1946. After changing his name and opening the Deanyer School of Hypnotism in Honolulu, he was indicted in 1956 on charges of sex trafficking underage girls. At his trial, prosecutors presented evidence that he'd used hypnotism to induce female students at his school to become prostitutes. Several police officers testified that when they interviewed the victims they still "appeared to be in a trance and would say nothing [redacted] and refused to testify against him."

369   her father teaching Manson: Author interview with Robin Border. In addition, I reviewed the transcript of a taped interview Martin Lee conducted with Deanyer in the seventies. Deanyer told Lee that he "talked to Manson frequently," adding, "the things, believe it or not, that he was asking me about were not on control . . . [but] expanded capabilities under hypnosis" (Lee interview with Deanyer, July 31, 1978; transcript courtesy of Philip Melanson).

369   "The most puzzling question of all": Bugliosi and Gentry, *Helter Skelter,* 626.

370   After midnight on July 4, 1954: The information in this section is from trial transcripts, newspaper clippings, West's personal file in the West Archive, and interviews with over fifty people who were connected to the case.

370   "dazed" and "trance-like": Charles L. Theall testimony, *Texas v. Jimmy N. Shaver,* case no. 2552, 409.

370 "What's going on here?": Ibid., 394.

371 "not expect him to be under these circumstances": J. A. Griswold testimony, ibid., 138.

371 "deepen the trance": Gilbert Rose testimony, ibid., 102.

371 "kill the evil girl Beth": United Press, "State Argues Shaver Insanity," Sept. 22, 1954, clipping in West Archive; West, "Transcript of Shaver 'Amytal Interview,'" Sept. 14, 1952, 16–18, ibid.

372 "quite sane now": Howard Hunt, "Shaver Confessed the Slaying After Hours of Questioning," *San Antonio Express*, Sept. 22, 1954, 1.

372 "sat through the strenuous sessions": United Press, "Shaver Won't Take Stand," Sept. 30, 1954, 1.

372 ice water: Mrs. Everett McGhee (Shaver's mother) testimony, *Texas v. Shaver*, 596–98; West, "'Amytal Interview,'" 10.

372 a two-year experimental program: West, "'Amytal Interview,'" 10.

372 whether Shaver had been treated: West testimony, *Texas v. Shaver*, 693.

372 "Sa" through "St" had vanished: Author interview with A1C Airman Trehearne, archivist at Lackland Air Force Base.

372 "practical trials in the field": West, letter to "Sherman R. Grifford," June 11, 1953, West Archive.

373 "took your clothes off, Jimmy": West, "'Amytal Interview,'" 6–14.

373 a play about it: Gilbert Rose, *The Eve of the Fourth: A Docudrama in Four Acts* (Madison, Conn.: International Universities Press, 1996). Rose also wrote an academic paper on the case: "Screen Memories in Homicidal Acting Out," *Psychoanalytic Quarterly* 29 (1960): 328–43.

374 maintained his innocence the whole time: Don Reid and John Gurwell, *Have a Seat, Please* (Huntsville: Texas Review Press, 2001), 37–40.

374 the day Shaver was sentenced to death: West, transcript of lecture about Shaver case, June 15, 1956, 8, West Archive.

374 against capital punishment: Milton Greenblatt, "LJ West's Place in Social and Community Psychiatry," in *Mosaic of Contemporary Psychiatry*, 9.

375 most surreal belonged to Tusko: Information in this section is primarily from news coverage, papers by West and other academics, and interviews with West's colleagues at the University of Oklahoma, including Chester M. Pierce, who assisted West in the experiment and coauthored their paper about it.

375 Sidney Gottlieb had funded it: Author interview with Gordon Deckert; Richard Green, "The Early Years: Jolly West and the University of Oklahoma Department of Psychiatry," *Journal of the Oklahoma State Medical Association* 93, no. 9 (Sept. 2000): 451.

374 during the rutting season: West and Chester M. Pierce, "Lysergic Acid Diethylamide: Its Effects on a Male Asiatic Elephant," *Science* 138, no. 3545 (Dec. 7, 1962): 1100.

375 "went into status epilepticus": Ibid., 1101.

375 The next morning's paper: Claire Conley, "Shot of Drug Kills Tusko," *Daily Oklahoman*, Aug. 4, 1962, 1.

375 he liked to inform his lecture audiences: Author interview with Roger Smith.

375 the *Medical Tribune*: Staff Report, "Oklahoma University Medical Center to Study Bull Elephant's Rampages," *Medical Tribune,* 1962, 8.

375 "recurring psychoses in humans": Conley, "Shot of Drug Kills Tusko," 1–2.

375 "individual personality": Staff Report, "Oklahoma University Medical Center."

376 "sexually capable but behaviorally tractable animal": West and Pierce, "Lysergic Acid Diethylamide," 1103.

376 "capricious"..."or purpose": Charles Savage, M.D., letter to the editor, *Science,* Dec. 18, 1962; Kenneth Kiedman, letter to the editor, *Science,* Dec. 20, 1962. The originals of both letters are in the West Archive.

376 "the department was worried": Author interview with Deckert.

376 "source was payment from the CIA": Ibid. Deckert also told me it was his understanding that West's objective was to create an "artificial musth."

376 Foundations Fund for Research in Psychiatry, Inc.: West and Pierce, "Lysergic Acid Diethylamide," 1103.

377 and again involving Lawrence Schiller: Jack Ruby and William Read Woodfield, "My Story," *Long Beach Press Telegram,* Jan. 28, 1964, 1, 8. According to multiple accounts, including the testimony of Ruby's brother, Earl Ruby, to the Warren Commission (14: 402–3) and a memoir by Ruby's first attorney, Melvin Belli (Belli with Robert Blair Kaiser, *My Life on Trial* [New York: William Morrow, 1976], 255–56), within seventy-two hours of Oswald's murder, Schiller had made a deal with the Ruby family to allow his associate, William Read Woodfield, to secretly obtain access to Ruby in jail and then publish a first-person account of the Oswald shooting.

377 Ruby "lost [his] senses": Ruby and Woodfield, "My Story," Jan. 29, 1969, 3, 8.

377 "a 'fugue state' with subsequent amnesia": Melvin Belli and Maurice C. Carroll, *Dallas Justice: The Real Story of Jack Ruby and His Trial* (New York; David McKay, 1964), 71.

377 On the advice of his attorney: Final Report of the Select Committee on Assassinations, U.S. House of Representatives, 95th Congress, 2nd Sess. (Washington, D.C.: G.P.O., 1979), 158. Ruby had written a note to one of his attorneys, Joe Tonahill, stating "Joe, you should know this. My first lawyer Tom Howard told me to say that I shot Oswald so that Caroline and Mrs. Kennedy wouldn't have to come to Dallas to testify. OK?"

377 "a blank spot in his memory": Belli and Carroll, *Dallas Justice,* 41.

377 Jolly West tried to insinuate himself: Gene L. Usdin, letter to Jack R. Ewalt, President, American Psychiatric Association, Jan. 6, 1964, West Archive ("A few days after the assassination, Jolly phoned me to ask if I would be willing to have my name submitted to the court in Texas as a possible psychiatric expert").

378 approaching Judge Joe B. Brown: Libby Price, dictated notes from West, outline for West's proposed book, *A Police Man at His Elbow: Psychiatric Reflections on Jack Ruby Case,* Feb. 16, 1967, ibid. Price was West's assistant; the relevant passage reads, "Chapter 2—How West was asked to set up panel of experts—psychiatrists—later that winter [1963] before Ruby trial started—turned down by Brown Court."

378 Three documents among his papers: Ibid. (third document is a second draft of chapter outline by West).

378 "targets will certainly be unwitting": "Memorandum from DDP Helms to DDCI Carter, 12/17/63," Kennedy-Inouye Hearings, Appendix A, 82.

378 "highly qualified" skills: Hubert Winston Smith, "Motion by Defense Counsel, for an Order by the Court...," *Texas v. Jack Ruby,* no. E–4010-J, Apr. 22, 1964, 5.

378 helping him land a teaching position: Smith was fired from his professorship at the University of Texas School of Law in 1965 for "disruptive" behavior and a "completely inadequate performance." "There is no question that the individual is ill," wrote a member of the school's Budget and Personnel Committee in a letter to the dean (Jerre Williams, letter to W. Page Keeton, June 15, 1965, West Archive), yet that didn't stop West from seeing that Smith was hired at Oklahoma that autumn.

379 the preceding "forty-eight hours": Libby Price, summary of West's testimony to the court, June 6, 1967, 13, ibid.

379 there were no witnesses: West, "Report of Psychiatric Examination of Jack Ruby," Affidavit submitted to Court, *Texas v. Ruby,* Apr. 27, 1964, 2.

379 "was now positively insane": United Press International, "Refuse Ruby Mental Test," *San Mateo* [Calif.] *Times and Daily News Leader,* Apr. 27, 1964, 1.

379 "unshakable" and "fixed": West, "LJW Talk on Jack Ruby," UCLA lecture, Oct. 30, 1978, 6, West Archive.

379 "He rubbed his head on the wall": Ronnie Dugger, "The Last Madness of Jack Ruby," *The New Republic,* Feb. 11, 1967.

379 every doctor who examined Ruby: The physicians were Robert Stubblefield (the only doctor who'd examined him both before and after West), Jan. 28, (approximately) Mar. 10, Apr. 30, May 1, May 11, 1964; William R. Beavers, Apr. 28, 30, May 1, 2, 31, 1964; Werner Tuteur, July 12–15, 1965; Emanuel Tanay, date unavailable; Gene Usdin, Sept. 29, 1965; and Andrew Watson, Sept. 17, 1965.

379 finding him essentially compos mentis: The psychiatrists were John T. Holbrook, Nov. 25, 1963; Manfred Guttmacher, Dec. 21–22, 1963 and Mar. 2–3, 1964; Roy Schafer, Dec. 28–30, 1963; Martin L. Towler, dates unavailable; Robert Stubblefield; and Walter Bromberg, Jan. 11, 20, 1964.

380 "earlier studies were carried out": West, "Report of Psychiatric Examination of Jack Ruby," 1.

380 "some real disinterested doctors": "Texas: Trying for the Truth of It," *Time,* May 8, 1964.

380 from Dr. William Beavers: W. R. Beavers, M.D., "Evaluation Report on Jack Ruby," Apr. 28, 1964, 2, Criminal Court District Court No. 3, Records Annex Building, Dallas.

381 a "devious man": Author interview with Libby Price.

381 "egotistical": Author interview with Bud Addis.

381 inveterate "narcissist": Bob Conrich, email with Dernburg.

381 "womanizer": Author interview with Addis.

382 Bay of Pigs invasion: Peter Grose, *Gentleman Spy: The Life of Allen Dulles* (Boston: Houghton Mifflin, 1994), 533–54.

382 "most important witness": Jeffrey H. Caufield, *General Walker and the Murder of President Kennedy: The Extensive New Evidence of a Radical-Right Conspiracy* (n.p.: Hillcrest, 2015), 539.

382 "The Jewish people are being exterminated": "Testimony of Jack Ruby," Warren Commission volumes, 5H208–211, June 7, 1964, 210.

382 "You have to get me": Arlen Specter with Charles Robbins, *Passion for Truth: From Finding JFK's Single Bullet to Questioning Anita Hill to Impeaching Clinton* (New York: William Morrow, 2000), 113.

382 CIA and FBI had obstructed: Associated Press, "Senator Says Agencies Lied to Warren Panel," *New York Times,* May 15, 1976, 12; David Binder, "F.B.I.–C.I.A. Laxity on Kennedy Found," *New York Times,* June 24, 1976, 1, 8.

383 failed CIA plots to assassinate: Binder, "F.B.I–C.I.A. Laxity," 8.

383 teamed up with anti-Castro Cubans: Church Committee, multiple references.

383 overseen those schemes: Richard Helms with Richard Hood, *A Look over My Shoulder: A Life in the Central Intelligence Agency* (New York: Ballantine, 2003), 203–4.

383 "their own conclusions about the assassination": Senate Select Committee to Study Governmental Operations with Respect to Intelligence, *The Investigation of the Assassination of President John F. Kennedy: Performance of the Intelligence Agencies* (book 5, final report; Senate Report 94-755), 94th Congress, 2d Sess. (Washington, D.C.: GPO, 1976).

383 make the Warren *Report* "persuasive": Jerry D. Rose, *The Fourth Decade: A Journal of Research on the John F. Kennedy Assassination,* Volumes 1–2, State University College, 1993, 27; see also Peter Dale Scott, *Deep Politics and the Death of JFK* (Berkeley: University of California Press, 1993), 69.

383 There was a "probable conspiracy": Final Report of the Assassinations Records Review, 1, Sept. 1998 [https://www.archives.gov/files/research/jfk/review-board/report/arrb-final-report.pdf Board]; see also Final Report of the Select Committee on Assassinations, 1.

383 didn't identify any potential coconspirators: HSCA Final Assassinations Report, 1.

383 "The murder of Oswald by Jack Ruby": G. Robert Blakey and Richard N. Billings, *The Plot to Kill the President: Organized Crime Assassinated J.F.K., The Definitive Story* (New York: Times Books, 1981), 339.

384 obstruct the Warren Commission: HSCA Final Assassinations Report, multiple references.

384 "Hoover lied his eyes out": Pamela Colloff and Michael Hall, "Hoover's Endgame, Conspiracy Theories: The FBI Theory," *Texas Monthly,* Nov. 1998.

384 rather than mounting its own: Grose, *Gentleman Spy,* 544.

384 "The President felt that [the] CIA": Associated Press, "Johnson Felt CIA Connected with JFK Slaying Files Show," Dec. 13, 1977.

384 in hopes of deposing the dictator: Blakey and Billings, *Plot to Kill the President,* 82–84.

384 Griffin and his partner approached: *Investigation of the Assassination of President John F. Kennedy,* Vol. Xia, 287.

385 "that Ruby was involved in illegal dealings": Blakey and Billings, *Plot to Kill the President,* 82.

385 "The CIA would be very limited": HSCA Appendix, Vol. XI, 62.

385 "An examination of Agency files": Ibid., 289.

385 "My Dear Mr. Chief Justice": West, letter to Earl Warren, June 23, 1964, JFK Collection, HSCA, National Archives (College Park, Md.): (RG 233), 005633.

385 "no need to do anything": Earl Warren to Burt Griffin, July 13, 1964, 004150, ibid.

386 Tuteur submitted: Werner Tuteur, "Psychiatric Report on Jack Ruby," July 22, 1965, 1–13, West Archive.

386 an edited version West had submitted: Werner Tuteur, "Report of Examination of Jack Ruby" (notarized), Sept. 3, 1965, 1–10, ibid.

386 "'They got what they wanted on me'": Tuteur, "Psychiatric Report," 7 (the passage had parenthesis drawn at either end of it and a black line drawn through the text); Tuteur, "Report of Examination," 7 (passage no longer on page).

386 his own book about Ruby: West, *A Police Man at His Elbow.* Libby Price, a graduate student at Oklahoma in the mid-1960s, shared a portion of the unpublished manuscript with me.

386 "The fact is that nobody knows": John Kaplan and Jon R. Waltz, *The Trial of Jack Ruby* (New York: Macmillan, 1965), 365.

386 "good quote": Note card, West Archive.

386 "the book-filled room": Don DeLillo, *Libra* (New York: Viking, 1988), 14–15.

387 Gerald Ford wasn't: Author correspondence with Ford staff.

387 Specter had joined the Warren Commission: Most of the information in this section is from Specter's memoir, *Passion for Truth.*

388 as the Single Bullet *Conclusion*: Ibid., 1.

12. Where Does It All Go?

392 "I didn't write the music": Vincent Bugliosi with Curt Gentry, *Helter Skelter* (New York: Norton, 1994), 512.

396 In 1968, Bugliosi fell into a scandal: The information in this section is from news articles, court documents, and interviews with the principals involved in the cases. Especially helpful was a 140-page manuscript called "The Vince Bugliosi Story," written by George Denny, the attorney who represented both the "milkman" (Herbert Weisel) and the "mistress" (Virginia Cardwell) in their civil lawsuits against Bugliosi. In a 1999 letter accompanying the manuscript, Denny explained that copies of it were "disseminated at the Beverly Hills Bar Association luncheon in May 1976 in connection with the DA's race that year...the matters set down in this document are factually accurate in every respect." Bugliosi refused to discuss both cases with me, claiming he was still bound by the nondisclosure agreements he'd signed as part of the settlements. That wasn't true, as Denny had explained to me in 1999. He, the Weisels, and Cardwell had all deliberately violated their NDAs in 1976 when Bugliosi made his last run for public office, in order to prevent him from getting elected. They knew he'd never sue them, Denny said, because he'd never go under oath again about his involvement in either case.

396 Bugliosi suspected his milkman: Bill Boyarsky and Robert A. Jones, "Former Milkman's Complaint Adds to DA Race Confusion," *Los Angeles Times*, Nov. 24, 1972, II-1.

396 Weisel had left his job in 1965: Arden Farms—Personnel Record, Herbert Weisel, Employment Record, "Date Terminated: 6/16/65" (copy courtesy of Denny).

396 eight months before Vincent Jr. was born: Ancestry.com, California birth record for Vincent Bugliosi Jr.

396 the evidence must've been in Weisel's personnel file: Anonymous letter to Weisel, postmarked Mar. 28, 1969 ("Dear Mr. Weisel, When I first spoke to you, you volunteered the statement that I could look at your records at Arden to verify that your leaving work there was unrelated to my wife's pregnancy. Now that I've accepted your offer, you refuse to grant me permission and won't even talk to me....").

396 demanding him to release his files: Rose Weisel, Declaration, Nov. 3, 1972, 1; Herbert Weisel, Declaration, Nov. 3, 1972, 1.

396 "changed your phone number" it said. "That wasn't nice": R. Weisel Declaration, 2; H. Weisel Declaration, 1.

396 the hopes that she could arrange: R. Weisel Declaration, 2; H. Weisel Declaration, 3.

396 "but that he wouldn't do it": R. Weisel Declaration, 2; Herbert Weisel, (Second) Declaration, Nov. 4, 1972, 2.

396 paternity and lie-detector tests: R. Weisel, (Second) Declaration, Nov. 4, 1972, 3.

397 "He's got a mental problem": Ibid., 2.

397 to take the bus to school: R. Weisel Declaration, 1; H. Weisel Declaration, 1.

397 They hired a lawyer: R. Weisel Declaration, 3; H. Weisel Declaration, 4.

397 civic duty to go public: H. Weisel Declaration, 4.

397 stolen money from his kitchen: Boyarsky and Jones, "Former Milkman's Complaint," 10.

397 Weisel sued him for slander: "Couple Sue Bugliosi for $7 Million," *Los Angeles Times*, A-25.

397 In depositions, Bugliosi and his wife: Denny, "Vince Bugliosi Story," 49–50.

397 The Weisels argued otherwise: Ibid., 49–52.

397 Bugliosi had twice used an investigator: Ibid., 49. David Correa, an investigator for the District Attorney's office, identified two requests in evidence, both by Bugliosi and both identifying Weisel as a material witness in a murder case; Denny's manuscript contained photocopies of the requests.

397 Bugliosi settled out of court: "Release Agreement," signed by Herbert and Rose Weisel, Vincent and Gail Bugliosi, George Denny (for Weisels), and Stephen W. Solomon (for Bugliosis), notarized March 21, 1973; Denny, "Vince Bugliosi Story," 53.

397 He paid in cash: Denny, "Vince Bugliosi Story," 53, 65–68; Denny included photocopies of his bank deposits for Bugliosi's two cash payments as well as copies of the personal checks he wrote to the Weisels.

397 a confidentiality agreement: "Liquidated Damages Agreement," signed by Weisels, Bugliosis, Denny, and Solomon, notarized March 22, 1973; Denny, "Vince Bugliosi Story," 53.

397 turn over the deposition tapes: Affidavit of Barbara Crooker, Court Reporter, May 6, 1973; Denny, "Vince Bugliosi Story," 53.

397 she was pregnant: Most of the information about what occurred is from Cardwell's police report, her declaration in the civil case, and Denny's manuscript.

397 he ordered Cardwell: Sgt. F. M. Sullivan, Santa Monica Police Department, Crime Report, Case 73 11072, Assault and Battery, Victim: Virginia Cardwell, June 25, 1973, 1–3; Cardwell Declaration, July 6, 1973; Denny, "Vince Bugliosi Story," 70–79.

398 photographed her bruises: Photos provided by George Denny.

398 in the next day's paper: "Bugliosi Accused of Assault," *Los Angeles Herald Examiner*, June 26, 1973, 1.

398 Bugliosi returned to Cardwell's apartment: Cardwell Declaration; Denny, "Vince Bugliosi Story," 79–89.

398 to forge a backdated bill for legal services: "Received from Virginia Cardwell one hundred dollars ($100.00) for consultation fee regarding child support for son Christopher. Barbara Silver—personal secretary to Vincent T. Bugliosi, Stanley, Steinberg & Bugliosi"—photocopy in Denny "Vince Bugliosi Story," 81; Cardwell Declaration.

398 He listened in on an extension: Denny, "Vince Bugliosi Story," 82.

398 Cardwell claimed that the bruises: Lt. M. Landis, Santa Monica Police Department, Crime Report, Case 73 11072, Assault and Battery, Supplementary report, June 26, 1973, 1.

399 "This outrageous charge": "Bugliosi Charge a Fake, Says Woman," *Los Angeles Herald Examiner,* June 26, 1973, 1–2.

399 in exchange for her confidentiality: Denny, "Vince Bugliosi Story," 86–93, 99–107; "Bugliosi Assault Said Settled Out of Court: Lawyer's Account," Santa Monica *Evening Outlook,* May 9, 1974, 7.

399 Cardwell story hit the papers in 1974: Mary Neiswender, "Charge Bugliosi Paid Hush Money," *Long Beach Press Telegram,* May 7, 1974.

399 Because of his clout in the DA's office: Denny, "Vince Bugliosi Story," 84; "SM Woman Escapes Prosecution," Santa Monica *Evening Outlook*, June 29, 1973.

404 "paralyze Melcher with fear": Bugliosi summation, *California v. Charles Manson, Susan Atkins, Leslie Van Houten and Patricia Krenwinkel,* case #22239, 21370.

405 "you will be free": David Felton and David Dalton, "Charles Manson: The Incredible Story of the Most Dangerous Man Alive," *Rolling Stone,* June 25, 1970, 60.

407 His letter arrived at Penguin: Vincent Bugliosi, letter to Scott Moyers, Penguin Press, July 3, 2006 (the letter had fifty-one pages of attachments).

407 Bugliosi sent another letter: Vincent Bugliosi, letter to Scott Moyers, Feb. 15, 2007.

407 And another: Vincent Bugliosi, letter to Editorial Section, Penguin Press, Nov. 18, 2008.

408 Bugliosi had detailed this allegation: Bugliosi to Moyers, July 3, 2006, 2.

409 forensic evidence of at least five bodies: Author interview with Paul Dostie.

409 authorized a dig in the desert: Louis Sahagun, "New Twist in Manson Tale," *Los Angeles Times*, May 20, 2008.

410   a ranch hand told police that Manson: Juan Flynn, LAPD Interview by Philip Sartuche, Aug. 18, 1970, Mike McGann files, 3; Bugliosi and Gentry, *Helter Skelter,* 440.

410   "may even exceed Manson's estimate": Bugliosi and Gentry, *Helter Skelter,* 615.

410   buried or staged to look like suicides: Most infamously, a Family member named John Philip Haught (also known as "Christopher Jesus" and "Zero") was found dead of a bullet wound to the face in a house in Venice in the presence of four Family members in November 1969. One of the group, Bruce Davis (later convicted in both the Hinman and Shea murders), told police Haught was playing a game of Russian roulette. When police checked the gun, however, all six chambers had been loaded and the barrel had been wiped clean of fingerprints. Nevertheless, the police declared the death a suicide (Bugliosi and Gentry, *Helter Skelter,* 619–20). In 1972, the body of nineteen-year-old Lauren Willett was found buried in the basement of a house occupied by Family members Nancy Pitman, Squeaky Fromme, and several others, in Stockton, California (the body of Willett's husband, James, twenty-six, had been discovered decapitated and partially buried in nearby Guerneville two days earlier; both had been shot in the head). One of the women's associates, Priscilla Cooper, told police that Lauren Willett had killed herself "playing Russian roulette." This time the ploy didn't work: two men (one later married to Pitman) and Pitman and Cooper went to prison for the murders (Bugliosi and Gentry, *Helter Skelter,* 622–23).

410   reopening an investigation: Author interview with Kathleen Sheehan (Chief of Police, Bishop, Calif.); author interview with Debra Tate; Garance Burke, "New Evidence Points to Manson Victims," *USA Today,* Mar. 20, 2008.

410   two with gardening shears: They were Nancy Pitman's son and "Country" Sue Bartell.

411   September 29, 1969: The information in this section is taken from original reports from police departments in Bishop and Culver City, California; sheriff's departments in Inyo and Los Angeles Counties; Parks Department; California Highway Patrol; and the Inyo DA's office; as well as news coverage; and interviews with investigators, witnesses to Tenerelli's time in Bishop, and friends and family members of Tenerelli from the Los Angeles area.

411   He was there to drive his car: The theory espoused by investigators after Tenerelli had been identified by medical records in late October was attributed in the *Inyo Register* (the paper serving Bishop, where the body was found) to John Preku, the chief of Bishop police, and in the *Inyo Independent* (the paper serving the county, where the car was found) to the county sheriff, Merrill Curtis. Both articles appeared on October 30, 1969. The *Independent*'s had about twice as much information, although, a week later, on November 6, the *Register* ran a second story with the information that had been left out of its first story, and this time, all the information was attributed to Sheriff Curtis, with no mention of Preku. The three articles are: "Suicide Victim Is Identified, Chief Reports," *Inyo Register,* Oct. 30, 1969, 1; "Suicide Victim Is Identified, Says Sheriff," *Inyo Independent,* Oct. 30, 1969, 1; "Suicide Victim Is Identified, Says Sheriff," *Inyo Register,* Nov. 6, 1969, 1.

412 "two Turkish bath towels": George Gordon, Coroner's Investigation, Brune Mortuary, Case 69-94, Oct. 3, 1969, 1.

413 a "motorcyclist killed in Bishop": Dial Torgerson and Ron Einstoss, "Possible Manson Victim: Search for Missing Stunt Man Pressed," *Los Angeles Times,* Dec. 11, 1969, 28.

413 might've been the Family's doing: Felton and Dalton, "Charles Manson," 30.

413 Tenerelli's suicide had been "purged": Author interview with Chris Carter.

413 the original Bishop Police Department investigative report: Files of Frank Fowles (former district attorney of Inyo County), Special Collections, Library, University of Nevada, Reno.

415 Tenerelli's name on it—misspelled: as "Tennerelli, Fillippo" on the generic 1969 registration form.

416 had no accent at all: Author interview with Bee Greer. In addition, no mention was made in the police reports of the people who had spoken with the person believed to be Tenerelli in Bishop saying he had an accent of any kind.

416 There was a lab report: A. L. Coffey, Chief, Bureau of Criminal Identification and Investigation, Department of Justice, letter to Donald H. Talmadge, Coroner of Inyo County, Oct. 9, 1969.

416 "similar or identical": Mary Hirsh, M.D., X Ray Report, Washington Hospital, Dept. of Radiology, to Talmadge, Inyo Coroner, Oct. 17, 1969.

417 identified the victim nearly two weeks earlier: Sgt. David Walizer, Supplementary Investigation Report, no. CR 69-472, Office of Sheriff, Inyo County, Oct. 28, 1969.

417 "not been at the location for more than two days": Walizer, Office of Sheriff, Inyo County, Supplementary Investigation Report, no. CR-69-472, Oct. 10, 1969.

418 "coming up from the wreck": Cox, Supplementary Investigation Report, Oct. 6, 1969.

418 "find a job": Kriens Complaint, 1. See also author interview with B. Greer.

418 "late model" blue Volkswagen: Hailey, Memo to Area Commander, Nov. 1, 1969, 1–2; Steuber, Supplemental Arrest—Investigation Report, 1.

418 a "hippie" type: Ibid. (both).

419 "was sure" that DeCarlo: Ibid. (both).

419 "prior to or on 10-1-69": Hailey Memo, 1.

419 DeCarlo was in Death Valley: According to trial testimony, investigation reports, and *Helter Skelter* and other books, Juan Flynn left Barker Ranch for the last time on September 29 or 30. The night before his departure, a "last supper" was held at which DeCarlo was present and, according to the testimony, made self-incriminating remarks concerning the murder of Donald "Shorty" Shea—but, more important, it put DeCarlo in the desert on the same day of Tenerelli's arrival to the area (Juan Flynn testimony, *California v. Manson et al.,* 11849, 11907, 12261, 12281; Jerry LeBlanc and Ivor Davis, *5 to Die* [Los Angeles: Holloway House, 1970], 161–69. In addition, in a 1999 taped interview with Bill Nelson, Barbara Hoyt recounted her first attempt to escape from Barker Ranch with Sherry Cooper on or around October 1, 1969: "Sherry made arrangements with Danny to meet us at bottom of Golar Wash...but we couldn't get down there that day. Danny told us later that he did make it and that they were kind of sneaking up a little bit, trying to meet us and we couldn't get down that time..." (Nelson

interview with Hoyt, audiotape). Cooper confirmed this to me, explaining that they were seven hours late, so DeCarlo left without them (author interview with Sherry Cooper).

419   to show to "Kitty": Fowles files, Folder 10.

419   she was "involved" with Tenerelli: Ibid.

420   predilection for Volkswagen Beetles: "28 'Hips' Nabbed in Death Valley, Goler Wash Raids," *Inyo Independent,* Oct. 16, 1969, 1.

420   "between the pages" of a *Playboy* magazine: Gordon, Coroner's Investigation, 1; Brune letter, Oct. 6, 1969.

420   "made of pubic hair": Bill Vance Notes (unsigned four-page document), LASO Files, 2.

420   arrested for stealing a gun: Redondo Beach Police Department, Courtesy Report to Inyo County Sheriff's Office, Oct. 6, 1969, Fowles Files. According to this report, two Redondo Beach residents filed a criminal report upon returning from a hunting trip to Death Valley, claiming that their parked auto had been robbed of a shotgun in the desert on October 4. After discovering the theft, they encountered five "hippies," one of whom—later identified at William Rex Cole (aka Bill Vance)—had the gun.

421   I received a response saying no records had been found: In response to my appeal to their response, Carter personally wrote to me on August 31, 2011 stating, "The department has been fully compliant and cooperative with you at each opportunity and will continue to do so, however further appeals or requests will not produce records which do not exist. Additionally, while you may have additional theories or ideas regarding this investigation, your accusations and posture of conspiracy or cover-up makes it very difficult for my office."

421   they'd never heard from the detectives: Among the most important witnesses who were willing to provide information but were never contacted: Bee Greer, Robert Denton, Dennis Cox, Frank Crom, and Leon Brune. They also could've interviewed Manson Family members, both incarcerated and not. One of them, Susan Atkins (who died a year after their "investigation" in September 2009), had told Ronnie Howard (the inmate who helped break the case) that the Family had killed more people then they'd been held accountable for, including "a guy in the desert—they can't identify him." According to LAPD detective Paul LePage's notes of the jailhouse interview with Howard (discussed in chapter 8: "Interview of Rena Howard—Sybil Brand Institute," Nov. 18, 1969, 1–4, LePage personal files), the conversation between Howard and Atkins took place on November 2, 1969, a few days after Tenerelli's body had been identified in Bishop. Evidently the news hadn't reached Atkins yet.

421   the six months between the reopening: The three people Jepson told me he interviewed were Billy Kriens (the Bishop police officer who conducted the two-day investigation of Tenerelli's death), Doug Manning (the CHP officer who told me the idea that Tenerelli committed suicide was a "bunch of malarkey"), and Ray Seguine (whose only connection to the case was he briefly owned the Sportsman's Lodge).

422   the scant record: David Jepson, fax to author, July 9, 2011.

423   Open Records Act Request: O'Neill Request, July 19, 2011.

423 no records had been found: Toni Fansler, Records Clerk, Bishop Police
Department, July 29, 2011.

423 The sheriff halted his dig in Death Valley: Associated Press, "Manson Site
Keeps Its Secrets," *Los Angeles Daily News,* May 24, 2008; author interview with
Dostie.

Epilogue

429 "exactly who did what to whom": Hadley Freeman, "The Second Summer of
Charles Manson: Why the Cult Murders Still Grip Us," *The Guardian,* Aug. 16,
2016.

430 Watson absconded to his parents' place: Tex Watson and Chaplain Ray, *Will You
Die for Me?* (Old Tappan, N.J.: Fleming H. Revell, 1978), 148. According to trial
transcripts and police reports, Watson left the Barker ranch between September
30 and October 2, the period during which Tenerelli arrived, then died, in
Bishop.

430 he turned himself in for questioning: The information in this section is taken
from two of my articles, both in the online journal *Medium*: "The Tale of the
Manson Tapes," Sept. 16, 2014; and "Charles Manson's Right-Hand Man Is Up
for Parole. Here's What to Watch For," Oct. 25, 1016.

433 "deep insight into environmental issues": Ted Rowland, "At 75, Charles Manson
Still Has Power to Influence Others," CNN.com, Nov. 12, 2009.

433 a seed gun called "the Savior": Jon Michael Jones (longtime friend of Manson),
correspondence with author.

433 cell phone to Manson: Gregory Blevins, "Local Lawyer Recalls Speaking with
Manson," *Visalia* [Calif.] *Times-Delta,* Nov. 20, 2017.

433 rechristened him "Dead Rat": Lis Wiehl with Caitlin Rother, "How Many
Uncounted Victims Did the Manson Gang Kill?," *The Daily Beast,* May 25, 2018.

435 as if some of it: Author interview with Hammond.